Computer Applications in the Earth Sciences

AN UPDATE OF THE 70s

COMPUTER APPLICATIONS IN THE EARTH SCIENCES

A series edited by Daniel F. Merriam

Computer Applications in the Earth Sciences

AN UPDATE OF THE 70s

Edited by

Daniel F. Merriam

Jessie Page Heroy Professor of Geology
Department of Geology, Syracuse University
Syracuse, New York

PLENUM PRESS • NEW YORK AND LONDON

Library of Congress Cataloging in Publication Data

Geochautauqua (8th : 1979 : Syracuse University). Computer applications in the earth
  sciences, an update of the 70s.

  (Computer applications in the earth sciences)
  Proceedings of the 8th Geochautauqua, which was held Oct. 26-27, 1979, at Syracuse
University, and which was sponsored by the Dept. of Geology, Syracuse University; the
Division of Marine Geology and Geophysics, University of Miami; and the International
Association for Mathematical Geology.
  Includes bibliographies and index.
  1. Earth sciences—Data processing—Congresses. I. Merriam, Daniel Francis. II. Syracuse
University. Dept. of Geology. III. University of Miami. Division of Marine Geology and
Geophysics. IV. International Association for Mathematical Geology. V. Title. VI. Series.
QE48.8.G44 1979   550'.28'54   81-10707
ISBN 0-306-40409-0   AACR2

Proceedings of the 8th Geochautauqua, held 26-27 October 1979,
at Syracuse University. The meeting was sponsored by the
Department of Geology at Syracuse University, the Division of
Marine Geology and Geophysics at the University of Miami, and
the International Association for Mathematical Geology.

© 1981 Plenum Press, New York
A Division of Plenum Publishing Corporation
233 Spring Street, New York, N.Y. 10013

in particular to our friends and colleagues

Lou Briggs
Milt Dobrin
Bill Krumbein

who contributed so much

LIST OF CONTRIBUTORS

F.P. Agterberg, Geological Survey of Canada, 601 Booth
     Street, Ottawa 4, Ontario, Canada KIA OE8

J.C. Brower, Department of Geology, Syracuse University,
     Syracuse, New York 13210

K.L. Burns, Department of Geology, Syracuse University,
     Syracuse, New York 13210

J.C. Davis, Kansas Geological Survey, 1930 Avenue "A",
     Campus West, University of Kansas, Lawrence, Kansas
     66044

M.B. Dobrin, Department of Geology, University of Houston,
     Houston, Texas 77004 (deceased: 22 May 1980)

J.C. Griffiths, Department of Geosciences, Pennsylvania
     State University, University Park, Pennsylvania
     16802

J.W. Harbaugh, Department of Applied Earth Sciences,
     Stanford University, Stanford, California 94305

W.W. Hay, Joint Oceanographic Institutions Incorporated,
     2600 Virginia Avenue, N.W., Suite 512, Washington,
     D.C. 20037 (formerly of: Division of Marine
     Geology and Geophysics, University of Miami, Coral
     Gables, Florida 33124)

G.S. Koch, Jr., Department of Geology, University of
     Georgia, Athens, Georgia 30602

R.W. Le Maitre, Department of Geology, University of
     Melbourne, Parkville, Victoria 3052, Australia

C.J. Mann, Department of Geology, University of Illinois,
     Urbana, Illinois 61801

D.B. McIntyre, Department of Geology, Seaver Laboratory,
     Pomona College, Claremont, California 91711

D.F. Merriam, Department of Geology, Syracuse University,
     Syracuse, New York 13210

A.T. Miesch, U.S. Geological Survey, Denver Federal Cen-
     ter, Mail Stop 925, Denver, Colorado 80225

D.M. Raup, Field Museum of Natural History, Roosevelt
     Road at Lake Shore Drive, Chicago, Illinois 60605

R.A. Reyment, Paleontological Institute, Uppsala Univer-
     sity, Box 558, S-751, 22 Uppsala 1, Sweden

P.G. Sutterlin, Canada Centre for Mineral & Energy Tech-
     nology, 555 Booth Street, Ottawa, Canada KIA OGl

E.H.T. Whitten, Department of Geological Sciences, North-
     western University, Evanston, Illinois 60201

PREFACE

In looking back at the 1970's, the decade may prove
to be a crucial one in the development of quantitative
geology. After quantification had lain fallow and essentially undeveloped for 120 years, introduction of the
computer in the 1950's revived interest and fostered advances in the subject. Developments continued through
the 1960's at a rapid pace and the state-of-the-art was
reported on in the proceedings of an international symposium held at the University of Kansas in June 1969
(Merriam, 1969).

The proceedings of the Kansas meeting, published
as the first contribution in this series on "Computer
Applications in the Earth Sciences" was one of 8 collo-
quia sponsored by the Kansas Geological Survey and the
International Association for Mathematical Geology in
the late 1960's. In a sense those international symposia were continued in the 1970's at Syracuse University
as a series of Geochautauquas sponsored by the Department of Geology at Syracuse University and the International Association for Mathematical Geology. These proceedings report the results of the 8th Geochautauqua
held in Syracuse on 26-27 October 1979.

The concept of the original meeting was simple -
those working in each subdiscipline of geology would
report on developments and activities in that field up
to the end of 1969 and project ahead. The rationale for
the first meeting was outlined in the preface by the
editor

Papers by leading experts in their field
stress the "status-of-the-art." Speakers will
discuss the use of computers in the earth sciences, past, present, and future. The meeting
is planned for those not acquainted with the

tremendous advancements made in quantitative
methods in recent years and those who are interested in future possibilities.

The concept behind the followup meeting also was
simple - those who had reported on their field at the
first symposium would do so again - an update of the 70's
so to speak - at the second meeting. Each contributor,
an expert in his area of interest, would recount developments and activity in that area for the 10-year period.
The idea of having the same "expert" report on his field
was excellent but in practice turned out to be not completely feasible. Some of the practitioners had moved
into other areas, some new areas had come on the scene,
and two of the original contributors unfortunately had
died in the intervening interval. The loss of Lou Briggs
and Bill Krumbein was sorely felt at the recent meeting
(Milt Dobrin died after the meeting in 1980).

Most of the objectives of the meeting - a review of
the decade and a look ahead for each field - were met.
It is hoped that those in attendance (and those who read
this volume) will benefit from exposure to the "experts".
The presentations by geologic subject creates some duplication in discussion of methods and techniques but the
duplication is minor.

Subjects covered by the speakers were biostratigraphy (J.C. Brower), geochemistry (A.T. Miesch), geophysics
(M.B. Dobrin), information systems (P.G. Sutterlin), map
analysis (J.E. Robinson), mineral- and fuel-resource forecasting (J.W. Harbaugh), mineral-resource evaluation
(F.P. Agterberg), mining geology (G.S. Koch, Jr.), oceanography (W.W. Hay), paleoecology (R.A. Reyment), paleontology (D.M. Raup), petroleum exploration (J.C. Davis),
petrology (R.W. LeMaitre), photointerpretation (K.L.
Burns), stratigraphic analysis (C.J. Mann), and structural geology (E.H.T. Whitten).

An introduction to the subject of geology and computing was given by D.B. McIntyre with his paper entitled "Developments at the Man-Machine Interface". The
stage was set for the meeting by the Dean of the Geomathematicians, J.C. Griffiths, with his presentation on
"Systems Behavior and Geoscience Problem-Solving." A
summation, based partly on the proceedings, is given
here in the written communication by the editor (but was
not presented orally at the meeting).

In summary - there were 7 authors who gave presentations at both meetings, 10 subjects were repeated and 3
were not (hydrology, petroleum engineering, and sedimentology), and 1 paper given orally is not presented
here, 1 paper printed here was not presented, and 1 paper
was available only as an abstract. So, some of the papers present only developments for the 10-year period,
others give developments from the beginning, some project into the future, but all give an idea of what is in
involved in that field as of the end of the decade of
the 70s.

Participants in the international symposium were
from many parts of the world. Countries represented
were Australia, Canada, Great Britain, India, Sweden,
United States, and West Germany.

About 17 percent of the participants were from industry, 56 percent from universities and colleges, 24
percent from government agencies, and 3 percent were
independent consultants. A change in background of
participants (e.g. contrast 60, 27, 12 and 1 % in those
categories in 1969) is certainly evident. That change
may reflect change in interest, differences in attitudes
by the profession, location or promotion of the meetings,
other considerations, or a combination of changes.

Many people helped with preparations for the meeting. In particular Ms. B.H. O'Brien, Janice Johnson,
and Deborah Blose, assisted with arrangements. Several
of the faculty and many of the students from the Department of Geology at SU helped with physical arrangements.
The University of Miami and IAMG kindly cosponsored the
meeting. Partial support for the meeting was given by
V.P. Volker Weiss of the Office of Research & Graduate
Affairs and was much appreciated. Janice Johnson typed
the proceedings and Jim Busis of Plenum Press arranged
for publication. Appreciation is expressed to all who
helped make the meeting a success.

It is hoped that in a small way the efforts of the
contributors may help stimulate interest and involvement
of the readers of this volume in computer applications
in the earth sciences. The truism that, as stated in
John Griffiths' paper, the computer "...can serve as an
intelligence amplifier..." seems to offer unlimited possibilities to geologists. Only the future will tell.

REFERENCE

Merriam, D.F., ed., 1969, Computer Applications in the
    Earth Sciences: Plenum Press, New York, 281 p.

Fontainebleau, France   D.F. Merriam
August 1980

Editor's Note: diacritical marks have been omitted

CONTENTS

SYSTEMS BEHAVIOR AND GEOSCIENCE PROBLEM-SOLVING

John C. Griffiths

Pennsylvania State University

"The power of reason must be sought not in the rules
that reason dictates to our imagination, but in the ability to free ourselves from any kind of rules to which we
have been conditioned through experience and tradition."
R. Reichenbach, 1963
(from Weinberg, 1975).

ABSTRACT

Pure and applied science can be considered as two aspects of the same system of accumulating knowledge, a process termed the scientific method. The scientific method
and its development may be viewed as a multitrack activity which includes cybernetics, operations research,
and a systems approach, all of which are necessary to
analyze and solve extremely complex problems. Advent
of the computer, which can serve as an intelligence amplifier, was timely in that it is available now to assist
in solving complex geological problems.

INTRODUCTION

It is proposed frequently that there are two types
of science, pure or basic and applied, but any hypothesis
built up by pure science is tested ultimately by its applications; I, therefore, consider that there is one
type of science and pure and applied merely are different aspects of the same system of accumulating knowledge
(see also Boulding, 1980).

Now the process of accumulating knowledge is termed
"the scientific method" although it is hardly a one-
track activity (Boulding, 1980, p. 533); it is more
similar to a business cycle and it possesses the usual
circadian rhythms. From time to time practitioners have
endeavored to write the rules of the game (e.g., Chamberlin, 1897; Fisher, 1942; Weinberg, 1975) but scientific
activity tends, in the long run, to evade these rules,
a feature epitomized in the quote from Reichenbach.

Sometime ago I endeavored to summarize the evolution
of the scientific method in a V-shaped figure (Griffiths,
1968a, fig. 1); in this view the trajectories, much simplified, converge upon General Systems Theory (von
Bertalanffy, 1968), a "covering" which includes cybernetics, computers, operations research and many other
recently developed activities. An alternative way of
representing the same feature was included in an article
on "Current Trends in Geomathematics" (Griffiths, 1970,
fig. 1) based on a "classification of systems" by Beer
(1964, p. 18) and again the convergence towards O.R.,
cybernetics, and systems approaches seem to be required
to analyze, and possibly to solve, the exceedingly complex problems which now seem about to overwhelm us.

Fortunately the advent of the computer and its relatively recent application to geological problem-solving
(Loudon, 1979) has served to offer us an intelligence
amplifier (Ashby, 1956); the impact of the computer is
captured in this masterpiece of understatement..."computers are almost certain to influence education deeply.
Mathematical and logical skills will be revolutionized
by it, in much the same way as the printing press led
to general literacy" (Rt. Hon. Lord Robens, 1969). Comparison with the printing press suggests the following
analog (Fig. 1).

Of course, for this level of development to be
achieved successfully, it is necessary to accept the
following recommendation; "The modern digital computer,
properly used as prosthetic intelligence, rather than
as a big adding machine doing faster what we always did
before, enables us to extend our ability to use algebraic
languages to describe and analyze the multidimensional
complexity of the world we live in." (Gould, 1979). Then
indeed the computer would become (a part of) a true intelligence amplifier system.

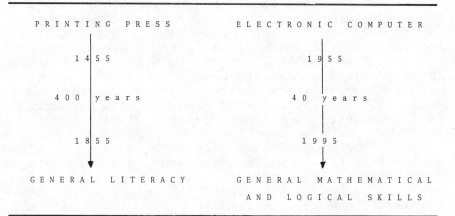

Figure 1. Analogous outcomes from effects
of printing press and computer.

SYSTEMS ANALYSIS

Because systems analysis seems to be central to the
procedure, it is as well to examine the concepts and some
of its paradigms to understand their implications. Following Churchman (1968) a system may be defined as "a
set of parts co-ordinated to accomplish a set of goals".
The boundaries of a system, are identified to differentiate it from its environment and this requires the definition of those features which affect the system but
which the system cannot affect. The system's environment
leads to its "fixed constraints" (Churchman, 1968).

A system possesses objectives and it is necessary
to postulate some manner of measuring the performance of
the whole system in terms of its progress, through time,
towards its objectives. In order to perform this activity the system must obtain certain resources which it
usually "metabolizes". System components may be identified and then it becomes necessary to specify their
activities, their goals and their measures of performance; finally there comes the "management of the system".

Such a system is easy to identify with individual
organisms and with corporate institutions of various
types and sizes; it is, however, less obvious that an
inanimate object may be looked upon as a system in this
sense. Nevertheless, because any object must be observed
(by someone?) to be identified at all, then the coupling

of the observer and observed achieves the level of a system. Furthermore if the idea of an inanimate object
having goals is inclined to be confusing think first of
the quote at the beginning and second because water "runs
down hill" it evidently may be considered to possess an
objective just as many processes which "strive to achieve
equilibrium" do! Some profound questions in teleology
and artificial intelligence arise at this juncture and
it is necessary to keep an open mind until these questions have been adequately discussed. To ventilate some
of these questions I have used such games as HEXAPAWN
(Gardner, 1962) in which one plays a trival game against
an "inanimate object" termed HER (Hexapawn Educable
Robot). The game consists of a board of 3 by 3 squares
and each of two players starts with three pawns; the objective of the game is to move one of the pawns from
one's own to the opponent's base line. HER is composed
of a set of 24 matchboxes organized so that they represent each of the decision points in the game; each
matchbox contains a number of beads of two different
colors, each of which corresponds to a possible move
which HER may make at an appropriate point in the game.
The two options are, move forward one square or take dia-
gonally an opponent's pawn. When a position in the game
requires a move by HER the matchbox corresponding to the
current decision point is selected and shaken and the
bead in the right-hand corner of the box determines HER's
move. Each matchbox used in the game remains open until
the outcome, win or lose, is attained. If HER wins, the
moves which led to the successful outcome are reinforced
by adding a bead of like color to each box; if HER loses
then the beads in the right-hand corner of the boxes are
removed. Thus appropriate moves are reinforced and
"wrong" moves are removed (aversive conditioning of
Skinner, 1971). In this manner HER "learns" and, after
some 20 to 30 games, cannot be beaten. The question
arises does HER have a purpose? If you answer yes what
is the difference between HER and you? If you deny HER
a purpose then can you demonstrate that you have a purpose? Before answering the question consider that "purposeful behavior requires that the acting object (i.e.
system in our situation) be coupled with the goal, that
is that the object registers messages from its surround-
ings" (i.e. be sensitive to its environment as HER is
because of the built-in rewards and penalties).   "If
a goal is to be attained some signals from the goal are
necessary at some time to direct the behavior, i.e. there
must be a goal" (quotes from Rosenbleuth and Wiener,
1950; and Rosenbleuth, Wiener, and Bigelow, 1943; words

in parentheses mine). These aspects of teology and artificial intelligence (such as learning) are described
entertainly by Michie (1961); and then the abstruse
question is raised "can a computer, or any machine,
think"? This question is unresolved yet although there
are strong opinions expressed in either direction (e.g.
Lucas, 1961) and it is as well to realize that although
the question seems to be simple enough the definitions
required for its ultimate solution prove elusive and the
question as usually stated may indeed be itself an example of Goedelian Incompleteness (Hofstedter, 1979).

Characteristic behavior of complex systems has been
described by Forrester (1968, 1970) and may be para-
phrased as follows: Complex systems tend

(1)   to be counter-intuitive
(2)   to be insensitive to changes in many of the
      (important) system parameters
(3)   to be resistant to policy changes
(4)   to possess influential pressure points usually
      in unanticipated places
(5)   to compenate for external applied effects
      (homeostasis)
(6)   to react to policy change in the short run
      opposite to the manner they react in the long
      run
(7)   towards low performance.

In summary, they tend to degenerate towards, what
I like to think of, as the Juggernaut Model, wherein
the juggernaut is a six-wheeled flatbedded vehicle upon
which is mounted a ten-ton idol surrounded by ceremonial
curtains around which the "leadership" parades. The objective is to encourage the "faithful" to drag this mon-
strosity through loose wet sand during the monsoon season
for some five miles from the jungle to the temple. There
is no steering mechanism apart from persuading the faithful to hurl themsleves under the wheels for the future
promise of great reward. This monster (i.e., model)
should be recognizable easily, at least to organization
theorists in academia, government, and industry. The
sequence of events is portrayed elegantly by Argyris
(1971). "In the social universe, where presumably there
is no mandatory state of entropy, man can claim the du-
bious distinction of creating, organizations that generate entropy, that is slow but certain processes leading
towards system deterioration". Expressed somewhat more
vehemently "the ever accelerating conversion of resources

into garbage, is, indeed, the chief characteristic of our
culture" (Caster, 1970) which reflects some of the roots
of the growing problem of "waste disposal". Apparently
our overall system seems to be running down!

SOME CHARACTERISTICS OF EXCEEDINGLY COMPLEX PROBABILISTIC SYSTEMS

The deterioration of many of the subsystems in
which we live emphasizes the feature that these systems
are not simple closed systems but, in the spirit defined
by Beer (1964), they are exceedingly complex probabilistic systems and they possess characteristics which are
important in geological problem-solving.

One of the features characteristic of this type of
system is it's memory; in geological terms the Principle
of Uniformitarianism implies, in some sense, a long,
almost infinite memory and many aspects of geological
(and other related sciences rely on this feature to justify their procedure. Yet it is considered difficult to
almost impossible to predict forwards in time for short
periods of from 5 to 10 years. Memory is discussed by
de Bono (1971) and from his description I have constructed
the examples in Figure 2. In this situation, faced with
the distribution of marbles, one has to reconstruct the
procedure and starting position used in obtaining their
disposition; in Figure 2A the substrate is loose (wet)
sand and the positions of the marbles show that they
were dropped at equal intervals on a straight line. In
Figure 2B the substrate is a corrugated surface and the
disposition of the marbles now is more complex; given
that the investigator knows that the surface "was" corrugated he may reconstruct the manner in which the peb-
bles were dropped. But, if the form of the substrate is
not known, then there is no unique solution to the problem. In this situation the observations solely of the
disposition of the marbles is insufficient to reconstruct
the events. Finally in the third example the marbles
were dropped on a concrete surface and the marbles end
up randomly distributed; in this situation it is not
possible to reconstruct the preceeding events. Obviously
memory becomes more and more limited from Figures 2A to
2C. How many geological processes possess these characteristics?

A second feature which is related closely to this
limited memory is the system's property known as

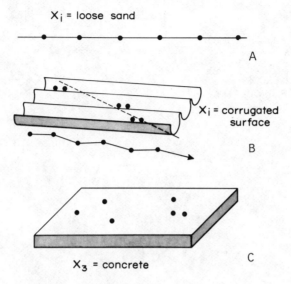

X_i = loose sand

A

X_i = corrugated surface

B

X_3 = concrete

C

Figure 2.   Exogenous versus endo-
            genous variability or
            interaction between
            heredity and environ-
            ment represented as
            disappearing memory
            trace (after de Bono,
            1969).

equifinality (von Bertalanffy, 1968) in which the same
outcome may be obtained from a series of events, or processes, by different routes or from different starting
states. The distribution of marbles dropped on concrete
is an example; the random disposition of the marbles may
be obtained by several different combinations of starting
states and procedures. Many processes with Markovian
memories possess these characteristics.

     Another characteristic of some importance is men-
tioned by Simon (1969, p. 23ff.) where he describes the
path of an ant to a goal (see Fig. 3) and deduces that
"an (ant) viewed as a behaving system, is quite simple,
the apparent complexity of its behavior over time is
largely a reflection of the complexity of the environment
in which it finds itself" (Simon, 1969, p. 25). He then
goes on to suggest that the word in parentheses may be
replaced by man, skier, sloop, or the search for a problem solution and the trajectory yet would be appropriate.
He states that "Only human pride argues that the apparent
intricacies of our path stem from a quite different

PATH OF "?" FROM
START TO GOAL

? = ANT, SKIER, SLOOP,
    SEARCH FOR PROBLEM
    SOLUTION

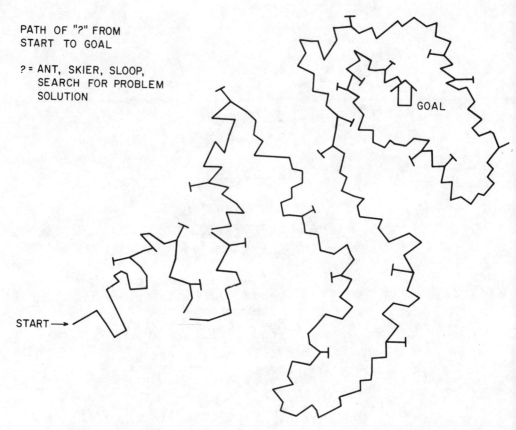

Figure 3.   Path of ant to goal (after Simon, 1969).

source than the intricacy of the ant's path" (Simon,
1969, p. 53). At an earlier stage he concludes that
"the possibility of building a mathematical theory of a
system or of simulating that system does not depend on
having an adequate microtheory of the natural laws that
govern the system components. Such a microtheory might
indeed be simply irrelevant" (Simon, 1969, p. 19), and
this leads me to consider the approach of using black-
box technology as an appropriate method of problem-
solving in exceedingly complex probabilistic geologic
systems.

     Consider for a moment the simple input-black box-
output model (Fig. 4); here the throughputs are linked
together in the normal manner from "cause" to "effect"
but there is a feedback loop which leads from the output
back to the black box or to the input or both. Therefore

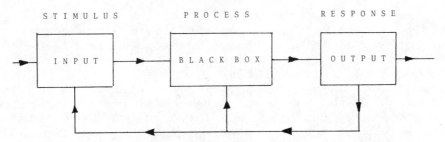

Figure 4.   Simple cybernetic model of input-
            black box-out (I-BB-O) system.

a simple unidirectional cause-effect relationship is inadequate to represent this system; here, again, a number
of geological processes may be modeled isomorphically
onto this black box model where they possess a source
material (input), process, and product (output).

   Most scientific investigations are aimed at evaluating what is in the black box and this pursuit may be labeled a search for "explanation". However it is not
obvious that this is the most appropriate procedure or
even that it is feasible in many situations (cf. Boulding, 1980). It is much simpler and may be more effective to study the association between input and output in
a stochastic or statistical relationship and let the box
remain black. This then leads back to Simon's claim
that a microtheory of what is inside the black box may
be irrelevant.

   As an example of a system which is likely to remain
black-box consider Ashby's discussion of the complexity
of a system (Ashby, 1964); his example consists of a
board of 20 by 20 lamps each of which may be on or off
leading to 2^{400} possible patterns. This number is very
large and so Ashby discusses what "very large" means in
this context and concludes with Ashby's Law: "Every-
thing material stops at 10^{100}" (Ashby, 1964, p. 163).
He then shows that 2^{400} is about 10^{120}, already exceeding
the limit of Ashby's Law. Suppose now we wish to sub-
divide this set of patterns into those which possess
some property P or not (i.e. suppose some are red) then
we are led to $2^{10^{120}}$ which is approximately $10^{10^{120}}$; in
other words in this rather simple system we are led to
a number the *exponent* of which is beyond Ashby's Law.
Such systems are likely to prove intractable to our present epistemological approaches (Ashby, 1964, p. 168);
and again there are many possible geological examples.

An alternate procedure for solving this type of
problem consists of relating the input to the output
through a transfer function (Box and Jenkins, 1970).
It is convenient to use matrix notation in this situation as in Griffiths (1966a) and it is there shown that
two matrices should be specified to determine a unqiue
third. When the input and output matrices are specified
appropriately, the black box (process) can be determined
in the form of a set of matrix equations, and the coefficients may be identifiable. On the other hand, whether or
not they are identifiable the relationships may be useful
in prediction, that is the "microtheory" may be relevant,
and the box may be left "black".

EXAMPLES OF SYSTEMS BEHAVIOR IN A GEOLOGICAL CONTEXT

As an initial example of these system properties
consider Vistelius' introduction of Markov models into
geological problems (1949); if the matrices of lithological changes are powered to follow their development
through various stages they may reach a final state in
a finite, relatively short, number of stages, (Griffiths,
1966b), that is they behave similar to regular ergodic
chains (Kemeny and others, 1959, p. 391 ff.). This
final state is composed of a constant probability vector
and no further powering will change it. For example, in
the Khev-grdzeli section the constant vector is reached
after 16 steps and consists of 33.8 percent sand, 41.5
percent silt, and 24.7 percent clay. Given this final
state it is not possible to retrace the steps followed
to achieve it, that is memory of the starting state and
specific process stages is lost; the outcome is equifinal
as in Figure 2C.

It is possible to represent the formation of detrital sediments as an input-black box-output model (see
Figure 5; and Griffiths and Ondrick, 1969, p. 75); the
input is equivalent to material from the source area
which passes through several processes, termed erosion,
transportation, deposition, and diagenesis, to emerge as
a detrital sediment (the output). Much attention has
been given to these processes but for convenience we may
look upon them as a black box or, if they are to be
treated individually, as a series of black boxes.

It is interesting to note that, as the source area
is eroded, if the output is allowed to accumulate it
gradually blankets the source area and inhibits further

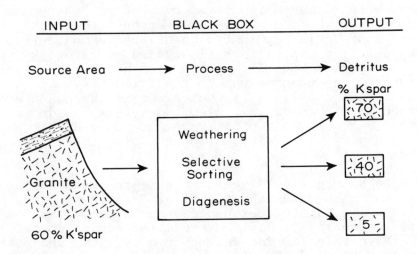

Figure 5. Petrogenetic system of arkosic detrital sediments represented as I-BB-O
system.

erosion; in other words there is a negative feedback loop
which gradually tends to reduce the effect of the continued process. Of course, if, as is usual, the eroded
material is removed, transported, and fresh source material continually is exposed, the process continues. In
practice, erosion is coupled with transportation and subsequently deposition and these, conceptually different
stages in the process, are difficult to separate because
they are obviously not independent. It is possible to
describe the performance in the black box as a process
of selective sorting on the basis of density (= type of
mineral), grain size, and shape, and it is possible to
study variation in this process in terms of the average
grain size and size sorting of the mineral constituents
in the detrital output.

    The petrogenetic system is represented in this man-
ner for the arkose rock type in Figure 5, following
Krynine's description (Krynine, 1948, 1950). The input
is represented as fresh and weathered granitic material
containing 60 percent K-spar. This material passes
through the black box labeled weathering, selective
sorting, and diagenesis and yields three types of output,
which differ in proportion of feldspar from much less, to

much more, than that in the source material; each of
these outputs may be achieved by changing the process in
the black box. The point to be emphasized is that
studies of variation in the quantitative composition of
the output, a typical arkosic sediment, is unlikely to
be unique to a specific source area unless the exact
nature of the process can be specified in *quantitative*
terms; this situation is equivalent to the example illustrated in Figure 2B. It also shows that to identify
uniquely a component of a system of the I-BB-O type, it
is necessary to specify at least two of these three components.

     An alternative situation is represented in Figure
6 in which the source material differs in proportion of
feldspar, a fairly reasonable expectation under "real
world" conditions, but the product contains no feldspar
and is equifinal. The fact that a detrital sediment
contains no feldspar does not permit us to infer that
there is no feldspar in the source area, another example
of the phenomenon of Figure 2C.

     When attempts are made to analyze variation in the
properties of detrital sediments by components analysis
(Griffiths, 1966a; Griffiths and Ondrick, 1969) and
attempts are made to identify the components, it is
determined that about 5 to 7 components account for the
major proportion (70 to 90 percent) of the total variation. Two of these, usually but not always, the dominant ones, are identifiable as grain size and size sorting and two more, the proportion of silica and carbonate
cements[1], usually are attributable to diagenesis. The
remaining components are weak, accounting for less than
10 to 15 percent of the variation, and are not readily
identifiable. In other words, the conceptual processes
represented by the operational agency of selective sorting plus the effects of diagenesis overprint the effects
of previous phenomena and destroy the memory of source
area and associated, weathering, processes.

     Because all detrital sediments follow a similar
geological history, that is there is always a source
area, a complex process or sequence of processes and a

_____

[1] The cementitious properties may be dominant over selective sorting but nearly always these four components represent the major proportion of the variation in all the
properties studied.

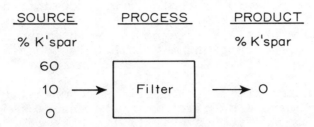

Figure 6.   Example of equifinality
in petrogenesis of detri-
tal sediments.

product; and because all the processes, physical and
chemical, generally reduce the complexity in composition
of the source material the end-product is usually a
quartzite as envisaged by Krynine (1948).   This end-
product, a quartzite, is equifinal; it has no memory of
its source or the trajectory by which it developed; it
is an example of Figure 2C.

On the basis of these several system characteristics
I have proposed to represent the classification of detrital sediments, using Krynine's philosophy and nomenclature with some modification in definition, in the form
of a cone (Griffiths, 1968b, 1972); this geometrical sym-
bolism permits the representation of the detrital sediments in a dynamic relationship as contrasted with the
conventional static arrangement in a square or rectangle.
It purports to show that all detritus irrespective of
original source area degenerates ultimately towards an
equifinal quartzite.   Each of the major tectonic environments of Krynine, which results in a specific type of
detrital sediment, such as an arkose, high-rank and low-
rank graywacke, is represented by a band from base to
apex along the cone.

To identify where a rock-specimen falls in the cone
it is necessary to recognize two features: first, irrespective of composition (i.e. type of source area) if a
specimen is from near the base of the cone (i.e. is near
its source area) the diversity in composition of *neighboring* grains will be large.   On the other hand, if the
specimen is from near the apex, the diversity in composition is small.   Because at the apex of the cone the product is equifinal, it may not be possible to assign the

specimen to its proper tectonic environment; hence all
such assignments are made by rock associations, that is
quartzites always are interbedded with associated rocks
which are more representative, that is possess better
"memories", of their tectonic environment.

To differentiate tectonic environments it is necessary to examine a specimen from the associated rock sequence which is from as near to the base of the cone as
possible; then the types of feldspar, if any, and rock
fragments usually may be used to assign the specimen to
one of the three clans. The critical features are:

(1) The sampling arrangement of selecting (a few)
     neighboring grains and observing their com-
     positional diversity is the essential proce-
     dure.
(2) Presence or absence of a specific type of
     constituent is more important than its pro-
     portions. Indeed quantitative proportions
     may be misleading for this purpose.
(3) Variation (diversity) in grains sizes of a
     specific detrital constituent, such as quartz
     for example, also will reflect the position
     of the specimen in the cone - if, and only
     if, the grains taken for measurement are con-
     tiguous.

The geometrical display as a cone also may be used
to illustrate that the progress from near to distant
from the source area in terms of time or space or both
is best measured by the arrangement of grains of different types, sizes, and shapes. Near source, diversity
among *neighboring* grains is high whereas distant from
source, diversity among *neighboring* grains is low. Progress is measured essentially by the degree of differentiation from undifferentiated near source to layered
strongly and laminated far from source, an example of a
gradual increase in negative entropy (Fig. 7). It seems
worth emphasizing that if a channel[1] sampling procedure
is used, there will be little difference in grain size
between the material which is near or distance from the
source area.

---

[1] In other words without carefully controlled stratigraphic sampling procedure (i.e. sedimentation unit sampling, Otto, 1938) the structure, and therefore degree of
intensity of the process, is lost.

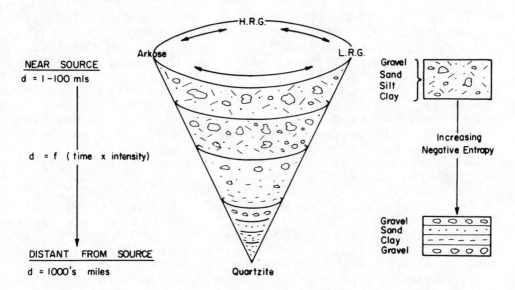

Figure 7.   Classification of detrital sediments represented in cone.

     This "conical" model which includes several differ-
ent starting states, trajectories which converge, and a
common equifinal end-product may be applied to the formation of igneous rocks as expressed for example, in
Bowen's Reaction Series (Bowen, 1928). The more modern
concept of "petrogeny's residua system" is the equifinal
end-product. Attempts to confine the origin of granite
to a single unidirectional process and a single starting
state led to the granite controversy (Gilluly, 1948);
this type of argument possibly reflects the fact that
rival hypotheses are represented in a form which insures
that they are examples of Goedel Incompleteness (Hofstedter, 1979). The solution requires the invention of
a metalanguage reflected in the change of question from
"How is granite formed?" to "How much granite is formed
in this manner and how much that?" - a feature emphasizing that the answerable question needs a language
which comprehends a quantitative answer.

     A similar model may be used to represent the origin
of clay minerals and the finer grained sediments of
which they are largely composed; there may be several
starting states (source materials) and the trajectories
converge towards the equifinal end-product, laterite
(Griffiths, 1952).

As a final example consider the procedure of mineral-
resource assessment represented as an I-BB-O model (Fig.
8; and Griffiths, 1978, fig. 1, p. 448); here the input
consists of two parts, one herited, the geological characteristics, and the other, the degree of commitment, an
acquired characteristic derived from the current socio-
economic infrastructure. Geological factors determine
the upper and lower bound of the amount of resource present in a region (Menzie, Labovitz, and Griffiths, 1977;
Labovitz, Menzie, and Griffiths, 1977); whereas the
amount produced is mainly a function of the degree of
commitment (Griffiths, 1978).

The geological factors are concepts and the actual
objects examined are the rocks which represent the memory
trace of geological events - "all we know of the past is
the record of it..." (Boulding, 1980, p. 834). The types
of rocks were standardized, by a transducing table (Fig.
2; Missan and others, 1978) based upon the classification
in Figure 7, into 13 different rock types and five ages;
this yields 65 different possible outcomes so that the
input may be characterized as chosen from 2^{65} possibilities. Similarly, the output is standardized into 77 commodities (Labovitz, Menzie, and Griffiths, 1977) and any
specific output therefore is chosen from 2^{77} possibilities. The black box contains therefore
$2^{65} \cdot 2^{77}$ combinations or approximately $10^{3 \times 10^{24}}$ which
comfortably exceeds Ashby's Law. Geological reasoning
and observation of the frequency of association is aimed
at reducing this enormous complexity by, for example,
observing that tin usually occurs in granite, a massive
reduction to a 1:1 mapping of rock type to commodity.
This reduction is an oversimplification because some 70
percent of the world's tin comes from "alluvium", actually
from detrital sediments derived from granite, or in our
terms, from arkoses. Tin also is associated with quartz
porphyry in Bolivia and with rhyolite in Mexico (Sainsbury, 1969). The major source of tin in North America
is as a by-product from the lead-zinc deposits at the
Sullivan Mine, Kimberley, British Columbia. It is clear
therefore that the input is at least 2^5 and because the
outputs frequently contain more than one other commodity
the output, let us say, also is composed of at least 2^5
possible alternatives leading to a set of
$2^5 \cdot 2^5 = 2^{160} = 1.46 \times 10^{48}$ possible combinations.

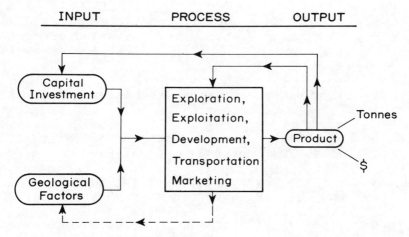

Figure 8.   Mineral-resource assessment as
           I-BB-O model.

It is possible that some ore deposits also may be
examples of equifinal products so that a black-box approach may be appropriate for studying the associations
of geological events (= rocks) with commodities.

CONCLUDING REMARKS

Elsewhere I have described several additional aspects of problem-solving in geoscience (Griffiths, 1969,
1974) and, in particular, the possible challenge arising
from the existence of Goedel Incompleteness (Beer, 1964)
in the formulation of geological questions. The equivalence of structure, characteristic of the systems view
of the epistemology of problem-solving, is displayed
delightfully, by Hofstedter (1979) in tracing the correspondence between the logic of Goedel, the art of
Escher, and the music of Bach. It would be surprising
indeed if the equivalence cannot be extended into various
other subject matter areas including geoscience.

REFERENCES

Argyris, C., 1971, Management and organizational devel-
     opment: McGraw-Hill Book Co., New York, 211 p.

Ashby, W.R., 1956, Design for an intelligence amplifier,
     in Automata studies: Ann. Math. Studies, no. 34,
     p. 215-234.

Ashby, W.R., 1964, Introductory remarks at panel discussion, *in* Mesarovic, M.D., ed., Views on general systems theory: John Wiley & Sons, Inc., New York, p. 165-169.

Beer, S., 1964, Management and cybernetics: John Wiley & Sons, New York, 211 p.

Boulding, K.E., 1980, Science: our common heritage: Science, v. 207, no. 4433, p. 831-836.

Bowen, N.L., 1928, The evolution of the igneous rocks: Princeton Univ. Press, Princeton, New Jersey, 334 p.

Box, G.E.P., and Jenkins, G.M., 1970, Time series analysis: Holden-Day, San Francisco, 553 p.

Caster, J.H., 1970, Etzioni's view of the environment: Science, v. 169, no. 3945, p. 529.

Chamberlin, T.C., 1897, The method of multiple working hypotheses: Jour. Geology, v. 5, no. 8, p. 837-848.

Churchman, C.W., 1968, The systems approach: Dell Publ. Co., Inc., New York, 243 p.

DeBono, E., 1971, The mechanism of mind: Penguin Books Ltd., London, 281 p.

Fisher, R.A., 1942, The design of experiments (3rd ed.): Oliver and Boyd Ltd., Edinburgh, 263 p.

Forrester, J.W., 1968, Planning under the dynamic influences of complex social systems: OECD Working Symposium on Long-range Forecasting and Planning (Bellagio, Italy) Mimeo. d-1123, 22 p.

Forrester, J.W., 1970, Counterintuitive behavior of social systems: Testimony for the Subcommittee on Urban Growth of the Committee on Banking and Currency, House of Representatives, Washington, D.C., d-1383-1, 27 p.

Gardner, M., 1962, Mathematical games: Scientific American, v. 206, no. 3, p. 138-144.

Gilluly, J., 1948, Origin of granite: Geol. Soc. America Mem. 28, 139 p.

Gould, P., 1979, Polyhedral dynamics: an introduction
    for social scientists, geographers and planners:
    Center de Etudes Geographicos, Inst. Nac. de Inves-
    tigacao Cientifica (Lisboa, Portugal), 51 p.

Griffiths, J.C., 1952, Reaction relation in the finer
    grained rocks: Clay Mins. Bull., v. 1, no. 8, p.
    251-257.

Griffiths, J.C., 1966a, A genetic model for the interpre-
    tive petrology of detrital sediments: Jour. Geology,
    v. 74, no. 5, pt. 2, p. 653-672.

Griffiths, J.C., 1966b, Future trends in geomathematics:
    Min. Ind., Pennsylvania State Univ., v. 29, no. 1,
    p. 1-8.

Griffiths, J.C., 1968a, Operations research in the min-
    eral industry: Proc. Symp. on Decision-Making in
    Mineral Exploration, Vancouver Research Council,
    p. 5-9, Western Miner., v. 41, p. 22-26.

Griffiths, J.C., 1968b, Classification of geologic data:
    Proc. Symp. on Decision-making in Mineral Explora-
    tion, Vancouver, British Columbia Res. Council,
    p. 37-42; Western Miner., v. 41, p. 37-42.

Griffiths, J.C., 1969, Cybernetics-geomathematics inter-
    action: Geol. Soc. America Sp. Paper 146, p. 87-
    94.

Griffiths, J.C., 1970, Current trends in geomathematics:
    Earth Science Rev., v. 6, no. 2, p. 121-140.

Griffiths, J.C., 1972, Some aspects of classification,
    in Protz, R., and Martini, I.P., eds., Classifica-
    tion of soils and sedimentary rocks: Proc. Symp.
    Dept. of Land Resource Science, Center for Resources
    Development, Univ. Guelph, p. 123-146.

Griffiths, J.C., 1974, Quantification and the future of
    geoscience, in Merriam, D.F., ed., The impact of
    quantification on geology: Syracuse Univ. Geol.
    Contr. 2, p. 83-101.

Griffiths, J.C., 1978, Mineral resource assessment using
    the unit regional value concept: Jour. Math. Geo-
    logy, v. 10, no. 5, p. 441-472.

Griffiths, J.C., and Ondrick, C.W., 1969, Modelling the
     petrology of the detrital sediments, *in* Merriam,
     D.F., ed., Computer applications in the earth sci-
     ences: Plenum Press, New York, p. 73-97.

Hofstedter, D.R., 1979, Goedel, Escher and Bach; an eter-
     nal golden braid: Basic Books Inc., New York, 777
     p.

Kemeny, J.G., Mirkil, H., Snell, J.L., and Thompson,
     G.J., 1959, Finite mathematical structures: Pren-
     tice-Hall, Inc., New Jersey, 487 p.

Krynine, P.D., 1948, The megascopic study and field
     classification of sedimentary rocks: Jour. Geology,
     v. 56, no. 2, p. 130-165.

Krynine, P.D., 1950, Petrology, stratigraphy and origin
     of the Triassic sedimentary rocks of Connecticut:
     Connecticut Gcol. and Natl. Hist. Survey Bull. 73,
     247 p.

Labovitz, M.L., Menzie, W.D., and Griffiths, J.C., 1977,
     COMOD: A program for standardizing mineral resource
     commodity data: Computers & Geosciences, v. 3, no.
     3, p. 497-537.

Loudon, T.V., 1979, Computer methods in geology: Aca-
     demic Press, New York, 269 p.

Lucas, J.R., 1961, Minds, machines and Goedel, *in* Sayre,
     K., and Crossan, F., eds., The modeling of mind:
     Univ. Notre Dame Press, South Bend, Indiana, p. 112-
     126.

Menzie, W.D., Labovitz, M.L., and Griffiths, J.C., 1977,
     Evaluation of mineral resources and the unit re-
     gional value concept, *in* Ramani, R.V., ed., Appli-
     cation of computer methods in the mineral industry:
     Soc. Min. Eng. America, Inst. Min. Metall. and
     Petrol. Eng. Inc., New York, p. 322-339.

Michie, D., 1961, Trial and error: Science survey, 1961
     (pt. 2): Penguin, Harmondsworth, p. 129-145.

Missan, H., Cooper, B.R., el Raba'a, S.M., Griffiths,
     J.C., and Sweetwood, C., 1978, Workshop on areal
     value estimation: Jour. Math. Geology, v. 10, no.
     5, p. 433-439.

Otto, G.H., 1938, The sedimentation unit and its use in
    field sampling: Jour. Geology, v. 46, no. 4, p.
    569-582.

Robens, RT. Hon., Lord, 1969, People and computers - part
    2: Computers and Automation, v. 18, no. 12, p. 53-
    55.

Rosenbleuth, A., Wiener, N., and Bigelow, J., 1943,
    Behavior, purpose and teleology: Phil. Sci.,
    v. 10, no. 1, p. 18-24.

Rosenbleuth, A., and Wiener, N., 1950, Purposeful and
    nonpurposeful behavior: Phil. Sci., v. 17, no. 4,
    p. 318-326.

Sainsbury, C.L., 1969, Tin resources of the world: U.S.
    Geol. Survey Bull. 1301, 55 p.

Simon, H.A., 1969, The sciences of the artificial:
    M.I.T. Press, Boston, Massachusetts, 123 p.

Skinner, B.F., 1971, Beyond freedom and dignity: A.A.
    Knopf, New York, 225 p.

Vistelius, A.B., 1949, On the question of the mechanism
    of the formation of strata: Doklady Akad. Nauk,
    SSSR., v. 65, p. 191-194.

von Bertalanffy, L., 1968, General system theory: G.
    Braziller, New York, 289 p.

Weinberg, G.M., 1975, An introduction to general systems
    thinking: John Wiley & Sons, New York, 279 p.

DEVELOPMENTS AT THE MAN-MACHINE INTERFACE

Donald B. McIntyre

Pomona College

ABSTRACT

Because early computers were expensive and had small
memories, attention had to be given to using them efficiently, although this made computer languages cumbersome
and unnatural for the human beings who used them. Computer programming had little connection with the development of mathematical concepts.

A summary of the evolution of computer hardware
shows that the power available for a fixed price has increased dramatically. Changes in computer languages and
in operating systems have gone along with changes in
hardware. As computers have become larger and cheaper,
more of the operating system has been transferred to
control storage. Scheduling of the use of computer resources, which used to be an important responsibility of
a human operator, is to an ever increasing extent taken
over by the machine itself. The complicated paging that
is performed to make efficient use of main memory and
auxiliary storage is transparent to the users, who therefore are freed to work on the problems that are their
proper concern.

Implementation of the concepts of virtual storage
and virtual machines allows many users to work simultaneously as if each had access to a dedicated computer
with a larger memory than possessed by the real machine.
This, combined with terminals that do not interrupt the

central processor unnecessarily, has been an important
trend in the past ten years. Terminals now are capable
of full-screen displays, which can be modified anywhere
on the screen. Card decks have become obsolete.

The most important development in language design
has been the implementation of the APL language, which
continues the historical evolution of mathematical notation. Its power comes from its use of functions and
operators (which are distinguished from one another),
from its extension of primary or primitive functions
(represented by single symbols), from its emphasis on
the use of arrays and the avoidance of much of the ap-
paratus of control statements that characterize most of
the other languages, and the use of workspaces in which
the user defines the environment. Although APL was considered expensive and inefficient on early computers,
this view is no longer justified, especially today when
emphasis must be on conserving skilled human resources.
APL is supported by all the major computer manufacturers
and can be obtained on some desk-top computers.

The development of Viewdata systems, notably the
British Post Office's Prestel, is bringing computer technology into the homes of those who have not considered
purchasing home computers. This trend will decrease
significantly the resistance to computers that is engen-
dered by fear of the unknown.

Online bibliographic searching has become a tool of
major importance in scientific research. The use of
Geo.Ref, GeoArchive, SCI, and SSIE are especially noted.
The growth of nonbibliographic online data bases has
raised the problem of how these can be indexed and made
more generally available.

I conclude that students of geology must know how
to use computers if they are to work effectively in a
world in which technology is changing so quickly. The
developments at the man-machine interface seem never to
have been so exciting or so vitally important.

EVOLUTION OF COMPUTER HARDWARE

The most obvious developments in the field of computing have been in hardware. Given the expenditure of
a constant sum of money, the computer power of the central processor has risen dramatically, as I can

illustrate from my own experience. Because I have been involved especially with IBM computers, and because of their importance in the market, my examples are mainly taken from IBM machines, but parallel development went on at other companies.

In 1960 the Geology Department at Pomona College purchased a Clary computer for $20,000. It had a drum memory capable of storing 32 integers, and its programs consisted of wired boards that controlled the processor when a mechanical device stepped through the sequence of instructions. Logarithms and trigonometric functions were performed by separate cartridges, only one of which could be plugged in at a time. Today our students carry more powerful computers (programmable calculators) in their pockets, and they cost between $100 and $500.

Prior to announcing System/360 in 1964, IBM had three principal types of computers:

(1) Computers that addressed individual characters. The parent of this series was the IBM 702, introduced in 1953, and from this root came such computers as the 705 (1954), the 1401 (1959), and the 7080 (1960).

(2) Computers that operated as true decimal machines. The parents of this series were the IBM 604, an electromechanical calculator introduced in 1948, and the 650, a vacuum-tube machine with a drum memory, introduced in 1953. From these were descended the 7070 (1958), the 7074 (1960), and the small 1620 (1959).

(3) Binary Computers.
These are the computers descended from the IBM 701 (1952) and 704 (1954). They included the 709 (1957), 7090 (1959), 7094 (1962), and 7094-II (1963); also the 7040/44 (1961), with two registers of 6-bit bytes, and the remarkable 7030 or Stretch computer (1960), which had 8-bit bytes and other features that in 1964 were included in the System/360.

In 1965 Pomona College installed one of the first IBM 360s shipped to a customer. It cost about 10 times what the Clary had cost, but it had a card-reader, a line-printer, and a disk drive. Its initial memory was

16K bytes, but this was increased in steps to 250K as
usage grew. In 1975 the Geology Department purchased an
IBM 5100 desktop computer for about $20,000. The APL
language (including a file system) was part of hardware,
and the user had a 64K workspace available. Because the
5100 is portable and can give displays on videomonitors,
it is useful especially in the classroom. Moreover students can be encouraged to use it freely as the whole
system of hardware and software is purchased and there
is no need for any type of accounting.

       In May 1979 Pomona College replaced the 360 with an
IBM 4331, the second one installed at a customer's site.
Unlike the 360/40, the 4331 supports terminals, and 30
of IBM's 3278 full-screen terminals are available for
free use by students and faculty. Although the 4331
operates as if it were a number of (virtual) machines,
the real memory is 1M; that is 1 Megabyte, or 1 million
bytes. The College accepted the 4331 as an interim processor to be used until the more powerful 4341 could be
delivered. The 4341 has a memory of 4M, but this can be
increased in the field to 8M.

       In less than 15 years the real computer memory
available in this small liberal arts college has increased 500 times, and the increase in disk storage is
equally spectacular.

EVOLUTION OF COMPUTER LANGUAGES AND OPERATING SYSTEMS

       The first computers could be programmed only in
their own machine language. But when assemblers were
developed, much of the detail was turned over to the
machine, thus sparing the human programmer. For example,
by using assembly language the programmer could refer to
a memory location by its symbolic address instead of
having to specify an absolute location, although registers had absolute addresses. In assembly language, instructions could be given in mnemonic code (such as CLA
for Clear and Add to the Accumulator) with enormously
improved readability of the code. Macros could be written in which several assembly-language instructions simulated a new and specialized machine instruction. The
development of higher level languages continued this
trend allowing the programmer to specify in a single
statement what the compiler would translate into many
machine instructions. More and more of the work was
given to the machine to perform, so that the programmer

could work at a level more suitable for the human mind
and more appropriate to the problem presented by the
user. FORTRAN, designed for scientific work, was developed for binary computers similar to the 704 and the
7090 series. COBOL, suitable for commercial work, was
developed for computers which address individual characters, such as the 705 and its descendents. The history
of development of these and other high-level languages
has been documented by the Association of Computing Mach-
inery (1978). No language of present interest was written for a decimal machine, although the popular 1620
used FORTRAN.

     The computer systems that supported FORTRAN and
COBOL not only invoked the language compilers needed to
translate source code into object code that could run on
the particular computer, but automatically fetched the
subroutines that were referred to in the program. They
also provided a linkage editor that built a coherent
package from the modules gathered by the system "librarian", which was part of the operating system.

     Before 1964 the computing world was divided into
two parts, the commercial and the scientific. There
were two types of machines which had entirely different
internal structures and which supported dissimilar high-
level languages, but the announcement of System/360 on
7 April 1964 changed this: a single general-purpose
computer, appropriately termed a 360 (for 'full-circle'),
could perform both commercial and scientific computing.
It could address an individual character stored in a
byte, whose size of 8 bits permitted an extension of the
basic character set from 64 (6-bit Binary Coded Decimal)
to 256 (Extended BCD). And it also could address a
group of contiguous bytes to form a Half Word, a Full
Word, or a Double Word (2, 4, or 8 bytes respectively).
Moreover all models of System/360 had a common instruction set, so that a program written for any one model
could run on any other, provided that time and space imposed no constraints. Unlike previous computers, whose
addressing structure necessarily restricted memory to
some small size, such as 32K in a 7090, by using the
method of addressing by base register and displacement,
System/360 had the ability to address memories as large
as 16M.

     Similar to today's pocket calculators, early com-
puters could do only one job at a time. Operating systems (sometimes termed supervisors or monitors) performed

only the simplest of tasks, and the human operator in
charge constantly had to intervene to initiate or terminate jobs, to decide the order in which jobs would be run,
to assign tape drives, and to mount tapes and load card
decks. Jobs were submitted to a batch stream presided
over by a human operator who tried to optimize the use
of the resources. But when a small job was running,
the operator was unable to allocate unused memory to
another program. Because every program loaded at an
absolute address, no flexibility was possible. But the
360 was a true System whose architecture made provision
for an operating system that enabled the computer to
direct its own activity. For example, it had a PSW
(Program Status Word) and 16 General Purpose Registers,
whereas the 7090 had had an Instruction Counter and three
Index Registers, which were not general purpose but used
only to control addressing.

When Pomona's 360 was delivered, neither we nor the
IBM employees with whom we worked understood the significance of the designation, System/360. We did not even
have an operator's console, and the only manner we could
run was under Basic Assembler, which required the card
deck to pass through the reader-punch twice. Because we
had no operating system, we used all the registers as
high-speed storage, and used privileged instructions,
such as LPSW (Load PSW), with complete freedom. We did
not appreciate that the reason for having "privileged"
instructions was to give the System control over the
work of several simultaneous users. Finally when we
realized what we would gain by giving up some of our
freedom to use parts of the hardware, we began to understand the revolution in the man-machine interface implied
by System/360.

Multiprogramming was possible on the 360 because the
system managed storage, and could assign job streams to
different partitions of memory. Because all addresses
were relative, the loader was free to put a program into
a different part of memory if it was resubmitted. Relative addressing, storage protection, and privileged instructions (used only by the system), were all needed
to provide the flexibility that made better use of the
machine.

VIRTUAL STORAGE AND VIRTUAL MACHINES

In 1970 IBM announced its 370/145, which not only
had monolithic storage instead of core memory, but had
control storage hardware. Addressing was provided for
16 control registers, although only 4 were implemented
in 1970. The implication of the announcement was that
IBM was preparing to announce Virtual Storage (VS).
This meant that the System was about to take a major
step forward. Whereas the operator of the 360 or 370
previously had to decide which jobs would run in different fixed partitions of real memory (foreground and background), the system would henceforth divide memory into
"pages", which would be swapped between main memory and
auxiliary storage as needed, so that many jobs could be
serviced simultaneously and the resources of the machine
used efficiently. The operation of the computer had become too complex for a human operator, and the System
had to be given the physical resources to do the job
itself.

When computers had small memories, a large job required segmentation and overlays, so that when one part
of the program had been completed it would call into
memory the next part, and destroy itself in the process.
The program for automatic contouring published by the
Kansas Geological Survey (McIntyre, Pollard and Smith,
1968), originally written for a 7090 and subsequently
modified for a small 360, had no fewer than 12 overlays
or phases. But VS permits the programmer to ignore the
restrictions of a finite real memory, and as long as
there is adequate disk memory, the virtual system, using
Dynamic Address Translation hardware, can bring into
real memory the pages as they are demanded by the program. The System, rather than the human operator or
programmer, takes care of the addressing requirements.
Programming of large jobs therefore is greatly simplified. Not only is there no need for overlays, but
every user can work with the full compiler, instead of
with only a subset as was often the situation formerly.
And debug aids are more powerful and more available to
the average user.

RCA announced VS in September 1970, but a year later
abandoned the manufacture of computers. In 1972 IBM announced VS and VM (Virtual Machines), so that the latent
power of the 370/145 was invoked. VS, or Virtual Storage, allows the programmer to proceed as if addressable
storage extended to 16M, although the real size of main

memory is less than this. The system takes care of swap-
ping information between main memory and auxiliary storage, usually on disk drives. Thus, the extended hardware
achieves more efficiently the overlaying of the program
or data, which previously consumed considerable human
effort and ingenuity. On the other hand, with VM a single computer simulates the concurrent operation of many
independent machines, each with its own operating system.
The user's terminal becomes the operator's console of a
private computer. For example, the user can display and
modify the contents of the PSW and registers of his virtual machine, exactly as the computer operator in the
machine room used to do for the real machine. But this
activity on a virtual machine does not affect other
users. When Pomona's 360 was new, I taught students how
to work in machine language by using the switches on the
console to control the contents of the registers and
PSW. We could step through a sequence of instructions
and observe the operation of the machine in detail.
This admirable teaching method required total dedication
of the computer, and when the work load on the 360 increased, we could no longer afford this luxury. But the
user of a virtual machine can perform these operations
without interfering with the work of other users. Thus,
everyone has the advantage of what seems to be a dedicated machine, unless, of course, the real resources are
inadequate for the total work involved. VM permits more
efficient use of the computer's power, and adds to the
security of individual users. With VM, interactive users
can do their work simultaneously with batch processing.

        To implement VM the computer must have Control
Storage (including Dynamic Address Translation) and a
Control Program. Today's control storage is likely to
be considerably larger than yesterday's main memory, and
more and more of the operating system is moving from
software to control storage.

IBM 4300, DESK-TOP COMPUTERS, AND FULL-SCREEN TERMINALS

        On 30 January 1979, IBM announced its long awaited
4300 series of middle-sized processors. The 360 (1964)
had used core memory and integrated logic circuits; the
370/145 (1970) had introduced the hardware to perform
Dynamic Address Translation, and used monolithic memory
in place of core; the 370/158 (1972) used Mosfet technology (Metal oxide silicon field effect transistor)
and implemented both VS and VM. The effect of the 4300

announcement was rather to decrease component size and
power requirements and to bring the cost down dramatically. Component chips went from a density of 2K to 64K
at a single step, and main memory for an IBM computer
was reduced from $75,000 to $15,000 for 1 Megabyte. It
was said that the number of first-day orders for the 4300
series exceeded the number of computers then existing.

IBM's 5100 desk-top computer, which became available
in 1975, demonstrated that the manufacturers of large
computers also intended to participate in the rapidly increasing market for desk-top minicomputers. Hewlett-
Packard claimed in October 1979 that its desk-top models
operated about 10 times faster than their 1974 counter-
parts and offered users memories that were 14 times larger. It was predicted that by 1984 desk-top systems
would reach 2M in user main memory, with 5M on floppy
disks, and 120M on hard disks. In 1979 Texas Instruments
reported the development of bubble memories with access
times twice as fast as previously, and memory chips with
more than one-million bits of storage, with automatic
error correction, in less than one square centimeter.

Already some students come to college with their
own computers, and wish to link them to the campus computer. It is obvious that desk-top computers will become
available in almost every home, where they will be taken
for granted, as the telephone and television are today.
Central computers will be more powerful and appropriate
aids for human thought. Terminals will be more elaborate, but perhaps cheaper. And as computers become more
numerous, there will be a greater premium on those who
know how to use them well.

From 1965 on it became increasingly usual for users
to communicate with computers interactively through terminals rather than by submitting a deck of cards to a
batch system. The IBM 2741 terminal was especially well
known, although there were numerous other brands. The
Selectric ball (typing element) permitted a wide range
of fonts, obtainable also by the later introduction of
the Diablo "daisy wheel". The 2741 was similar to an
IBM Selectric typewriter, and its characteristic sound
was familiar, not only to computer users, but to the
many people who heard them in action at airline counters.
The output was typed, and enormous quantities of paper
were consumed, usually only to end up in the waste bas-
ket when a particularly intractable problem was being
explored. Consequently many manufacturers introduced

Cathode-Ray Tube (CRT) displays that eliminated the need
to print the entire dialogue with the computer.

All these terminals operated in a start/stop mode;
that is, every action necessitated an interrupt on the
Central Processing Unit (CPU). To make the interaction
with the system more efficient, IBM replaced the 2741
with the 3270 type of terminal, which have CRT screens,
but which operate differently from the older, start/stop
terminals. The user does not have to work one line at a
time, but rather can move the cursor to any part of the
screen to enter or modify data. Thus, the user may
spend several minutes entering data on the screen, without having to wait for the computer to respond to the
many interrupts that would have occurred under the old
system. Moreover, only the changes that have been made
in the screen are transmitted to and from the computer.
Thus, by providing more power in the terminals and their
controllers, the system allows the CPU more machine
cycles to do its proper job.

Terminals that behave in this manner are termed
"full screen" terminals, and they are supported by an
operating system, such as IBM's Conversational Monitor
System (CMS), that provides full-screen editing and
other utilities, such as file management. The result is
greatly increased productivity. Because several terminals are supported by a single controller, it is economical to have several terminals in a cluster. They then
can share a printer, such as an IBM 3287. With such a
system available, punched cards are obsolete.

IBM now has color terminals, and users are just beginning to explore the possibilities, just as TV produ-
cers did when color TV became popular. Graphic display
also is becoming more accessible to users, although the
term "computer graphics" has different meanings to different people. Plotting of graphs of all types is no
longer a problem, and students in beginning chemistry
classes, for example, can use the computer to plot the
results of their experiments. A few firms, such as
Evans and Sutherland, have carried true interactive
graphics to an extraordinary degree of sophistication,
and it is impossible to convey in writing the spectacular results that can be achieved: under the command of
a light pen, objects can be "picked up" and moved on the
screen, scales can be changed, and the objects can be rotated in three dimensions. This type of application
usually is supported on a minicomputer, such as a PDP-11,
dedicated to the purpose.

THE APL LANGUAGE AS AN INTELLECTUAL TOOL

We have seen that the evolution of computers in the past 20 years has been towards more complex operating systems that take much of the burden of allocating machine resources away from the human operator. The complicated addressing needed to support paging is transparent to the user. Thus, computers are constantly becoming simpler to use, and one can expect that users will find it easy to write their own programs instead of delegating the job to a programmer who is not an expert in the user's own field. In short the computer should be used as a tool of thought.

The earliest computers had small memories, and only those who knew the internal structure intimately could hope to program and use one of them. As a result of this physical constraint, programming became detached from the mainstream of development of mathematical thought. During the 19th Century, mathematicians such as Cayley and Sylvester developed what the latter termed the "Algebra of Multiple Quantity". They emphasized how important it was to escape from the tyranny of scalars by conceiving of and working with arrays. Sir William Rowan Hamilton was the first to use "vector" in its modern sense, and Sylvester introduced the term "matrix" into mathematics.

Unfortunately much of this experience and tradition was necessarily set aside when computers were developing. Languages such as FORTRAN require the user to manipulate scalars. Loops are built into the program, so that what should be thought of as an array is treated as a succession of operations on scalars. John Backus (1978), the leader of the FORTRAN design team, has said that the development of languages of this type held back the progress of computing for 20 years. The programmer had to concentrate on control statements, loops, and Dimension and Declaration statements, and much of a typical program had little apparent relevance to the subject matter that is properly the user's concern.

The APL language originated as an extension and systematization of mathematical notation, and it is the only computer language that existed independently of the computer and would continue to be used were computers to disappear. In its earliest form, it was used by its inventor, K.E. Iverson, as a method of describing complex systems (Iverson, 1973). It came to the attention of a general audience in Iverson's book "A Programming Language" (1962), in which the first example is an

exact account of the architecture of IBM's 7090, then
one of the principal computers used for scientific work.

Iverson notation was used in 1964 to give a formal
description of the newly announced System/360, and in
1965 the notation was implemented on a 7090 as the language that came to be known as APL. The language is
distinguished by its extension of the number of functions
recognized in mathematics by a single symbol, such as
+ -. The ball on the Selectric typewriter provided an
introduction to these symbols on the machine, and the
extension of the character set on the 360, achieved by
going from a 6-bit to an 8-bit code, made internal storage of the symbols possible. Today APL is supported not
only by IBM but by almost every major computer manufac-
turer.

Being dynamic, APL does not bother the user with
Declarations and Dimensions, and instead of huge programs, good APL typically consists of single-line functions consistent with mathematical tradition (McIntyre,
1978). Because APL distinguishes between functions and
operators (which modify functions), the language possesses extraordinary power and brevity. APL character-
istically works on arrays, which can be of any shape and
rank, and consequently loops and control statements are
usually absent. The user of APL learns to think in
terms of arrays, just as Sylvester urged mathematicians
to do a century ago. For example, an APL function to
compute the mean should work on a matrix or an array of
higher rank by summing over the last axis: thus

$$MEAN:(+/\omega) \div 0 \bot \rho \omega$$

APL is consistent, more so than ordinary mathematical notation, and it provides a generality that ensures
uniform treatment of special situations, such as empty
arrays. Through APL, boolean functions become an integ-
ral part of algebra, where they properly belong, and unlike other computer languages, APL has an intellectual
content that is well worth studying for the insight it
brings (McIntyre, 1979, 1980).

The manner in which APL is implemented also is different from that of other languages. Not only is it dynamic and interactive, but it provides an environment,
termed a Workspace, which can contain the user's functions and variables, as well as control of the index

origin, print precision, etc. A workspace can be saved
on disk, and individual objects can be copied from it.
Moreover, although APL could claim to be the highest
level of all existing languages, its power enables APL
to be used for tasks that would be considered close to
machine language. For example, one of my students has
used APL (with auxiliary processors for shared variables)
to read and use a star-catalog tape issued by the Smithsonian Institution, although it is written in the internal BCD code of a 7094 computer.

My own experience in teaching the use of computers
to students and colleagues in many different disciplines
is that APL increases productivity because, once the
problem is clearly defined, the APL solution is usually
evident. It therefore is possible to begin writing and
testing the solution at the same time that one endeavors
to formulate the problem. This is one of the most important developments at the man-machine interface.

VIEWDATA, CEEFAX, ORACLE, AND PRESTEL SYSTEMS

Almost every home in a country such as Britain has
a telephone and at least one television set, which with
little or no modification could be used as the display
screen for a computer. Indeed it is possible now to buy
a keyboard that can use an ordinary TV set for its display, and which can act as a terminal to a remote computer through a simple modem and the existing telephone
line. However it takes some knowledge to make the connection to a remote computer, and the online charge for
use of the computer probably is too great for most potential users.

A step in this direction was taken by the BBC when
it introduced its Ceefax service in 1974, and this was
followed in 1975 by the Oracle service produced by Britain's independent television company ITA. A television
picture with 575 lines, each with 700 picture elements,
and a gray scale of 64 levels (which can be represented
by 6 bits), is equivalent to 2.4M bits. Large amounts
of information therefore are transmitted over a television channel. Because not all the possible channels
are used currently for transmission of pictures, the
BBC is able to transmit frames of information that can
be displayed on a slightly modified TV set. This is
the Ceefax system. About 100 frames are transmitted in

a continuous cycle, so that the user who wishes a particular frame has to wait for an average of about 12 seconds
before that frame comes round. Once the frame is displayed, it remains on the screen as long as the viewer
wishes.

In 1976 there were 500 sets in Britain that could
display the frames transmitted by the BBC and ITA. By
1980 it was possible to purchase or lease a set in any
major city in the country, and it is forecast that in
ten years 25 percent of the homes will be using the service.

Although it must be emphasized that Teletext systems such as Ceefax and Oracle are not interactive, they
are, however, free (once the equipment is installed),
and they serve as a powerful introduction to computing
in the home. It is certain that any family accustomed
to these systems will not be afraid of a computer terminal.

Of greater significance is Prestel, a product of the
British General Post Office, which also is responsible
for Britain's telephone service. The user of Prestel has
an account, which similar to a telephone account, charges
for use made of the system. The modified television set
is linked to the user's telephone, and a connection can
be made to the Post Office's computer at any time that
the television and telephone are not otherwise being
used. A remote control unit, rather similar to a pocket
calculator, enables the user to activate the system in
the same manner that a change might be made in the TV
channel being viewed. Some 200,000 frames, from more
than 200 suppliers, are accessible online. If the user
has a directory, he can request the display of a particular frame by entering its code number. Otherwise he
can display the first frame of a menu and locate the desired frames by a tree (root) system with 10 branches
at each node. Each frame contains 880 characters arranged in 22 rows and 40 columns, so that the library
of 200,000 frames is equivalent to 176 million characters. This compares with an estimated 55 million characters in the London telephone directory. However the
amount of useful information is less. In order to
achieve readability, there are probably less than 100
words on an average frame. Because all frames are accessible constantly, access time is better than with
Ceefax and Oracle, which depend on cyclic transmission.

Prestel marks an electronic revolution in the transmission of information. The user can obtain information on such diverse topics as Air Travel, Ancient Monuments, Automobiles, Betting, Bible Society, Careers, Contraception, Dishwashers, Divorce, Jobs, Jokes, Legal Advice, Maternity Benefits, Medieval Banquets, Night Life, Pregnancy, Pubs, Science, Sports, and Weather.[1] Some frames are provided free of charge, whereas for others there is a charge. For example, the car buying guide costs 3P per frame and the maximum price per frame is 50P (Cawkell, 1977b; Berkovitch, 1979).

Development of Prestel started in the early 1970s and a public test began in 1976. I was told that in 1979 there were about 1500 users, presumably all using the test site in the London area. It is claimed that by the end of 1980, 60 percent of the people in Britain will be able to connect to Prestel with a local call.

Prestel provides information at the user's request, but it is not truly interactive. Of course, Prestel could be adapted to provide computing power for its users, but the load on the system probably would be intolerable if more than simple calculations were allowed. As the system grows in popularity and computers become cheaper, regional centers may be created where Prestel's information service can be combined with true computing power for the users.

Although the British Post Office has been the leader in developing a computer-based information service for its customers, there is widespread interest in the idea. Germany and Holland have purchased the Prestel service, and rival systems have been created in other countries. Because Prestel is a registered trademark, it is necessary to have a generic name for systems similar to it, and the term Viewdata (Videotex in the US) is used in this sense. The first international conference and exhibition of Viewdata was held in London in March 1980. The British Radio and Electrical Manufacturers Association predict that eventually all television sets made in Britain will be able to be used for Viewdata reception.

---

[1]The Prestel Users Guide and Directory: Eastern Countries Newspaper Group Ltd., Norwich, England.

ONLINE BIBLIOGRAPHIC SEARCHING

Online bibliographic searching has grown in recent
years to be a major research tool and marks an important
step in the development of man-machine interaction. The
principal suppliers of the service are Systems Development Corporation, in Santa Monica, California, and Lockheed Information Systems, Palo Alto, California. These
firms use their computer power and knowledge to make
available data bases created by a variety of suppliers.
The number of these data bases is great and constantly
growing. To make use of this service one needs to have
an account number and a terminal, such as the portable
Texas Instruments Silent-700. Charges are made only
when the service is actually used, and then the price,
which differs with the data base, is about $1.20 per
minute of connect time. If a large bibliography is
desired, it is more economical to have it printed off-
line and mailed.

The principal geological data base used in the
United States is Geo.Ref, which is produced by the
American Geological Institute. Geo.Ref has been available only through SDC's Orbit System, but Lockheed plans
to make Geo.Ref available on its Dialog System early in
1981.

GeoArchive is similar in intent to Geo.Ref. It is
produced by GeoSystems, London, England, and has been
available in the United States only through Lockheed's
Dialog System. This is not the place to discuss the relative merits of Geo.Ref and GeoArchive, the details of
search strategy, or the Orbit and Dialog commands, but for
those interested I recommend that some of the same references be found on both data bases and printed out in
full. One then can see which search strategies would
recover these articles in each data base, and which
strategies would fail. The user should be equipped with
the Thesaurus and Guide for the data base in order to
work effectively, but it is remarkable how successful
one can be in using a new data base without these aids
provided that one is familiar with the computer system.

Other bibliographic data bases that I find particularly useful are Science Citation Index, SCI, and the
Smithsonian index to funded research, SSIE. SCI is an
excellent data base to search if you know a key reference, because you can find out who has since cited it.
SSIE is valuable if you wish to know who currently is
doing research on a topic.

As a simple example of a Geo.Ref search, I entered
"1755" as the key for searching, and retrieved the following references, among others:

Isoseismal map of the 1755 Lisbon earthquake
(1979)

A discussion of the 1755 Lisbon earthquake
(1977)

The earthquake of November 1, 1755 (1968)

This is hardly a sophisticated search, and it did
yield some papers that were not relevant to Lisbon (such
as one on Moon rock number 1755), but it is certainly
successful in gaining entry into published modern views
about the Lisbon earthquake of 1755. With these successful "hits" in hand, one then can consult the references
that they in turn cite.

During the Geochautauqua, one of the speakers referred to the work of Crain on the distribution of cra-
ters on Mars. Being interested in the topic, but not
knowing Crain's work (or even the spelling of his name),
I used a portable terminal to search Geo.Ref during a
break in the sessions.

I asked for any author "Crane" or "Crain" that was
combined with the word "Mars". I got one hit, namely
the paper by Ian K. Crain on "Statistical Methods for
Geotectonic Analysis" that was an abstract in the International Geological Congress resumes (1972).

I next used SCI to see who had cited any paper published by "Crain IK" in 1972, and found the paper by
Buckley and Buckley on "The Packing of Royal Tern Nests",
published in Auk 94 (1977) 36-43.

Returning to Geo.Ref, I asked what variants of the
author "Crain I" were present, and by combining "Crain,
I.K." with "Crain, Ian K." I found 25 papers. One of
these was Crain's paper on "The Monte-Carlo Generation
of Random Polygons", in Computers & Geosciences 4 (1978)
131-141. I also found that the author had moved from
Canberra, Australia, to Ottawa, Canada. It took only a
few minutes to obtain this information.

In order to find out more about Prestel, Viewdata,
Teletext, Ceefax, and Oracle, I used the INSPEC file on
SDC. I found papers such as the following, all with

short abstracts which I do not reproduce here:

    Prestel - the UK Post Office's Viewdata service
      (1978)
    Strengths and weaknesses of Prestel (1979)
    Teletext systems: a review (1979)
    Rivals of Viewdata and Teletext in the Inter-
      national field (1978)
    The coming of age of Viewdata (1978)
    The technical side of Viewdata (1978)

Although I had not previously used the INSPEC data base, and did not have the thesaurus or the manual, I was nevertheless able to find a number of informative recent articles on the subject of my search.

Interesting uses of the Citation Index are given by Garfield (1974), Cawkell (1977a), and Scrutton (1977), who show how SCI can be a tool in the study of interrelationships in scientific work.

NONBIBLIOGRAPHIC DATA BASES

Nonbibliographic data bases are important also, but I have found it difficult to discover the existence of many of those that are available. The only one that I use myself is the file of X-ray Diffraction data for crystalline substances available from the Joint Committee on Powder Diffraction Standards. The magnetic tape is available for purchase, and I have described a simple search program that can be used to help in the identification of minerals by X-ray diffraction methods (Glazner and McIntyre, 1979).

An example of a large nonbibliographic data base that is available online from a commercial time-sharing firm is IMPORTS, available from I.P. Sharp Associates, Toronto. It gives information on every shipment of crude oil or petroleum products into the U.S.

I should note here that Felix Chayes is engaged in a praiseworthy project to construct a worldwide data base on the chemical compositions of igneous rocks. The difficulty in having access to data of this type is that the information is not supported financially by commercial applications.

Indexes are available for online data bases, and I have found the following to be useful:

Directory of Online Databases
Cuadra Associates

Information Sources
Information Industry Association

But there is a great need for a compilation of non-bibliographic data bases relevant to geology. The National Oceanic and Atmospheric Administration (NOAA) is one example of a source that can supply machine-readable geologic data, such as gravity anomalies, heat-flow values, etc.

CONCLUSION

Computers have become a vital part of modern culture, and their use affects many aspects of geologic work. I believe that it is essential for students of geology who hope to survive in this fast changing and exciting world to be taught how to work at this interface between man and machine, so that they will put these powerful tools to proper use and avoid the fears, pitfalls, and abuses that come from ignorance.

REFERENCES

ACM, 1978, History of Programming Languages Conference, Los Angeles, California (June 1-3, 1978): ACM Sigplan Notices, v. 13, no. 8, 310 p.

Backus, J., 1978, Can programming be liberated from the Von Neumann style?: Comm. ACM, v. 21, no. 8, p. 613-641.

Berkovitch, I., 1979, Building a science magazine within Prestel: Phys. Technol., v. 10, 3 p.

Cawkell, A.E., 1977a, Science perceived through the Science Index. Endeavour: New Ser. 1, no. 2, p. 57-58.

Cawkell, A.E., 1977b, Developments in interactive on-line television systems and Teletext information services in the home: On-Line Review, v. 1, p. 31-38.

Glazner, A.F., and McIntyre, D.B., 1979, Computer-aided
    X-ray diffraction identification of minerals in
    mixtures: Am. Miner. v. 64, p. 902-905.

Iverson, K.E., 1973, APL in exposition: IBM Tech. Rept.
    320-3010 (Available from APL Press), 61 p.

McIntyre, D.B., 1978, Experience with direct definition
    one-liners in writing APL applications: I.P. Sharp
    Assoc. Ltd., An APL Users Meeting, Proceedings,
    p. 281-297.

McIntyre, D.B., 1979, Computer Corner: Computers & Geo-
    sciences, v. 5, no. 2, p. 273-275.

McIntyre, D.B., 1980, APL in a Liberal Arts College:
    I.P. Sharp Assoc. Ltd., An APL Users Conference,
    Proceedings, p. 544-574.

McIntyre, D.B., Pollard, D.D., and Smith, R., 1968, Com-
    puter programs for automatic contouring: Kansas
    Geol. Survey Computer Contr. 23, 75 p.

Scrutton, R.A., 1977, Fragments of the earth's continen-
    tal lithosphere: Endeavour, New Ser. 1, no. 2,
    p. 58-62.

COMPUTERS AS AN AID IN MINERAL-RESOURCE EVALUATION

Frederik P. Agterberg

Geological Survey of Canada

ABSTRACT

Separate flowcharts have been constructed for (1)
some computer-based techniques for mineral-resource estimation; (2) different types of input for computer-based
mineral-resource estimation and statistical exploration;
and (3) quantification and analysis of geoscience map
data. Several examples are presented to illustrate the
geostatistical modeling of results obtained by image
analysis, and the interpretation of probability index
maps derived by multivariate statistical analysis of systematically quantified data on the geological framework
of a region.

INTRODUCTION

For planning purposes it may be necessary to acquire
knowledge about the mineral potential of regions where
undiscovered ore deposits may be found in the course of
future exploration operations. This paper is concerned
with the contribution that computers can make to resource
evaluation. Special attention will be paid to the subjects of quantification and multivariate analysis of geoscience map data.

The information for a region consists not only of
published geoscience maps and reports but also of an intricate network of concepts regarding the geological

history of the region considered and the modes of occurrence of the undiscovered deposits. In the past, these
concepts were frequently in conflict with one another.
For example, one geologist would advocate the hydrothermal
origin of a given type of mineral deposit. In exploration
operations he would emphasize the significance of deep-
seated fractures. At the same time another geologist,
assuming a synsedimentary origin for this deposit type,
may have stressed the importance of lithological features.
Especially if the evidence is scarce, it remains necessary to entertain mutually contradictory genetic concepts,
and scientific investigations then should be guided by
Chamberlin's method of multiple working hypotheses. However, concepts on the genesis of ore deposits are being
refined continuously through the acquisition of new information and through better insight into geological processes. This leads to a reduction of the variance of the
opinions and allows the usage of more precise metallogenic
concepts in statistical resource estimation.

Because of the continuing advancement of geophysical
and geochemical methods which produce systematic data, it
is tempting to base quantitative resource appraisals on
these measurements only. However, this would seem to be
a risky procedure. Although certain types of mineral deposits may have direct geophysical signatures - as, for
example, radiometric measurements for uranium and thorium,
aeromagnetic responses for iron deposits, and airborne
electromagnetic methods for massive sulphide deposits -
the inherent difficulties in interpreting such signatures
directly in terms of economic concentrations of minerals
are well known. In the example of indirect interpretations of such data there are difficulties also. Although
many types of quantitative geophysical and geochemical
measurements are continuous, they generally are influenced by the characteristics of the near-surface geology
which, in any given area, is likely to be nonuniform because of the presence of discontinuities separating different rock types. The heterogeneous nature of the geological framework will be reflected in the quantitative
measurements. Although the boundaries between geological
rock units may not be exposed, the available knowledge
about them should be used as much as possible and integrated with the geophysical and geochemical data. In
general thus, it seems that, as is the situation in effective exploration for mineral deposits, effective and
realistic resource appraisal based on predictive models
will require a judicious blend of geological, geophysical,
and geochemical data on a base of sound metallogenic concepts.

In the past, mineral-resource appraisals usually were made by experienced geologists who, in general, formulated their opinions using the language of subjective probabilities. For example, an electromagnetic anomaly may indicate the existence of a massive sulphide deposit which is rich in copper and zinc but simple probabilities would suggest that this is not generally the situation. It might indicate equally the occurrence of a graphite deposit or perhaps the presence of a pyrite body without copper and zinc sulphides, or even merely a geological structure such as a fault. Hence it would be unwise to use the language of certainty when asked whether an undiscovered orebody is present. Either a subjective or an objective probabilistic answer is required.

During the past ten years, computers have been employed increasingly as a tool in mineral-resource evaluation. They are being used for file-building and information management, manipulation of subjective probabilities, image analysis of geoscience map data, and multivariate statistical analysis. These applications can be considered as components of resource analysis, a relatively new topic where the more speculative geological concepts regarding the genesis of mineral deposits are joined with the inductive logic of mathematical statistics and the data-processing capabilities of digital computers.

COMPUTER-BASED MINERAL-RESOURCE ESTIMATION
AND STATISTICAL EXPLORATION

Some computer-based techniques for mineral-resource estimation are shown in Figure 1. Different types of input for resource evaluation and statistical exploration are listed in Figure 2. Most of the techniques of Figure 1 have been discussed in more detail in a review of statistical exploration methods by Agterberg and David (1979). Other recent publications concerned with the subject include a review of resource-appraisal methods by Harris (in press), a compendium of Russian resource-estimation techniques by Rundkvist and others (1979), and the final report on "Prospector", a computer-based consultant for mineral exploration which consists of semantic networks encoding subjective models developed by economic geologists (Duda and others, 1979). The close relationship between quantitative regional mineral-resource estimation and exploration which is aimed specifically at the discovery of new deposits is shown schematically in Figure 2. Findlay and Walsh (1979) have argued that the

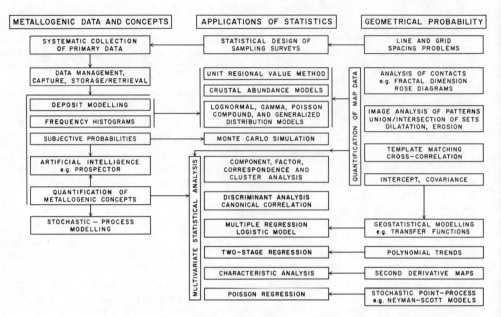

Figure 1.   Some computer-based techniques for mineral-
resource estimation.

application of computer-based statistical techniques is
valid only towards the end stages of a regional-resource
analysis after a firm data base has been established.
These authors also have pointed out that the relationships
between the processes leading to exploration on the one
hand and resource estimation on the other are close but
the end-products are different because exploration hopefully results in discovery and the other merely places
prognostications in quantitative terms.

The headings of Figure 1 are (1) metallogenic data
and concepts, (2) applications of statistics, and (3)
geometrical probability. It can be attempted to use the
geoscience map data of a region for a resource appraisal
in which little or no use is made of metallogenic concepts. Then the procedure which can be followed consists
of two stages: (a) quantification of map data; and (b)
multivariate statistical analysis. We would be concerned
primarily with geometrical probabilities and statistical
techniques. The advantage of this approach is restricted
to its objectivity; however, in practical applications,
it turns out that the number of combinations of map patterns that can be tested systematically for their

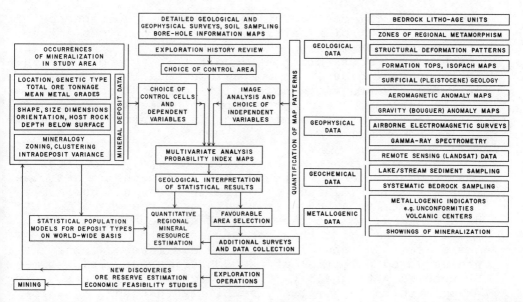

Figure 2.   Different types of input for computer-based
            mineral-resource estimation and statistical
            estimation.

correlation with a pattern for occurrences of mineral deposits is limited severely. In general, the choice of
variables for statistical analysis should be guided by
metallogenic concepts in order to obtain improved results.
This approach is shown schematically in Figure 1 by the
arrow leading from the quantification of metallogenic
concepts to multivariate statistical analysis which consists of the manipulation of quantified map data and other
inputs derived from concepts of geometrical probability.
Studies such as the one by Divi, Thorpe, and Franklin
(1979) in which metallogenic concepts are modeled and
tested statistically will be helpful in resource evaluation for deciding on the types of variables to be used
and the choice of control areas.

      It can be attempted to perform resource appraisals
on the basis of metallogenic data and concepts without
any use of statistical models. In fact, this procedure
is close to a conventional geological practice of which
the objective is to attempt to identify target areas that
duplicate as much as possible with the available data the
areas in which deposits are known. Other geologists with
knowledge of the same area generally would appreciate that

any geometrical configuration proposed in the absence of
sufficient control remains hypothetical and does not represent necessarily the exact true which is unknow.   It
is, however, difficult to transmit this type of uncertainty to nongeologists.   In comparison, statistical models
have the advantage of their built-in uncertainty which
can be estimated.   The step from deterministic geological
modeling to statistical modeling is illustrated in the
following example.

Suppose that in a well-developed area, n mineral deposits with T tons of ore are known to occur in association with a metallotect of which the combined surface
area amounts to A km^2.   In the target area which is to
be appraised, the surface area of the metallotect is
equal to B km^2.   It then can be useful to argue that
there are nB/A tons of ore.   This estimate neglects the
undiscovered potential of the control area.   It also may
be necessary to qualify it by geological arguments, for
example there may be the possibility that the "metallotect" in the target area is not comparable completely
with its counterpart in the control area because of the
absence of a critical but unknown factor that controlled
the mineralization.

The preceding deterministic model can be made probabilistic by introducing additional assumptions regarding
the nature of the random distribution according to which
the mineral deposits are distributed with respect to the
metallotect.   These assumptions can be tested statistically for a control area.   For example, suppose that the deposits are distributed randomly across the metallotect
according to a simple Poisson process.   This model can
be visualized easily as follows.   Let the surface area
of the metallotect be subdivided into many small equal-
area cells by superimposing a grid.   A random distribution according to the simple Poisson process then indicates that each of the small cells has an equal probability of containing a mineral deposit.   Under these conditions the expected number of deposits $\lambda_x = \lambda x$ for an area
of x km^2 underlain by the metallotect remains equal
to that computed by the deterministic model.   In this
formula λ is a constant which is independent of the size
of the area underlain by the metallotect.   We have $\lambda_x =$
n = λA for the control area, and $\lambda_x = nB/A = \lambda B$
for the target area.

Although the expected number of deposits calculated
by our statistical model is equal to that of the deter-

ministic model, the method of prediction is entirely
different because the number of deposits is assumed to be
a random variable K with the Poisson distribution:

$$P(K = k) = e^{-\lambda_x}\lambda_x^k/k! \tag{1}$$

For example, if λ_x = nB/A = 2.7 in the target area, then
the statistical model predicts that there is a probability P(K=3) = 0.220 that there are exactly 3 undiscovered deposits. Suppose that after development of the
target area it turns out that it contains only one mineral deposit. This outcome would prove that the deterministic model is wrong but it is compatible with the statistical model because P(K=1) = 0.181. Of course, the
statistical model could lead to the acceptance of an
erroneous hypothesis regarding the analogy between target
and control areas. For this reason, it should be attempted not only to test the goodness of fit of the statistical
model but also to perform geological interpretation of
estimates of expected values resulting from the statistical analysis.

In order to predict the total tonnage of ore in the
target area, we can assume that the ore tonnage of a single deposit is a random variable of which the mean value
is equal to T/n (=average amount of ore per deposit in
the control area). If the random variables for deposit
density and ore tonnage are statistically independent,
the new statistical model will yield an expected ore
tonnage of TB/A for the target area which is equal to
the amount predicted by means of the deterministic model.
However, the statistical estimate is subject to a considerable uncertainty depending on the form (e.g. lognormal)
assumed for the deposit size distribution.

The preceding statistical model for prediction of
total amount of ore in the larger area makes use of a
so-called generalized random variable (cf. Fig. 1). A
so-called compound random variable (also see Fig. 1)
arises if it can be assumed that the amount of metallotect per larger equal-area cell also satisfies a random
variable whereas the number of deposits per unit of area
underlain by the metallotect remains controlled by a
simple Poisson process. When the random variable for
amount of metallotect has the gamma distribution, the compound random variable for number of mineral deposits per
larger equal-area cell satisfies the negative binomial
model (cf. Agterberg, 1977).

In some applications of multivariate analysis to data
quantified from different types of maps, it is useful to
separate local features (e.g. anomalies) from regional
trends or gradients. Agterberg and Cabilio (1969) fitted
polynomial trend surfaces to a number of lithological variables showing that favorable environments for precious
metal telluride ores in the Abitibi volcanic belt of the
Canadian Shield are defined more precisely by residuals
after elimination of regional trends. For similar reasons, Botbol and others (1979) have applied characteristic
analysis which is a special type of principal-components
analysis to binary patterns extracted from second derivative maps for many geochemical variables. It would be
useful to attempt when the conceptual models will have
been developed further to model the genesis of some types
of ore deposits as stochastic processes in a manner previously employed for sedimentological processes (Schwarzacher, 1975). This stochastic-process modeling (cf.
Fig. 1) also may become helpful for deciding on the types
of transformations and combinations to be applied to the
variables used in multivariate analysis.

Figure 2 shows that the primary inputs for resource
analysis are of three different types. The information
on the mineral deposits leads to the definition of patterns of cells with known deposits and dependent variables
which are correlated with the independent variables consisting of combinations of patterns for geological, geophysical, and geochemical data. The choice of control
area which is based on an exploration history review is
of great importance during the multivariate analysis.
However, as discussed in Agterberg (1974), the quantification of the amount of exploration per cell can present
a difficult problem because our knowledge about the presence or absence of mineral deposits in a given volume of
rock is itself a function of the independent variables.

QUANTIFICATION OF MAP DATA

Methods for coding geoscience data for large regions
are shown in Figure 3. Traditionally, the spatial variability of almost any type of variable is displayed on a
map. Although this practice facilitates our understanding, it may involve a significant amount of interpretation and generalization. In many types of statistical
analysis, the map data are coded for equal-area cells
belonging to a grid. For example, Agterberg and others
(1972) coded the pattern of acidic volcanic rocks in

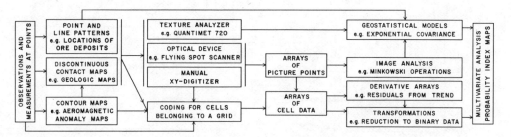

Figure 3.   Quantification and analysis of geoscience
             map data.

east-central Ontario shown in Figure 4 for cells measuring
10 km on a side. Every 10 km cell was subdivided into
400 subcells measuring 500 m on a side and presence of
the rock type at the centers of these subcells was point-
counted. During the past 10 years significant progress
has been made in the field of image analysis and map patterns now can be quantified to give arrays of picture
points which, in turn, can be processed using digital
computers (cf. Fabbri, and Kasvand, 1978). An example
of texture analysis applied to geological map data (from
Agterberg, 1978) is shown in Figure 4. The pattern of
Figure 4A was used as input for a Quantimet 720 with
linear correlator module. Geometrical covariances measured on the Quantimet for the east-west and north-south
directions are shown in Figures 4C and 4D. In order to
obtain these results the pattern of Figure 4A was shifted
with respect to itself for a sequence of distances
(d = ka) equal to multiples (k = 1,2,...,28) of a constant
sampling interval equal to a = 4.694 km. The area of
overlap between the original pattern and the shifted pattern was measured after each shift yielding the covariance
which is expressed in number of picture points divided
by 500,000 in Figures 4C and 4D. Apart from measurement
errors, the covariance for k = 0 provides a measure of
the proportion (= 7.2 percent) of the total area of Figure 4A which is underlain by acidic volcanics. The geometrical covariance can be transformed into an autocorrelation coefficient (r_d) shown in Figure 4B in four directions for small   shifts only using a logarithmic
scale in the vertical direction. The exponential model
provides a good fit to these results. This enables us
to use Matheron's geostatistical formulae (see e.g.
Journel and Huijbregts, 1978) for estimating the variance
of the amount of the rock type contained in a cell of

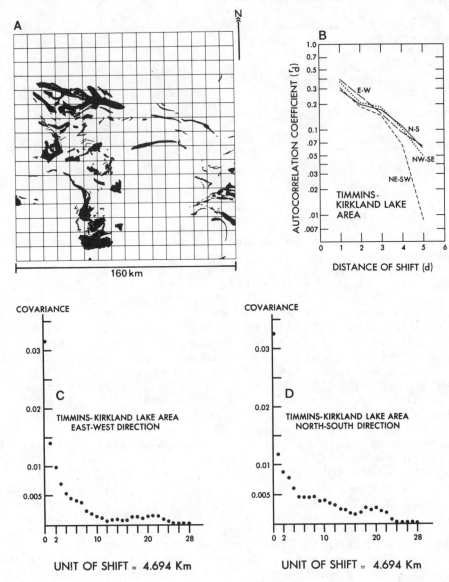

Figure 4. Image analysis of acidic volcanics in Timmins-
          Kirkland Lake area, Ontario (from Agterberg,
          1978). (A) Original pattern with superimposed
          grid (10 km cells). (B) Autocorrelation coef-
          ficients for four directions for pattern of Fig-
          ure 4A. Distances of shifts as on left side
          of Figures 4C and 4D. (C) Covariance (=area of
          overlap after shift) in picture points divided
          by 500,000 for east-west direction. (D) Ditto
          for north-south direction.

variable size and shape randomly superimposed on the pattern.

The geostatistical modeling illustrated in Figure 4
can be taken a step further as shown by Agterberg and
Fabbri (1978) and Agterberg (in press). For the purpose
of multivariate statistical analysis of map data quantified for cells belonging to a grid, we are interested in
the frequency distributions of variables such as cell proportion underlain by a specific rock type. If the cells
are small, this frequency distribution is U-shaped. For
the somewhat larger (e.g. 10 km) cells used in multivariate analysis, it is h-shaped, assuming zero value in
cells where the rock type is absent and a positive value
less than one in cells where it is present in the region.
These sequences of frequency distributions can be modeled
if the variance is known. In Figure 5, observed frequency
distributions and estimated model distributions are shown
for nine examples including the examples of Agterberg and
Fabbri (1978) for percentage of acidic volcanies in 10 km
and 20 km cells in the Bathurst area of New Brunswick.
Suppose that a rock type percentage value x (as plotted
in the vertical direction of Fig. 5) is transformed into a
a value y by the inverse of the relationship $x = \Phi(y)$
where Φ denotes a fractile of the standard normal distribution. Then

$$y = (rz - b)(1 - r^2)^{-\frac{1}{2}} \qquad\qquad (2)$$

where z denotes a value obtained by application of the
same type of transformation to $p = \Phi(z)$ with p being the
frequency percentage value as plotted in the horizontal
direction of Figure 5. The parameter b in Equation (2)
satisfies $\bar{x}=1-\Phi(b)$ where $\bar{x}$ denotes the average cell proportion value. The parameter r follows from $\bar{x}$ and the
variance $s^2(x)$. A nomogram for the relationship between
r, $\bar{x}$, and $s^2(x)$ is given in Agterberg (in press).

Simply stated, the experimental data of Figure 5
imply that a "probit" transformation of cell proportion
data helps to normalize them. Because of the similarity
between "logits" and "probits" (see e.g. Fisher and Yates,
1963), the transformation of cell proportion data into
logits would have a similar effect. This type of transformation is applied to the dependent variable only in
the logistic model of multivariate analysis to be discussed in the next section.

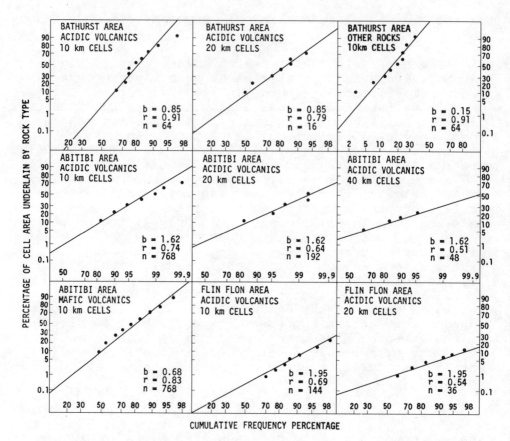

Figure 5.   Straight-line fits for various rock types
in three areas in Canada. Lines satisfy
Eq. (2) with b and r computed from mean $\bar{x}$
and variance $s^2(x)$ of proportion values in
n cells. Both axes have normal probability
scales.

MULTIVARIATE STATISTICAL ANALYSIS OF CELL DATA

Some of the multivariate techniques that can be used
to correlate the occurrences and characteristics of mineral deposits to variables systematically quantified for
the geological framework in a region were shown in Figure
1. Figure 6 represents a contoured probability index map
for copper deposits constructed by Agterberg and others
(1972) using multiple regression analysis. The quantified
map data consisted of rock types including the acidic volcanics of Figure 4A and geophysical (Bouguer and aeromagnetic anomaly) data.

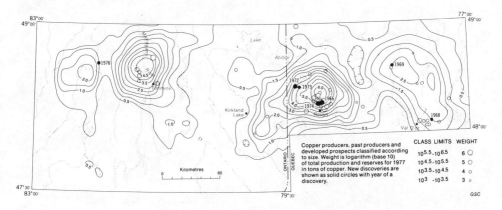

Figure 6.   Contoured probability index map for number
            of events per 40 km unit area in Abitibi
            area of Canadian Shield (after Agterberg,
            and others, 1972) with "new" discoveries
            shown for comparison. Event represents
            one or more copper deposits per 10 km
            cell.

     Also shown in Figure 6 are "new" discoveries of cop-
per deposits on which no data were available when the map
was constructed. A more detailed discussion of this hindsight study has been given in Agterberg and David (1979).
In this section, we will investigate in more detail the
basic assumptions which have to be made in order to construct a probability index map for occurrences of both
known and undiscovered deposits.

     Figure 7A shows the locations of a number of strati-
form massive sulphide deposits in Archean rocks in the
vicinity of Noranda, western Quebec. It also shows the
locations of the 10 km cells of the grid (UTM grid) used
for multivariate statistical analysis. Sets of probabilities computed by using (stepwise) multiple regression
and the logistic model are shown in Figures 7B and 7C.
These cells were used as "control cells". In the linear
model of multiple regression, the dependent variable was
set equal to one for control cells while it was kept equal
to zero in all other cells. It is likely that a number
of these other cells contain undiscovered deposits and
this complicates the statistical estimation procedure.
Recently, some properties of the estimators resulting in
this situation have been studied by Chung and Agterberg
(1980).

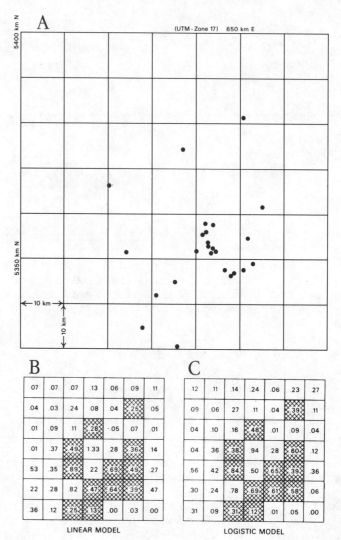

Figure 7.   (A) Stratiform massive sulphide
deposits in vicinity of Noranda,
Quebec with 10 km cells for multivariate analysis.   (B) Each number
represents probability that a 10 km
cell contains one or more deposits
computed by multiple regression.
(C) Ditto for logistic model.
Hatched pattern in Figures 7B and
7C indicates control cells with
one or more known deposits (from
Agterberg, 1975).

The estimated probabilities arising from the linear
model were divided by a constant (f) before plotting them
in Figure 7B. The constant f was set equal to the sum of
all estimated probabilities in a control area divided by
the total number of control cells in this control area.
It can be regarded as an approximation of the probability
of discovery in the entire area of study. An analogous
method was used to correct the probabilities initially
resulting from the logistic model. Figures 7B and 7C
represent, for each 10 km cell, the probability of occurrence of an "event" which consists of one or more deposits. By using Poisson regression, each of the deposits
shown in Figure 7A could be considered separately. However, it may be advantageous to reduce the weights of individual deposits when there is a tendency toward relatively strong local clustering as in the situation of
Figure 7. The linear model can be used as an approximation for either the logistic model of the Poisson model.
The logistic model results in probabilities (Fig. 7C)
which cannot be negative or greater than one whereas unconstrained multiple regression can give negative values
or values greater than one as shown in Figure 7B. The
estimated probabilities of events can be interpreted as
the expected values of random variables. Consequently,
they can be added for larger unit areas and this may
yield contourable patterns as the one in Figure 6.

The contours of Figure 6 are for the expected value
of a random variable representing number of events per
square unit area measuring 40 km on a side. This random
variable was interpreted as a positive binomial variable
in Agterberg and others (1972) and as a Poisson variable
in Agterberg (1975). These two interpretations yield
sequences of probability values for actual numbers of
events per unit which are approximately equal to one another in most practical applications. Neither model can
be satisfied exactly in a strict sense. The Poisson model
has the advantage that it is fully additive as illustrated
by the following example. Suppose that the number of deposits in some area A has a Poisson distribution with parameter λ_a and that in area B it has a Poisson distribution with parameter λ_b. Then the number of deposits
in the combined area C(=A+B) satisfies a Poisson
distribution with paramter $\lambda_c = \lambda_a + \lambda_b$. In the Poisson
model, a 10 km cell can contain more than
one deposit. In the situation of Figure 6, however, the
effect of local clustering was reduced by defining
"events". Suppose that a 40 km unit area in Figure 6 is
subdivided into sixteen 10 km cells none of which could

be indicative of more than a single event. It follows
that the Poisson model cannot be exactly satisifed for
the 40 km unit area.

If it is assumed that the logistic model is valid,
then the occurrence of an event consisting of one or more
deposits per 10 km cell is controlled by a Bernouilli variable. The combination of a number of Bernouilli variables would give a so-called "subnormal" variation of the
binomial distribution of which some properties have been
summarized by Johnson and Kotz (1969, p. 80). It is interesting to compare the preceding three models for the
random variable of which the expected value is shown on
the contour map. From a practical point of view the
Poisson and binomial models are easier to use than the
subnormal binomial model.

For a larger region, the preceding three models can
be approximated by normal distribution models which facilitates the comparison. For example, the sum of all
n = 49 probabilities shown in Figure 7C is Σp_i = 13.75.
Consequently, according to each of the three mo-
dels, about 14 events are expected in the area of Figure
7 and this is rather close to the observation of 12 control cells in this area of 49 cells. According to the
Poisson model, the variance is equal to 13.75. The positive binomial approximation would have parameter p =
$\Sigma p_i/n$ = 0.2806 because n = 49. Hence its variance would
be np(1-p) = 9.89 which is less than the variance of
the Poisson variable.

The subnormal binomial distribution has variance
np(1-p) - n·var(p_i) = 7.05 where var(p_i) denotes the variance among the p_i (i = 1,2,...,n) values. If the
three discrete distributions are approximated by
normal distributions with mean values equal to 13.75, the
standard deviations which are equal to the square roots
of the preceding variances become 3.7, 3.1, and 2.7, respectively. These values are relatively close to one
another, especially in view of other uncertainties associated with the selection of variables and choice of control area in the multivariate statistical approach.

                        CONCLUDING REMARKS

Practitioners of mineral-resource analysis should
appreciate the great uncertainty generally associated
with any attempt to predict the occurrence of undiscovered deposits. This applies even to relatively simple

applications of geological analogy for the extrapolation
from an area with known mineral deposits to a similar area
without known deposits of the same type.

Computers can facilitate greatly the work of the geoscientist engaged in resource analysis by providing (1)
access to a more extensive data base; (2) automating
quantification of map features; and (3) accessing many
types of statistical techniques. In multivariate analysis, it is imperative to test each model by changing the
input variables in order to investigate the stability or
lack of stability of the results. These repetitive tasks
can be performed only with the aid of computers. The
choice of variables and the interpretation of statistical
results should as much as possible be based on metallogenic concepts.

REFERENCES

Agterberg, F.P., 1974, Geomathematics: Elsevier, Amster-
    dam, 596 p.

Agterberg, F.P., 1975, Statistical models for regional
    occurrence of mineral deposits, *in* Schriften fur
    Operations Research und Datenverarbeitung im Berg-
    bau 4: Gluckauf, Essen, p. C-1, 1-15.

Agterberg, F.P., 1977, Frequency distributions and spa-
    tial variability of geological variables, *in* Proc.
    14th Symp. Applications of Computer Methods in the
    Mineral Industry: Soc. Min. Eng. AIME, New York,
    p. 287-298.

Agterberg, F.P., 1978, Quantification and statistical
    analysis of geological variables for mineral re-
    source evaluation, *in* Sciences de la Terre et Me-
    sures, Colloque Jean Goguel: Bur. Rech. Geol. Min.
    Memoire No. 91, p. 399-406.

Agterberg, F.P., 1979, Mineral resource estimation and
    statistical exploration, *in* Facts and Concepts of
    World Oil Occurrence: Can. Soc. Petr. Geol. Mem.
    6, p. 301-318.

Agterberg, F.P., in press, Cell value distribution models
    in spatial pattern analysis, *in* Future Trends of
    Geomathematics, J.C. Griffiths Volume: Pion, Ltd.,
    London.

Agterberg, F.P., and Cabilio, P., 1969, Two-stage least
    squares model for the relationship between mappable
    geological variables: Jour. Math. Geology, v. 1, no.
    2, p. 137-153.

Agterberg, F.P., Chung, C.F., Fabbri, A.G., Kelly, A.M.,
    and Springer, J.S., 1972, Geomathematical evaluation
    of copper and zinc potential of the Abitibi area,
    Ontario and Quebec: Geol. Survey Canada Paper 71-
    41, 55 p.

Agterberg, F.P., and David, M., 1979, Statistical explora-
    tion, *in* Computer Methods for the 80's: Soc. Min.
    Eng. AIME, New York, p. 90-115.

Agterberg, F.P., and Fabbri, A.G., 1978, Spatial correla-
    tion of stratigraphic units quantified from geologi-
    cal maps: Computers & Geosciences, v. 4, no. 3,
    p. 285-294.

Botbol, J.M., Sinding-Larsen, R., McCammon, R.B., and
    Gott, G.B., 1978, A regionalized multivariate ap-
    proach to target selection in geochemical explora-
    tion: Econ. Geology, v. 73, no. 4, p. 534-546.

Chung, C.F., and Agterberg, F.P., 1980, Regression models
    for estimating mineral resources from geological map
    data: Jour. Math. Geology, v. 12, no. 5, p. 473-
    488.
Divi, S.R., Thorpe, R.I., and Franklin, J.M., 1979, Ap-
    plication of discriminant analysis to evaluate com-
    positional controls of stratiform massive sulfide
    deposits in Canada: Jour. Math. Geology, v. 11,
    no. 4, p. 391-406.

Duda, R.O., Hart, P.E., Konolige, K., and Reboh, R.,
    1979, A computer-based consultant for mineral ex-
    ploration: Final Rpt. Project 6415, SRI Interna-
    tional, Menlo Park, Cal., 185 p.

Fabbri, A.G., and Kasvand, T., 1978, Picture processing
    of geological images: Geol. Survey Canada Paper
    78-1B, p. 169-174.

Findlay, D.C., and Walsh, J.H., 1979, Canadian applica-
    tions in resource analysis: Resources Policy,
    March 1979, p. 61-70.

Fisher, R.A., and Yates, F., 1963, Statistical tables
    for biological, agricultural and medical research
    (6th ed.): Hafner, New York, 145 p.

Harris, D.C., in press, Mineral endowment - geostatistical
    theory and methods for appraisal: Paper prepared
    for Symposium on Methods for Broad Mineral Resource
    Appraisal, Univ. West Virginia, Main 1978, 85 p.
    (in press, Univ. West Virginia Press).

Johnson, N.L., and Kotz, S., 1969, Distributions in
    statistics, discrete distributions: Houghton Miff-
    lin, Boston, 328 p.

Journel, A.G., and Huijbregts, Ch. J., 1978, Mining geo-
    statistics: Academic Press, London, 600 p.

Rundkvist, D.V., ed.-in-chief, 1979, Quantitative fore-
    casting in regional metallogenic investigations:
    VSEGEI, Leningrad, 88 p. (in Russian).

Schwarzacher, W., 1975, Sedimentation models and quanti-
    tative stratigraphy: Elsevier, Amsterdam, 382 p.

QUANTITATIVE BIOSTRATIGRAPHY, 1830-1980

James C. Brower

Syracuse University

ABSTRACT

　　Charles Lyell (1830-1833) became the first quantitative biostratigrapher when he proposed his method for determining the relative age of Tertiary fossil assemblages
by calculating the percent of living species in them.
Quantitative biostratigraphy languished for about 125
years but a major renaissance began in the late 1950's
which is continuing at an accelerating pace.

　　Methods of quantitative biostratigraphy can be
grouped into several categories. The first category consists of the quantification of the index-fossil concept
including measurement of the attributes of an index fossil as well as the relative biostratigraphic values of
the species concerned.

　　The second category represents the treatment of assemblage zones with multivariate analysis. The basic
data may represent proportions of different species in a
series of samples but presence-absence data also are
used. The unweighted presence-absence data may be analyzed but the presences also can be weighted by the
amount of biostratiqraphic information conveyed by the
species involved. Most of the techniques applied here
are well-known multivariate methods such as cluster
analysis, multidimensional scaling and some forms of
archeological seriation.

In the third category, the biostratigrapher is faced with a plethora of methods for determining the most likely sequence of biostratigraphic events based on observations from numerous stratigraphic sections. Most schemes are concerned with point events which consist of the highest and lowest occurrences of the species treated. Several techniques are concerned with entire range zones. Sequencing algorithms produce either average sequences or are intended to give the stratigraphically highest possible estimate of the top of a range zone and the stratigraphically lowest possible estimate of the base of that range zone. Once the most likely sequence of events is ascertained, it can serve to correlate the individual samples and stratigraphic sections. Some of the techniques are elaborate whereas others are simplicity carried to the ultimate.

Although numerous methods of quantitative biostratigraphy have been proposed which do produce excellent results, most biostratigraphers have resisted successfully the impact of quantification. There are several reasons for this. First, most practicing biostratigraphers are basically nonquantitative. Secondly, many of the methods involve logic and algorithms which are not familiar to biostratigraphy. Thirdly, biostratigraphers learn that nonquantitative techniques produce acceptable results although only after long periods of time and much effort. Essentially quantitative biostratigraphy has proven unpalatable to the intended consumers.

Therefore, in the fourth category, we have cast about for super-simple methods of quantitative biostratigraphy, almost without numbers, which closely replicate the logic of biostratigraphers. One such technique is archeological seriation which can work directly on a species by samples data matrix to simultaneously produce a range chart as well as correlation of the samples. Both additive and nonadditive models are applicable. Another is a sequencing method which involves comparison of lists of events in a series of stratigraphic sections and resolving the inconsistencies between the different sections in such a manner as to produce a composite zonation.

Lastly, paleontologists have studied evolutionary sequences in a numerical context using a smorgasbord of techniques for many years. The statistical methods range from the simplest univariate to the most complicated multivariate types with or without the aid of

time-series analysis. Although evolution provides the
basis for biostratigraphy, it is surprising that many
evolutionary sequences are approached through a strictly
biological point of view rather than in a biostratigraphic context.

Through the past 150 years, biostratigraphers have
proposed many numerical schemes for quantitative correlation. It is unfortunate that most of these methods have
not been tested rigorously on numerous actual and simulated data sets. Hopefully, during the next decade quantitative biostratigraphers will evaluate systematically
the available algorithms by case studies to ascertain
which techniques provide the best results with various
types of data. Thus the 1980's should represent an interval of consolidation instead of a decade in which a
new horde of algorithms will be invented.

INTRODUCTION

Biostratigraphic correlation provides the foundation
for many studies in stratigraphy, both of an applied and
theoretical nature. The basis of historical geology is
the relative time scale which is founded on biostratigraphy. Without this time scale, earth history could not be
reconstructed because any historical science involves the
placement of events in a matrix defined by time and
space. The time scale is essential to studies in evolutionary biology because ancestors and descendents could
not be recognized without such a scale. Biostratigraphic
correlation also is useful in the search for fossil fuels.
Coal, oil, and gas are concentrated in certain zones and
depositional environments which are localized in time and
space. Biostratigraphy represents one of the main wea-
pons in the search for these elusive targets.

An obvious question is: why bother to quantify biostratigraphy. Three major reasons can be listed. The
first is the massive amounts of biostratigraphic data.
Data matrices may include hundreds of species and samples and these cannot be comprehended simultaneously by
the human mind. Any systematic treatment of biostratigraphic data should use, evaluate, and screen all the information available. This requires efficient algorithms
and the memory bank of a large computer. A second is
that quantitative methods have the potential for providing a higher degree of biostratigraphic resolution than
do qualitative techniques. Thirdly, some of the

quantitative methods provide information about the statistical probabilities associated with various biostratigraphic hypotheses. Such data cannot be obtained from
qualitative methodology.

It is with this in mind that IGCP (International
Geological Correlation Program) Project 148 on Quantitative Stratigraphic Correlation was established several
years ago. As far as biostratigraphy is concerned, three
goals have been set: first is to devise quantitative
techniques for biostratigraphy. The numerous available
methods will be outlined subsequently. The second involves the implementation of computer programs for those
methods and to make the programs available to the scientific public at large. Third is to utilize case studies
of actual and simulated data to test and compare the
various methods. Furthermore, it seems reasonable to
evaluate quantitative biostratigraphy and to present a
prognosis for future work based on these goals and how
well they have been realized to date.

                    HISTORICAL BACKGROUND

Consideration of the history of stratigraphy indicates that a series of breakthroughs have lead to all of
the correlation methods, both qualitative and quantitative, used in biostratigraphy. Excellent reviews of the
development of biostratigraphy are given by Hancock (1977)
and Mallory (1970). The obvious prerequisite for any
biostratigraphic methodology is the recognition that fossils could be used for correlation. This concept originated with William Smith and was published in tables,
maps, and writings in 1799, 1815, and 1816-1819. Smith
realized that the strata could be arranged in stratigraphic order and that each stratum was characterized by an
assemblage of fossils. The faunal zones cataloged by
Smith thus are assemblage zones.

Frederick Quenstedt (e.g., 1856-1858) was probably
the first individual to systematically record detailed
data and attempt to compile the range zones of fossils.
However, it was left to his student Albert Oppel (1856-
1858) to exploit fully the potential of range zones.
Oppel advocated compiling range-zone charts of suites of
species. These were scrutinized then to determine intervals characterized by assemblages of taxa that occurred
together as well as overlap zones between two or more
taxa. This allowed him to refine considerably the

zonations proposed by earlier workers. Two major types
of quantitative methods can be tied to the concepts first
laid out by Smith, Quenstedt, and Oppel. These are the
quantification of assemblage zones as well as the analysis
of the most likely sequence of events.

    Index fossils were known and used to trace and iden-
tify zones long before the time of Darwin, but the exact
root of the idea is uncertain. According to Eicher (1976)
and Donovan (1966), the concept of an index fossil can be
traced back to Albert Oppel (1856-1858) who named each of
his zones after a particularly abundant and characteristic
species which was termed the "index." The origin of the
idea could be even earlier. For example, William Smith
wrote in 1817 (on p. iv of the Stratigraphical System of
Organized Fossils):

        By the tables it will be seen which fossils are
        peculiar to any stratum and which are repeated
        in others.

At any rate and from whatever origin, correlation by index fossils became usual practice by the late 19th century and is employed yet by many biostratigraphers.

    The last major revolution in biostratigraphy is the
doctrine of organic evolution which can be attributed to
Charles Darwin in 1859. Evolution obviously provides the
mechanism for morphological changes in organisms and
therefore is the vital basis for biostratigraphy. It is
interesting to note that much biostratigraphical methodology developed long before the doctrine of evolution was
accepted by paleontologists (e.g. Gould, 1977). As far
as biostratigraphy is concerned, the essential facts lie
in the changes in the organisms - not the mechanisms involved. At any rate, once evolution and natural selection began to permeate the paleontological community,
paleontologists could start to analyze lineages of fossils
in a meaningful manner.

    Charles Lyell (1830-1833) probably was the first
quantitative biostratigrapher when he defined several of
the Tertiary epochs based on percentages of living molluscan species. These percentages consisted of: Eocene, 3
percent; Miocene, 18 percent; and Pliocene, 49 percent.
The Lyellian method is statistical for two reasons.
First, the percentages were derived from massive amounts
of data, namely some 8,000 species and 40,000 specimens.
Second, the definitions furnished an identification rule

for determining the age of unknown samples. Lyell's zonation of the Tertiary provided the first quantified assemblage zones. Subsequent developments are covered later
in this paper.

Several reviews on quantitative techniques in biostratigraphy have been published recently, namely those
of Brower and Millendorf (1978) and Hay and Southam
(1978). Hazel (1977) summarized the state of the art in
the quantification of assemblage zones whereas Miller
(1977) outlined the graphical correlation approach of
Shaw (1964). Reyre (1974) reviewed many quantitative
studies in palynology, most of which were done by European workers. Nevertheless, developments have been proceeding rapidly and these reviews are outdated, at least
partially, hence this paper.

Four general approaches have been employed in biostratigraphy. These include: (1) treatment of the index-
fossil concept, (2) quantification of assemblage zones,
(3) determination of the most likely sequence of biostratigraphic events, and (4) study of lineages.

INDEX-FOSSIL CONCEPT

Index fossils were used before Darwin's time to distinguish and trace biostratigraphic zones, and correlation
by such fossils currently is in widespread practice.
However, Jeletzky (1965) argued against the possibility
of quantified biostratigraphy because he believed it was
impossible to express numerically the degree of biochronological usefulness of fossils. He concluded (1965, p.
135), "Any attempt at the quantification of biochronological correlation is, thus, precluded by the fundamentally
qualitative and *non-statistical* nature of its most valuable data (index fossils)." Subsequent discussion will
show that this is not true. The first practical attempt
at a quantification of the index fossil concept was that
of Hazel (1970). A novel approach was presented by Cockbain (1966) who proposed the entropy function as a numerical measure of the relative biostratigraphic usefulness
of a fossil. This method, as McCammon (1970, p. 49)
pointed out, is inefficient.

The three attributes of an index fossil, namely
facies independence (F), geographical persistence (G),
and vertical range (V), are measured easily as discussed
by McCammon (1970), Brower, Millendorf, and Dyman, (1978);
and Millendorf, Brower, and Dyman (1978).

The work of McCammon (1970) was a major breakthrough
in quantification of the index-fossil concept and provided
a method for determining a numerical index of the amount
of biostratigraphic information conveyed by the presence
of a particular fossil taxon or species. These indices
are termed relative biostratigraphic value (RBV) and they
are scaled through a range of 1.0 for the ideal index fossil to 0.0 for a species with no useful biostratigraphic
information. The index designed by McCammon (1970)
weighted all three parameters equally. Two types of taxa
could have RBV's of almost 1.0. In the first instance, a
classic index fossil would be valued for three attributes,
that is a high degree of facies independence and geographical persistence in conjunction with a short vertical
range. Secondly, a geographically widespread species
that is restricted to a single facies also will have a
high RBV. Such a taxon will be useful for its ability
to trace a biofacies laterally and vertically and the RBV
of this form is not influenced strongly by its vertical
range. Thus, the McCammon index represents a compromise
between time-stratigraphic correlation on one hand, and
establishing the physical continuity and geographical
persistence of a particular biofacies on the other.

Brower, Millendorf, and Dyman (1978) advocated another index in which the parameters were weighted in a different manner. The geographical persistence and facies
independence were weighted equally but the vertical range
was given double weight relative to either of the other
two parameters. This index was designed specifically to
identify taxa that would be most useful for time-stratigraphic correlation. Brower, Millendorf, and Dyman (1978)
also point out that other RBV's can be structured which
incorporate the desired properties.

Once the index fossils have been quantified, the information can be used in several contexts. The appropriate number of index and near-index fossils can be selected
to construct a reasonable zonation of biostratigraphic
events or samples. For example, McCammon (1970) demonstrated that only about 10 percent of the species with
the highest RBV's were needed to provide a useful zonation of some Tertiary strata from the Gulf Coast. This
essentially is a search for parsimony, that is a reasonably effective zonation based on the smallest possible
number of taxa. McCammon (1970) also devised simple
classification or identification functions to assign
samples to the faunal zones. In another approach,
Brower, Millendorf, and Dyman (1978) and Millendorf,

Brower, and Dyman (1978) successfully used several of
these RBV's to weight the data for species in the multivariate analysis of assemblage zones as discussed later.
The RBV's and the biostratigraphic attributes also can be
used to test biostratigraphic hypotheses. For example,
are the biostratigraphic properties of bottom dwellers
different from those of pelagic organisms? Have the biostratigraphic parameters of one or more groups of organisms changed with time? Do species living in different
types of habitats have the same properties?

QUANTIFICATION OF ASSEMBLAGE ZONES

Assemblage zones were the first type of zone to be
recognized in biostratigraphy. As mentioned before the
zones of William Smith and Charles Lyell basically are
assemblage zones. After the quantitative definition of
the Tertiary epochs by Lyell, no advances were made in the
quantification of assemblage zones for about 125 years
(see Mallory, 1970, and Hancock, 1977 for reviews).
This interval of quiescence was ended when Simpson (1947,
1960) and Sorgenfrei (1958) initiated work on similarity
coefficients to measure faunal resemblance. Although
Simpson (1947, 1960) studied these coefficients in the
context of biogeography, he was aware of the implications
for biostratigraphy. Similar indices were used by Sorgenfrei (1958) for correlation of the Middle Miocene of Jut-
land with the Miocene of other areas. These pioneering
works have given rise to numerous studies that have attempted to define time zones or ecological zones which
can be employed in correlation.

Assemblage zones are characterized by a particular
suite of taxa regardless of their ranges, and yield typically a combination of stratigraphical and ecological information. Assemblage zones show the distribution of
faunal discontinuities in time and space. The techniques
for depicting such zones are numerous and many are rooted
in conventional multivariate analysis and numerical taxonomy. Comprehensive papers on biostratigraphy which outline some of the methods, present examples of applications, and compare results from various techniques include Hazel (1970, 1971, 1977), Brower, Millendorf, and
Dyman (1978), and Millendorf, Brower, and Dyman (1978).
The reader should note that many of the techniques of
quantitative paleoecology and biogeography are similar
to those of biostratigraphy; examples of such allied
publications include Ali, Lindemann, and Feldhausen

(1976), Blackith and Reyment (1971), Buzas (1970), Ellison
(1963), Feldhausen (1970), Fox (1968), Gill, Boehm, and
Erez (1976), Henderson and Heron (1977), Imbrie (1964),
Kaesler (1966), Lynts (1971, 1972), Lynts and Stehman
(1971), McCammon (1966), Oltz (1969, 1971), Park (1974),
Raup and Crick, (1979), Rowell and McBride (1972), Rowell,
McBride, and Palmer (1973), Scott (1970), Simpson (1960),
Sorgenfrei (1958), Stone (1967, 1973), Symons and DeMeuter
(1974), Valentine and Peddicord (1967), and the volume
edited by Scott and West (1976).

The primary data matrices of biostratigraphy are
rectangular with species or taxa along one axis and samples arrayed on the other. Generally the data consist of
presences and absences of the taxa in the samples but
Reyre (1972, 1974) analyzed relative abundances or proportions of various species. However, presence-absence
data contain all the information needed for most biostratigraphic studies. For simplicity, it is easiest to
discuss the analysis of assemblage zones in the following
order: Q-mode analyses between samples, R-mode analyses
between taxa, and methods which treat both taxa and samples in a single sequence of operations.

Q-Mode Analyses

Study of the relationships between samples involves
a series of steps, each of which presents decisions that
must be made by the biostratigrapher.

In Step 1, if the data are presence-absence, as is
the usual situation, one must decide whether to convert
the data to the range-through form or work with the original data. In the range-through method of data treatment, a taxon is listed as present in all samples within
its local range zone for each stratigraphic section.
This helps to eliminate sampling problems and minimizes
bias toward whatever other factors, such as environmental
parameters, that could dictate the presence of a particular organism. The time duration of the species is of
interest, not the vagaries of its distribution. This type
of data is used by most biostratigraphers. In some situations the range-through method can lose pertinent information such as where several biofacies intertongue re-
peatedly. The range-through technique is not applicable
for data consisting of relative abundances.

The question for Step 2 is whether to calculate the
relative biostratigraphic values (RBV). The course of

action involved here depends on the purpose of the analysis. If stratigraphical groupings are desired, the RBV's
can be useful. If the RBV's are to be determined, one
must measure the attributes of an index fossil and elect
the RBV index of interest (see previous discussion). The
RBV's can be employed in several manners. The presences
can be weighted by the RBV's. If so the presence of a
species will contribute an amount of similarity between
samples that is proportional to its RBV. This usually
produces clusters that are tighter and stratigraphically
more homogeneous. Another strategy is to discard the
taxa with lower RBV's and to complete the analysis only
on the species with the highest RBV's. This results in
a parsimonious solution consisting of a reasonable zonation based on the smallest possible number of species
(McCammon, 1970).

Step 3 comprises the computation of a similarity or
difference matrix between all pairs of samples. For binary data, the presences and absences may suffice or the
presences can be weighted by the RBV's. Absences cannot
be evaluated completely for biostratigraphic data because
a taxon can be absent from a sample for various reasons.
Therefore similarity coefficients based on mutual presences or positive matches are preferred by most authors.
Various similarity coefficients are employed such as the
Jaccard, Dice, Otsuka, or Simpson although middle-of-the
road types such as the Dice coefficient usually are recommended. However other types of coefficients have been applied in quantitative biostratigraphy such as the correlation coefficient of the Pearson product-moment type. Useful reviews of these coefficients are available in
Cheetham and Hazel (1969), Hohn (1976), Sepkoski (1974),
and Sneath and Sokal (1973). Recently, several probabilistic similarity coefficients have been formulated by
Henderson and Heron (1977) and Raup and Crick (1979).
Although not tested on biostratigraphic data, these may
yield excellent results in the quantification of assemblage zones.

Many varieties of similarity and difference coefficients are available for data on relative abundances.
Coefficients that are used in paleoecologic studies and
could be used in biostratigraphy consist of the quantified association coefficients of Sepkoski (1974), correlation coefficients, such as that of Sorenson and the Pearson product-moment type, and a legion of distance coefficients.

The last step in the analysis is to extract the main themes from the similarity or difference matrix. Methods that have been employed for biostratigraphic or paleoecologic data include agglomerative cluster analysis (Hazel, 1977; Millendorf, Brower, and Dyman, 1978), divisive clustering in the form of association analysis (Gill, Boehm, and Erez, 1976) and dissimilarity analysis (Gill and Tipper, 1978; Tipper, 1979), principal components (Hazel, 1977), factor analysis (Symons and DeMeuter, 1974), correspondence analysis (see Reyre, 1974), principal coordinates (Hazel, 1977), nonlinear mapping and multidimensional scaling (Millendorf, Brower, and Dyman, 1978), and lateral tracing (Millendorf, Brower, and Dyman, 1978).

Plant ecologists have developed some methods which are useful especially for nonlinear data (Whittaker, 1973 outlines some of these techniques). Cisne and Rabe (1978) applied several of these direct and indirect ordination algorithms (polar ordination, principal components, and reciprocal averaging) to numerous samples from Middle Ordovician rocks in New York which could be correlated in time by position relative to a series of bentonites. The data consist of percentages of common taxa, all of which range throughout the time interval studied. The problem thus is basically paleoecological. The different samples could be characterized by their position on a depth gradient. Plots of ordination scores on a time-stratigraphic diagram permit the identification of transgressions and regressions which could be used for time correlation. The ordination scores also serve to calculate rates of change with respect to distance along transects and to estimate the slope of the basin. Other geological examples of such ordination techniques are presented by Ali, Lindemann, and Feldhausen (1976), Feldhausen (1970), and Park (1974).

Shier (1978) outlines a simple technique termed sample ordering which produces a one-dimensional ordination of samples that can be used for paleoecological analysis. This strategy also could be applied to biostratigraphic data.

R. Christopher (1978, pers. comm.) has contoured matrices of similarity coefficients derived from samples in two stratigraphic sections (see also Reyre, 1974).

Biostratigraphers profitably might borrow some of the techniques developed by archeologists. For many years archeologists have faced problems closely allied to those

of biostratigraphy. Samples containing various objects
must be arranged into a sequence which represents time or
an evolutionary series. Examples of such problems are
numerous and embrace such fascinating case studies as
artifacts in graves, sentence structure, and word frequency in manuscripts written through the ages, etc.
Strangely enough, few of these methods have been noticed
by biostratigraphers. General discussions of these techniques are in Cowgill (1972), Doran and Hodson (1975),
Hodson, Kendall, and Tautu (1971, especially the articles
by Gelfand and Kendall), Johnson (1972), and Marquardt
(1978). These methods range from the exceedingly simple
where one just rearranges the rows and columns of the matrix to concentrate the most similar samples along the
diagonal to exceedingly complex methods which combine
multidimensional scaling with principal components.
Schuey and others (1978) calculate an evolutionary scale
from similarity coefficients based on an autocorrelation
function.

      For the studies done by Millendorf, Brower, and Dyman
(1978), the best results were obtained from agglomerative
cluster analysis of the UPGM type, multidimensional scaling shows the major features of the faunal zones and discontinuities between these whereas lateral tracing provides detailed correlations within the zones. Techniques
restricted to linear relationships such as principal components are not adequate in many instances. Most authors
(e.g. Hazel, 1970, 1971, 1977) have worked only with the
entire data set. However, Brower, Millendorf, and Dyman
(1978) and Millendorf, Brower, and Dyman (1978) adopted a
more sophisticated two-fold approach. First, the entire
data set is treated in order to gain an overall picture.
Hopefully, the desired correlations or zones can be extracted from the clusters or ordinations. Second, the
analysis focuses on pairs of adjacent sections to prepare
a line of sections or a fence diagram showing more detailed correlations.

R-Mode Analyses

      An R-mode analysis can be performed on the taxa with
the same techniques except for several details. For example, lateral tracing is not applicable in the R-mode.
The data can be presence-absence, either in the original
or range-through form. There is no purpose in weighting
the data by the relative biostratigraphic values. Relative abundance data also can be processed for the species.

      R-mode results can be difficult to interpret in
terms of the stratigraphic distribution of the taxa.

Hazel (1970, 1977) presents some results in the form of dendrograms and principal components. Species which are confined to one assemblage zone generally cluster or group together. However long-ranging forms which occur in several or more assemblage zones obscure the structure of the data and introduce distortion into the dendrogram or ordination plot. Another problem with R-mode analyses is that they mainly disclose information about the "center of gravity" or "centroid" of the individual range zones rather than the endpoints or upper and lower limits of the taxa. Thus the endpoints of the range zones may be of more interest to biostratigraphers than the centroids.

Sequential Analyses in R- and Q-Modes

The only example of a dual-space technique in biostratigraphy known to me is that of Hazel (1977). A matrix of correlation coefficients was computed for presence-absence data of the range-through type for 24 species of Cambrian trilobites. Extraction of the principal components of this matrix produced four rather loosely structured assemblage zones along with several species that could not be definitely assigned. The first three principal components account for 59 percent of the variance in the correlation matrix. Although the plot of the first three principal components does show the assemblage zones, these are not in stratigraphical order unless they lie along a rather complex spiral. Principal-component scores array the relationships between the samples. Generally, principal components seem to have been adequate for this rather simple data set consisting of 24 species and 65 samples. However, such eigenvector methods probably would not be adequate for more complex data with ordination axes that are strongly nonlinear. The results obtained from other similar techniques, such as factor and correspondence analysis, probably would be similar to those derived from principal components.

Archeologist Cowgill (1972) outlines a seriation technique which might be useful in biostratigraphy. The data matrix includes the presence-absence of a series of objects in numerous samples or units. A similarity matrix was formed for the units, after which two axes were obtained from this matrix by multidimensional scaling. The two axes were reduced to a single dimension by "graphical regression" although formal regression or principal components would have served the same purpose (Kendall, 1971). This produced coordinates for a one-

dimensional seriation of the objects. For biostratigraphical data of the range-through type, the coordinates
would give roughly the midpoints of the zones. Scores
are determined for each sample based on the seriation
coordinates for the objects, the number of samples containing each object, and the objects present and absent
in each sample. These scores arrange the samples with respect to the seriation sequence which should give the desired stratigraphy. The experience of Millendorf, Brower,
and Dyman (1978) with multidimensional scaling in the Q-
mode suggests that this scheme might be successful for
biostratigraphical information.

MOST LIKELY SEQUENCE OF EVENTS

     As discussed earlier, the idea of using sequences of
biostratigraphic events for correlation dates from at
least the days of Quenstedt (1856-1858) and Oppel (1856-
1858). Numerous methods are available to the biostratigrapher for determining sequences of events that are observed in many stratigraphic sections. These can be divided into two categories based on the type of events to
be sequenced. The first set of schemes is concerned with
point events, consisting of the highest and lowest occurrences of any given species. This has the advantage that
one can develop separate zonations based on either highest or lowest occurrences of the species concerned. The
second category involves methods designed to determine
sequences of entire range zones.

     Sequencing methods either produce average sequences
or are designed to give the stratigraphically highest
possible estimate of the top of a range zone and the
stratigraphically lowest possible estimate of the base
of a range zone. I will term the latter as "conservative
zonations." Both philosophies are subject to mixed advantages and disadvantages. An average sequence gives
the most probable zonation for a particular suite of
data; such sequences of events are reasonable in many
situations and operational within a particular area.
Much statistical theory is applicable directly to average zonations which therefore are on reasonably firm
statistical ground. For example, one can estimate confidence intervals and reliabilities for some of the
average zonations as discussed later (e.g. Hay, 1972;
Southam, Hay, and Worsley, 1975; Hay and Southam, 1978).
Alternatively, maximizing the tops and minimizing the
basis of range zones yields a conservative zonation which

is consistent with the nature of error in biostratigraphic data. The reasoning is as follows.

If reworking and misidentification are ignored as sources of error, the only possible estimates of a range zone will be either the true range zone, an unlikely situation, or an underestimate thereof. For an underestimate, either the base of the range zone will be too high in the sequence or the top of the range zone will be too low in the sequence. It therefore follows that the best estimate of a true sequence of biostratigraphic events is the one that places the tops of the range zones as high as possible in the sequence and assigns the bases as far down as possible in the sequence of events (e.g., Shaw, 1964; Edwards, 1978; Rubel, 1978). Thus conservative zonations are intuitively and theoretically appealing. Unfortunately, the methods for most conservative zonations tend to be rather ad hoc schemes which cannot be tied directly to statistical theory. After the sequence of events has been determined, it can be used to correlate the samples in the various stratigraphic sections (e.g., Blank, 1979; Shaw, 1964).

Average Sequences for Point Events

W.W. Hay in conjunction with John Southam and Thomas Worsley devised a technique based on binomial probability (Hay, 1972; Southam, Hay, and Worsley, 1975; Southam and Hay, 1978). For any two events, say I and J, only two possibilities are allowed. Event I is over J or J is over I. If the two events are located at the same level, the occurrence is ignored. The frequencies are recorded in matrix form for all possible pairs of events. The information required includes the number of stratigraphic sections in which event I is over J and the number of sections containing both events. These data then are structured into a matrix which gives the probabilities for row events over column events. The events can be sequenced in different manners which are used by statisticians in paired comparisons. For example, the row sums of the probability matrix or a matrix containing the frequencies of event I over J could be used. Worsley and Jorgens (1977) and Blank (1979) employed simple row and column operations on the latter matrix. If element a_{ij} exceeds a_{ji} then row j is interchanged with column i. Approximate confidence limits can be assigned to all pairs of events based on incomplete beta functions, etc. These data are used to determine the most reliable zonation consisting of the required number of events.

One practical problem may arise with this technique.
Biostratigraphic data are typically incomplete. Also,
Hay, Southam, and Worsley ignore ties where events I and
J occur together which introduces additional missing
data into the system. Consequently, cycles of three or
more inconsistent events may occur. An example with
three events, A, B, and C, would be where A is over B
which is over C where C also is over A. Misidentifica-
tions and other sources of error can result in inconsistencies. These inconsistencies produce great difficulties
in determination of the most likely sequence of events.

F. Gradstein and F.P. Agterberg (manuscript in preparation) have improved the binomial probability method.
First, if events I and J occur at the same level, the
probabilities are allocated on the basis of 0.5 for I
over J and 0.5 for I under J. This reduces the number of
blanks in the data. In addition, cycles of inconsistent
events are identified and eliminated during the sequencing of the data. The second modification is concerned
with the method of reporting the sequence of events. The
usual practice is simply to list the sequence from oldest
to youngest. However, Gradstein and Agterberg have applied probability theory to estimate the distances between events along the relative time scale. All events
are assumed to have the same variance; the variance of
the events is set arbitrarily equal to one because the
time scale is relative. Thirdly these authors perform
cluster analysis on the distance scale between all of the
events. These clusters then outline assemblage zones
which can be employed for large-scale correlation.

Edwards and Beaver (1978) outlined an algorithm
which allows three possibilities for events I and J. I
would be over J or J could occur above I. Both events
could occur at the same level, a possibility that is not
tolerated by the binomial method. Trinomial probability
is clearly a logical extention of the binomial method.
A modification of the Bradley-Terry model for paired
comparisons serves to determine the position of the individual events in the entire sequence. Although theoretically and intuitively appealing, there are several
practical problems to this technique. The equations for
the Bradley-Terry model are cumbersome and complex which
restricts this technique to relatively small numbers of
events. Also any event that is always located in the
same position in the sequence must be deleted from the
analysis.

Millendorf and Brower (unpublished data) have attempted to create composite sections based on simple averages of footages or proportional distributions of events in stratigraphic sections. These authors also experimented with ranking the events and treating the information with nonparametric statistics. Both methods resulted in reasonable zonations.

I. Dienes has formalized definitions for stratigraphic and biostratigraphic phenomena in the rubric of set theory. In addition, he has proposed several methods for sequencing point events. One of these advocates multidimensional integer kriging as a solution whereas the other uses spatial and temporal precedence matrices (Dienes, 1977, 1978).

Conservative Zonations for Point Events
Based on Correlation and Regression

In one of the first works on quantitative biostratigraphy, Shaw (1964, see recent review by Miller, 1977) applied correlation and regression in a graphical context. The data consist of the vertical distances above a particular datum plane for the upper and lower occurrences of a group of taxa in a set of stratigraphic sections. In the first step data from two stratigraphic sections (X and Y) are plotted on a bivariate graph with the section on the X axis serving as the reference. Changes in rates of sedimentation, unconformities, faults, etc. produce various types of segments or "doglegs" on the graph. The data are segmented visually although computer algorithms could be used for this operation. Originally, straight lines of the least-squares type were fitted to the linear segments on the graph although the errors of the data points do not fit the assumptions made by least squares (Shaw, 1964). However as currently practiced by many individuals, the endpoints for the line segments are selected by the biostratigrapher (e.g., Miller, 1977).

An individual data point, that is either a highest or lowest occurrence of one particular taxon, might be subject to two types of error. A lowest occurrence could represent an unfilled base which is too high in the reference section. Alternatively, the highest occurrence could be too low in the reference section. These errors are updated by projecting the errant points onto the trend line and eventually onto the reference section. All projections are parallel to the X and Y axes. The purpose of such updating of the data is to place the tops

of the range zones as high as possible in the sequence of
events and move the lowest occurrences or bases as far
down as possible in the sequence of events. In this manner, the method attempts to provide the most likely true
sequence of events in the two sections in which the updated reference section becomes the composite for the
two sections.

In the next and subsequent stages, new sections are
incorporated gradually into the composite for the first
two sections until a composite is created for all sections. As new sections are added, the composite or reference section is updated so that the base and top of
the range zone of each taxon are minimized and maximized
respectively as just mentioned for the first two sections.
The composite section gives the order or sequence for all
events as well as their elevations above the datum in
composite section units. Once formulated, the composite
can serve to correlate unknown sections and samples.

Edwards (1978; see also Murphy and Edwards, 1977)
notes that in many instances only the relative order of
the events is necessary and that the absolute spacing between the events need not be determined. Consequently,
Edwards presented a nonparametric version of Shaw's (1964)
graphical correlation approach which avoids the problem
of fitting regression lines. The algorithm results in a
simple sequence of events of the conservative type.
Similar to Shaw and his followers, Edwards treats two
sequences of events at a time which are plotted on the X
and Y axes of a bivariate scatter plot. Unfortunately,
this method of presentation is difficult to visualize.
As mentioned later, displaying the two sequences of events
side by side yields data which are more familiar to biostratigraphers.

Hohn (1978) generalized Shaw's method by using principal components. His approach is ingenious in terms of
computer-core requirements because the principal components are extracted from a correlation matrix between the
stratigraphic sections. Missing data are interpolated
and the scores for the first principal component give the
zonation of the events. An alternative and less efficient
approach tried by Brower (unpublished data) is to calculate a correlation matrix between the events; the first
principal component of this matrix would list the necessary zonation. It is important to observe that principal
components result in an average zonation rather than the
conservative zonation of the Shaw algorithm.

Sequences of Range Zones

The next group of methods is designed to organize sequences of entire range zones. At least some of the concepts of set theory are applied to the operations.

Guex (1977, 1978a, 1978b, 1979; Davaud and Guex, 1978) proposed a simple technique which has some features of archeological seriation. A taxon by taxon matrix of associations, here termed A, is formed. If taxa I and J occur together in one or more of the stratigraphic sections studied, a 1 is recorded for a_{ij}. If I and J are not known to occur together a_{ij} becomes 0. The association matrix then is analyzed in a manner that is essentially the same as in some of the simpler types of archeological seriation in which the rows and columns of the matrix are reordered. This concentrates the 1's and the associated pairs of taxa along the diagonal of the association matrix. The 0's which denote taxa that do not occur together are placed in the off-diagonal elements. The concentration principle also is organized to produce the largest possible square submatrices which contain blocks of species that are consistently associated. After these row and column operations, range charts of taxa and assemblages of species are read directly from the matrix.

Rubel (1976, 1978) devised a scheme for treating entire range zones in terms of set theory. Four possibilities are visualized for the range zones of I and J. I can be over J or vice versa. The two range zones can overlap or intersect in different manners. For example the top of I could occur above that of J or vice versa; also one range zone might occur within the other one or the two range zones might be located at the same horizon or horizons. All of these possibilities fall into the category of overlapping or intersection. Also one or both range zones could be missing. The range zone data are recorded for all sections separately and then summed for all sections following simple algebraic rules derived from set theory that were developed by Rubel. Thus summation provides the most likely sequence of range zones. The algebraic rules for summation are designed so that the estimated positions of the tops of the zones are placed as high as possible in the sequence of events whereas the bases are minimized and placed as low as possible. The algorithm is not probabilistic and reliabilities or confidence limits are not assigned to the zones. Also Rubel did not present any algorithm designed to extract systematically the sequence of range zones.

Davaud (Davaud and Guex, 1978) combined some aspects
of the methods of Guex and Rubel with some new ideas in
an ingenious manner. As done by Guex, a species by species association matrix is calculated in the first step.
Unlike Guex and similar to Rubel, Davaud recognizes four
types of association: taxon I over J, taxon I under J,
coexistence of I and J if the two occur together at least
once, and the indeterminate situation where I and J do
not occur in the same stratigraphic section. Although
the association matrix is asymmetrical, only the upper
half need to be treated because the information in the
lower half of the matrix is redundant. The next stage
resolves as many of the indeterminate situations as possible. The remaining indeterminations are discarded.
In the third step, the association matrix is reorganized
in a similar fashion to that employed in the Guex technique. Lastly the range charts and associations of taxa
can be tabulated in stratigraphic order.

Several common denominators underlie these three algorithms. The methods are not probabilistic in the sense
that estimates of the accuracy or reliability of the zonation of the events are not presented. Also the techniques
can lose some pertinent information. As mentioned before,
if taxa I and J occur together, a 1 is assigned for this
relationship. However it might be the situation that the
base of the range zone of I could be consistently above
that of J. This and similar information is not always
recovered by these methods.

SIMPLE METHODS FOR QUANTITATIVE BIOSTRATIGRAPHY

Most nonquantitative biostratigraphers have resisted
stubbornly numerical methods. Essentially, quantitative
biostratigraphy has proved unpalatable to the intended
consumers, in spite of the fact that many methods of
quantitative biostratigraphy have produced effective results with large, cumbersome, and complex data sets. I
believe the lack of palatability is due to two causes.
First, many of the quantitative methods are complex
whereas most biostratigraphers are not quantitatively
oriented. Secondly, most of the quantitative techniques
utilize methodologies that basically are foreign to biostratigraphers.

Consequently, through the past year I have concentrated my attention on simple methods of quantitative
biostratigraphy. Some of these techniques literally

almost remove the numbers from quantitative biostratigraphy. It is hoped that these simple techniques will prove
more palatable to biostratigraphers than the more elaborate methods that have been developed to date. Furthermore, these simple methods share at least some features
in common with other biostratigraphic methods.

Method 1

Begin by considering the true range zone of a taxon.
If reworking and misidentification can be discarded as
possible sources of error, then, the only possible estimates of the range zone are either the actual or true
range or an underestimate thereof. Underestimates are
obviously the most likely possibility. In underestimates,
the base or lowest occurrence of the range zone can be
placed too high or the top of the range zone can be
placed too low. Thus if a relative zonation of the
events is considered, the most likely estimate of a series
of range zones is that which places the tops of the range
zones as high as possible in the zonation and places the
bases of the range zones as low as possible in the zonation. Shaw (1964) and Edwards (1978) made use of this
reasoning in their parametric (Shaw) and nonparametric
(Edwards) correlation and regression-based approaches.
This method is a somewhat different version of the Edwards
(1978) scheme. Point events are treated, that is highest
and lowest occurrences of a series of taxa. One lists
the sequence of events, from lowest to highest in the n
stratigraphic sections.

The algorithm is exceedingly simple. First a composite sequence of the events is determined. For any
two stratigraphic sections, the lists of events are
placed side by side and the similar events are connected
with tie-lines. If the events are in the same order, all
tie-lines will be parallel and the events in the two sections are consistent with one another. If the events are
not in the same order in the two sections, some of the
tie-lines will cross indicating that the events are inconsistent with one another in the two sections. The resolution of the inconsistencies is conducted by placing
the bases of the range zones (lowest occurrence events)
as low as possible in the zonation and the tops of the
range zones (highest occurrence events) as high as possible in the zonation. This revised or updated information is used to create a composite zonation of events for
the two sections. Next the first composite then is
matched with the series of events in a third stratigraphic

section and a second composite section created as outlined; the second composite contains the revised zonation
for the first three sections. Information from all other
sections gradually is assembled into the data until a
composite series of events is ascertained for all stratigraphic sections.

     In the second step, the composite serves as a stan-
dard to correlate all of the individual sections, much
as done by Shaw (1964) and Edwards (1978). The events
are matched between the composite and the individual
sections and tie-lines are drawn. Tie-lines that cross
emphasize the inconsistencies in the sequences of biostratigraphic events between the composite and the individual sections. These "false" correlations then can be
ignored. The "goodness of fit" between the individual
events in the composite zonation and the local sections
can be measured in several manners; for event I the
amount of mismatch might be determined by (number of sections in which event I is inconsistent with the composite/
total number of sections) or by a simple type of "stan-
dard-deviation" such as the following:

$$\text{"Standard-deviation" for event } I = \sqrt{\frac{\sum\limits_{J=1}^{n}\left(\begin{array}{c}\text{Number of events crossed}\\ \text{by event } I \text{ in section } J\end{array}\right)^2}{(\text{Number of sections, } n)}}$$

Higher "standard deviations" denote the events with lesser
consistencies that will be less useful in correlating
the sections. This method basically is the same as that
used by many practicing nonquantitative biostratigraphers
who usually do not update their data in the form of a
composite or explicitly delete false correlations.
Also, nonquantitative biostratigraphers do not formalize
estimates of the error inherent in the zonations which
they produce. This method also is essentially the same
as that of Edwards (1978). However, Edwards plots the
two series of events as the axes of a bivariate scatter-
plot. As mentioned before, data presented in this fashion
are difficult for biostratigraphers to visualize. Plotting the series of events side by side displays the data
in a form more familiar to biostratigraphers. Also,
Edwards and I resolve some of the inconsistent events in
a slightly different manner.

Method 2

This category of techniques is borrowed from archeological seriation. As discussed earlier, archeologists
may encounter the problem of arranging various objects,
such as graves and Iron Age brooches, into one-dimensional
sequences which generally represent either time or "evolutionary" series. Mathematical solutions to this problem
date back to Flinders Petrie (1899). Useful reviews of
many of these techniques are given in Cowgill (1972),
Doran and Hodson (1975), Gelfand (1971), Hodson, Kendall,
and Tautu (1971), Kendall (1963, 1971), Johnson (1972),
Marquardt (1978), and Wilkinson (1974). One can perform
seriation on a p x p matrix of distances or similarities
measured between objects or samples as mentioned earlier
under the quantification of assemblage zones. Original
data matrices (say n x m) including both objects and samples can be seriated and it is this type of seriation that
is of interest here.

Scott (1974) first suggested that archeological seriation could be applied usefully to biostratigraphic
data. Doveton (1978, pers. comm.) seriated some paleoecological data on Pennsylvanian conodonts (see also
Doveton, Gill, and Tipper, 1976). I thank John Doveton
for a copy of his unpublished manuscript and for calling
my attention to the possibility of seriation on original
data matrices. Tipper (1977) also applied seriation to
original data matrices of ecological and paleoecological
data. Although the data were discussed in the context
of networks, Smith and Fewtrell (1979) seem to have
adopted a seriation approach for microfossil data.

The biostratigraphic data to be considered represent
presences and absences of various taxa or species in a
series of samples observed in different stratigraphic
sections. Presences can be scored as 1.0 and absences
as 0.0. The data also could be viewed in black and
white. The intuitive appeal of black and white data
rather than various shades of dingy gray should be obvious. The data are ordered as follows. The presences
and absences are arranged with the taxa in the columns
and samples in the rows. The samples are put in a pre-
liminary sequence so that the data from the different
sections are placed in sequential blocks; for each section, the samples are listed from top to bottom. The
range-through method of data recording is used for each
stratigraphic section. Thus each taxon is scored as present in all samples within its range zone for each section.

The object of the exercise is simple. Consider,
first, the full seriation model which utilizes both first
and last occurrences. Here the rows and columns of the
matrix are interchanged in such a manner as to concentrate the presences along the diagonal of the matrix; the
absences are located as far away from the diagonal as
possible. This is referred to as the "concentration
principle" by archeologists. It also minimizes the range
zones of the taxa among the samples as suggested by Scott
(1974). The rearranged matrix has the taxa in the columns
and the samples in the rows of the matrix. The taxa with
the most similar range zones will be in adjacent columns
of the rearranged matrix. Also the most similar samples
will be grouped in the adjacent rows. Thus, the technique
groups both taxa and samples simultaneously. Two types of
of solutions can be obtained. The unconstrained solution
ignores all information about the stratigraphic position
of the samples and taxa within the stratigraphic sections.
Data on the stratigraphic position for the samples within
the individual sections are introduced into the analysis
for a constrained solution. This constraint forces the
samples within each section to remain in stratigraphic
order. Such is not true for the unconstrained solution
in which two samples within a single section can be seriated out of stratigraphic order.

Some biostratigraphers only work with one type of
event, either highest or lowest occurrences. This sim-
plifies the seriation to a largely additive model. The
more usual situation, that is concerned with highest occurrences, will be outlined briefly. The data are arranged as before. For each section, a taxon is recorded
as present in all samples below its highest occurrence.
One simply shuffles or interchanges the rows and columns
of the matrix until all the presences are located below
the diagonal of the matrix and all absences are concentrated above the diagonal. As for the full seriation
model, the rearranged matrix both correlates the samples
and gives the sequence of events.

These seriation methods have two major advantages.
First they share the virtue of simplicity. Second, they
roughly duplicate the procedures followed by many nonquantitative biostratigraphers. It is hoped that nonquantitative biostratigraphers will adopt some of these
simple methods if not the more complex algorithms.

EVOLUTIONARY SEQUENCES

The study of lineages in paleontology can be traced back at least as far as 1899 when Rowe systematically examined the evolution of *Micraster* from the Cretaceous chalks of England. Some early examples of statistical analyses of evolutionary sequences are those of Carruthers (1910; see also Swinnerton, 1921) on Carboniferous corals, Trueman (1922) on Jurassic oysters, and the monumental work of Brinkmann (1929) on Jurassic ammonites. The latter study especially is interesting because of the large samples involved and also for the plots of morphology versus stratigraphic position which were used to make correlations and infer the existence of unconformities. The statistical techniques are derived from a broad menu including such recipes as simple univariate and bivariate statistics (e.g., Gingerich, 1976; Kellogg, 1975; and Ozawa, 1975), principal components or factor analysis (see Kaesler, 1970; Malmgren, 1974, 1976; and Rowell, 1970 for simple and clear examples), principal coordinates (Blackith and Reyment, 1971), discriminant analysis (Reyment, 1978a, 1978b, 1978c; Reyment and Banfield, 1976; Campbell and Reyment, 1978; Blackith and Reyment, 1971; Symons and Ringele, 1976), various numerical taxonomic techniques (Cheetham, 1968; Kaesler, 1970; and Rowell, 1970), and cladistic analysis (Kesling and Sigler, 1969). An evolutionary sequence shows the distribution of size and shape in a framework defined by time and space. Therefore other methods also are important such as time-series analysis (Southam and Hay, 1978; Reyment, 1978a, 1971), Fourier analysis of shapes (e.g., Waters, 1977; Christopher and Waters, 1974; Kaesler and Waters, 1972), optical-data processing (see Srivastava, 1977 for applications to geological maps; the same scheme also could be used for fossils), quantified transformation grids (e.g. Sneath, 1967), and many other methods used for pattern analysis.

One of the main problems concerning the analysis of lineages and its utility in biostratigraphy is the nature of evolutionary changes. Two end-member models, "punctuated equilibria" and "phyletic gradualism," have been proposed. The concepts and many case studies are reviewed by Eldredge and Gould (1977) and Gould and Eldredge (1977). These authors strongly advocate the punctuated equilibria model but Gingerich (1976, 1979) argues persuasively for phyletic gradualism. According to punctuated equilibria evolutionary changes are abrupt. If so, then lineages can be segmented definitely and used to show chronostratgraphy. Conversely if species tend to change gradually

as predicted by the phyletic gradualism model, then lineages become difficult to breakdown into their component
species or other morphological units because any divisions
of a true continuum are ultimately arbitrary. Either of
these patterns can be complicated by the fact that the
appearance and disappearance of a species or morphological trait need not be synchronous throughout the area in-
habited by a lineage. At least some examples of both
phyletic gradualism and punctuated equilibria are known.
For example, even Gould and Eldredge (1977) concede that
the proloculus of a Permian foraminifer studied by Ozawa
(1975) constitutes an example of phyletic gradualism.
Gingerich (1976, 1979) presents other examples of grad-
ualistic change but these are debated by Gould and Eldredge (1977). Situations which probably fit the punc-
tuational model are Pleistocene land snails and hominids
(Gould, 1969, 1976) and many fossil brachiopods (e.g.,
Johnson, 1975).

Evolution obviously provides the basis for biostratigraphy. Ironically, many evolutionary sequences are approached in a paleobiologic context rather than from a
biostratigraphical point of view (for example, see most
of the studies in Gould and Eldredge, 1977). However,
some studies of lineages have been oriented strongly toward biostratigraphy. One example of such is the examination of the Cretaceous of the Western Interior of the
USA by Kauffmann (e.g., 1970, 1977) and various colleagues
including Cobban (e.g., 1951, 1958) and Sohl (1977). Detailed study of rapidly evolving lineages can result in
well-defined species that are short lived in time. Kauffmann (1977) reports average durations of Cretaceous species of ammonites and pelecypods that range from 0.19 to
3.1 million years. Based on a combination of the lineages and range charts, Kauffmann (1970, 1977) documents
regional composite assemblage zones in these Cretaceous
rocks that range from 0.08 to 0.5 million years in duration as determined by radioactive dating. The data
treatment may be qualitative or relatively simple statistics are involved. More powerful statistical algorithms
might yield a higher degree of resolution of both the
lineages and the range charts.

Reyment has been developing methodology for the
analysis of morphometric chronoclines. A brief review
was published in 1978 and full details are in a book on
"Morphometric Methods in Quantitative Biostratigraphy"
(Reyment, 1980). The data studied represent such
things as morphometric variables on a lineage, ecologically caused changes in size, shape, or frequency of

various taxa, etc. Typically multivariate statistics are
combined with time-series techniques such as cross-correlation and slotting (e.g., Gordon and Reyment, 1978).
Southam and Hay (1978) also are experimenting with time
series for paleontological data.

SUMMARY

Numerical methods in biostratigraphy can be grouped
into four basic categories. Firstly, although index fossils were used long before the time of Darwin, the measurement of the attributes of an index fossil did not begin until the 1960's. The quantification of index fossils allows the identification of the taxa which convey
the largest amounts of biostratigraphic information.
These data can be employed in several manners.

The second one represents the analysis of assemblage
zones, typically by multivariate statistics. Quantified
assemblage zones give data about both paleoecology and
stratigraphy. The locations of faunal discontinuities
in time and space are emphasized. Correlations, both
between and within the assemblage zones, can be determined.

The third group embraces the numerous methods which
are available for determining the most likely sequence
of biostratigraphic events recorded in different stratigraphic sections. The zonations can be of either the
average or conservative types. Assemblage zones, overlap
zones, etc., are derived easily from dissecting the series of all events. The sequencing methods produce lists
of events which are efficient for correlation but yield
little information about environments. Once ascertained,
the sequence of events can be used to correlate the various stratigraphic sections.

The analysis of evolutionary sequences is placed in
Category 4. A complete numerical approach requires mor-
phemetric statistics which are used in conjunction with
time-series algorithms. Careful examination of lineages
may pay off with well-documented taxa that are short
ranged in time. Another advantage is that the endpoints
of the range zones can be known definitely.

Although they belong in the other categories,
several simple techniques are treated separately in the
hope that they may entice nonquantitative biostratigraphers to try numerical techniques. *Method 1* determines

a conservative sequence of events. The techniques of
Method 2 are borrowed from archeological seriation and
these schemes simultaneously produce range charts and
correlations of the samples.

The annotations given earlier indicate that the various algorithms are data oriented. They require different types of input data, make different assumptions and
usually produce results which are more or less different.
The biostratigraphic information which can be derived
from the various techniques covers a wide spectrum, ranging from the biostratigraphic properties of taxa or biostratigraphic events, to the distribution of taxa and
morphology in an evolutionary and time-stratigraphic context.

The previous discussion denotes that quantitative
biostratigraphers have fulfilled the first two goals of
IGCP Project 148 reasonably well. To date, numerous algorithms have been developed and computer programs for
many of these generally are available. Unfortunately,
most of these techniques have only been tried on a few
case studies. Only a few data sets have been examined
with more than one technique. One of the exceptions is
the Cambrian fossils of Shaw (1964, graphical correlation) which have been treated by Edwards (1978, pers.
comm., nonparametric "regression"), Edwards and Beaver
(1978, trinomial probability), Guex (1977, a seriation-
type method), and Hohn (1978, principal components).
Hazel (1977) and Millendorf, Brower, and Dyman (1978)
applied a battery of techniques to several case studies
on assemblage zones.

A PREDICTION FOR THE 1980's

Thus far, the status of quantitative methods in biostratigraphy has been reviewed up to 1980. The next question is what will the future bring?

The 1960's and 1970's have brought a plethora of
algorithms. Many of these work effectively, particularly
on certain types of data, but the problems of biostratigraphy remain far from being resolved. In one sense,
this period constitutes an adaptive radiation of techniques. It is possible that a major algorithm, which is
yet to be written and may be capable of resolving all of
the trials and tribulations of biostratigraphical data,
is just about to be discovered. However, writing as a

self-acknowledged skeptic, I doubt it. (I may eventually
regret these words.) Rather than continue to create
another horde of algorithms in the 1980's, I would prefer
to see this decade as an interval of consolidation. The
adaptive radiation of techniques should cease. Now is
the time to begin to weed out the methods that are determined unfit by rigorous case studies. Accordingly, I
hope the 1980's will concentrate on the third goal of
IGCP Project 148, namely to evaluate the methods of quantitative biostratigraphy through case studies of both
real and simulated data.

REFERENCES

Ali, S.A., Lindemann, R.H., and Feldhausen, P.H., 1976,
    A multivariate sedimentary environment analysis of
    Great South Bay and South Oyster Bay, New York:
    Jour. Math. Geology, v. 8, no. 3, p. 283-304.

Blackith, R.E., and Reyment, R.A., 1971, Multivariate mor-
    phometrics: Academic Press, London, 412 p.

Blank, R.G., 1979, Applications of probabilistic bio-
    stratigraphy to chronostratigraphy: Jour. Geology,
    v. 87, no. 5, p. 647-670.

Brinkmann, R., 1929, Statistisch-biostratigraphische unter-
    suchungen an mitteljurassischen Ammoniten uber Art-
    begriff und Stammesentwicklung: Abhandlungen der
    Gesellschaft der Wissenschaften zu Gottingen, Mathe-
    matisch-physikalische Klasse, Neue Folge Bd. 13,
    249 p.

Brower, J.C., and Millendorf, S.A., 1978, Biostratigraphic
    correlation within IGCP project 148: Computers &
    Geosciences, v. 4, no. 3, p. 217-220.

Brower, J.C., Millendorf, S.A., and Dyman, T.S., 1978,
    Quantification of assemblage zones based on multi-
    variate analysis of weighted and unweighted data:
    Computers & Geosciences, v. 4, no. 3, p. 221-227.

Buzas, M.A., 1970, On the quantification of biofacies:
    Proc. North Am. Paleont. Conv., Chicago, 1969, pt.
    B, p. 101-116.

Campbell, N.A., and Reyment, R.A., 1978, Discriminant
    analysis of a Cretaceous foraminifer using shrunken
    estimators: Jour. Math. Geology, v. 10, no. 4, p.
    347-359.

Carruthers, R.G., 1910, On the evolution of *Zaphrentis
    delanouei* in Lower Carboniferous times: Geol. Soc.
    London Quart. Jour., v. 66, p. 523-538.

Cheetham, A.H., 1968, Morphology and systematics of the
    bryozoan genus *Metrarabdotos*: Smithsonian Misc.
    Coll., v. 153, no. 1, Publ. 4733, 121 p.

Cheetham, A.H., and Deboo, P.B., 1963, A numerical index
    for biostratigraphic zonation in the mid-Tertiary
    of the eastern Gulf: Gulf Coast Assoc. Geol. Soc.
    Trans., v. 13, p. 139-147.

Cheetham, A.H., and Hazel, J.E., 1969, Binary (presence-
    absence) similarity coefficients: Jour. Paleontology,
    v. 43, no. 5, p. 1130-1136.

Christopher, R.A., and Waters, J.A., 1974, Fourier series
    as a quantitative descriptor of microspore shape:
    Jour. Paleontology, v. 48, no. 4, p. 697-709.

Cisne, J.L., and Rabe, B.L., 1978, Coenocorrelation:
    gradient analysis of fossil communities and its ap-
    plications in stratigraphy: Lethaia, v. 11, no. 4,
    p. 341-364.

Cobban, W.A., 1951, Scaphitoid cephalopods of the Colorado
    Group: U.S. Geol. Survey Prof. Paper 239, 39 p.

Cobban, W.A., 1958, Late Cretaceous fossil zones of the
    Powder River Basin, Wyoming and Montana, *in* Wyoming
    Geol. Assoc. Guidebook, 13th Ann. Field Conf., 1958,
    Powder River Basin, p. 114-119.

Cockbain, A.E., 1966, An attempt to measure the relative
    biostratigraphic usefulness of fossils: Jour.
    Paleontology, v. 40, no. 1, p. 206-207.

Cowgill, G.L., 1972, Models, methods and techniques for
    seriation, *in* Models in archaeology, Clarke, D.L.,
    ed.,: Methuen and Co. Ltd., London, p. 381-424.

Davaud, E., and Guex, J., 1978, Traitement analytique
    (manuel) et algorithmique de problemes de correla-
    tions biochronologiques: Eclogae Geol. Helvetiae,
    v. 71, no. 3, p. 581-610.

Dienes, I., 1977, Formalized stratigraphy and its use on
    the Dorog Basin area, in Matematicke Metody v Geo-
    logii: Hornicka Pribram ve vede-technice (Pribram,
    Czechoslovakia), p. 626-645.

Dienes, I., 1978, Methods of plotting temporal range
    charts and their application in age estimation:
    Computers & Geosciences, v. 4, no. 3, p. 269-272.

Donovan, D.T., 1966, Stratigraphy: an introduction to
    principles: Rand McNally and Co., Chicago, 199 p.

Doran, J.E., and Hodson, F.R., 1975, Mathematics and
    computers in archaeology: Harvard Univ. Press,
    Cambridge, 381 p.

Doveton, J.H., Gill, D., and Tipper, J.C., 1976, Conodont
    distributions in the Upper Pennsylvanian of eastern
    Kansas; binary pattern analyses and their paleoeco-
    logical implications (abst.): Geol. Soc. America,
    Abstracts with Programs, v. 8, no. 7, p. 842.

Edwards, L.E., 1978, Range charts and no-space graphs:
    Computers & Geosciences, v. 4, no. 3, p. 247-255.

Edwards, L.E., and Beaver, R.J., 1978, The use of a
    paired comparison model in ordering stratigraphic
    events: Jour. Math. Geology, v. 10, no. 3, p. 261-
    272.

Eicher, D.L., 1976, Geologic time (2nd ed.): Prentice-
    Hall, Inc., New Jersey, 150 p.

Eldredge, N., and Gould, S.J., 1977, Evolutionary models
    and biostratigraphic strategies, in Concepts and
    methods of biostratigraphy, Kauffman, E.G., and
    Hazel, J.E., eds.: Dowden, Hutchinson & Ross,
    Stroudsburg, Pennsylvania, p. 25-40.

Ellison, R.L., 1963, Faunas of the Mahantango Formation
    in south-central Pennsylvania: Pennsylvania Topog.
    and Geol. Survey, General Geology Rept. G 39, p.
    201-212.

Feldhausen, P.H., 1970, Ordination of sediments from the
    Cape Hatteras continental margin: Jour. Math. Geo-
    logy, v. 2, no. 2, p. 113-129.

Fox, W.T., 1968, Quantitative paleoecologic analysis of
    fossil communities in the Richmond Group: Jour.
    Geology, v. 76, no. 6, p. 613-640.

Gelfand, A.E., 1971, Rapid seriation methods with archaeo-
    logical applications, *in* Mathematics in the archaeo-
    logical and historical sciences, Hodson, F.R., Ken-
    dall, D.G., and Tautu, P., eds.: Edinburgh Univ.
    Press, Edinburgh, p. 186-201.

Gill, D., Boehm, S., and Erez, Y., 1976, ASSOCA: FORTRAN
    IV program for Williams and Lambert association
    analysis with printed dendrograms: Computers &
    Geosciences, v. 2, no. 2, p. 219-248.

Gill, D., and Tipper, J.C., 1978, The adequacy of non-
    metric data in geology: tests using a divisive-
    omnithetic clustering technique: Jour. Geology,
    v. 86, no. 2, p. 241-259.

Gingerich, P.D., 1976, Paleontology and phylogeny: pat-
    terns of evolution at the species level in early
    Tertiary mammals: Am. Jour. Sci., v. 276, no. 1,
    p. 1-28

Gingerich, P.D., 1979, The stratophenetic approach to
    phylogeny: reconstruction in vertebrate paleontol-
    ogy, *in* Phylogenetic analysis and paleontology,
    Cracraft, J., and Eldredge, N., eds.: Columbia
    Univ. Press, New York, p. 41-77.

Gordon, A.D., and Reyment, R.A., 1979, Slotting of bore-
    hole sequences: Jour. Math. Geology, v. 11, no. 3,
    p. 309-327.

Gould, S.J., 1969, An evolutionary microcosm: Pleisto-
    cene and Recent history of the land snail *P. (Poeci-
    lozonites)* in Bermuda: Bull. Mus. Comp. Zoology,
    v. 138, no. 7, p. 407-531.

Gould, S.J., 1976, Ladders, bushes, and human evolution:
    Nat. Hist., v. 85, no. 4, p. 24-31.

Gould, S.J., 1977, Ontogeny and phylogeny: The Belknap
    Press of Harvard Univ. Press, Cambridge, Massachu-
    setts, 498 p.

Gould, S.J., and Eldredge, N., 1977, Punctuated equili-
    bria: the tempo and mode of evolution reconsidered:
    Paleobiology, v. 3, no. 2, p. 115-151.

Guex, J., 1977, Une nouvelle methode d'analyse biochrono-
    logique: note preliminaire: Bull. Soc. Vaud. Sci.
    Nat., v. 73, no. 351, p. 309-322.

Guex, J., 1978a, Le Trias inferieur des Salt Ranges (Pak-
    istan): problemes biochronologiques: Eclogae
    Geol. Helvetiae, v. 71, no. 1, p. 105-141.

Guex, J., 1978b, Influence du confinement geographique
    des especes fossiles sur l'elaboration d'echelles
    biochronologiques et sur les correlations: Bull.
    Soc. Vaud. Sci. Nat., v. 74, no. 354, p. 115-124.

Guex, J., 1979, Terminologie et methodes de la biostrati-
    graphie moderne: commentaires critiques et proposi-
    tions: Bull. Soc. Vaud. Sci. Nat., v. 74, no. 355,
    p. 169-216.

Hancock, J.M., 1977, The historic development of concepts
    of biostratigraphic correlation, *in* Concepts and
    methods of biostratigraphy, Kauffman, E.G., and
    Hazel, J.E., eds.: Dowden, Hutchinson & Ross, Inc.,
    Stroudsburg, Pennsylvania, p. 3-22.

Hay, W.W., 1972, Probabilistic stratigraphy: Eclogae
    Geol. Helvetiae, v. 65, no. 2, p. 255-266.

Hay, W.W., and Southam, J.R., 1978, Quantifying biostrati-
    graphic correlation: Ann. Rev. Earth Planet. Sci.,
    v. 6, p. 353-375.

Hazel, J.E., 1970, Binary coefficients and clustering in
    biostratigraphy: Geol. Soc. America Bull., v. 81,
    no. 11, p. 3237-3252.

Hazel, J.E., 1971, Ostracode biostratigraphy of the York-
    town Formation (Upper Miocene and Lower Pliocene)
    of Virginia and North Carolina: U.S. Geol. Survey
    Prof. Paper 204, 13 p.

Hazel, J.E., 1977, Use of certain multivariate and other techniques in assemblage zonal biostratigraphy: examples utilizing Cambrian, Cretaceous, and Tertiary benthic invertebrates, *in* Concepts and methods of biostratigraphy, Kauffman, E.G., and Hazel, J.E., eds.: Dowden, Hutchinson & Ross, Inc., Stroudsburg, Pennsylvania, p. 187-212.

Henderson, R.A., and Heron, M.L., 1977, A probabilistic method of paleobiogeographic analysis: Lethaia, v. 10, no. 1, p. 1-15.

Hodson, F.R., Kendall, D.G., and Tautu, P., eds., 1971, Mathematics in the archaeological and historical sciences: Edinburgh Univ. Press, Edinburgh, 565 p.

Hohn, M.E., 1976, Binary coeffients: a theoretical and empirical study: Jour. Math. Geology, v. 8, no. 2, p. 137-150.

Hohn, M.E., 1978, Stratigraphic correlation by principal components: effects of missing data: Jour. Geology, v. 86, no. 4, p. 524-532.

Imbrie, J., 1964, Factor analytic model in paleoecology, *in* Approaches to paleoecology, Imbrie, J., and Newell, N., eds.: John Wiley & Sons, Inc., New York, p. 407-422.

Jeletzky, J.A., 1965, Is it possible to quantify biochronological correlation?: Jour. Paleontology, v. 39, no. 1, p. 135-140.

Johnson, J.G., 1975, Allopatric speciation in fossil brachiopods: Jour. Paleontology, v. 49, no. 4, p. 646-661.

Johnson, L., 1972, Introduction to imaginary models for archaeological scaling and clustering, *in* Models in archaeology, Clarke, D.L., ed.: Methuen and Co. Ltd., London, p. 309-379.

Kaesler, R.L., 1966, Quantitative re-evaluation of ecology and distribution of Recent Foraminifera and Ostracoda of Todos Santos Bay, Baja, California, Mexico: Kansas Univ. Paleont. Contr., Paper 10, 50 p.

Kaesler, R.L., 1970, Numerical taxonomy in paleontology:
    classification, ordination and reconstruction of
    phylogenies: Proc. North Am. Paleont. Conv., Chica-
    go, 1969, pt. B, p. 84-100.

Kaesler, R.L., and Waters, J.A., 1972, Fourier analysis
    of the ostracode margin: Geol. Soc. America Bull.,
    v. 83, no. 4, p. 1169-1178.

Kauffman, E.G., 1970, Population systematics, radiometrics,
    and zonation - a new biostratigraphy: Proc. North
    Am. Paleont. Conv., Chicago, 1969, pt. F, p. 612-666.

Kauffman, E.G., 1977, Evolutionary rates and biostrati-
    graphy, *in* Concepts and methods of biostratigraphy,
    Kauffman, E.G., and Hazel, J.E., eds.: Dowden,
    Hutchinson & Ross, Inc., Stroudsburg, Pennsylvania,
    p. 109-141.

Kellogg, D.E., 1975, The role of phyletic change in the
    evolution of *Pseudocubus vema* (Radiolaria): Paleo-
    biology, v. 1, p. 359-370.

Kendall, D.G., 1963, A statistical approach to Flinders
    Petrie's sequence dating: Intern. Statistical Inst.
    Bull., no. 40, p. 657-680.

Kendall, D.G., 1971, Seriation from abundance matrices,
    in Mathematics in the archaeological and historical
    sciences, Hodson, F.R., Kendall, D.G., and Tautu,
    P., eds.: Edinburgh Univ. Press, Edinburgh, p. 215-
    252.

Kesling, R.V., and Sigler, J.P., 1969, *Cunctocrinus*, a
    new Middle Devonian calceocrinid crinoid from the
    Silica Shale of Ohio: Univ. Michigan, Mus. Paleon-
    tology Contr., v. 22, no. 24, p. 339-360.

Lyell, C., 1830-33, Principles of geology: J. Murray,
    London, 3 vols.

Lynts, G.W., 1971, Analysis of the planktonic Foraminifera
    fauna of core 6275, Tongue of the ocean, Bahamas,
    Micropaleontology, v. 17, no. 2, p. 152-166.

Lynts, G.W., 1972, Factor-vector analysis models in ecol-
    ogy and paleoecology: 21st Intern. Geol. Congress
    (Montreal) Sect. 7, Paleontology, p. 227-237.

Lynts, G.W., and Stehman, C.F., 1971, Factor-vector models
    of middle Eocene planktonic foraminiferal fauna of
    core 6282, Northeast Providence Channel, Bahamas:
    Rev. Espanola Micropaleontol., v. 3, p. 205-213.

Mallory, V.S., 1970, Biostratigraphy - a major basis for
    paleontologic correlation: Proc. North Am. Paleont.
    Conv., Chicago, 1969, pt. F, p. 553-566.

Malmgren, B.A., 1974, Morphometric studies of planktonic
    foraminifers from the type Danian of southern Scan-
    dinavia: Stockholm Contr. Geol., v. 29, p. 1-126.

Malmgren, B.A., 1976, Size and shape variation in the
    planktonic foraminifer *Heterohelix striata* (Late
    Cretaceous, southern Scandinavia): Jour. Math. Geo-
    logy, v. 8, no. 2, p. 165-182.

Marquardt, W.H., 1978, Advances in archaeological seria-
    tion, *in* Advances in archaeological method and the-
    ory, v. 1, Schiffer, M.B., ed.: Academic Press,
    London, p. 257-314.

McCammon, R.B., 1966, Principal component analysis and
    its application in large-scale correlation studies:
    Jour. Geology, v. 74, no. 5, pt. 2., p. 721-733.

McCammon, R.B., 1970, On estimating the relative bio-
    stratigraphic values of fossils: Bull. Geol. Inst.
    Univ. Uppsala (n.s.), v. 2, p. 49-57.

Millendorf, S.A., Brower, J.C., and Dyman, T.S., 1978,
    A comparison of methods for the quantification of
    assemblage zones: Computers & Geosciences, v. 4,
    no. 3, p. 229-242.

Miller, F.X., 1977, The graphic correlation method in
    biostratigraphy, *in* Concepts and methods of bio-
    stratigraphy, Kauffman, E.G., and Hazel, J.E., eds.:
    Dowden, Hutchinson & Ross, Inc., Stroudsburg, Penn-
    sylvania, p. 165-186.

Murphy, M.A., and Edwards, L.E., 1977, The Silurian-
    Devonian Boundary in central Nevada: Univ. Calif.,
    Riverside Campus Museum Contr., no. 4, p. 183-189.

Oltz, D.F., Jr., 1969, Numerical analysis of palynological
    data from Cretaceous and early Tertiary sediments in
    east central Montana: Palaeontographica, pt. B, v.
    128, p. 90-166.

Oltz, D.F., Jr., 1971, Cluster analyses of Late Creta-
    ceous-Early Tertiary pollen and spore data: Micro-
    paleontology, v. 17, no. 2, p. 221-232.

Oppel, A., 1856-1858, Die Juraformation Englands, Frank-
    reichs und des sudwestlichen Deutschlands, nach
    ihren einzelnen gliedern eingntheilt und verglichen:
    von Ebner and Seubert, Stuttgart (originally pub-
    lished in three parts in Abdruck der Wurttemb.
    naturw. Jahreshefte 12-14; 1856, 1-438; 1857, 439
    bis-594 + map; 1858, 695-857 + table).

Ozawa, T., 1975, Evolution of *Lepidolina multiseptata*
    (Permian foraminifer) in East Asia: Mem. Fac. Sci.
    Kyushu Univ., Ser. D, Geol., v. 23, p. 117-164.

Park, R.A., 1974, A multivariate analytical strategy for
    classifying paleoenvironments: Jour. Math. Geology,
    v. 6, no. 4, p. 333-352.

Petrie, W.M.F., 1899, Sequences in prehistoric remains:
    Jour. Anthropol. Inst., v. 29, p. 295-301.

Quenstedt, F.A., 1856-1858, Der Jura: H. Lauppschen,
    Rubingen, 842 p.

Raup, D.M., and Crick, R.E., 1979, Measurement of faunal
    similarity in paleontology: Jour. Paleontology,
    v. 53, no. 5, p. 1213-1227.

Reyment, R.A., 1971, Spectral breakdown of morphometric
    chronoclines: Jour. Math. Geology, v. 2, no. 4,
    p. 365-376.

Reyment, R.A., 1978a, Biostratigraphical logging methods:
    Computers & Geosciences, v. 4, no. 3, p. 261-268.

Reyment, R.A., 1978b, Quantitative biostratigraphical
    analysis exemplified by Moroccan Cretaceous ostra-
    cods: Micropaleontology, v. 24, no. 1, p. 24-43.

Reyment, R.A., 1978c, Graphical display of growth-free
    variation in the Cretaceous benthonic foraminifer
    Afrobolivina afra: Palaeo., Palaeo., Palaeo., v.
    25, no. 4, p. 267-276.

Reyment, R.A., 1980, Morphometric methods in biostratigra-
    phy: Academic Press, London, 176 p.

Reyment, R.A., and Banfield, C.F., 1976, Growth-free
    canonical variates applied to fossil foraminifera:
    Bull. Geol. Inst. Univ. Uppsala, (n.s.), v. 7, p.
    11-21.

Reyre, Y., 1972, Application de l'informatique a la
    <<gestion>> et a l'interpretation stratigraphique
    des donnees paleontologiques quantitatives: BRGM
    Bull. (2nd ser.), Sec. 4, no. 2-1972, p. 49-65.

Reyre, Y., 1974, Les methodes quantitatives en polyno-
    logie, in Elements de palynologie, applications
    geologiques, Chateanueuf, J.-J., and Reyre, Y.,
    eds.: BRGM, Orleans, p. 271-312.

Rowe, A.W., 1899, An analysis of the genus Micraster, as
    determined by rigid zonal collecting from the zone
    of Rhynchonella Cuvieri to that of Micraster cor-
    anguinum: Geol. Soc. London Quart. Jour., v. 55,
    p. 494-547.

Rowell, A.J., 1970, The contribution of numerical taxonomy
    to the genus concept: Proc. North Am. Paleont. Conv.
    Chicago, 1969, pt. C, p. 264-293.

Rowell, A.J., and McBride, D.J., 1972, Faunal variation
    in the Elvinia Zone of the Upper Cambrian of North
    America - a numerical approach: 21st Intern. Geol.
    Contress (Montreal), Sect. 7, Paleontology, p. 246-
    253.

Rowell, A.J., McBride, D.J., and Palmer, A.R., 1973,
    Quantitative study of Trempealeauian (Latest Cam-
    brian) trilobite distribution in North America:
    Geol. Soc. America Bull., v. 84, no. 10, p. 3429-
    3442.

Rubel, M., 1976, On biological construction of time in
    geology: Eesti NSV Tead. Akad. Toimetised. Keemia.
    Geoloogia, v. 25, nr. 2, p. 136-144 (in Russian).

Rubel, M., 1978, Principles of construction and use of
    biostratigraphical scales for correlation: Compu-
    ters & Geosciences, v. 4, no. 3, p. 243-246.

Schuey, R.T., Brown, F.H., Eck, G.G., and Clark, F.C., 1978, A statistical approach to temporal biostratigraphy, *in* Geological background to fossil man: Recent research in the Gregory Rift Valley, East Africa, Bishop, W.W., ed.: publ. for the Geol. Soc. London by Scottish Academic Press and Univ. of Toronto Press, p. 103-124.

Scott, G.H., 1974, Essay review: stratigraphy and seriation: Stratigraphy Newsletter, v. 3, p. 93-100.

Scott, R.W., 1970, Paleoecology and paleontology of the Lower Cretaceous Kiowa Formation, Kansas: Univ. Kansas Paleont. Contr., Art. 52 (Cretaceous 1), 94 p.

Scott, R.W., and West, R.R., eds., 1976, Structure and classification of paleocommunities: Dowden, Hutchinson & Ross, Inc., Stroudsburg, Pennsylvania, 291 p.

Sepkoski, J.J., Jr., 1974, Quantified coefficients of association and measurement of similarity: Jour. Math. Geology, v. 6, no. 2, p. 135-152.

Shaw, A.B., 1964, Time in stratigraphy: McGraw-Hill Book Co., New York, 365 p.

Shier, D.E., 1978, Sample ordering - a new statistical technique for paleoecological analysis: Trans. Gulf Coast Assoc. Geol. Soc., v. 28, p. 461-471.

Simpson, G.G., 1947, Holarctic mammalian faunas and continental relationships during the Cenozoic: Geol. Soc. America Bull., v. 58, no. 7, p. 613-687.

Simpson, G.G., 1960, Notes on the measurement of faunal resemblance: Am. Jour. Sci., v. 258a, p. 300-311.

Smith, D.G., and Fewtrell, M.D., 1979, A use of network diagrams in depicting stratigraphic time-correlation: Geol. Soc. London Quart. Jour., v. 136, pt. 1, p. 21-28.

Smith, W., 1815, A memoir to the map and delineation of the strata of England and Wales, with part of Scotland: John Cary, London, 51 p.

Smith, W., 1816-1819, Strata identified by organized fos-
     sils, containing prints on coloured paper of the
     most characteristic specimens in each stratum: The
     author, London, 32 p, (parts 1 and 2 in 1816; part
     3 in 1817; part 4 in 1819).

Smith, W., 1817, Stratigraphical system of organized fos-
     sils, with reference to the specimens of the origin-
     al geological collection in the British Museum:
     explaining their state of preservation and their use
     in identifying the British strata: E. Williams,
     London, 118 p.

Sneath, P.H.A., 1967, Trend-surface analysis of transfor-
     mation grids: Jour. Zoology London, v. 151,
     p. 65-122.

Sneath, P.H.A., and Sokal, R.R., 1973, Numerical taxonomy:
     W.H. Freeman & Co., San Francisco, 573 p.

Sohl, N.F., 1977, Utility of gastropods in biostratigra-
     phy, *in* Concepts and methods of biostratigraphy,
     Kauffman, E.G., and Hazel, J.E., eds.:   Dowden,
     Hutchinson & Ross, Inc., Stroudsburg, Pennsylvania,
     p. 519-539.

Sorgenfrei, T., 1958, Molluscan assemblages from the ma-
     rine Middle Miocene of South Jutland and their en-
     vironments: Geol. Survey Denmark (2nd ser.), no.
     79, 2 vols., 503 p.

Southam, J.R., and Hay, W.W., 1978, Correlation of strati-
     graphic sections by continuous variables: Computers
     & Geosciences, v. 4, no. 3, p, 257-260.

Southam, J.R., Hay, W.W., and Worsley, T.R., 1975, Quan-
     titative formulation of reliability of stratigraphic
     correlation: Science, v. 188, no. 4186, p. 357-
     359.

Srivastava, G.S., 1977, Optical processing of structural
     contour maps: Jour. Math. Geology, v. 9, no. 1,
     p. 3-38.

Stone, J.F., 1967, Quantitative palynology of a Cretaceous
     Eagle Ford exposure: Compass, v. 45, no. 1, p. 17-
     25.

Stone, J.F., 1973, Palynology of the Almond Formation
    (Upper Cretaceous), Rock Springs Uplift, Wyoming:
    Am. Paleontology Bull., v. 64, no. 278, 135 p.

Swinnerton, H.H., 1921, The use of graphs in palaeontol-
    ogy: Geol. Mag., v. 58, p. 357-364, 397-408.

Symons, F., and De Meuter, F., 1974, Foraminiferal asso-
    ciations of the mid-Tertiary Edegem sands at Terha-
    gen, Belgium: Jour. Math. Geology, v. 6, no. 1,
    p. 1-15.

Symons, F., and Ringele, A., 1976, Study of time-related
    variability within the genus *Astarte* (Bivalvia):
    Jour. Math. Geology, v. 8, no. 2, p. 113-136.

Tipper, J.C., 1977, Some distributional models for fossil
    marine animals (abst.): Geol. Soc. America, Ab-
    stracts with Programs, v. 9, p. 1202.

Tipper, J.C., 1979, An algol program for dissimilarity
    analysis: a divisive-omnithetic clustering tech-
    nique: Computers & Geosciences, v. 5, no. 1, p.
    1-13.

Trueman, A.E., 1922, The use of *Gryphaea* in the correla-
    tion of the Lower Lias: Geol. Mag., v. 59, no. 6,
    p. 256-268.

Valentine, J.W., and Peddicord, R.G., 1967, Evaluation of
    fossil assemblages by cluster analysis: Jour.
    Paleontology, v. 41, no. 2, p. 502-507.

Waters, J.A., 1977, The quantification of shape by use of
    Fourier analysis: the Mississippian blastoid genus
    Pentremites: Paleobiology, v. 3, no. 3, p. 288-
    299.

Whittaker, R.H., ed., 1973, Ordination and classification
    of communities, *in* Handbook of vegetation science,
    pt. 5: Junk, The Hague, 737 p.

Wilkinson, E.M., 1974, Techniques of data analysis-seria-
    tion theory: Archaeo-Physika, v. 5, p. 1-142.

Worsley, T.R., and Jorgens, M.L., 1977, Automated bio-
    stratigraphy, *in* Oceanic micropaleontology, Ramsay,
    A.T.S., ed.: Academic Press, London, p. 1201-1229.

COMPUTERS IN GEOLOGICAL PHOTOINTERPRETATION

K.L. Burns

Syracuse University

ABSTRACT

Computer processing of digital remote-sensing data can produce imagery of high spectral and geometric fidelity without the degradation associated with photographic reproduction. This is a significant advance in quality control in the data-acquisition system.

However progress in the interpretation system lags considerably. In one specific application, interpretation for geological lineaments, there occur low correlations between annotations which have hindered the acceptance of geological photointerpretations as reliable data.

Recently, perception models have been developed which radically alter our understanding of the properties of annotations. In particular the models imply that presence-absence data associated with the existence of lineaments is not a ranked binary variable and correlation measures are meaningless as indicators of data quality.

Computer processing now seems to be essential in geological photointerpretation. The procedures developed to date comprise estimation of operator resolution, digitization of annotations to arrays of cells, fitting perception models, and using the model parameters to assign probability estimates to quality maps written as shade prints or on filmwriters.

INTRODUCTION

At the present time the most widely used method of extracting spatial information from imagery for geological purposes is by human photointerpretation. The method is cheap, simple, and adaptable in terms of targets and operating conditions, and is the main source of information from imagery for a wide range of purposes. The human interpreter, therefore, is an essential link in an information-processing system and his characteristics are important in design of the total system.

In geology, a target of some importance is the discrete, linear feature termed a *lineament*. The interpreter marks their location by a line drawn on the image, so that the result of the interpretation process is a network of intersecting lines termed an *annotation*.

A persistent difficulty with information extracted in this manner is the lack of reproducibility between annotations made on the same image by different interpreters, or by the same interpreter on different occasions. Burns, Huntington, and Green (1977, fig. 1) and Burns and Brown (1978, fig. 2) show repeated interpretations of the same image, and how that although there is some similarity between them, there is nowhere precise agreement. This situation also is illustrated by the comparative plates of Kelley and Clinton (1960) and measurements reported by Podwysocki, Moik, and Sharp (1975) and Siegal and Short (1977). In addition, field examinations at locations indicated by the annotations may yield confirmation in ground-observables of the existence of structures, but sometimes do not. Practical experience is that lineaments interpreted from imagery may or may not be meaningful in terms of the ground geology. As a result of varying experience with annotations, some geologists regard lineaments as in the same class as the Martian Canals - imaginary lines perceived in random spatial noise (Crain, 1972), whereas for others, lineaments are meaningful and their study is incorporated in engineering and mining investigations.

This paper reviews some recent work on the human perception of geological lineaments. Annotations have been shown to have properties rather different to those of signals ordinarily encountered in geophysics, and it is this anomalous behavior that causes much of the difficulty in evaluating their significance. Examination of those properties suggests that annotations could be

made more reliable by changes in photointerpretation
practice.

PROPERTIES OF ANNOTATIONS

"Resolution"

An annotation may be digitized into a large number
of small regions termed *cells*. The appropriate cell size
for any annotation is governed by the ability of the observer to discriminate between adjacent lineaments, which
is a function of the physical resolution of the system
and the human resolution of the observer.

The smallest resolvable object, a criterion used
in measurement of physical resolution, is not appropriate
for annotations. For example, some high-contrast linear
features, such as roads, with widths on the ground of 15
m, have been detected on LANDSAT imagery with pixel dimensions of approximately 30 by 60 m. Their detection
rests upon their effect on reflected intensity across
the whole of a pixel; the observer cannot locate them
with greater precision than "somewhere within" a pixel,
so that mere detectability is insufficient as a measure
for features with decision boundaries, such as lineaments.

The spatial resolution of an annotation is defined
here as the distance between the closest pair of linear
features which are visually separable. Burns, Shepherd,
and Berman (1976) printed LANDSAT MSS imagery at a scale
of 1:500,000 at which scale the pixel size (approximately
0.06 x 0.12 mm) matches human resolution at normal view-
ing distances (approximately 8 to 10 lines/mm), to eliminate those problems that might arise from a mismatch,
and demonstrated two different methods of measuring annotation resolution.

In the first method, interpreters were asked to
classify pairs of adjacent lineaments into two states,
nonseparable (state 1) or separable (state 2). The number of observations of each state can be written $n_1(a)$
and $n_2(a)$ which are functions of a, the measured
distance between features in a pair. A discriminant function, $d(\infty)$ then is erected, where

$$d(\infty) = \frac{\int_0^\alpha n_1(a) \ da + n_2 \int_\alpha^\infty n_2(a) \ da}{\int_0^\infty n_1(a) \ da + \int_0^\infty n_2(a) \ da}$$

which is the empirical probability that two adjacent
lineaments can be classified correctly as distinct or not
when distance ∞ apart. Measurements yielded a maximum
value of $d(\infty)$ at 0.85, 0.90, for LANDSAT imagery corresponding to ∞ = 205, 275 m, respectively, at ground
scale (Burns, Shepherd, and Berman, 1976, fig. 5). Thus
maximum discrimination was obtained at separations of
about 250 m and the accuracy of classification was about
90 percent.

In the second method, the agreement between two
different annotations of the same scene was estimated by
a parameter R, the "reproducibility" which is a multistate measure of association discussed further later.
Where w is the width of lineaments, arguments can be
made that R should increase rapidly as w increases from
0, then dR/dw should decline to be approximately constant, and the resolution of the annotation is the value
of w at the beginning of the latter stage. Measurements
showed that dR/dw was approximately constant from w=300
to w=600 m, implying a resolution of about 300 m, in
reasonable agreement with the result obtained by different methods. This second method is not as precise as
the first as it the result is influenced by the geometrical pattern of the features, a factor which can be excluded in the first method. However it does not require
observer characterization so is more objective.

At the scale of imagery used for these experiments,
the results imply an *interpretation cell* of dimensions
approximately 0.5 x 0.5 mm as the area of the image
viewed by an observer in deciding whether a pattern is
two separate lineaments or only one. This "decision
area" corresponds to a "decision level" of about 0.9.
It is regarded as significant that the decision area
contained approximately 5 x 5 pixels and that this corresponds to the 9 x 6 or 7 x 5 dot matrices used for
alphanumeric character representation in dot-matrix
printers. The observer makes classifications on the
basis of a pattern formed by arrays of resolvable elements.

Perception Vectors:

When an interpreter draws a feature on the image he is classifying cells in the field of view into one of two states - a state denoted a_1 for cells which are occupied by a feature and a state denoted a_0 for cells which do not contain a feature. Because lineaments intersect, cells under crossing points are multiply classified (Burns, Shepherd, and Berman, 1976, fig. 1) but the number is small and may be neglected, thus a single annotation is a binary classification of the cells into two states, a_0 and a_1.

If an image is annotated several (say k) times, to give a series of different annotations, each cell is classified several times. The classification state of each cell then may be described by a *perception vector* $v = (v_1, v_2, v_3, \ldots.)$ where each component v_i takes the states a_0 or a_1. Thus, for example, the perception vector $v = (a_0, a_1, a_0, a_0, a_1)$ indicates the cell was assigned state a_0 on the first, third, and fourth annotations and state a_1 on the second and fifth.

It is convenient to define a scalar, V, termed the *perception level* as the number of states v_i such that $v_i = a_1$, that is,

$$V = |(v_i | v_i = a_1, v_i \neq a_0)|$$

PERCEPTION MODELS

Burns and Brown (1978) introduced a perception model to explain the process of image interpretation. The image is conceived as consisting of several disjoint sets of cells termed *messages* of different types. The interpreter has a certain probability of perceiving a given message correctly and assigning the correct classification or of not perceiving the message correctly and assigning an incorrect classification.

There could be a number of messages and a number of classification states, and the perception probabilities may change from trial to trial, and complex models can provide close fits to the data (e.g. Burns and Brown, 1978, model B). However it is shown in that paper that an approximation which is adequate for practical purposes is a simple two by two classification (Burns and

Brown, 1978, model A). It was determined that perceived lineaments are not drawn from a mononomial distribution and the simplest model which provides anything approaching an adequate fit is binomial, with the perceived lineaments being drawn from two disjoint distributions with substantially different perception properties. In the simple model, the cells of the image comprise two disjoint sets, termed *positive message* and *negative message* respectively. The positive message is that set of cells which lie on lineaments, the negative message is that set which do not.

This result is contrary to traditional concepts in geological photointerpretation and seems to run counter to line-finding methods which search for a positive message only (e.g. Vanderbrug, 1975) but is in accord with recent work in psychology (Estes, 1975; Sperling and Melchner, 1978).

There are two independent probabilities, a probability P_0 that a cell of the negative message will be assigned the correct perception state a_0 and a probability P_1 that a cell of the positive message will be assigned its correct perception state, a_1. These correspond to the marginal probabilities or empirically estimated attention operating characteristics of Sperling and Melchner (1978, fig. 1). The probabilities of incorrect identification are $(1-P_0)$ and $(1-P_1)$ respectively.

If v is the perception level as defined previously and α is the proportion of positive message in the image, then the simple model may be written as follows:

$$n(k,v) = N\alpha\binom{k}{v}P_0^{k-v}(1-P_0)^v + N(1-\alpha)\binom{k}{v}(1-P_1)^{k-v}P_1^v \quad (1)$$

Where n(k,v) is the number of cells with perception level v after k repeated annotations and N is the total number of cells in the image.

For any particular situation there are two solutions, the correspondence between a solution and its dual being

$$
\left.
\begin{array}{l}
\alpha \iff 1 - \alpha \\
P_0 \iff 1 - P_1 \\
P_1 \iff 1 - P_0
\end{array}
\right]
\qquad (2)
$$

The solution is decided between these alternatives on intuitive grounds.

The perception model may be inverted to provide the probability that a message of either type exists at a cell. Burns and Brown (1978) define the *quality* of an annotation as the probability that any cell is classified correctly. For a single interpretation (that is, k = 1) in a typical situation, it is determined that the quality of the annotation is 0.66 for the positive portion and 0.78 for the negative. This indicates that approximately 34 percent of the lineaments drawn on the experimental annotations were spurious, being negative messages interpreted as positive.

This quantifies the field geologist's problem. About one-third of the lineaments he seeks to verify in the field could be "artifacts of the interpreter's imagination" in the same category as the Martian Canals. Because the annotations as usually supplied provide no guide as to which of the lineaments may be in that category, we have the strange situation in mineral exploration where men and machines are moved about in the field to determine which lineaments are projections of an interpreter's imagination and which have substance.

The obvious absurdity of this procedure has led to the introduction by Burns, Huntington, and Green (1977) of methods of processing annotations to produce *quality maps* which show the probability of a message existing at any given location. This is one method of message extraction termed the *perception-level method*.

If a series of k annotations are superposed in such a manner as to generate the set intersection of the lineaments, the size of the intersection set decreases approximately geometrically with k. This is a property of other types of geological targets than the discrete lineaments considered here. This situation corresponds to the application of the condition k = v in expression (1), as follows:

$$n(1,1) = N\alpha(1-P_0) + N(1-\alpha)P_1$$

$$n(2,2) = N\alpha(1-P_0)^2 + N(1-\alpha)P_1^2$$

$$n(3,3) = N\alpha(1-P_0)^3 + N(1-\alpha)P_1^3$$

and so on. As a result, the common area of lineaments
dwindles away to nil, in practical situations, when k >
6. This is illustrated in Table 1 and by Burns and Brown
(1978, fig. 3).

If a series of k annotations is superposed in such a
manner as to take the set union of the lineaments, the
size of this union set increases with k. This corresponds to the situation v = 0 in expression (1), as follows

$$N - n(1,0) = N[1-\alpha p_0 - (1-\alpha)(1-P_1)]$$

$$N - n(2,0) = N[1-\alpha P_0^2 - (1-\alpha)(1-P_1)^2]$$

$$N - n(3,0) = N[1-\alpha P_0^3 - (1-\alpha)(1-P_1)^3]$$

and so on. As a result, the combined area of lineaments
increases to occupy almost the whole image. This is
illustrated by Table 1.

This behavior of the annotations confronts the industrial geologists with a severe problem. Expressed in
practical terms, it indicates the more sources of advice
he employs, the smaller the area of mutual agreement.
It also indicates that each new adviser will canvass new
possibilities until eventually they are all covered. He
will never obtain a consensus on a limited number of
choices. This behavior is in contrast to geophysical
signals of other types where repeated acquisition cycles
tend to reinforce the signal at the expense of the noise.

However a real signal exists in annotations as shown
by the correlation peak at registration obtained by Burns
Shepherd, and Berman (1976, figs. 7 and 8) so the annotations cannot be discarded as random patterns as proposed by Gilluly (1976, p. 1512) but contain real information. At the present time it seems essential to accept
the perception process as generating information with
curious properties and process them by computer.

                    REPRODUCIBILITY OF ANNOTATIONS

We consider the simplest situation, which is two
different annotations by a single observer. The perception vector for each cell then has the form $V = (v_1, v_2)$

Table 1.   Expected proportion of image occupied by lineaments when k annotations are combined by set intersection (column 2) and set union
(column 3).   In first situation
combined area dwindles away to
nil as k increases, in second it
increases to (eventually) fill
whole image.   Perception parameters used are $\alpha = 0.6987$,
$P_0 = 0.9129$, $p_1 = 0.3883$.

k	n(k,1)/N	[N-n(k,0)]/N
1	.178	.178
2	.051	.305
3	.018	.399
4	.007	.473
5	.003	.531
6	.001	.580
7	.000	.621
8	.000	.657

where $v_i = a_0$ or a_1.   This gives rise to four
situations, which are (a_0,a_0),
(a_0,a_1), (a_1,a_0), and $(a_1 a_1)$.   We denote the
number of cells in each set by n_{00}, n_{01}, n_{10}, n_{11} respectively.   Table 2 shows the   values
these are expected to take under the perception model.

The general form of the produce-moment correlation
coefficient is

$$R_{a\bar{a}} = \sum_{i=1}^{\ell} (x_1 - \bar{x})^2$$

$$R_{bb} = \sum_{i=1}^{\ell} (Y_i - \bar{Y})^2 \qquad (3)$$

$$R_{ab} = \sum_{i=1}^{\ell} (x_i - \bar{x})(Y_i - \bar{Y})$$

where x_i, Y_i are random variables taking any of ℓ states such as x_1, x_2,...x_ℓ, and similarly for Y.

In this situation, X_i, Y_i take only two values, which for the moment we differentiate by denoting the states of X by a_0, a_1 and the states by Y by b_0, b_1.

The definitions of $\bar{X}$ and $\bar{Y}$ are as follows

$$\bar{X} = [(n_{00}+n_{01})a_0 + (n_{10}+n_{11})a_1]/n$$

$$\bar{Y} = [(n_{00}+n_{10})b_0 + (n_{01}+n_{11})b_1]/n$$

(4)

It then follows, after some manipulation, that

$$R_{aa} = (n_{00}+n_{01})(n_{10}+n_{11})(a_0-a_1)^2/n$$

$$R_{bb} = (n_{00}+n_{10})(n_{01}+n_{11})(b_0-b_1)^2/n$$

$$R_{ab} = (n_{00}n_{11}-n_{01}n_{10})(a_0-a_1)(b_0-b_1)/n$$

This yields the binary reproducibility of Burns, Shepherd, and Berman (1977) which is

$$R = \frac{n_{00}n_{11} - n_{01}n_{10}}{[(n_{00}+n_{01})(n_{10}+n_{11})(n_{00}+n_{10})(n_{01}+n_{11})]^{\frac{1}{2}}}$$

(5)

If we substitute for the perception parameters from Table 2, this becomes

$$R = \frac{\alpha(1-\alpha)[(1-p_1)(1-p_0) - p_1p_0]^2}{[\alpha p_0+(1-\alpha)(1-p_1)][\alpha(1-p_0)+(1-\alpha)p_1]}$$

(6)

In a practical situation, $\alpha = 0.6987$, $p_0 = 0.9129$, and $p_1 = 0.3883$, from which we estimate R as 0.1306. This is a typical figure. Usually R lies in the range

Table 2.   Expected number of pixels n_{ij} with given perception states $a_0 a_j$, in terms of parameters, N, α, p_0, p_1 of simple perception model.

Perception vector	Expected Number		
	Symbol	Contribution from negative message	Contribution from positive message
a_0	n_0 =	$n\alpha p_0$	$+ N(1-\alpha)(1-p_1)$
a_1	n_1 =	$n\alpha(1-p_0)$	$+ N(1-\alpha)p_1$
$a_0 a_0$	n_{00} =	$N\alpha p_0^2$	$+ N(1-\alpha)(1-p_1)^2$
$a_0 a_1$	n_{01} =	$N\alpha p_0(1-p_0)$	$+ N(1-\alpha)(1-p_1)p_1$
$a_1 a_0$	n_{10} =	$N\alpha(1-p_0)p_0$	$+ N(1-\alpha)p_1(1-p_1)$
$a_1 a_1$	n_{11} =	$N\alpha(1-p_0)^2$	$+ N(1-\alpha)p_1^2$

0.10 to 0.15 with values up to 0.30 representing exceptional agreement.

The reproducibility is an extension of the product-moment correlation coefficient to ordered, multistate variables. As such, it should be comparable to correlation and coincidence measures of Shepherd and Gaskell (1977), Huntington and Raiche (1978), Siegal and Short (1977), and others. It was shown by Burns, Shepherd, and Berman (1976) that R differs with the degree of freedom so that azimuths, lengths, and areas yield different measures. If account is taken of this difference, the results of various authors are comparable and R, or equivalent measures of association, is low if the annotations seem, intuitively, to be in fairly good agreement.

Expression 6 explains the low value for R. It reduces to zero in circumstances when $p_0 + p_1 = 1$, that is, when the probability of correctly perceiving

Table 3. Reproducibility as function of probabilities p_0, p_1 of correct recognition of negative and positive messages, respectively for $\alpha = 0.6987$.

		P_1									
		0	0.1	0.2	0.3	0.4	0.5	0.6	0.7	0.8	0.9	1.0
P_0	0	1	.863	.736	.620	.512	.411	.318	.230	.149	.072	0
	0.1	.731	.600	.481	.375	.280	.196	.123	.063	.019	0	.032
	0.2	.547	.426	.321	.231	.155	.092	.044	.012	0	.015	.070
	0.3	.413	,304	.213	.138	.080	.037	.010	0	.011	.046	.114
	0.4	.311	.213	.135	.076	.034	.009	0	.009	.038	.089	.167
	0.5	.232	.143	.078	.034	.008	0	.008	.034	.078	.143	.232
	0.6	.167	.089	.038	.009	0	.009	.034	.076	.135	.213	.311
	0.7	.114	.046	.011	0	.010	.037	.080	.138	.213	.304	.413
	0.8	.070	.015	0	.012	.044	.092	.155	.231	.321	.426	.547
	0.9	.032	0	.019	.063	.123	.196	.280	.375	.481	.600	.731
	1.0	0	.072	.149	.230	.318	.411	.812	.620	.736	.863	1

the negative and positive message are complementary. In the example cited, $p_0 + p_1 = 1.3$ and the low reproducibility is due to the proximity of the sum to 1. This is illustrated further in Table 3. The diagonal zeros corresponding to the situation $p_0 + p_1 = 1$ are unaffected by changes in ∞. Table 3 shows that R does not increase monotonically as p_0, p_1 both increase.

DISCUSSION

The obstacles to annotations being accepted as reliable sources of data may be quantified in terms of the low values of the reproducibility R. There seem to be two remedies: replace R with some other method of measuring a comparison that monotonically increases with each of p_0 and p_1 and does not have a minimum at $p_0 + p_1 = 1$, or change the interpretation procedures to take better account of the properties of the information and ensure that the latter condition is avoided.

The first possibility is to redefine the reproducibility. The present definition may be regarded geometrically as an inner product in a space with axes defined by

the ordered pairs (a_0,a_1) and (b_0,b_1). However, the perception model shows   there is no basis
to this ordering. That is, there is no property of the
cells incorporated into the model which enables a relation between states of the type $a_0 < a_1$. In previous work,
by getting $a_0=0$ and $a_1=1$ we have   incorporated such
a   relationship. This now is seen
to be unjustified. Although the terms in a_0,a_1,b_0,b_1
cancel out in the manipulations leading
from expressions (3) to (5) they enter into the treatment. The problem is illustrated by the mean values
given by expression (4). The mean is, in fact, meaningless, if a_0 and a_1 cannot be assigned numerical values
on some   common scale. It is contended that
the perception model of Burns and Brown (1978) differ-
entiates the two states and implies that they cannot be
ordered on a common scale, so that the mean is an unde-
finable quantity.

Accordingly, it is considered that the reproducibility should be replaced by quantities which are concerned with each class of information separately. The
quality measures introduced by Burns and Brown (1978)
serve this purpose and have the advantage of being
probabilities. The probability that a given pixel was
interpreted correctly as being part of the positive message and assigned the state a_1 is, for k annotations,
$Q_1(v,k)$ where

$$Q_1(v,k) = \frac{\binom{k}{v}(1-\alpha)p_1{}^v(1-p_1)^{k-v}}{\binom{k}{v}(1-\alpha)p_1{}^v(1-p_1)^{k-v} + \binom{k}{v}\alpha p_0{}^{k-v}(a-p_0)^v}$$

The corresponding probability for the negative message
is

$$Q_0(v,k) = 1 - Q_1(k-v,k)$$

where v is the perception level as defined previously.

The second possibility is to revise the interpretation procedures to avoid the condition $p_0+p_1 =1$. These
methods may be described as searching   the imagery
for lineaments with a strong criterion, that is, the most
obvious lineaments are found first and annotated. The
annotation effectively removes them from further consideration and the criterion then is changed to select
more subtle features from the residual area. This process is continued in steps, until subtle features are

being extracted. The negative message then is presented
as simply the residue after all possible lineaments have
been found.

This procedure will be familiar to photointerpreters
and I draw attention to one noticeable psychological phenomenon.   As soon as all the strongly defined lineaments
are covered by annotation which obscures them from vision,
there is a discrete shift in perception criteria and a
whole new group of lineaments become visible.

The interpretation procedures reflect this psychological phenomenon and with the aim of extracting as much
information as possible, advantage is taken of the
heightened perception to pursue the signal to low
thresholds. Generally, results show that it is pursued
too far, and some 34 percent of the positive annotation
is lineaments generated from random noise in the negative
message area.

This problem may be avoidable by one of two procedures. The first is to establish two strong criteria,
one for the recognition of a lineament, and another for
the recognition of areas free of lineaments. At a first
pass, the two regions are blocked out leaving a residual
zone of uncertainty in between. This requires annotating
by two methods instead of one, such as a pen to mark
lineaments and a brush to shade in areas which are lineament free. The recognition threshold is lowered and a
second pass is made over the residual region. This procedure would be repeated several times, with the recognition criteria being made increasingly subtle only as
the residual area decreases. This technique may ensure
that the two probabilities, p_0 and p_1, are maintained at
a comparable level and that p_1 is not raised at the expense of p_0 which is the present situation. The elimination of   clearly negative areas by a different annotation procedure should considerably reduce the opportunity
for generation of spurious lineaments in the negative
region towards the end of the annotation process, which
is what seems to happen in present techniques.

Another solution may be search the imagery for the
boundary between lineaments and the remaining area.
This is a method suitable for geographic themes but does
not seem to be practicable for lineaments which tend to
be numerous and of small width. Also, there have been
no perception models erected for boundary recognition
and it is not known what new complications may occur.

It is considered therefore, that the first procedure is
to be preferred.

GEOMETRIC CORRELATIONS

For studies of geological structures derived from
both ground observation and interpretation of imagery,
correlation measures have been used widely to quantify
associations between the geometric parameters, such as
length and trend, of structural features. Examples from
remote sensing include Renner (1968), Schulz and Ingerson (1973), Shepherd and Gaskell (1977), and Huntington
and Raiche (1978).

If the annotation is divided into cells and L is
the length of lineament in a cell, from Table 2 it may
be expected that the length drawn from the positive
message is

$$\frac{L(1-\alpha)p_1}{\alpha(1-p_0)+(1-\infty)p_1}$$

whereas the length drawn from the negative message is

$$\frac{L\alpha(1-p_0)}{\alpha(1-p_0)+(1-\alpha)p_1}$$

A problem in geometric correlations has been how to
treat cells containing no lineaments. If these are included in measurements of correlation, the correlation
becomes extremely high due to the large number of cells
of zero length, particularly if the cell size is small.
The data are mixed in that it contains two multistate
variables (the states of the positive and negative messages) and the parameters, length, and trend, of the
lineaments perceived.

If we take the length L as an ordinate, then for a
single annotation,

$$\text{for } 0 < L \leq \infty, \quad V = (a_1)$$

$$\text{for } 0 = L \quad , \quad V = (a_0)$$

Hence the region from $0 < L \leq \infty$ corresponds to one-half
space in the perception state and the region L = 0 to

the other. Because geometric measurements are defined
only in the former one-half space, they are restricted
validly to cells in which L is finite, so that zero-
length cells may be ignored.

For geometric correlations between two annotations,
if the suffix X refers to the first observer, and Y to
the second, the observation space has fields defined as
follows:

(i) for $0 < L_x \leq \infty$, $0 < L_y \leq \infty$, $V_x = a_1$, $V_y = b_1$

(ii) for $0 = L_x$, $0 < L_y \leq \infty$, $V_x = a_0$, $V_y = b_1$

(iii) for $0 < L_x \leq \infty$, $0 = L_y$, $V_x = a_1$, $V_y = b_0$

(iv) for $0 = L_x$, $0 = L_y$, $V_x = a_0$, $V_y = b_0$.

It is immaterial to the perception states whether
zero cells are discarded or whether cell size is increased until there are no zero cells.

GENERAL IMPLICATIONS

It is general practice in computer processing of
mixed-mode data in the natural sciences to quantify presence-absence data by assigning it to a scale in which
absent is 0 and present is 1. However, the physical
properties of annotations described here and the analysis
of Burns and Brown (1978) show that this is not an appropriate assignment for perception data.

Cluster analyses based on similarity measures (e.g.
Wishart, 1969; Sepkoski, 1974; Lance and Williams, 1967)
therefore should be treated with considerable caution if
the procedures require assigning numeric values to multistate perception data (e.g. Wishart, 1969, table 3a).

This caution has wider implications than remote
sensing as much geological field data depends upon perception processes (Chadwick, 1975) and the natural sciences generally are characterized by a dependence upon
multistate variables where the states are determined by
visual inspection of phenomena.

CONCLUSIONS

A model of human perception of geological lineaments in aerial and satellite imagery shows that the output of a photointerpreter (an "annotation") has characteristics which indicate that he perceives two disjoint messages, a *positive message* corresponding to presence of a lineament and a *negative message* corresponding to the absence. This model explains properties of the annotations such as the approximately geometric change in lineament area as multiple annotations are combined, decreasing to zero if the method of combination is set intersection or increasing to fill the whole image if the method is set union, and the anomalously low correlations between intuitively similar annotations. The low opinion of photointerpretations held in some parts of geology is considered to be a consequence of this latter property and not of a lack of meaningful information, although it is shown that some 34 percent of lineaments in a single annotation are "artifacts of the imagination" construed out of spatial noise in regions where probably no lineaments exist.

The two states of cells represented in an annotation, generally "presence" and "absence" of a detectable lineament, cannot be ordered on these properties alone and cannot be assigned values 0 to 1 on a common arithmetic scale. As a result, correlation coefficients are not meaningful measures of comparison, and in addition, do not increase monotonically with increases in the three perception parameters. Annotation quality is better measured in terms of two quality parameters for negative and positive messages respectively, rather than by a single coefficient. Quality parameters which estimate the probability of correct classification of each cell provide a measure of data quality suited to the perception properties of the image.

Interpretation procedures which treat the two types of message separately should improve the reproducibility of the output.

ACKNOWLEDGMENTS

Some of this work was done while the author was Principal Research Scientist at the Division of Mineral Physics, Commonwealth Scientific and Industrial Organization (CSIRO), Sydney, Australia. The author was grateful for comments from Drs. N. Fisher and A. Green of the

CSIRO and W.S. Kowalith of the Department of Applied
Earth Sciences, Stanford University, but this acknowledgment does not imply that they necessarily agree with the
views expressed here. I am grateful to Dr. N.M. Short
of NASA for his encouragement to publish this review.

REFERENCES

Burns, K.L., Shepherd, J., and Berman, M., 1976, Repro-
    ducibility of geological lineaments and other dis-
    crete features interpreted from imagery: measure-
    ment by a coefficient of association: Remote Sens-
    ing of the Environment, v. 5, no. 4, p. 267-301.

Burns, K.L., Huntington, J.F., and Green, A.A., 1977,
    Computer assisted photointerpretation of geological
    lineaments: perception method, *in* Lynch, A.J., ed.,
    APCOM 77: 15th Intern. symp. on application of
    computers and operations research in the mineral
    industries (Brisbane): Aust. Inst. Min. Metall.
    (Melbourne), p. 275-285.

Burns, K.L., and Brown, G.H., 1978, The human perception
    of geological lineaments and other discrete features
    in remote sensing imagery: signal strengths, noise
    levels and quality: Remote Sensing of the Environ-
    ment, v. 7, no. 2, p. 163-176.

Chadwick, P.K., 1975, A psychological analysis of obser-
    vations in geology: Nature, v. 256, no. 5518, p.
    570-573.

Crain, I.K., 1972, A statistical approach to the analysis
    of tectonic elements: unpubl. doctoral dissertation,
    Australian National Univ., 72 p.

Estes, W.K., 1975, Human behaviour in mathematical per-
    spective: Am. Scientist, v. 63, no. 6, p. 649-655.

Gilluly, J., 1976, Lineaments--ineffective guide to ore
    deposits: Econ. Geology, v. 71, no. 8, p. 1507-
    1514.

Huntington, J.F., and Raiche, A.P., 1978, A quantitative
    method for comparing geological lineament patterns:
    Remote Sensing of the Environment, v. 7, no. 2,
    p. 145-161.

Kelley, V.C., and Clinton, N.J., 1960, Fracture systems and tectonic elements of the Colorado Plateau: Univ. New Mexico Publ. in Geology, Univ. New Mexico Press, Publ. No. 6, 104 p.

Lance, G.N., and Williams, W.T., 1967, Mixed-data classificatory programs. I. Agglomerative systems: Aust. Computer Journal, v. 1, no. 1, p. 15-20.

Podwysocki, M.H., Moik, J.G., and Sharp, W.C., 1975, Quantification of geologic lineaments by manual and machine processing techniques: Proc. NASA Earth Res. Symp. v. 1B, NASA TM X-58168, p. 885-904.

Renner, J.G.A., 1968, The structural significance of lineaments in the eastern Monsech area, province of Lerida, Spain: Publ. Intern. Inst. Aerial Survey and Earth Sciences (Ser. B) No. 45, p. 12-25.

Schulz, P.H., and Ingerson, F.E., 1973, Martian lineaments from Mariner 6 and 7 images: Jour. Geophys. Res., v. 78, no. 35, p. 8415-8427.

Sepkoski, J.J., 1974, Quantified coefficients of association and measurement of similarity: Jour. Math. Geology, v. 6, no. 2, p. 135-152.

Shepherd, J., and Gaskell, J.L., 1977, Trend analysis of fractures and fissure vein mineralization in the Drake Volcanics of NSW, Australia: Trans. Inst. Min. Metall. (Sect. B), v. 86, p. 9-16.

Siegal, B.S., and Short, N.M., 1977, Significance of operator variation and the angle of illumination in lineament analysis on synoptic images: Modern Geology, v. 6, no. 1, p. 75-85.

Sperling, G., and Melchner, M.J., 1978, The attention operating characteristic: examples from visual search: Science, v. 202, no. 4365, p. 315-318.

Vanderbrug, G.J., 1975, Line detection in satellite imagery: Symp. Machine Processing of Remotely Sensed Data, Purdue Univ., p. 2A-16 to 2A-21.

Wishart, D., 1969, FORTRAN II programs for 8 methods of cluster analysis (CLUSTAN I): Kansas Geol. Survey Computer Contr. 38, 112 p.

LOOKING HARDER AND FINDING LESS--USE OF THE COMPUTER IN PETROLEUM EXPLORATION

John C. Davis

Kansas Geological Survey

ABSTRACT

The decade of the 70's was marked by steady, if un-spectacular, progress in the use of computers by the pet-roleum industry. Digital seismic processing in the field of geophysics was the single most significant development, and promises to alter many basic procedures in explora-tion. Programs and techniques for computer mapping have improved significantly during the decade; contour mapping now is probably the most important application of compu-ters to geologic aspects of petroleum exploration. Data banks have grown tremendously, and rapid interactive re-trieval systems permit display of combined seismic and geologic information as maps and cross sections. Mini-computer systems are promising to bring dramatic changes to log-interpretation procedures and to the making of subsurface lithofacies maps, increasingly valuable ex-ploration tools for defining stratigraphic traps. Com-putational advances in the area of petroleum resource assessment allow modeling of economic potential for large areas. These techniques include both economic and geo-logic considerations.

Data banking, log analysis, and contour mapping are extremely basic procedures, routinely required for almost all exploration activities. Aside from the more exciting geophysical applications, the use of computers in petro-leum exploration seems to have advanced during the past decade through the determined refinement of such basic techniques.

INTRODUCTION

The past decade has been one of turmoil in the petroleum industry, marked by shortages, record prices and
profits, public and governmental criticism, and Herculean
efforts to develop new exploration tools and to find more
oil. Without doubt, the most significant development in
the application of computers to exploration has been in
the geophysical field of digital seismic processing, allowing enhanced resolution of stratigraphy and three-
dimensional seismic interpretation and mapping. Use of
large-scale color displays of seismic output has proved
especially appropriate because the achievements have
themselves been so spectacular. Important, although less
dramatic, advances also have been made in the use of computers for treatment of geologic (rather than geophysical)
data.

Geologic data banks now are at a highly developed
state, and include almost all well and seismic information
available for most of the petroleum provinces of North
America. Sophisticated interactive retrieval programs
allow information to be extracted quickly, and displayed
as cross sections and maps. Some systems permit the geologist to adjust and modify the contents, and to store
them back in the bank. The ability to commingle seismic
information with other forms of geologic data is an especially significant advance.

Contour mapping probably is the second most important
application of computers to geologic aspects of petroleum
exploration, and contour mapping programs have been improved significantly in the past decade. Most programs
operate by constructing a regular meshwork of interpolated
points across a map area, but new developments include
fast routines to create triangular meshes in which each
node corresponds to a control point. This insures that
the mapped surface passes exactly through each grid point,
and minimizes problems of aliasing and smoothing that occur when mapping nonuniformly distributed data. Faults
and other discontinuities in the mapped surface can be
accommodated easily, a valuable feature which also is included in new versions of contour programs that operate
by gridding.

Log interpretation procedures have changed dramatically in recent years, in large part due to the proliferation of interactive minicomputers. Combining a digitizer,
minicomputer, disk drive, CRT display screen, and small

plotter, these relatively inexpensive systems allow a log
analyst to experiment with trial solutions in real time.
By using matrix algebra rather than table look-up procedures, fast interpretations can be achieved, even from
underdetermined or incomplete log suites. Several wells
may be processed simultaneously, and lithofacies or other
properties mapped in three dimensions by including trend-
surface equations in the matrix of log equations. Because
stratigraphic traps are increasingly important as exploration targets, subsurface lithofacies maps based on log
interpretations also are increasingly valuable as exploration tools.

Methods of petroleum resource assessment are undergoing active development, at scales ranging from the regional to the prospect. Approaches include use of subjective appraisals, Monte-Carlo simulation, and probabilistic estimation based on multivariate observations.
Some statistical models are dependent heavily upon geologic input while others are based on geometric considerations and search theory. To date, no single technique
has been established clearly as superior (or even as
satisfactory), and there seems to be no relationship between computational complexity and success.

In summary, the past decade has been a time of increasingly effective utilization of computers by explorationists. Geologists now recognize that computers can do
certain things extremely well, such as maintaining files,
making contour maps, or processing well logs. There is
also a realization that no "miracle method," regardless
of mathematical elegance, will overcome the shortcomings
of most geological data and make the finding of oil an
easy task.

DEVELOPMENTS

To determine the decade's most significant advances
in computing in oil exploration, the opinions of five
persons long associated with the use of computers in
exploration were sought. Each expert was requested to
provide three nominations. A consulting geologist, the
manager of a large independent, a member of the exploration division of a domestic major, a geologist in the research center of another major, and the manager of the
long-range planning division of an international oil company offered 10 different suggestions, and one on which
all agreed.

There is a single outstanding development in petroleum exploration in the past decade that easily ranks as
the most significant advance of all. It came about because of computers, and was an impossibility until computers had advanced to their modern state. This development
of course is digital seismic processing. No other technological or methodological advance has so revolutionized modern petroleum exploration. By discrete sampling
and digital encoding, modern seismic equipment in principle has unlimited dynamic range. In practice, there
are electronic limitations, but nevertheless, digital recording is a tremendous advance over analog methods.

Digital encoding also opened the way for digital signal processing, and it is in this area that exciting developments are occurring. The application of the Fast
Fourier Transform (FFT) made complex signal analysis and
decomposition a practical reality. The design of digital
filters has become a high art in the geophysical profession. The display of specific components of the seismic
wavelet has provided new insights, and holds a promise
for the eventual direct detection of hydrocarbons. For
example, Figure 1 (originally in color in Becquey, Lavergne, and Willm, 1979), shows the acoustic impedance
along a 3½ km seismic section over an offshore gas field.
The low-impedance gas-bearing sand can be traced easily
along the seismic profile, where it stands out in strong
contrast to the higher impedance sediments in which it
is enclosed. The downward trend in increasing acoustic
impedance caused by compaction of the sedimentary column
also can be seen on the section.

Another new development is three-dimensional seismic
surveying, whereby it is possible to create "pictures" or
"maps" of the subsurface at any desired depth, from a
processed grid of seismic lines. Interpretations are no
longer confined to a seismic profile, but may be displayed
as horizontal surfaces, as in Figure 2, originally published in a color advertisement by Geodigit. The illustration shows an area 5 x 6 km; the dips of units at a
depth of 3600 m are shown in color. Steepest dips are
dark gray, gentlest dips are light gray, and in white
areas there is no local gradient. Draping over a channel feature is clearly apparent.

In their original forms, both of these examples also
illustrate a hardware advance that has occurred primarily
because of the requirements of geophysicists. These are
large-size, relatively inexpensive, color-display units

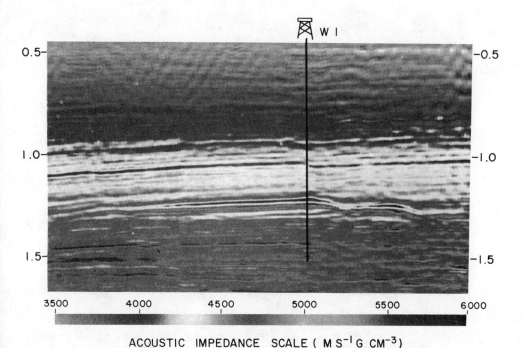

ACOUSTIC IMPEDANCE SCALE (M S^{-1} G CM^{-3})

Figure 1.   Acoustic impedance along marine seismic
            traverse across gas field (after Becquey,
            Lavergne, and Willm, 1979).

in the form of plotters, film and electrostatic printers,
and video consoles. These now are becoming available in
formats appropriate for other uses, and the routine use
of color display devices can be anticipated for all types
of geologic applications in the next decade. This will
be possible, in large part, because of the market provided by the geophysical industry.

     These exciting developments belong to the realm of
the geophysicist, and are covered in greater depth by
others in this volume (Dobrin, 1980). In contrast, the
first among the other nominations for most significant
advance in computer applications in exploration did not
spring from a dramatic breakthrough in equipment or methodology, does not involve esoteric mathematics, and
seldom results in spectacular color displays. However,
the evolutionary development of geologic data banks during
the 1970's has resulted in significant advances in petroleum exploration, particularly on the domestic scene.

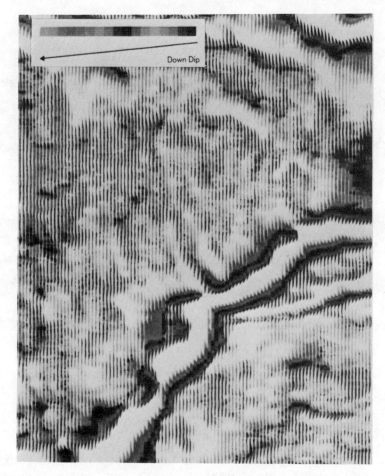

Figure 2.   "Map" of subsurface at depth of
            3600 m in area 5 x 6 km, ob-
            tained by Tomoseis three-
            dimensional seismic technique
            (from advertisement by GEODIGIT).

     Every major oil company has devoted millions of dol-
lars to develop data storage and retrieval programs, and
to encode the geologic, engineering, and geophysical information which they have stored in these banks. Service
companies have assembled well-data files, through the
cooperation of oil companies, geological surveys, and
societies, that cover most of the oil-producing regions
of the United States and Canada. Typically, an industrial
well-data file will contain about a million records, each
of which will include numerous items of information such

as the tops of formations, production and DST tests, bot-
tomhole temperatures and pressures, notes on lithologies,
geographic coordinates, and legal descriptions. Extensive
files now exist containing digital well logs, either of
new wells logged in digital mode, or of old wells whose
paper traces have been digitized. Such information is
becoming increasingly valuable, as procedures used for
seismic interpretation are applied to the analysis of
acoustic logs.

The need to store and retrieve vast quantities of
information quickly and easily has led to the purchase of
large computing systems by the oil industry. It is likely
that the oil companies operate the largest computers in
use outside the military and government spheres, and much
of the impetus for the acquisition of these machines has
stemmed from the need to handle geological data banks.
In fact, some esoteric types of mass storage devices,
such as the laser read-only memory, have been developed
in direct response to industry needs, and with oil-company
support.

A recent innovation in data banking involves the
ability to merge disparate types of information, such as
well data and seismic profiles, into a single working
file. Through an interactive terminal, an exploration
geologist then can manipulate the data, correlating and
creating subsurface interpretations, which then are incorporated back into the data bank. In 1977, the AAPG
sponsored one of its most successful ever research sem-
inars, titled "Exploration Data Synthesis," on the topic
of merging different types of exploration data into a
single whole within a computer.

Some companies use a large host computer linked to
smaller machines or remote job entry (RJE) stations in
field offices; often the links extend, via satellite,
across international boundaries or even across oceans.
This provides the most isolated of field offices with
access to the computational power and data-bank resources
at the corporate headquarters, as well as an almost instantaneous communications link. Such capabilities are
not confined to the large multinational oil companies.
Service bureaus and commercial computer networks offer
timesharing services at rates which are affordable by
even the smallest companies. A small user cannot only
purchase computing power, but also can purchase access
to software and to commercial data banks. Some of these
banks are maintained by commercial organizations; others

such as the PDS files at the University of Oklahoma are
in the public domain (Tracy, 1978).

The development of petroleum data files has been
paralleled through the past decade by an evolution in
minicomputer hardware. Ten years ago, a minicomputer was
an expensive poor cousin of a mainframe computer. Usually,
these machines were limited to 32K core, had a primitive
operating system whose high-level language was a feeble
subset of that available on larger computers, and were
extemely slow by modern standards. Thanks to the technology of LSI - Large Scale Integration - minicomputer
hardware now is significantly cheaper in both absolute
as well as real terms. Cores have expanded to gargantuan
proportions, and operating systems have increased in sophistication to a level rivalling that of the mainframe
machines. Indeed, the distinction between a minicomputer
and a full-sized machine is mostly arbitrary, and may depend more on pedigree than performance.

These changes have resulted in the explosive proliferation of minicomputers throughout the exploration industry. Usually, these machines are installed originally
for a specialized purpose, such as well-log interpretation, but soon become a versatile component of an interactive network. Increasingly, mainframe computers are re-
served for mass data storage and retrieval, transmitting
working files to peripheral minicomputers for further processing and display under the interactive control of a
geologist or geophysicist.

Minicomputers have played a critical role in another
advance in exploration geology. Several interactive log
analysis systems have been developed by the major oil
companies (Smith and Souder, 1975) and by other research
organizations. Typically, these systems run on a stand-
alone mini, equipped with tape and disk drives, a digitiz-
ing table, a small plotter, and a display screen. A log
analyst can retrieve digitized well information from the
disk, display the various tool responses as cross plots,
and estimate the coefficients of the logging equations
either by eye or by fitting regressions.

Most log-analysis programs mimic human interpreters
in the manner they operate. The programs contain digitized charts, taken from service company chart books, which
are stored in core. Interpreted values are found by table
look-up procedures, entering data from the digitized logs.
However, at least one program (Doveton and Cable, 1979)

uses a more direct approach, setting up and solving a
series of matrix equations which relate log responses to
the interpreted petrophysical quantities. The process is
faster than might be supposed, because the unknown coefficients of the logging equation need only be found once
for an interval of consistent composition. Then, the
entire interval can be interpreted simply by multiplying
the matrix of coefficients by the array of digital log
values.

     The program can solve overdetermined suites of logs,
where there are more logging tool responses than unknown
constituents to be estimated, by using least squares. If
the number of digitized logs exactly equals the number of
constitutents being estimated, the matrix equation is
solved directly. Unfortunately, the most common situation occurs when the number of lithologies to be determined exceeds the number of available logs. Approximate
solutions can be determined even in such circumstances
by using a maximum likelihood procedure.

     Petrophysical analysis of well records is increas-
ingly important in exploration, especially on the domestic
scene. Much of the remaining undiscovered oil is in
stratigraphic, rather than structural, traps. It is essential that the industry be able to map lithofacies and
changes in porosity in order to locate areas which are
prospective. From interpreted well logs, it is possible
to create many lithologic descriptors which can be mapped
(Bornemann, 1979). These include average lithology, percent sandstone or limestone, number of beds per interval,
degree of mixing or entropy, and the like. These properties can be created easily by a logging program and then
stored in a computer file for later display by a mapping
program (Fig. 3).

     A recent development in the mapping of lithofacies
defined from well logs stems from use of the matrix algebra approach to log interpretation. The lithologic components are estimated using a series of simultaneous
equations that relate them to the various log readings.
Trend surfaces are estimated from a set of simultaneous
equations that can relate these same lithologic components to geographic coordinates. Therefore, the two sets
of equations can be combined, and solved at one time.
The result is a trend-surface map of a lithologic component, derived from a set of well logs which are interpreted and mapped in a single operation.

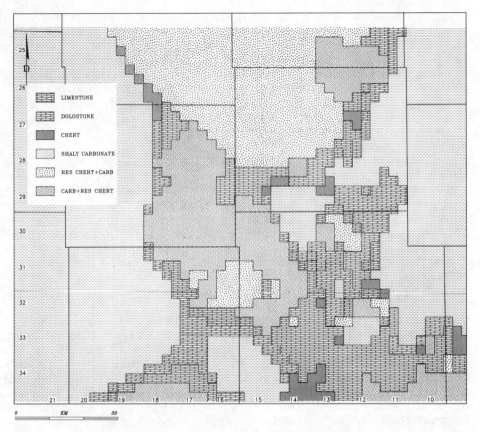

Figure 3.   Lithofacies in Viola Limestone (Ordovician)
            of south-central Kansas. Map drawn by com-
            puter from well-log interpretations made
            using interactive log-analysis system
            (Bornemann, 1979).

     Well-log interpretation programs also are invaluable
for purposes other than lithofacies mapping. These include dipmeter analysis, for reservoir studies and paleo-
current mapping; construction of synthetic seismographs
from acoustic logs for integrating well information into
geophysical sections; and the calculation of porosity/
permeability estimates for reservoir studies.

     The subject of lithofacies mapping introduces another
of the topics nominated by the panel of exploration experts: the construction of maps by computer. A decade
ago, computer contour mapping was a controversial

operation, regarded with suspicion by many explorationists.
Today, computer mapping is a routine part of the preparation of an exploration play, and many of the shortcomings
of earlier contouring programs have been overcome. Indeed, second only to data retrieval, mapping is probably
the greatest use of computers made by exploration geologists.

Two contouring problems which were especially troublesome in the past now have been at least partially
overcome, using a number of different approaches. Contouring programs always have had troubles with geophysical data, because these generally consist of dense arrays
of control points along widely spaced lines. Most contouring programs operate by interpolating from the data
to a regular grid, through which the contour lines are
drawn (Davis, 1975). The interpolation process averages
control points in a small neighborhood around each grid
node. With typical seismic data, nodes which are near
the traverses are close to many data points, resulting
in excess averaging and smoothing of the mapped surface.
Grid notes in the areas between seismic lines are controlled only poorly, because there is no local information. The resulting maps may have the appearance of contoured egg crates, because of rapid changes in the slope
of the map between the seismic lines.

Modern contouring programs approach this problem in
different ways. Some generate "pseudopoints" inside the
holes between the seismic lines. These points are created
by some type of global estimation procedure that includes
all of the points along the bounding traverses. Other
programs operate by altering the number of grid nodes
according to the density of control points in the immediate vicinity. Along the traverses a dense network is
created, allowing the surface to be modeled with great
fidelity. Between the traverses, only a few grid nodes
are used, so the surface, and correctly, has a generalized
form.

The other major problem encountered when using contouring programs is representing discontinuous, or
faulted, surfaces. Again, several approaches have been
developed which can be used to resolve the difficulites
which arise, provided the traces of the faults along the
mapped surface can be digitized and provided to the contouring algorithm. Detecting unknown faults yet is beyond the capabilities of current procedures.

The most usual procedure involves treating a surface
bounded by faults as a separate map, defined only by the
control points on that fault plate. In other words,
faults are regarded in the same manner as are the margins
of the map. This approach, although simple, has certain
drawbacks because there may be too few control points on
a plate for adequate control. Additional "pseudopoints"
may be created along the fault traces by interpolation
from points where the throw of the fault is known, usually
along seismic traverses (ACI, 1971).

A most sophisticated approach (Berlanga, 1979) for
contouring seismic data from faulted surfaces attempts to
resolve the system of faulted plates into its original
unfaulted form. First, all of the fault intersections
along the seismic traverses are connected into a set of
fault traces which are defined by spline equations. Next,
a linear-programming procedure attempts to iteratively
"move" each fault plate until the discontinuities along
the seismic traces disappear. Usually, this cannot be
accomplished completely, because faulting and folding may
not be independent. If this is the situation, the program
allocates the residual discontinuities among all of the
faults. Then, the restored surfaces are evaluated along
the fault traces, using information from both sides of
the faults. Finally, the faults are restored, but now
the faults are defined on both their upthrown and down-
thrown sides by an array of control points. This array
is included, along with the original set of control
points, in contouring. The advantage of this somewhat
complicated process is that trends which are evident on
one fault plate continue in a logical fashion onto adjacent plates. In the mapping of complexly faulted surfaces, such as those over salt domes, the method creates
much more realistic maps than can be generated by other
techniques (Fig. 4).

Recent developments in mathematics (Brassel and Reif,
1979) have led to an algorithm which allows irregularly
distributed points in a plane to be connected into a
unique set of triangles, termed Delauney triangles, that
form an optimal partition of the space. The new algorithm
(McCullagh and Ross, 1980) is extremely fast, and has
permitted revival of the procedure of contouring by tri-
angulation. It has been known for a long time that contouring on an irregular triangular mesh offered significant advantages over conventional gridding procedures
(SCA, Inc., 1975). The surface, by definition, would be
self-weighted because the grid size conforms exactly to

Figure 4.   Contour map of seismic reflection
            times over part of faulted Sitio
            Grande structure, Tabasco Basin,
            Mexico.   Contour interval is 0.05
            sec, mapped area is 15 x 15 km
            (Berlanga, 1979).

to the point distribution. Because all control points
coincide with grid nodes at the vertices of the triangular
mesh, the contoured surface must pass exactly through each
control point. The surface itself is defined by triangular spline plates, which blend into adjacent plates (Fig.
5). This produces a smooth surface with continuous first
and second derivatives (McCullagh, 1979). Because each
part of the surface is defined by a single triangular
plate, maps may be joined without discontinuities or
changes in trends simply by overlapping a common row of
triangles.

    Because the surface is defined locally, it is easy
to accommodate faults or other discontinuities. Points
along the fault trace are flagged, indicating that the
conditional requirement for continuity of the surface is

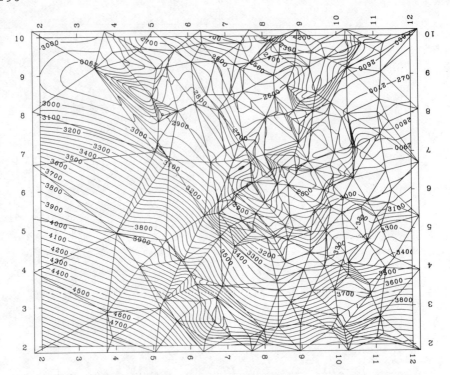

Figure 5.   Contour map of subsurface structure on top
             of Viola Limestone (Ordovician) of south-
             central Kansas, mapped using contouring
             program which fits Delaunay triangles to
             data.

removed. The program then will contour each side of the
fault independently, constructing the surfaces from elevations and trends in plates two layers deep on each side
of the fault. At the ends of faults, where the discontinuities die out, the surface becomes continuous again.

    This new approach to triangular contouring has two
significant, practical advantages. First, it is extremely
fast. It is possible to construct a triangular mesh, calculate the surface, and then estimate the values of this
surface at a regular grid of points faster than many conventional contouring programs can estimate the grid points
directly. Secondly, the program will run on extremely
small computers, as small as 32K minicomputers. This is
because the surface at any point is defined on the basis
of a single triangular plate and the adjacent plates. A
large mesh need not be held in core, but can be "rolled
through" the computer and processed in strips. The strips

will fit together without discontinuities or abrupt changes in slope.

This new program should have a significant impact on petroleum exploration, because it can be run on the numerous minicomputer systems already installed for log interpretation. Any field office which is performing automated log analysis will be able to carry the interpretative process to its next logical step, and to map the results of their interpretations (Bornemann, 1979). This capability will be valuable especially as the search for stratigraphic traps intensifies.

The computational advances discussed so far have been concerned with improving exploration at the prospect scale. That is, the locating and defining of a specific drilling site. Within the past decade, computers also have enjoyed wide use in petroleum exploration at an entirely different scale. This application is in petroleum-resource appraisal; the modeling of large areas, usually equalling or exceeding sedimentary basins in size, for the purpose of estimating their economic potential for the long run. These computational tools are not designed for the individual oil finder, but rather for corporate management, and increasingly, government planners. Because the ultimate concern of management is profitability, and the ultimate concern of government seems to be taxes, these techniques have strong economic, as well as geologic, components.

Economic theory, if not its practice, is better established in quantitative form than is geologic theory. Therefore, there are a wide variety of models in use today, most of which are similar in their economic components. Typically, the economic elements include routines to calculate discounted net cash flows, given assumed costs, expenses, and incomes. Usually, these are broken down into a myriad of individual items, which may be specified as probability distributions to account for the uncertainties in their true values. The costs involved in exploration and development may be forecast with relative assurance. Similarly, income can be forecast reasonably well, given that production is discovered. The great uncertainty is in the amount of oil or gas that will be found, if indeed any is discovered at all.

One of the most widely used procedures is the tract evaluation model used by the U.S. Geological Survey (Akers, 1976) to fix the fair market value of offshore leases.

Similar programs are used by many major oil companies for prospect evaluation. The geologic components of these programs consist of a Monte-Carlo multiplication of various reservoir engineering variables to yield the barrels of recoverable oil in place in a perceived structure. These variables include elements of volume such as height of closure, area of closure, thickness of the reservoir unit, porosity, gas/oil ratio, and the like. The USGS model uses 17 such geologic variables which must be specified in the form of triangular or other probability distributions. The computed volume is weighted by a risk, or "dryhole" factor, to account for the possibility of failure. The expected production distribution then is passed to the economic model, which computes the expected worth of the prospect or lease.

This method is identical to techniques used to evaluate reservoirs, and to test alternative reservoir development schemes (Newendorp, 1977). However, petroleum engineers do not evaluate reservoirs until after they are discovered, at which time something is known about their characteristics. In applying this model to prospects in advance of drilling, or even leasing, the geologist must provide distributions about which he has no information. It should be no surprise that, despite the complexity of the model, it yields imprecise answers in the Louisiana Gulf Coast OCS region (Uman, James, and Tomlinson, 1979). A critique (Davis and Harbaugh, 1980) of this study pointed out that the confidence bands around tract evaluations covered two orders of magnitude. Nevertheless, this model is used widely, and may have a significant effect on federal leasing policy, and on government/industry interaction.

Other techniques for regional assessment include modeling based on assumed distributions of sizes of reservoirs, scattered according to some spatial model within the area being evaluated (Drew, 1974). Models of discovery rate and order of discovery, such as those formulated by Kaufman, Balcer, and Kruyt (1975) are used to generate possible scenerios of exploration in the region. An elaborate model of this type is being used to assess the National Petroleum Reserve in Alaska, where the geographic locations of any reservoirs discovered will have a profound effect on their economic viability (L. White, 1979, personal comm.). The modeling goes so far as to calculate the costs of alternative pipeline systems that would be necessary to produce from this region. A similar but less complex, model has been proposed for the Atlantic OCS, to allow the Department of Energy to experiment with alternative leasing programs without actually implementing these alternatives.

Another alternative assessment procedure has been suggested (Harbaugh, Doveton, and Davis, 1978), and has been implemented by several oil companies in Latin America. This scheme recognizes several troublesome but inescapable facts of regional assessment. First, a guess is just a guess, and terming it a "subjective Bayesian estimate" will not improve its accuracy or likelihood of correctness. Secondly, no prospect is going to be drilled, at least in offshore and frontier regions, unless *something* shows up on the seismic profiles over the prospect location. Therefore, the assessment of a region reduces to the sum of the assessments of the perceived seismic prospects. These seismic prospects have a limited number of attributes, most of which are geometric. They include perceived size, height of closure, area of drainage, and the like.

Thirdly, exploration is a game of reasoning by analogy, either with better explored parts of the same region, or with other regions believed to be similar. Therefore, the suggested regional assessment model (Davis and Harbaugh, 1980) relies upon simple statistical relations between the perceived characteristics of seismic prospects in analogue areas and the results of the subsequent drilling of these seismic prospects. The statistical relationships then are used to predict the outcome of drilling that may be done in the exploration area, using the attributes of seismic prospects in that area (Fig. 6). As exploration proceeds, Bayesian conditional relationships may be used to modify the predictions in light of the experiences gained.

This simple predictive model is not good, but it seems to perform at least as well as alternative evaluation procedures, and its simplicity suggests that it may be inherently better, or at least easier to use. Its greatest drawback is that it requires a modicum of study in areas that have been explored already, in order to establish the initial statistical relationships. For some reason, geologists seem reluctant to rake through the cold ashes of their past adventures. Perhaps it is because they fear that the lessons which they may learn will prove instructive, but in too painful a manner.

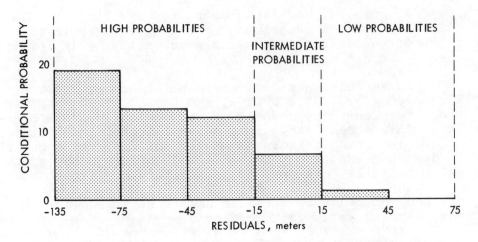

Figure 6.   Conditional probability distribution
            showing likelihood of success in drill-
            ing prospects which are defined by seis-
            mic residuals in Calafate Basin of
            Chile.   Residuals are computed from seis-
            mic interpretations of top of Tobifera
            Series (Jurassic) which underlies pro-
            ducing interval (internal report, Empresa
            Nacional del Petroleo, by R.M. Erazo
            and E.H. Vieytes, 1979).

SUMMARY

There are a multitude of other computer applications
which have been made to petroleum exploration, but most
have not proved themselves through widespread use.   It
is significant that the panel of experts nominated procedures which, for the most part, are extremely basic:
data banking, log analysis, and contour mapping.   This
suggests that the use of computers in exploration has
advanced in the past decade, not because of esoteric
mathematics, but through the determined refinement of
basic techniques.   Explorationists now realize that there
is no computational panacea; rather, the computer is a
powerful and useful tool for an exceedingly difficult
tasks.

REFERENCES

ACI, 1971, Contouring with faulting: Applications Con-
     sultants, Inc., Houston, Texas, 36 p.

Akers, H., Jr., 1977, Monte Carlo range-of-values program
    description: Internal Memorandum [May 1977], Con-
    servation Division, U.S. Geol. Survey, 73 p.

Becquey, M., Lavergne, M., and Willm, C., 1979, Acoustic
    impedance logs computed from seismic traces: Geo-
    physics, v. 44, no. 9, p. 1485-1501.

Berlanga, J.M., 1979, Oil exploration outcome probabili-
    ties in the Tabasco Basin, Mexico, as estimated by
    use of seismic information: unpubl. doctoral dis-
    sertation, Stanford Univ., 120 p.

Bornemann, E., 1979, Well-log analysis as a tool for
    lithofacies determination in the Viola Limestone
    (Ordovician) of south-central Kansas: unpubl. doc-
    toral dissertation, Syracuse Univ., 151 p.

Brassel, K.E., and Reif, D., 1979, A procedure to gener-
    ate Thiessen polygons: Geographical Analysis, v.
    11, no. 3, p. 289-303.

Davis, J.C., 1975, Contouring algorithms, in Aangeenbrug,
    R.T., ed., Auto-Carto II, Proc. Intern. Symp. on
    Computer-Assisted Cartography: U.S. Dept. Commerce,
    Bureau of the Census, Washington, D.C., p. 352-359.

Davis, J.C., and Harbaugh, J.W., 1980, Comment on oil and
    gas in offshore tracts: Estimates before and after
    drilling: Science, v. 209, no. 4460, p. 1047-1048.

Dobrin, M.B., 1980, Computer processing of seismic re-
    flections in petroleum exploration, in Merriam, D.F.,
    ed., Computer applications in the earth sciences, an
    update of the 70's: Plenum Press, New York, this
    volume.

Doveton, J.H., and Cable, H.W., 1979, Fast matrix methods
    for the lithologic interpretation of geophysical
    logs, in Gill, D. and Merriam, D.F., eds., Geomathe-
    matical and petrophysical studies in sedimentology:
    Pergamon Press, Oxford, p. 101-116.

Drew, L.J., 1974, Estimation of petroleum exploration
    success and the effects of resource exhaustion via
    a simulation model: U.S. Geol. Survey Bull. 1328,
    25 p.

Harbaugh, J.W., Doveton, J.H., and Davis, J.C., 1977,
    Probability methods in oil exploration: John Wiley
    & Sons, New York, 269 p.

Kaufman, G.M., Balcer, Y., and Kruyt, D., 1975, A probab-
    ilistic model of oil and gas discovery, *in* Haun,
    J.D., ed., Methods of estimating the volume of un-
    discovered oil and gas resources: Am. Assoc. Pet-
    roleum Geologists Studies in Geology No. 1, p. 113-
    142.

McCullagh, M.J., 1979, Creation and application of vari-
    able density grids to oil exploration data (abst.):
    Am. Assoc. Petroleum Geologists Bull., v. 63, no. 3,
    p. 494.

McCullagh, M.J., and Ross, C.G., 1980, The Delaunay tri-
    angulation of a random data set: in preparation.

Newendorp, P.D., 1975, Decision analysis for petroleum
    exploration: Petroleum Publ. Co., Tulsa, Oklahoma,
    668 p.

SCA, Inc., 1975, Mapping-contouring system: Scientific
    Computer Applications, Inc., Tulsa, Oklahoma, 39 p.

Smith, M.B., and Souder, W.W., 1975, Minicomputers for
    maxi analysis: Soc. Prof. Well Log Analysts, 16th
    Ann. Logging Symp., R1-13.

Tracy, P.A., 1978, Petroleum Data System--A network of
    energy information: Proc. 12th Ann. Mtg., Geoscience
    Information Society, Seattle, Washington, v. 8, p.
    25-30.

Uman, M.F., James, W.R., and Tomlinson, H.R., 1979, Oil
    and gas in offshore tracts: Estimates before and
    after drilling: Science, v. 205, no. 4405, p. 489-
    491.

USE OF COMPUTERS IN SEISMIC REFLECTION PROSPECTING

Milton B. Dobrin

University of Houston

ABSTRACT

During the past decade the digital computer has
brought about revolutionary improvements in our capability
to study geology by the seismic reflection method. New
recording and processing technology has brought us much
closer than anyone would have predicted ten years ago to
our ultimate goal of extracting the same geological information that would be retrievable if there were a borehole
to the maximum depth of interest at every shot point.

These improvements in the seismic art have made it
possible to map structural features with more accuracy
and to present them more correctly; they also have enhanced our ability to identify lithology and deduce strat-
tigraphic relationships from reflection data.

Perhaps the most spectacular development of the past
decade in seismic exploration has been the capability
under proper conditions of detecting gas deposits on seismic record sections, making use of the fact that reflections from the top of gas-filled sands have a higher amplitude than those from water- or oil-filled sands.
Digital recording and processing makes it possible to
preserve relative reflection amplitudes on seismic records. This could not be done with analog techniques
because of their limited dynamic range.

Geologic structures can be mapped with more precision by automatic techniques for transferring reflections

from their apparent positions based on reflection times
alone to their true positions in space. Wave-equation
and frequency-domain methods are employed for such migration. Three-dimensional recording and processing procedures require computers with high storage capacity but
they greatly increase the accuracy with which complex
structures, particularly in areas of tectonic disturbances
can be mapped.

New capabilities made possible by digital processing
now allow the geophysicist to derive lithological and
stratigraphic information of a type that was not obtainable previously from seismic reflection records. Filtering programs are available for extracting from complex
source signals simple symmetrical wavelets that enhance
resolution of reflections and allow better discrimination
of stratigraphic relations. True amplitude registration
facilitates determination of reflectivities at lithologic
boundaries that permits construction of synthetic velocity logs. Presentation of such logs for all shot points
in record-section form allows mapping of velocity, which
with proper well ties can be converted to a lithologic
cross-section comparable to that which could be obtained
from closely spaced boreholes. Such presentations give
valuable information on stratigraphy in areas where conditions are favorable. Computer determination of parameters such as instantaneous frequency and instantaneous
phase, carried out by complex analysis of waveforms, may
provide information on lithology and hydrocarbon content
not obtainable from conventional processing.

Important progress has been made in computer modeling of seismic data. This involves ray-path modeling for
precise structure interpretation and stratigraphic modeling to relate waveforms and amplitudes to subsurface lay-
ering. With the introduction of three-dimensional recording, modeling techniques have been determined particularly
useful in the interpretation of the data thus obtained.

INTRODUCTION

At the time of the Lawrence, Kansas conference in
1969, where I last spoke on this subject, the digital
computer had been in use for commercial recording and
processing of seismic reflection data for less than six
years but it already had made a substantial impact on
the art of seismic prospecting for oil and gas. Digital
filtering had led to significant improvements in data

quality of suppression of undesired signals. Programs
for determining seismic velocities from reflection records had made it possible to obtain such information
with greater accuracy than ever before. In spite of its
many capabilities for processing seismic data, however,
the computer did not extract any information from seismic
signals that was fundamentally different in nature from
that which had been obtainable with the analog systems in
use at the time digital technology was introduced.

The primary objective of seismic surveys at that time
was, as it had been since the earliest days of the art,
to map the *geometry* of subsurface boundaries with the object of locating structural entrapments of hydrocarbons.
To accomplish this, it was only necessary to observe
times of correlative reflection events and to convert
these times into depths that could be mapped. Wave forms
and amplitudes were only of secondary interest, as they
were seldom relevant to the mapping of geologic structures.

Today, thanks to improved digital techniques, it is
possible to map structures with considerably greater precision than in 1969. But the most spectacular developments during the past decade have extended the capabilities of seismic reflection beyond the mapping of subsurface geometry into stratigraphic analysis, identification
of lithology, and the detection of certain types of hydrocarbons. Many potentially productive stratigraphic features such as pinchouts, truncations, sand bodies and facies changes can now be resolved, when conditions are
appropriate, because of better waveform definition and
improved suppression of noise, both brought about by computer capabilities introduced over the past decade.

The better structural, stratigraphic, and lithological information which modern digital technology allows us
to extract from seismic records makes it seem that we
have come much closer to the ultimate goal of seismic
prospecting than anyone would have predicted ten years
ago. This goal is to obtain geological information equivalent to that retrievable from a series of conceptual
boreholes extending to the maximum depth of interest at
each shot point.

IMPROVEMENTS IN STRUCTURAL MAPPING

Migration

Let us first consider the improvements that the computer has brought into structural mapping. To obtain a
true picture of the subsurface from reflection data, we
must correct for distortions in our records that are inherent in the raypath geometry. Conventional record sections show all reflections as originating vertically below the position of the shot-receiver pair where they are
generated and recorded, even though the paths of reflections from dipping boundaries, being perpendicular to
them, cannot be vertical and the reflection points should
be displaced laterally from their plotted positions. Figure 1 illustrates the difference between the *apparent*
position of a reflector on a seismic time section and its
true position in space. The error thus introduced is
usually not significant when dips are gentle, but in
areas that are disturbed highly structurally, particularly
here there are sharp synclines, the distortions can be so
great that the observed geometry on the section will be
meaningless structurally, or even misleading. The process
of transferring reflections from their apparent position
on a record section to a section which shows the events
in their true positions is termed *migration.*

The deviation between actual structure and apparent
structure may be associated with dipping reflectors in
the vertical plane of the shooting line or else with reflecting surfaces not in this plane at all. Reflections
from such out-of-plane sources cannot be distinguished
from those with vertical ray paths and thus can give rise
to erroneous structural interpretations.

During the past decade the computer has made two developments possible for overcoming these limitations.
One is automatic migration, the plotting of record sections on which reflection events are represented on each
trace at times corresponding to their proper positions in
space. The other innovation, three-dimensional recording
and migration, usually involves special recording techniques in the field as well as new types of presentation.

Let us first consider the techniques for automatic
migration of reflection data shot along a linear profile.
In Fresnel, or diffraction, migration is it assumed that
each reflecting point along a boundary is the source of
a diffraction for which the time of arrival at a surface

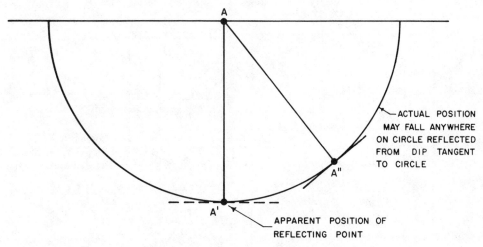

Figure 1.   Unmigrated and migrated positions of single reflecting point with source and receiver at coincident position on surface
(Lindseth, 1974).

position is related to the horizontal separation of that
position and the source point by a hyperbolic curve of
the type illustrated in Figure 2. All recorded events
which lie along this curve are transferred by computer
summation to the vertex of the hyperbola, which is the
true position of the source of diffractions on the time
section.

     If a diffracted event is stored actually at sampled
positions which lie along the hyperbola, the summation,
by adding values in phase, will yield a high amplitude
which is put into storage at the position of the vertex
on the record section constituting the output. If no
event lies along the line the summation yields an amplitude which will be at background level. If a dipping
reflection is stored, each sampled point along it could
be considered the source of a new hyperbola. By transfer through summation of each of these hyperbolas to the
position of its vertex, the output channels, representing
the results of the summation, will show the true position
of the reflection along the section.

     In the example in Figure 2, amplitudes sampled along
the hyperbola on all channels from 1 to 99 are added to
give a sum which is plotted at time 1.200 sec on channel
50. The same type of compositing is carried out for all

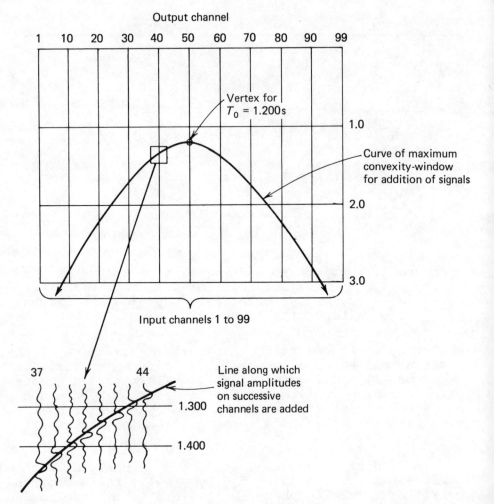

Figure 2.   Principle of computer migration based on
             Fresnel diffraction. Signals on each trace
             are added at times determined by intersection
             with trace of hyperbolic curve. If source
             is at vertex, sum will have observable strength
             when plotted at that position on output trace.
             If not, signal amplitudes cancel and no event
             appears (Dobrin, 1976).

other sample times (every .002 sec) on channel 50 and then
for all samples on channel 51, for which the window now
extends from channel 2 to channel 100. This process is
repeated one output trace at a time until all channels
are swept. The record section thus plotted is the migrated section.

Figure 3 illustrates the results of Fresnel migration. It compares the conventional and the migrated sections for synclinal structure. The "bow-ties" are observed when the curvature of each synclinal reflection is greater than that of the wave-front at the same depth, leading to a crossover of the rays on their way to the surface.

A more recently introduced technique of automatic migration involves the introduction of the observed data into the wave equation using finite-differences instead of derivatives (Claerbout, 1976). Conceptually, the technique follows the reflected waves observed at the surface downward into the earth for a time equal to one-half the two-way reflection time. At this instant the wave should have reached the reflecting surface and its position should be equivalent to that of the reflector.

Figure 4 illustrates the principle. Assume a geologic section with three conformable synclinal surfaces at different depths, each generating a reflection. With source and receiver pairs evenly spaced along a profile at the surface, the resultant seismic record shows that the shape of the shallowest synclinal pattern on the time-horizontal-distance display is similar to that of the synclinal surface in space but that the resemblance gets poorer as the depth of the structure increases. The "bow tie" pattern previously noted becoming more pronounced as the syncline gets deeper.

We could reproduce the shape of the depth section on the time section if we conceptually or mathematically determined what the geophone would record if it and the shot were lowered a distance into the earth corresponding to the wave travel for half the reflection time. Figure 5 shows how the time section as recorded at the surface is transformed to true structure if brought down to the slanting surface. The events displayed on this curved surface when projected upward to the x-t plane constitute the migrated time section.

Figure 6 shows how a complex section can be made more meaningful geologically if it is transformed by wave-equation migration. The "bow ties" become synclines as the diffraction patterns are collapsed. Irregularities remain, due to sampling errors and lack of complete information on velocities, but there is no question that the migration gives a more realistic representation of true structure.

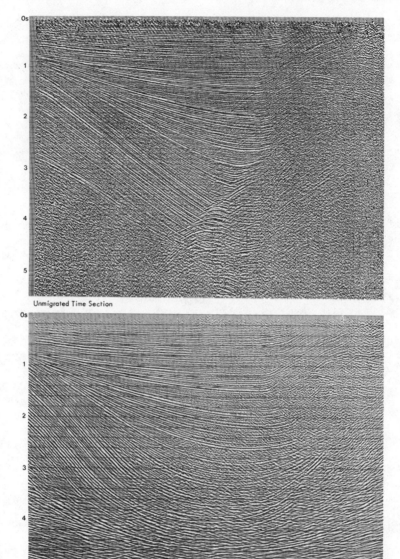

Figure 3.   Results of computer migration
            using diffraction method. Un-
            migrated section (above) shows
            "bow ties" at greater depths.
            Migrated section (below) shows
            true geometry of synclinal struc-
            ture (Prakla-Seismos).

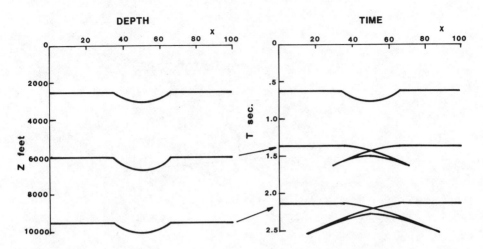

Figure 4.   Synclinal structure shown at these levels
            on depth section is observed with increasing
            distortion on time section (unmigrated re-
            cord) as depth gets greater.

A recent variation upon wave-equation migration con-
verts the pattern on the record section from the space
domain into the spatial-frequency domain by Fourier transformation, carries out the migration in the frequency domain, and then transforms the results back into spatial
coordinates (Stolt, 1978). One advantage of this technique is that it allows accurate migration of steeper
dips than conventional wave-equation techniques can handle.

Three-Dimensional Presentation

Conventional seismic surveys involve shooting and
recording along lines and each record section thus produced shows structures which are presumed to be in the
vertical plane of the recording line. If there are substantial dips in directions that cross the line of the
profile it would be difficult to present the true structure on conventional vertical sections. A more accurate
recording system for structurally disturbed areas involves mapping on regular two-dimensional grids instead
of along linear profiles. A simple operational technique for producing such a grid is to shoot at closely
spaced intervals along one line and to receive at comparable intervals on a line perpendicular to the shooting profile. This arrangement gives a uniform grid of
reflection points which makes a rectangle with sides

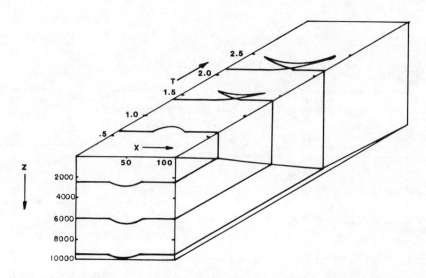

Figure 5.   Principle of wave-equation migration. Wave
             field recorded in time is continued down-
             ward into earth until position correspond-
             ing to one-half of reflection time is reached.
             Along sloping surface having trace on t_1x
             plane indicated by inclined line, time
             structure has same shape as structure in
             depth. Projection of this configuration
             yields migrated time section.

one-half as long as the respective shooting and receiving
lines. Another approach is to shoot a large number of
parallel conventional profiles more closely spaced than
in regular mapping. The latter technique is the only
practical one for offshore three-dimensional surveys.

     In order to realize the full potential of three-
dimensional recording, it is necessary to migrate the
reflections observed in the field to their true positions
in space. This involves the same principles as two-
dimensional migration, but it is considerably more tedious
and requires a computer having a large storage capacity.

     All reflection points are put into computer storage
at their correct positions in the x, y plane and their
amplitudes for a given reflection time are presented as
variable-density or variable-area patterns in the horizontal plane corresponding to that time. Comparing the

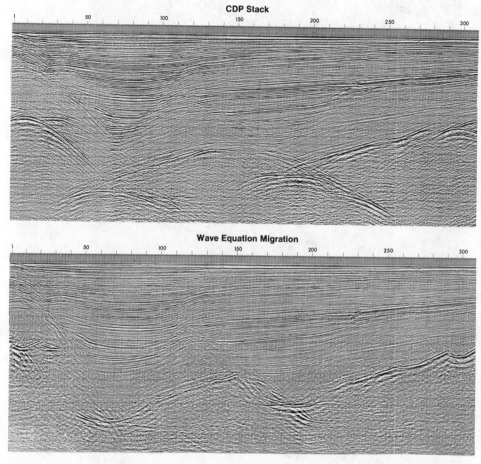

Figure 6.   Example of wave-equation migration. Un-
            migrated section (above) shows diffraction
            patterns and "bow-ties" that are collapsed
            in migrated section (below) (Seiscom-Delta).

patterns on these horizontal "slices" for times that are
close together, it is possible to follow faults and other
structural features downward into the earth. Figure 7
shows a typical "slice" presentation (both unmarked and
interpreted) for a three-dimensional survey over the Gulf
of Thailand (Dahm and Graebner, 1979). It shows the reflection pattern over the horizontal plane corresponding
to a reflection time (two-way) of 1.384 sec. The fault
pattern can be followed upward and downward by comparison with other slices for nearby depths.

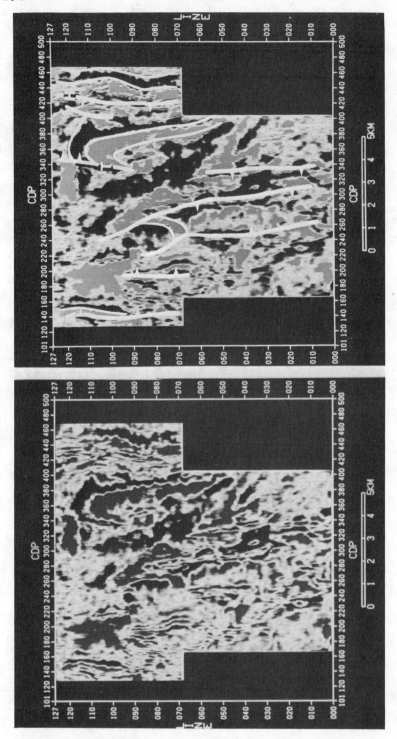

Figure 7. Presentation of three-dimensional migrated data. Variable density
image is "slice" for time of 1.384 sec plotted from seismic coverage in
Gulf of Thailand. Slice on left is uninterpreted. Faults and folds are
superimposed on right (Dahm and Graebner, 1979).

In profile shooting over three-dimensional structures, the interpretation may be facilitated by modeling,
either physical or mathematical. Figure 8 shows a series
of sections obtained by mathematical modeling along six
lines over a hypothetized structure that could be a reef
or similar build-up. Note how indications of the feature
can be observed on lines laterally displaced from it by
substantial distances. In such modeling, the seismic
data obtained over a hypothesized subsurface configuration
is compared with that observed in the actual field measurements. The structure of the model is changed progressively until the best possible agreement is obtained
between the two. The positions of the receiving lines
must have the same geometrical relation to the subsurface feature in the two examples.

USE OF SEISMIC REFLECTION FOR LITHOLOGIC

AND STRATIGRAPHIC STUDIES

When only analog techniques were available for recording reflection signals, the dynamic range of the
ground-motion velocities to be recorded was so much
greater than that of the recording systems that it was
not possible to reproduce true relative amplitudes, and
a great amount of compression was necessary to register
all events without distortions due to saturation. Digital
recording can accommodate such large dynamic ranges that
it is possible to register the true relative amplitudes
of most reflection signals. This new capability has
turned out to be valuable in ways that were not visualized at the time that digital recording first appeared
on the scene. It has made it possible to measure *reflectivities* of subsurface geological boundaries, a type of
information that has led to the development of practical
techniques for identifying lithology and also for detecting hydrocarbons.

Direct Detection of Hydrocarbons

The fact that the contrast in acoustic impedance
(velocity times density) between an impervious shale and
a gas-filled sand underlying it is greater than if the
contact were with a water- or oil-filled sand should make
the reflection from the top of the gas sand stronger than
that from the top of a sand containing water or oil.
This is the basis for the "bright spot," an anomalously
strong reflection on a record section which is diagnostic of the presence of gas.

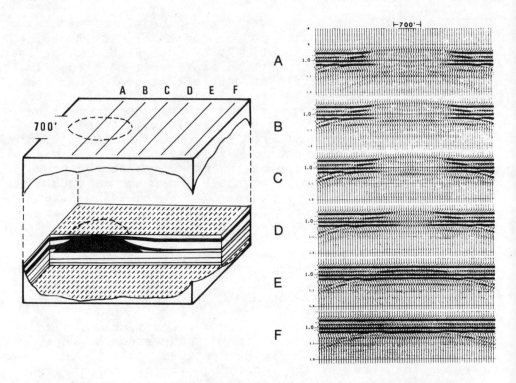

Figure 8.   Seismograms obtained by computer modeling
            along lines crossing buried structure at
            various lateral distances. Note how in-
            dications of the subsurface features can
            be observed on lines displaced from it
            farther than its diameter.

It is evident from the reflectivities shown on the
schematic cross-section in Figure 9 that the amplitude
of a reflection from the top of a gas sand should be
about two-and-a-half times that at the top of an oil
sand and nearly three times that at the top of a water
sand. The principle has been known for a long time and
there are numerous papers in the Soviet literature, dating
from the early 1960's, proposing that it be applied for
detecting hydrocarbons directly.

In spite of the simplicity of this concept, it could
not be put to use on a practical basis until computer programs could be developed that would separate out reflectivity from many other factors, such as distance from the
source (spherical spreading) and attenuation. Figure 10
shows a conventionally processed section over a known gas

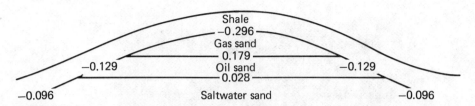

Figure 9.   Reflection coefficients at top and bottom
            surfaces of gas sand and oil sand and at
            contact between shale and salt-water sand
            (Dobrin, 1976).

accumulation, whereas Figure 11 illustrates the section
obtained when true amplitudes are extracted. The "bright
spot", the high-amplitude reflection which shows the position of the gas sand, is obvious after the special
processing but it hardly stands out at all on the conventionally processed section.

Wavelet Processing

        In working with reflection amplitudes, it is desir-
able to show every reflection signal as a simple symmetrical pulse rather than as a multicycle train of peaks
and troughs. "Wavelet processing" (Neidell and Poggiagliolmi, 1977) is an automatic filtering technique for
converting the complex reflection pulse actually recorded at the surface to a symmetrical wavelet on which
only a central peak and two lower amplitude troughs on
opposite sides of it are observable. The added resolution this procedure allows is valuable particularly in
mapping stratigraphic features.

        Figure 12 illustrates some of the stages in the pro-
cess of extracting a simple symmetrical wavelet from a
broad, complex signal observed from a marine source.
Phase and amplitude spectra are determined first. Then
the phases are shifted to zero at all frequencies, yielding a symmetrical but multicycle wavelet. The final step
is a filtering operation that will concentrate the energy
in the center pulse, reducing amplitudes of side lobes to
the point that they fall below noise level. The result-
tant signal has no frequencies outside the range encom-
passed by the input pulse. The amplitude of such an extracted wavelet should be proportional to the reflection
coefficient at the boundary from which the reflection
originates.

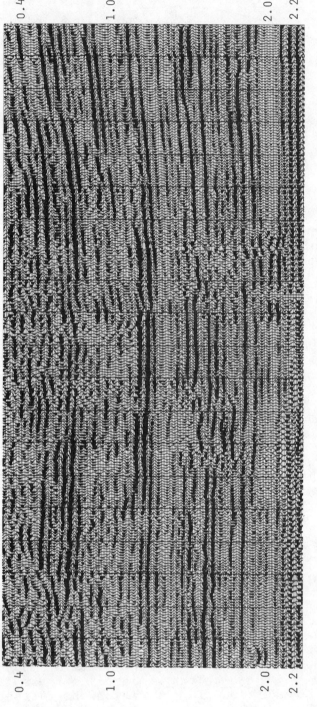

Figure 10. Conventionally processed section shot over gas accumulation. Amplitude equaliation makes it impossible to distinguish reflection originating at surface of gas sand at 1.4 sec from other reflections (Western Geophysical Co. of America).

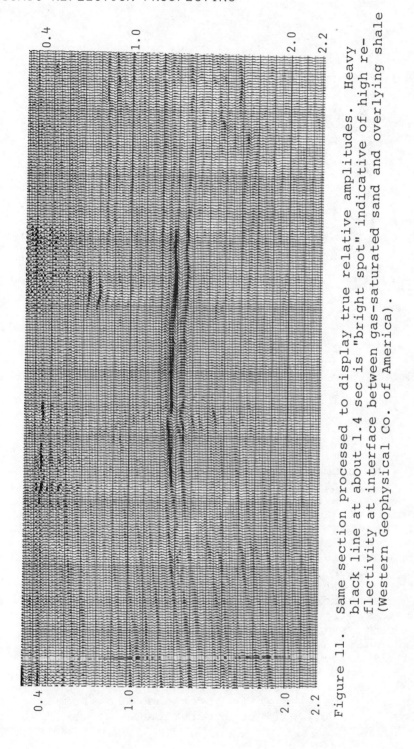

Figure 11. Same section processed to display true relative amplitudes. Heavy
black line at about 1.4 sec is "bright spot" indicative of high reflectivity at interface between gas-saturated sand and overlying shale
(Western Geophysical Co. of America).

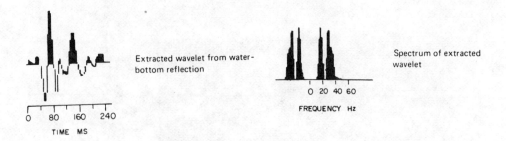

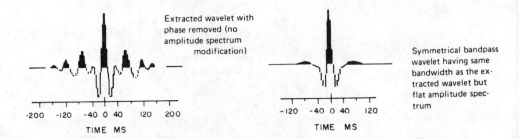

Figure 12. Conversion of complex wavelet from marine
source into symmetrical wavelet by appropriate phase correction and filter operator (Neidell and Poggiagliomi, 1977).

Synthetic Sonic Logs

The capability of recording amplitudes of reflections thus processed and relating them to acoustic-impe-
dance contrasts at interfaces makes it possible to determine velocity as a function of depth from reflection signals alone because the reflectivity (proportional to the
amplitude observed) is equal to the difference of the
acoustic impedances (velocity times density) across the
interface divided by their sum. We can solve for the
velocity below each reflector if we know the reflectivity
and the velocity above it and assume an empirical velo-
city-density relation. The resulting information when
plotted as velocity vs time or vs depth could be looked
upon in the same light as a velocity log and may be referred to as an "inverse velocity log" or sometimes as a
"pseudovelocity log."

An important difference between a real sonic log and
a synthetic one lies in the fact that the frequency of
the synthetic log will be lower because of the filtering

effect of the earth upon the reflection signals from which
the latter is made (Lindseth, 1979). Figure 13 shows a
comparison between a sonic log and a synthetic velocity
log from a record shot over the logged well. The maximum
frequency of the sonic log is obviously higher. The
agreement is good but there are differences that show
some of the limitations of the method.

If a series of adjacent seismic traces constituting
a record section is converted to a corresponding series
of synthetic velocity logs a new type of geologic section
can be constructed which shows seismic velocity vs position along the profile and also vs time on the record
(which is convertible to depth). The velocities are represented on the sections by a color code (e.g., the low
velocities are blue, intermediate ones yellow, higher
ones orange, and highest velocities red.) Such sections
are available commercially under a number of trademarks
such as "Seislog." Where well ties are available it is
possible to associate the color bands corresponding to
different ranges of velocity with types of lithology,
such as sand or shale, or with porosity variations which
may be correlative with velocity changes in limestones.

Figure 14 shows an example of a synthetic seismic
log where a number of stratigraphic units are characterized on the basis of velocity. Each "wiggly line" is a
plot of velocity vs depth. The color patterns here are
replaced by different types of cross-hatching which represents various types of lithology. The advantage of
having such information in stratigraphic studies hardly
can be overstated. There are enough hazards to this approach, however, that one should have restricted confidence in any such lithologic projections of indicated
velocities in the absence of well ties.

Complex Analysis as Source of Geologic Information

A new seismic technique which facilitates stratigraphic interpreation has been described recently by Taner,
Koehler, and Sheriff (1979). It involves complex analysis of the seismic waveform with calculation of a quadrature (imaginary) trace for every real trace observed on
a seismogram. The transformation is carried out by computing the Hilbert transform of the real signal.

By comparing the amplitudes of the real trace and
imaginary trace at a given time, it is possible to determine reflection strength, phase, and frequency as functions of time on the record. These attributes are

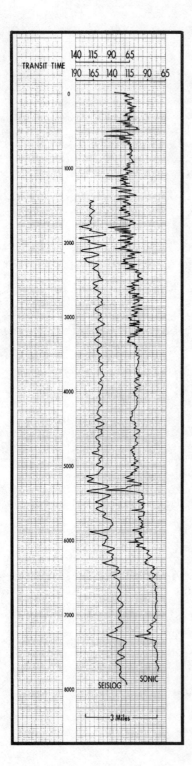

Figure 13.
   Comparison of sonic
log and Seislog from
reflection record shot
over well in which log
was made (Teknica, Ltd.).

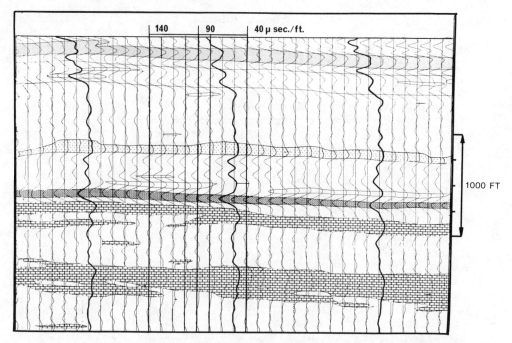

Figure 14.   Typical Seislog made from record section.
             Lithology indicated by cross-hatching
             based on velocity indications from Seis-
             log traces (Teknica, Ltd.).

represented by a color code and bands with various colors
corresponding to various ranges of the attribute values
are superimposed on the conventional variable-area section in black and white.   The reflection strength gives
information on reflectivity and might be used to locate
hydrocarbons by the "bright-spot" approach.   Instantaneous phase when superimposed on a record shows the degree
of continuity of reflection.   Record sections showing
phase are good particularly for pointing up faults as
well as depositional patterns.   Hydrocarbon accumulations
may be associated with anomalously low frequencies (although the reason is not understood) and color superposi-
tion based on frequency can show up deposits of oil or
gas under favorable circumstances.

SEISMIC PROSPECTING IN THE 1980'S

Finally, let us try to project the developments in
seismic reflection in the 1980's in geophysics for the
past decade as far as we dare into the next decade.

What might we predict about the state of the geophysical art by the end of the 1980's? In making such predictions there is no better way to look into the future than to examine present trends and speculate where they may be leading us.

One new development that may have a great impact on future technology is the use of shear waves instead of compressional waves for reflection work. A comparison of shear and compressional reflections could provide valuable information not otherwise obtainable on lithology and fluid content. Another is the introduction of many more recording channels in the field than are used conventionally in current operations. This increase (up to 1024 channels in one system now operating commercially) allows more effective three-dimensional coverage and also enhances resolution by allowing correction of individual signals before compositing groups of them for noise cancellation. Many of the systems designed for recording a large number of channels at once use a smaller number of bits than are employed conventionally in recording. This allows transmission of more multiplexed signals on a single conductor in the field than would be possible with the full complement of bits. The most extreme level of such reduction is to confine each recorded sample to a single bit indicating the sing of the signal. Amplitude is built up by compositing of many identical signals, generally from Vibroseis sources.

A major limitation upon the number of channels that can be recorded at the same time without drastic reduction in the number of bits is the large capacity that would be needed to put all the information into storage. A 500-channel full-bit record of standard length would require the capability of storing 10 million bits per second. Such a recording rate is not practical even with 1600 bit-per-inch tape, although a 2-inch video tape of the type used in color television recording may allow fast enough storage to meet these requirements. Even then the processing of such a concentration of data is not feasible presently because no existing computer will accept data at the necessary rates.

The increase in recording channels will improve the accuracy of structural mapping and should increase resolution to some extent but the principal limitation on resolution is in the earth, where absorption of seismic signals increases exponentially both with frequency and with distance traveled. As resolution of reflection

signals is limited by the frequency that can be transmitted to the reflector, we must expect it to decrease
rapidly as reflector depth increases. Digital filtering
can only optimize the resolving power of the waves that
earth materials will pass but cannot improve it further.
Thus, we will never be able to map all productive pinchouts and truncations at depths of many thousands of meters.

In spite of these real limitations imposed by nature,
we can look forward to substantial progress over the next
decade toward the ultimate goal of geophysics, which is
to determine, as was said before, exactly what the drill
would find at any specified location and depth. This
goal will never be attained fully but sophisticated computer technology as developed for geophysical applications has brought us much closer to it than anyone would
have dreamed ten years ago.

The rapid rate of technological progress in exploration geophysics for the past decade can be attributed to
two factors. One is the rapid growth during this period
in the capabilities of digital computers. The other is
the incentive and support resulting from the world-wide
energy shortage to improve geophysical exploration techniques in ways that can take advantage of these capabilities. Although alternative forms of energy will have
to provide a long-term solution to our present problems,
the only practical short-term alleviation (i.e., through
the next few decades) will be in more effective exploration for the undiscovered oil and gas yet in the earth.
It is fortunate that the progress in geophysical technology, much of it computer-based, which has characterized the past decade gives every indication of continuing
through the next decade. The result should be an increased effectiveness in locating new hydrocarbon supplies
so greatly needed to maintain the world's economy until
new types of energy resources can be developed in sufficient quantities to meet the world's needs.

REFERENCES

Claerbout, J., 1976, Fundamentals of geophysical data
    processing: McGraw-Hill Book Co., New York, 274 p.

Dahm, C.G., and Graebner, R.J., 1979, Field development
    with three-dimensional seismic methods in the Gulf
    of Thailand - a case history: Offshore Technology
    Conference, 11th Ann. Proc., Houston, Texas, v. 4,
    p. 2591-2606.

Dobrin, M.B., 1976, Introduction to geophysical prospect-
    ing (3rd ed.): McGraw-Hill Book Co., New York,
    630 p.

Lindseth, R.O., 1974, Recent advances in digital process-
    ing of geophysical data: Teknica, Ltd., Calgary.

Lindseth, R.O., 1979, Synthetic sonic logs - a process
    for stratigraphic interpretation: Geophysics, v.
    44, no. 1, p. 3-26.

Neidell, N., and Poggiagliolmi, E., 1977, Stratigraphic
    modeling and interpretation - geophysical principles
    and techniques, *in* Seismic Stratigraphy, Applica-
    tions to Hydrocarbon Exploration: Am. Assoc. Pet-
    roleum Geologists Mem. 26, Tulsa, Oklahoma, p. 389-
    416.

Stolt, R.H., 1978, Migration by Fourier transform: Geo-
    physics, v. 43, no. 1, p. 23-45.

Taner, M.T., Koehler, F., and Sheriff, R.E., 1979, Complex
    seismic trace analysis: Geophysics, v. 44, no. 6,
    p. 1041-1063.

REGIONAL MINERAL- AND FUEL-RESOURCE FORECASTING - A MAJOR

CHALLENGE AND OPPORTUNITY FOR MATHEMATICAL GEOLOGISTS

John W. Harbaugh

Stanford University

ABSTRACT

Mathematical geologists need to exert a stronger influence on government policy with regard to forecasts of
mineral- and energy-resource commodities. The problems
of forecasting inherently are statistical, and they
should be based on geological, geophysical, and mineral-
production data insofar as possible. Thus, the problems
are both geological and statistical, or in other words,
strong "geostatistical".

There are three main categories of problems in applying and using geostatistical methods in resource forecasts, namely (1) problems of policy, (2) problems of
philosophy, and (3) problems of direction. The problems
of policy, for example, are centered principally on the
failure of governmental policy makers to incorporate
appropriately statistical undertainty in energy-resource
policies. If effective, long-term forecasts of the
world's energy and other mineral resources are to be
made, geomathematicians must take a leading role. Three
major tasks lie ahead of them, namely: (1) prepare comprehensive inventories of present resources that incorporate geological considerations and which, in turn, may
be analyzed from a statistical standpoint; (b) develop
formal optimization methods to guide exploration; and
(c) promote policies that will make available publicly
much of the exploration data that now are "frozen" because they are kept confidential by industry and government.

INTRODUCTION

My purpose in this paper is to emphasize that mathematical geologists need to make themselves heard with regard to pressing national and global problems that involve forecasting of mineral and fuel resources. Governmental planning should be facilitated greatly if effective procedures for forecasting petroleum, coal, uranium, and metallic resources were applied on a systematic regional, national, and world-wide basis. Unfortunately, such procedures are developed either inadequately or are not being applied to any significant extent.

Assessing a mineral or energy resource on a regional or national basis requires that geology be incorporated in the assessment processes. Furthermore, assessment processes are inherently "probabilistic", and demand use of the statistician's tools because realistic forecasts necessarily incorporate statistical uncertainty in the estimates. The skills needed are both geological and statistical, and thus are "geostatistical" in the broad sense and lie much within the mathematical geologists' domain. Now, let us turn to some major problems.

THREE MAIN CATEGORIES OF PROBLEMS

Let us begin by discussing three main categories of problems, namely *Problems of Policy*, *Problems of Philosophy*, and *Problems of Direction*. It seems appropriate to focus on these classes of problems before considering some of the technical details.

Problems of Policy. If resource forecasts are to be used properly for public policy making, it is essential that the policy makers understand the nature of the forecasts. Unfortunately, few policy makers in government seem to have much appreciation for the fact that any realistic resource forecast necessarily must incorporate a substantial degree of uncertainty. In fact, forecasts of any of the major energy mineral resources - oil, natural gas, coal, and uranium - are beset with enormous uncertainties. Yet the policy makers at the Federal level in the United States seem reluctant to allow for uncertainty in their resource policy. For example, the U.S. Congress seems to have assumed that by simply establishing a large exploration program (with public funds) that they could establish firmly the petroleum-resource potential of the National Petroleum

Reserve in Alaska, which spans a large area in northwestern Alaska. There seems to have been no appreciation by the Congress of the immense uncertainty surrounding the undertaking, and that at best there would be a high probability of not finding any commercial oil or gas accumulations in spite of an investment of many hundreds of millions of dollars. We witness similar misunderstanding concerning the large uncertainty that surrounds the United States' uranium resource potential. Thus, a major problem of policy concerns allowence for uncertainty in national decisions that are affected by resource estimates.

A second major policy issue concerns the planning of Federal energy-resource programs. For example, how much debate and professional attention have we mathematical geologists directed toward two of the U.S.'s major current energy-resource forecasting programs, namely the assessment of the petroleum potential in the nation's outer continental shelves (OCS's), and the National Uranium Resource Evaluation (NURE) program. These programs have involved a number of highly talented geologists, engineers, and other professionals, but it cannot be said there has been appropriate input from the fraternity of mathematical geologists. In hindsight, it is clear that we as mathematical geologists should be involved in planning the acquisition, coordination, and analysis of data.

Problems of Philosophy. My next main concern is to point out persistent problems in philosophy that affect geologists (and policy makers, too). First, the geological fraternity as a whole seems to adhere more or less stubbornly to "cause-and-effect" philosophy. By this I mean the belief that decrees that we may understand ultimately any geological phenomenon if we are given sufficient information. Cause-and-effect philosophy, for example, seems to dominate oil exploration, where it may be argued that if we knew enough about the origin, migration, and entrapment of petroleum, that we could predict with perfect assurance the location of undiscovered oil and gas pools. The truth of it is that even with our highly advanced technology, we are incapable yet of making forecasts that are more or less "assured". Witness the disappointing results in the Atlantic OCS and the Gulf of Alaska. Most oil explorationists will admit that exploration remains a risky, "chancy" business, but exploration strategies and plays seem to be guided by mechanistic cause-and-effect procedures which do not incorporate uncertainty in a formal manner.

A second major problem of philosophy is the reluctance to accept that there may be some irreducible level of uncertainty in a resource forecast, and that this uncertainty may be large. Again, the view seems to be that given enough information, uncertainty can be eliminated.

The third problem of philosophy is unwillingness to treat uncertainty from a quantitative analytical standpoint. The counter argument is that if uncertainty exists, we should take steps to measure and quantify it and appreciate the fact that the analytical treatment of uncertainty is the business of statisticians and geostatisticians.

A fourth problem of philosophy is the reluctance of policy makers and business decision makers to incorporate formally uncertainty in their decision-making procedures. Even if the uncertainty is fully acknowledged, the traditional "seat-of-the-pants" decision-making procedures generally fail to use formalized, rigorous methods that are available. Part of the problem is that procedures to quantify uncertainty (such as expressing an exploratory well outcome or a resource forecast as an objectively obtained probability distribution) have been slow in materializing.

Problems of Direction. There should be concern with problems of direction. I see three main problems in this context. First, there is widespread confusion between "economic geology" and the "geology of economic deposits". The distinction between the two is important. For example, most technical papers labeled "economic geology" do not address questions of economics at all. There is nothing wrong with study solely of the geology of economic deposits as long as the objective is understood clearly. In general, however, the goal of the study of the geology of economic deposits is an understanding of the origin and occurrence. By contrast, the goal of economic geology is drastically different because it is both economic and geologic. In a profit-seeking enterprise, the ultimate role of the economic geologist is to provide information which will facilitate decision making in the quest to maximize profits. Thus, we can generalize that the ultimate role of economic geology is to facilitate decision making.

A second problem, which is related closely, is the general failure to focus on the manner in which geology is employed in making economic, financial, public policy

decisions. How many papers can be cited that analyze
critically the manner in which geology was used in making
economic or financial decisions? The answer is that
there are surprisingly few, and there are almost no papers
that dissect the decision-making process from a rigorous,
analytical standpoint. On a more general level, there
are papers that are concerned with the role of geology
in its affect upon decisions, but the actual decision
processes themselves are not presented. We can argue
that there is a strong need for research at this interface between geology and formalized decision analysis,
it being a no-man's land between two seemingly disparate
disciplines, bridged by only a few researchers.

A third main problem of direction concerns the need
for research on geological "sample design" from an optimization standpoint. For example, how should the optimum
spacing of boreholes be established to block out a commercial coal seam? For example, we might apply techniques
of universal Kriging to estimate the variance of the coal
seam's thickness between boreholes, and then space the
holes close enough so that the maximum acceptable variance is not exceeded. However, the problem actually is
one of financial optimization because we must compare the
financial value of the information obtained from each
borehole, with the cost of the borehole. The cost of the
borehole is easy to forecast, but estimating the financial
value of the information in the form of the reduced variance is more difficult. The problem of an optimum
borehole spacing arises daily in many exploration contexts, but it remains essentially unstudied in many applications.

SOME ISSUES INVOLVING FORECASTING

To return to the theme of resource forecasting, let
us consider three more important issues. First, there
is a major difference between a resource forecast (on
a regional basis) and a forecast of the result of an
exploration campaign. If we were to design a program
to forecast the resources of a region, it should differ
substantially from a program to explore the region commercially. We can argue that a program to obtain a resource forecast in a frontier region should concentrate
on gathering information throughout the region that has
to do with the occurrence of the commodity being sought,
for example petroleum. By contrast, an exploration campaign should concentrate on finding petroleum that may be
be exploited profitably. In a regional petroleum

forecast, it is as important to estimate where oil does not occur as it is to estimate where it does occur. By contrast, in exploration the objective is to focus on those localities where oil may be profitably extracted and ignore the rest.

The second issue concerns the magnitude of the effort that should be directed toward resource forecasting on a national basis (in the U.S., for example). We can argue that major decisions are being made (for example, the U.S.'s 20-billion dollar synthetic fuels program) with grossly inadequate information about supplies of both conventional and nonconventional hydrocarbon resources. Would a 100 million dollar resource forecasting study be adequate to confirm or deny the need for a synthetic fuels program? We do not know because we have little experience in forecasting the results of large- vs. small-scale resource forecasting programs. The issue itself is pertinent to the discipline of economic geology, however, because it is basically an economic issue.

The third issue is whether resources can be forecast effectively without incorporating exploration methodology. One point of view is that the resource should be estimated without regard to the procedures used to explore for it. An alternative view (to which I subscribe), is that a resource estimate that does not consider exploration methodology (and economics, in turn) is of little use. For example, if we are to forecast the hydrocarbon resources of the Atlantic OCS in terms of its commerically producible oil and gas, we can be assured that present exploration practices will require that an exploratory well be drilled only where there is an attractive seismic prospect present. It can be argued that a useful resource forecast of the Atlantic OCS's hydrocarbon potential depends heavily on knowledge of seismic prospects, plus the results of exploratory drilling to date. Thus, a resource forecast for the Atlantic OCS might consist of the estimated sizes of the fields discovered to date, plus the sum of the probability distributions assigned to each seismic prospect presently discernible, plus a probability distribution for the "wild card" factor for the rest of the region. The summation process would require Monte-Carlo methods. Such a definition of a resource forecast is obviously a restricted one that may not satisfy everyone. The fact that there are differences of opinion emphasizes the need for satisfactory, alternative definitions of resource potential; however, any definition is necessarily both semantic and statistical.

RESOURCE INVENTORIES

Forecasts of undiscovered resources require that we know what we have discovered already. In other words, we need inventories of our existing resources. Surprisingly, the United States lacks an effective inventory of its mineral and fuel resources. I suggest that there are five categories of inventories that should be created, namely, one for the nation's oil and gas resources, a second for its nonmetallic resources, a third for its metallic resources, a fourth for its uranium resources, and a fifth for its coal resources.

What should be included in a resource inventory? An inventory should be more than a listing of deposits. Ideally it should contain information pertaining to size, grade, quality, critical geological characteristics, and cumulative production and remaining reserves. Unfortunately, few existing resource inventories contain this much information. Let us now consider the information that should be incorporated in an inventory of the oil and gas fields of a region. For each field the inventory should contain the following:

(1)   The field's cumulative production
(2)   Area size
(3)   Producing horizons, with cumulative production allocated to each horizon
(4)   Type or types of trap
(5)   Year of discovery
(6)   Depth ranges
(7)   Number of producing wells
(8)   Well spacing
(9)   Oil and gas initially in place (expressed as a probability distribution)
(10) Reserves, expressed as a series of probability distributions for different economic and engineering scenarios
(11) Reservoir characteristics segregated by producing horizon, including thickness, porosity, permeability, and relative permeability

Such an inventory would be immensely useful. For example, it would enable us to determine the form of the frequency distributions of field sizes in the region, either for the region as a whole, or for specific subregions, or for specific periods of discovery, or for specific producing horizons, and so forth. Obtaining frequency distributions is essential in resource forecasting,

because knowledge of the form of field size frequency
distributions is fundamental in forecasting the remaining,
undiscovered resources of the region. Thus, the current
lack of appropriate resource inventories seriously ham-
pers our efforts in making effective forecasts.

Several regional resource-inventory efforts have
been completed recently. One involves both the metallic
and the nonmetallic resources of the California Desert
Conservation Area (CDCA) in southeastern California.
This effort has been undertaken on behalf of the U.S.
Bureau of Land Management, and involves a compilation of
all reported mineral occurrences in the CDCA. It is a
major undertaking because the CDCA embraces about one
fifth the area of California, and lies within a region
that has been explored extensively for more than a century.

SOME BROAD RESEARCH AREAS

There are some general, broad areas for research
that should provide challenges for mathematical geologists. I shall speak of four areas which are all interrelated and to which I have alluded previously. The
first concerns methods for estimating exploration outcome
probabilities, as for example, forecasting the outcome of
an exploratory well drilled in search of oil and gas.
The forecast should be expressed as a probability distribution, which provides for a dryhole probability, plus a
spectrum of oil and gas field sizes. The probability
statement produced should be conditional upon the geological and geophysical data which form the rationale
for drilling the prospect. Such a procedure for estimating well-outcome probabilities would have immediate relevance for exploration. They also would be relevant in
resource forecasting because resource forecasts necessarily are based on information supplied mainly by exploration. Furtherfore, if there is agreement that resource
forecasts should incorporate exploration methodology,
then a regional resource forecast may be regarded in part
as the Monte-Carlo sum of probability distributions at-
tached to individual prospects.

The second general research area involves application of formalized optimization methods in exploration,
particularly in the design of borehole drilling programs.
The third and fourth involve, respectively, the interfaces between exploration geology and formalized decision

analysis, and the interfaces between regional resource appraisal and public policy making. As I stated earlier, these are no-man's lands which have received little attention, perhaps as a consequence of their seeming tenuous nature.

A CAVEAT: "FROZEN" DATA

Before proceeding, let me touch on a sobering fact that affects the whole issue of regional resource appraisal. Many of the data are "frozen" in that they are inaccessible because of government or industry policies. The reasons for their inaccessibility are familiar and include the proprietary nature of information which may have large financial value. For example, most seismic data obtained in oil exploration are highly sensitive and are accessible only to their owners. Even seismic data which have been submitted to the United States government in OCS operations virtually are inaccessible, even to Federal agencies other than the agency receiving the data. There are historical reasons for such security policies, but it would seem that some of the data, particularly in relatively thoroughly explored areas, could be made accessible for inventory analysis purposes.

We encounter similar problems in the use of ore-deposit data. For example, data pertaining to uranium ore reserves on a property-by-property basis is totally inaccessible, yet much of the data reside in Federal files and many of the ore deposits are on public lands.

What can be done about this? We could argue that companies that explore and produce on public lands ought to make their data eventually accessable to the public. This would involve a compromise between the need to withhold public inspection of the data during an interim period, with the long-term public good provided by eventual accessibility of the data. Many in industry will argue that eventual release of the data is of greatest value to industry itself. Witness the value to the oil industry of the voluntary public exchange of electric logs of virtually all oil wells drilled in the United States. I have heard only praise for this system from persons in industry. Therefore, we can ask if well logs are that different from seismic data? It would be appropriate for a committee that includes IAMG members to prepare a proposed policy statement that would provide standards for release of exploration and exploitation data that pertain to the public lands.

A SPECIFIC RESEARCH OPPORTUNITY

Before concluding, let me outline a somewhat more specific research opportunity. There is a strong need to explore the statistical relationships that presumably exist between seismically perceived structures and hydrocarbon occurrences. The OCS regions would provide good opportunities to examine these relationships, particularly in offshore Louisiana and Texas. Onshore regions, however, need to be analyzed similarly for comparison purposes. Consider the problems of assessing the petroleum potential of the Atlantic OCS. There is a large body of seismic information available for the Atlantic OCS, but most of the seismically detected structures are untested. If these untested structures are to be incorporated in an appraisal of the Atlantic OCS's hydrocarbon potential, they should be compared with similar structures that have been perceived seismically elsewhere and have been tested by drilling. Such a comparison would provide a structure-by-structure forecast of the Atlantic OCS's hydrocarbon potential under present exploration technology. Although a forecast would be influenced strongly by drilling results in the Atlantic OCS to date, it also would be highly uncertain because we are not sure where the best analogs to the Atlantic OCS are. The Louisiana and Texas OCS is suitable partly because it contains many structures that are similar to those of the Atlantic OCS. But the Atlantic OCS is lithologically more similar to the rocks of the northern part of the Gulf Coastal Plain (northern Louisiana and southern Arkansas) where the oil-producing rocks (Cretaceous and Jurassic) also are more nearly equivalent in age to those of the Atlantic OCS.

RECOMMENDATION

Mathematical geologists need to involve themselves to a greater degree in resource forecasting by providing guidance on a sustained basis. There are many interesting technical challenges and there also is a strong social need. It is a unique opportunity for mathematical geologists.

COMPUTERS IN OCEANOGRAPHY

William W. Hay

Rosenstiel School of Marine and Atmospheric
Science, University of Miami

ABSTRACT

Oceanography is a broad topic encompassing not only
marine geology and geophysics but also physical, chemical, and biological oceanography. Computers are used for
data storage, analysis, and modeling. Data storage for
this field is centralized in the National Oceanographic
Data Center which archives a vast amount of data in a
variety of forms. Many of the oceanographic institutions
also archive sets of data of particular interest at that
institution. The Deep Sea Drilling Project (DSDP) archives measurements and observations on the cores that
have been recoved by drilling, and this constitutes the
largest body of homogenous computer-accessible data in
geology. The DSDP computer files have been transferred
by duplication to Germany and to the USSR. Computer
analysis ranges from complex processing problems, such
as multichannel seismics and satellite images, to relatively simpler current dynamics, paleoecologic interpretations, lithologic analysis, and construction of age-
depth curves in marine stratigraphic sequences. Modeling
is most sophisticated in physical oceanography and atmospheric science, where the general circulation models require large computing facilities. Process modeling is
developing rapidly in marine chemistry. Ecological modeling is an active area in biology, with much interesting work being carried out on analog computers. A unique
development in oceanographic computing is the use of
satellites to transmit data from ships and buoys to

shore laboratories for processing and return by satellite
of the processed data to the ships in time to permit
modification of experiments in process as conditions
change.

COMPUTER APPLICATIONS IN EXPLORATION AND MINING GEOLOGY:

TEN YEARS OF PROGRESS

G.S. Koch, Jr.

University of Georgia

ABSTRACT

Although many applications of computers to exploration and mining geology had been developed prior to 1969,
their use and acceptance in mining was limited, even by
the technologically advanced countries. Today, most
mining companies and governmental agencies concerned
with natural resources apply computers extensively.

During the decade, Matheron's French geostatistics
has undergone extensive theoretical expansion on the one
hand, and reduction to understandable form, through several textbooks, on the other hand. Classical statistics
for mining geology has been refined further as the result
of many detailed applications with much feedback from
industrial practice.

The manipulation by computer of large data bases
has made possible a closer relationship between geology
and mine systems analysis, and between geology and mining.

Whereas in 1969 the contribution of statistics and
computers to geological exploration for mineral deposits
was in its infancy, today these methods are used widely,
although the most extensive applications are in the mining of known ore deposits. Particularly influential have
been (1) the development of models for drillhole exploration and (2) operations research methods to conceptualize
and organize exploration effort.

A significant step has been the development of many
computer programs, some relatively large and complex,
for the computer analysis of data from the mineral industry. Some of these programs are proprietary, but many
have been published in technical journals.

Exploration geochemistry and geophysics grew at an
explosive rate. Today, many computer applications have
been made for the organization, display, and interpretation of these data.

INTRODUCTION

When I wrote "Computer applications in mining geology" in 1969 for the previous symposium volume, the
application and acceptance of computers and statistics
was limited, even in the technologically advanced countries; today, most mining companies and government agencies concerned with natural resources apply computers
extensively. I am sure that this trend will continue;
as data increase dependence on computers necessarily
follows. Computers will become easier to use, and the
results of their use will be easier to understand.

A decade ago (Koch, 1969), I could attempt a summary
of the literature. Today it is impossible to summarize
or even mention all of the significant publications, nor
is there a book that integrates the advances made; excellent papers in "Computer methods for the 80's in the
mineral industry," (Weiss, 1979a) cover many phases.
The time-consuming work of developing models and running
computers has occupied most of us during the decade; we
have been more engrossed with "doing our own thing" than
with sharing and clarifying our goals and our progress.

Moreover, words have never been as well-matched to
our field as are graphic displays and data. This explains much of the current emphasis on computer graphics,
data-base development, and manipulation, and man/machine
interaction. Many new devices, including touch sensing,
terminals, and minicomputers are going to make communication easier, quicker, and more accurate.

In this article, I mention some published and unpublished articles with which I am familiar; most of
those cited are recent but they in turn refer to earlier
ones. Sixteen International Symposia on the Applications
of Computers and Operations Research in the Mineral

Industries (APCOM) have been held since 1961; many computer applications discussed in this paper were first
published in the proceedings of these symposia (listed
in Table 1). Because most are out of print, they may
not be easy to find.

EXPLORATION

Planning of Exploration

Computers are used widely by mining companies and
to some extent by governmental agencies for exploration
planning, but I am not aware of much published work with
a geological component. Helpful are papers by Weiss
(1979b, 1979c), Griffiths (1974), Gabelman (1976),
Guarascio and Turchi (1976), Mackenzie (1972), Mackenzie
and Bilodeau (1977), and Gaucher and Gagnon (1973).

Champigny, Sanders, and Sinclair (1980) provide an
interesting example of structured property exploration
evaluated by measures of "relative information gain."
Much of the work done in the 1970's was proprietary;
I hope that some of this will be published soon.

Resource Evaluation

Shortages of petroleum and other commodities have
added to the new emphasis on resource evaluation. Because of the large amounts of data and the multivariate
statistical analyses required, computers have been essential for these investigations.

The proceedings of two recent meetings of the International Geological Correlation Program Project 98,
"Standards for Computer Applications in Resource Studies"
(Cargill and Clark, 1977, 1978) are sources for recent
developments. Also valuable is a book by Harris (1977),
one of the pioneers in the subject.

Harris continued his work of the 1960's on classification and evaluation of gridded areas; he applied his
methods to several parts of North America to establish
generality (Harris, 1973). Later, he and colleagues
(Harris and Brock, 1973) introduced concepts of subjective probability. Harris' current work stresses probabilistic interpretatins of inferences made by geologists applying scientific methodology consistently in
regional evaluation. Thus, the discipline imposed by

Table 1. Summary of symposia on applications of computers and operations research in the mineral industries (APCOM). Sponsors: AIMM, Australasian Institution of Mining and Metallurgy; CIM, Canadian Institution of Mining and Metallurgy; CSM, Colorado School of Mines; EP, Ecole Polytechnique (Montreal); McG, McGill University; SAIMM, South African Institution of Mining and Metallurgy; SME, Society of Mining Engineers of the American Institute of Mining Engineers; PSU, the Pennsylvania State University; SU, Stanford University; TUC, Technische Universitat Clausthal; UA, University of Arizona. For each symposia, the proceedings volume was published by the first-listed sponsor.

No.	Year	Sponsor(s)	Location	Name of proceedings volume	Editor(s) of proceedings volume
1	1961	UA	Tucson, Arizona	Short course on computers and computer applications in the mineral industry	J.C. Dotson
2	1962	UA, SU	Tucson, Arizona	Computer short course and symposium on mathematical techniques and computer applications in mining and exploration	J.C. Dotson
3	1963	SU, UA	Stanford, California	Computers in the mineral industry	George A. Parks

No.	Year	Sponsor(s)	Location	Name of proceedings volume	Editor(s) of proceedings volume
4	1964	CSM, SU, PSU, SME, UA	Golden, Colorado	International symposium on application of statistics, operations research, and computers in the mineral industry	Sherman W. Spear
5	1965	UA, SU, CSM, PSU, SME	Tucson, Arizona	Short course and symposium on computers and computer applications in mining and exploration	J.C. Dotson, W.C. Peters
6	1966	PSU, SU, CSM, SME, UA	University Park, Pennsylvania	Proceedings of the symposium and short course on computers and operations research in mineral industries	Pamela L. Slingluff, Theresa A. Fike
7	1968	CSM, SU, PSU, SME, UA	Golden, Colorado	Seventh international symposium on operations research and computer applications in the mineral industries	Charles O. Frush
8	1969	SME, SU, CSM, PSU, UA	Salt Lake City, Utah	A decade of digital computing in the mineral industry -- a review of the state-of-the-art	Alfred Weiss

No.	Year	Sponsor(s)	Location	Name of proceedings volume	Editor(s) of proceedings volume
9	1970	CIM, McG, EP, SU, CSM, PSU, SME, UA	Montreal, Canada	Decision-making in the mineral industry	J.I. McGerrigle
10	1972	SAIMM, SU, CSM, PSU, SME, UA	Johannesburg South Africa	Application of computer methods in the mineral industry: proceedings of the tenth international symposium	M.D.G. Salamon, F.H. Lancaster
11	1973	UA, SU, CSM, PSU, SME	Tucson, Arizona	Eleventh symposium on computer applications in the minerals industry	John R. Sturgul
12	1974	CSM, SU, PSU, SME, UA	Golden, Colorado	Twelfth symposium on the applications of computers and mathematics in the minerals industry	Thys B. Johnson, Donald W. Gentry
13	1975	TUC, SU, CSM, PSU, SME, UA	Clausthal, West Germany	Thirteenth international symposium on the application of computers and mathematics for decision making in the mineral industries	F.L. Wilke

No.	Year	Sponsor(s)	Location	Name of proceedings volume	Editor(s) of proceedings volume
14	1976	SME, PSU, SU, CSM, UA	University Park, Pennsylvania	Application of computer methods in the mineral industry: proceedings of the fourteenth symposium	R.V. Ramani
15	1977	AIMM, SU, CSM, PSU, SME, UA	Brisbane, Australia	Apcom 77: papers presented at the fifteenth international symposium on the application of computers and operations research in the mineral industries	Alban Lynch
16	1979	SME, UA	Tucson, Arizona	Sixteenth application of computers and operations research in the mineral industry	T.J. O'Neil

the inflexibility of the computer has helped to emphasize
the importance of systematic geological observation; the
computer has made possible a consistency of application
of scientific methodology.

The Geological Survey of Canada also was active in
resource evaluation. Agterberg and others (1971) made
a geomathematical evaluation of copper and zinc potential
in the Abitibi area of Ontario and Quebec. In this study,
they established a data base for geological and geophysical parameters measured in small cells. Through multivariate statistics, they then compared these measurements
to metal content for cells containing ore bodies and predicted metal endowment in other cells. They showed that
meaningful data could be obtained from geological maps,
that these data were incomplete, and that effective
statistical methods could be devised. Later, they
(Agterberg, 1975; Chung, 1978) refined their models and
established their generality by applying them to other
geographic areas and to large blocks of the earth's
crust. Recently, Agterberg and Divi (1978) modeled the
frequency distribution of concentration values for a
chemical element in blocks of constant weight sampled
at random from a segment of the earth's crust and developed statistical models to describe clustering of mineral
deposits of a given type in a region.

Griffiths and his students, at the Pennsylvania
State University, continued work on resource studies
(e.g., Griffiths and Singer, 1973; Menzie, Labovitz,
and Griffiths, 1976). Griffiths (1978) further developed his idea of unit regional value, a concept that has
influenced greatly other investigators.

At the U.S. Geological Survey, in Reston, Virginia,
the Office of Resource Analysis emphasized petroleum
rather than mineral-resource geology. However, much of
their work is directly relevant to mineral deposits,
and their papers on mineral deposits as such have been
influential. One approach, the discovery process model
(Drew, Schuenemeyer, and Root, 1980; Barouch and Kaufman, 1977) estimates undiscovered petroleum resources in
a partially explored region based upon characteristics of
the discovery process; another, is a classification
technique (Botbol and others, 1978) named characteristic
analysis. A recent one is a study of rock geochemical
data related to possible concealed porphyry copper mineralization (McCammon and others, 1979). All of these
models have been successful for various geological

situations; further work will define more clearly their
generality.

Other models developed in the 1970's include abundance estimation (Celenk and others, 1978), volumetric
estimation (Kingston and others, 1978), and subjective
probability, using the Delphi method (Baxter and others,
1978; Miller and others, 1975). In explored areas, deposit modeling (Sinding-Larsen and Vokes, 1978) has been
used successfully for resource estimation. Beauchamp
and others (1979) applied discriminant analysis to identify favorable areas for uranium. Singer and Overshine
(1979) assessed resources in Alaska, providing an example
of suitable methodology for a poorly explored area.

Data bases for resources first were developed extensively during the 1970's; typically, geologists and engineers wrote the specifications for the bases, which
were completed by computer and information scientists.
Examples of large systems are those of the Geological
Survey of Canada (Robinson, 1972; Eckstrand, 1977) and
the U.S. Geological Survey and Bureau of Mines (1976);
the systems allow these organizations and other geologists to retrieve easily and use valuable information.

Gill and others (1977) discussed the design of geological data systems for developing nations. Thompson
(1975) described a computer-oriented system to portray
minerals availability for policy planners in the U.S.
government. Cargill and Clark's (1977) previously
cited publication also contains papers on data bases.

Sampling Designs for Exploration

Most sampling designs for exploration are drilling
plans. Progress on two-dimensional models (begun by
Slicher in the 1950's and by Griffiths and his students
in the 1960's) continued with Singer's work (1975);
with Drew's (1979) procedures for determining the areal
influence of drillholes; and with Shurygin's (1976)
mathematical analyses.

Three-dimensional models are less developed than the
two-dimensional ones and apply to a narrower range of
physical situations. Koch, Link, and Schuenemeyer (1974)
use simulation to locate exploration drillholes for ore
bodies that can be represented as ellipses. Malmqvist
and Malmqvist's (1979) model explores for three-dimensional folded targets.

Exploration Geochemistry

Exploration geochemistry developed rapidly in both
scope and in volume of data, as costs of chemical analysis decreased and extensive regional surveys were undertaken. Rose, Hawkes, and Webb (1979, p. 520) point out
that "for both data handling and a great deal of statistical interpretation of the results of large-scale geochemical surveys, computer-processing methods are virtually mandatory. Furthermore, the field is developing
rapidly with the appearance of new statistical concepts
and with computer services becoming progressively less
expensive." McCammon (1974) provides another excellent
summary chapter on the subject.

Several workers developed sampling designs and
methods of statistical analysis implemented by computers.
Excellent papers that will lead the reader to other references are by Miesch (1976) and by Garrett (1979).
Sinclair (1976) developed probability graphs that have
been used widely for determining thresholds. Govett and
coworkers (Govett, 1972; Govett and others, 1975) were
active in statistical analyses of data sets from Cyprus,
New Brunswick, and elsewhere.

Regional geochemical surveys required a systematic
collection of samples, analytical work, and presentation
of results. Webb and others (1978) present work done in
Great Britain; Howarth and others (1980) describe some
of the techniques that were used for this atlas, and also
for study of exploration data collected by the U.S. Department of Energy in the search for uranium.

MINING GEOLOGY

Geostatistics

Geostatistics provides a way to analyze variables
that are distributed in space (or time); it was devised
by G. Matheron, who published a book in French in 1962.
Geostatistics could be considered an extension of the
weighting schemes such as inverse distance (long used in
ore-reserve calculations) and of trend-surface analysis
(developed in the United States and South Africa in the
1950's and 1960's). Because Matheron's book required
intensive study of a complicated system, it was difficult reading, even for those with a good knowledge of
French.

In the 1970's the theory and practice of Geostatistics became accessible to English-speaking geologists and engineers through many short courses. Four books published in English were the following: "Geostatistical Ore Reserve Estimation," by Michel David (1977) explains the subject using a relatively small amount of mathematics; more mathematical, "Mining Statistics" by Andre G. Journel and C.J. Huijbregts (1978, is comprehensive and suitable for reference as well as a textbook; "An Introduction to the Geostatistical Methods of Mineral Evaluation," is a summary by J.M. Rendu (1978); "Practical Geostatistics" by Isobel Clark (1979) provides a short, relatively nonmathematical approach. The first three are by Matheron's students; Clark presents an independent view.

Many of the articles written on geostatistics during the last decade are thoroughly referenced in the extensive bibliographies in these books.

Other Developments in Ore-Reserve Estimation

During the 1970's, D.G. Krige and H.S. Sichel of South Africa continued the work they began in the 1950's on statistical and computer methods of ore reserve estimation. Krige summarized his results in a 1978 book entitled "Lognormal-de Wijsian geostatistics for ore evaluation." Sichel (1972) wrote on the statistical valuation of diamondiferous deposits, a difficult subject because of the extremely low grade of these deposits and their high variability. De Wijs, of the Netherlands, wrote (1972) on the method of successive difference applied to mine sampling.

In two papers, Parker and coauthors (Parker and Switzer, 1975; Parker, Journel, and Dixon, 1979) discuss the use of conditional probability distributions in ore-reserve estimation; the second is a case study for estimation of open-pit reserves in stratabound uranium deposits.

CONCLUSIONS

During the next decade, I anticipate continued rapid growth. Among the authors who have commented on the technological and human factors in this future development are Agterberg (1979), Krige (1977), and Merriam (1980). The role of Matheron's geostatistics and

classical statistics will become more clearly defined.
Many additional methods of data analysis, particularly
those of the exploratory data-analysis school of Tukey
(1977), will be employed widely and familiar to all
practitioners. Enough information will be at hand from
completed exploration studies in which statistics and
computers played a part to allow appraisal of the models
and their refinement. Planning for geochemical and geophysical surveys will be a necessity and methods of data
interpretation will be better understood and more
straightforward than at present. Methods for the routine development and handling of large data bases will
be available and used, and they will be efficient. I
believe that the application of computers in exploration
and mining geology will be as beneficial in the years
to come as it has been in the past.

REFERENCES

Many of the references in this list come from one
of the sixteen symposia on the Application of Computer
Methods in the Mineral Industry. For brevity, these references are identified in the following list by the
number of the symposium and the acronym APCOM. Table 1
gives the bibliographic details necessary to identify
fully the editors and publishers of these symposia volumes.

Agterberg, F.P., 1975, Statistical models for the region-
     al occurrence of mineral deposits: 13th APCOM,
     p. CI1-CI15.

Agterberg, F.P., 1979, Statistics applied to facts and
     concepts in geoscience: Geol. en Mijnbouw, v. 58,
     no. 2, p. 201-208.

Agterberg, F.P., Chung, C.F., Fabbri, A.G., Kelly, A.M.,
     and Springer, J.S., 1971, Geomathematical evalua-
     tion of copper and zinc potential of the Abitibi
     area, Ontario and Quebec: Geol. Survey of Canada
     Paper 71-41, 55 p.

Agterberg, F.P., and Divi, S.R., 1978, A statistical
     model for the distribution of copper, lead, and
     zinc in the Canadian Appalachian region: Econ.
     Geology, v. 73, no. 2, p. 230-245.

Barouch, E., and Kaufman, G.M., 1977, Estimation of un-
    discovered oil and gas in mathematical aspects of
    production and distribution of energy: Proceedings
    of Symposium in Applied Mathematics, v. 21, Am.
    Math. Soc., p. 77-81.

Baxter, G.G., Cargill, S.M., Chidester, A.H., Hart, P.E.,
    Kaufman, G.M., and Urquidi-Barrau, F., 1978, Work-
    shop on the Delphi method: Jour. Math. Geology,
    v. 10, no. 5, p. 581-588.

Beauchamp, J.J., Begovich, C.L., Kane, V.E., and Wolf,
    D.A., 1979, Application of discriminant analysis
    and generalized distance measures to uranium explor-
    ation: Union Carbide Technical Report K/UR-28,
    Oak Ridge, Tennessee, 58 p.

Bilodeau, M.L., and MacKenzie, B.W., 1977, The drilling
    investment decision in mineral exploration: 14th
    APCOM, p, 932-949.

Botbol, J.M., Sinding-Larsen, R., McCammon, R.B., and
    Gott, G.B., 1978, A regionalized multivariate ap-
    proach to target selection in geochemical explora-
    tion: Econ. Geology, v. 73, no. 4, p. 534-546.

Cargill, S.M., and Clark, A.L., eds., 1977, Standards
    for computer applications in resource studies:
    Jour. Math. Geology, v. 9, no. 3, p. 205-337.

Cargill, S.M., and Clark, A.L., 1978, "Standards for
    computer applications in resource studies," Pro-
    ject 98: Jour. Math. Geology, v. 10, no. 5, p.
    405-642.

Celenk, O., Clark, A.L., de Vletter, D.R., Garrett, R.G.,
    and van Staaldvinen, C., 1978, Workshop on abun-
    dance estimation: Jour. Math. Geology, v. 10, no.
    5, p. 473-480.

Champigny, N., Sanders, K.G., and Sinclair, A.J., 1980,
    Sepcogna gold deposit of Consolidated Cinola Mines -
    an example of structured property exploration:
    Western Miner, June, p. 35-44.

Chung, C.F., 1978, Computer program for the logistic
    model to estimate the probability of occurrence of
    discrete events: Geol. Survey of Canada Paper 78-
    11, 23 p.

Clark, I., 1979, Practical geostatistics: Applied Sci.
    Publ., Ltd., London, 129 p.

David, M., 1977, Geostatistical ore reserve estimation:
    Elsevier Sci. Publ. Co., Amsterdam, 364 p.

de Wijs, H.J., 1972, Method of successive differences
    applied to mine sampling: Trans. I.M.M., v. 81,
    p. A78-A81.

Drew, L.J., 1979, Pattern drilling exploration: optimum
    pattern types and hole spacings when searching for
    elliptical shaped targets: Jour. Math. Geology, v.
    11, no. 2, p. 223-254.

Drew, L.J., Schuenemeyer, J.H., and Root, D.H., 1980,
    Resource appraisal and discovery rate forecasting in
    partially explored regions: Part A, an application
    to the Denver Basin: U.S. Geol. Survey Prof. Paper
    1138, 13 p.

Eckstrand, O.R., 1977, Mineral resource appraisal and
    mineral deposits computer files in the Geological
    Survey of Canada: Jour. Math. Geology, v. 9, no.
    3, p. 235-244.

Gabelman, J.W., 1976, Expectations from uranium explora-
    tion: Am. Assoc. Petroleum Geologists, v. 60, no.
    11, p. 1993-2004.

Garrett, R.G., 1979, Sampling considerations for regional
    geochemical surveys, *in* Current research, part A,
    Geol. Survey of Canada Paper 79-1a, p. 197-205.

Gaucher, E., and Gagnon, D.C., 1973, Compilation and
    quantification of exploration data for computer
    studies in exploration strategy: Can. Inst. Min.
    Met. Bull., Sept., p. 113-117.

Gill, D., Beylin, J., Boehm, S., Frendel, Y., and
    Rosenthal, E., 1977, Design of geological data
    systems for developing nations: Jour. Math.
    Geology, v. 9, no. 2, p. 145-158.

Govett, G.J.S., 1972, Interpretation of a rock geochem-
    ical exploration survey in Cyprus - statistical
    and graphical techniques: Jour. Geochem Expl.,
    v. 1, no. 1, p. 77-102.

Govett, G.J.S., Goodfellow, W.D., Chapman, R.P., and
    Chork, C.Y., 1975, Exploration geochemistry - dis-
    tribution of elements and recognition of anomalies:
    Jour. Math. Geology, v. 7, no. 5/6, p. 415-446.

Griffiths, J.C., 1974, Quantification and the future of
    geosciences: Syracuse Univ. Geology Contr. 2,
    p. 51-66.

Griffiths, J.C., 1978, Mineral resource assessment using
    the unit regional value concept: Jour. Math. Geo-
    logy, v. 10, no. 5, p. 441-472.

Griffiths, J.C., and Singer, D.A., 1973, Size, shape and
    arrangement of some uranium ore bodies: 11th APCOM,
    p. B82-B1112.

Guarascio, M., and Turchi, A., 1976, Exploration data
    management and evaluation techniques for uranium
    mining projects: 14th APCOM, p. 451-464.

Harris, D.P., 1973, A subjective probability appraisal
    of metal endowment of Northern Sonora, Mexico:
    Econ. Geology, v. 68, no. 2, p. 222-242.

Harris, D.P., 1977, Mineral endowment, resources, and
    potential supply: theory, methods for appraisal,
    and case studies: MINRESCO, TUSCON, Arizona,
    various pages.

Harris, D.P., and Brock, T.N., 1973, A conceptual baye-
    sian geostatistical model for metal endowment: 11th
    APCOM, p. B113-B184.

Howarth, R.J., Koch, G.S., Jr., Chork, C.Y., Carpenter,
    R.H., and Schuenemeyer, J.H., 1980, Statistical
    map analysis techniques applied to regional distri-
    bution of uranium in stream sediment samples from
    the southeastern United States for the National
    Uranium Resources Evaluation Program: Jour. Math.
    Geology, v. 12, in press.

Journel, A.G., and Huijbregts, C., 1978, Mining geo-
    statistics: Academic Press, New York, 600 p.

Kingston, G.A., David, M., Meyer, R.F., Ovenshine, A.T.,
    Slamet, S., and Schanz, J.J., 1978, Workshop on
    volumetric estimation: Jour. Math. Geology, v. 10,
    no. 5, p. 495-500.

Koch, G.S., Jr., 1969, Computer applications in mining geology, *in* Merriam, D.F., ed., Computer applications in the earth sciences: Plenum Press, New York, p. 121-140.

Koch, G.S., Jr., Link, R.F., and Schuenemeyer, J.H., 1974, A mathematical model to guide the discovery of ore bodies in a Coeur d'Alene lead-silver mine: U.S. Bureau of Mines, Rept. Invest. No. 7989, 43 p.

Krige, D.G., 1977, The human element in APCOM's development: 15th APCOM. p. 1-6.

Krige, D.G., 1978, Lognormal-de Wijsian geostatistics for ore evaluation: South African Institute of Mining and Metallurgy Monograph Series, Geostatistics 1, 50 p.

Mackenzie, B.W., 1972, Corporate exploration strategies: 10th APCOM, p. 1-8.

Mackenzie, B.W., 1972, and Bilodeau, M.L., 1977, A model to assess the economic characteristics of base metal investment in Canada: 15th APCOM, p. 463-470.

Malmqvist, K., and Malmqvist, L., 1979, A feasibility study of exploration for deep-seated sulphide ore bodies: 16th APCOM, p. 25-37.

Matheron, G., 1962, Traite de geostatistique appliquee: Editions Technip, Paris, Tome 1 (1962), 334 p.; Tome 2 (1963), 172 p.

McCammon, R.B., 1974, The statistical treatment of geochemical data, *in* Levinson, A.A., Introduction to exploration geochemistry, Applied Publishing, Ltd., Calgary, Canada, p. 469-508.

McCammon, R.B., Botbol, J.M., and McCarthy, J.H., 1979, Drill-site favorability for concealed porphyry copper prospect. Rowe Canyon, Nevada based on characteristic analysis of geochemical anomalies: Fall Meeting, Soc. Mining Engineers, Tucson, Arizona, preprint, 13 p.

Menzie, W.D., Labovitz, M.L., and Griffiths, J.C., 1976, Evaluation of mineral resources and the unit regional value concept: 14th APCOM, p. 322-339.

Merriam, D.F., 1980, Some future developments in geology:
     Nature and Resources, v. 16, no. 2, p. 2-5.

Miesch, A.T., 1976, Geochemical survey of Missouri -
     methods of sampling, laboratory analysis, and repro-
     duction of data: U.S. Geol. Survey Prof. Paper
     954-A, 39 p.

Miller, B.M., Thomsen, H.L., Dolton, G.L., Coury, A.B.,
     Henricks, T.A., Lennartz, F.E., Powers, R.B., Sable,
     E.G., and Varnes, K.L., 1975, Geological estimates
     of undiscovered recoverable oil and gas resources
     in the United States: U.S. Geol. Survey Circ. 725,
     78 p.

Parker, D.H., and Switzer, P., 1975, Use of conditional
     probability distributions in ore reserve estimation:
     13th APCOM, p. MIII1-MIII16.

Parker, H.M., Journel, A.G., and Dixon, W.C., 1979, The
     use of conditional lognormal probability distribu-
     tion for the estimation of open-pit ore reserves
     in stratabound uranium deposits - a case study:
     16th APCOM, p. 133-148.

Rendu, J.M., 1978, An introduction to geostatistical
     methods for mineral evaluation: Monograph, South
     African Inst. Min. Metall., Johannesburg, 100 p.

Robinson, S.C., 1972, The role of a data base in modern
     geology, *in* Merriam, D.F., ed., The impact of
     quantification in geology: Syracuse Univ. Geology
     Contr. 2, p. 67-82.

Rose, A.W., Hawkes, H.E., and Webb, J.S., 1979, Geochem-
     istry in mineral exploration: Academic Press,
     New York, 657 p.

Shurygin, A.M., 1976, The probability of finding deposits
     and some optimal search grids: Jour. Math. Geology,
     v. 8, no. 3, p. 323-330.

Sichel, H.S., 1972, Statistical valuation of diamondifer-
     ous deposits: 10th APCOM, p. 17-25.

Sinclair, A.J., 1976, Application of probability graphs
     in mineral exploration: Spec. Vol. no. 4, Associa-
     tion of Exploration Geochemists, 95 p.

Sinding-Larsen, R., and Vokes, F.M., 1978, The use of
    deposit modelling in the assessment of potential
    resources as exemplified by Caledonian stratabound
    sulfide deposits: Jour. Math. Geology, v. 10, no.
    5, p. 565-580.

Singer, D.A., 1975, Relative efficiencies of square and
    triangular grids in the search for elliptically
    shaped resource targets: U.S. Geol. Survey, Jour.
    Research, v. 3, no. 2, p. 163-167.

Singer, D.A., and Ovenshine, A.T., Assessing metallic
    resources in Alaska: Am. Scientist, v. 67, no. 5,
    p. 582-589.

Thompson, G.G., 1975, A computer-oriented minerals
    availability system: 13th APCOM, p. GII1-GII14.

Tukey, J.W., 1977, Exploratory data analysis: Addison-
    Wesley, Reading, Massachusetts, 499 p.

U.S. Geol. Survey and U.S. Bureau of Mines, 1976, Prin-
    ciples of the mineral resource classification sys-
    tem of the U.S. Bureau of Mines and U.S. Geological
    Survey: U.S. Geol. Survey Bull. 1450-A, p. A1-A5.

Webb, J.S., Thornton, I., Thompson, M., Howarth, R.J.,
    and Lowenstein, P.L., 1978, The Wolfson geochemical
    atlas of England and Wales: Clarendon Press, Oxford,
    69 p.

Weiss, A., ed., 1979a, Computer methods for the 80's:
    Soc. Mining Engineers, New York, 975 p.

Weiss, A., 1979b, Mining information systems planning and
    project management, introductory review, *in* Weiss,
    A., ed., Computer methods for the 80's: Soc. Mining
    Engineers, New York, p. 1-2.

Weiss, A., 1979c, Project management in mineral informa-
    tion technology, *in* Weiss, A., ed., Computer methods
    for the 80's, Soc. Mining Engineers, New York, p.
    15-30.

SOME DEVELOPMENTS IN COMPUTER APPLICATIONS IN PETROLOGY

R.W. Le Maitre

University of Melbourne

ABSTRACT

During the last decade most of the computer applications in petrology have been concerned with data bases,
petrological mixing models, the use of multivariate statistical techniques and, more recently, the modeling of
igneous differentiation trends.

The characteristics of three of the major data bases,
that is RKNFSYS (approximately 16,000 analyses), CLAIR
(approximately 26,000 analyses), and PETROS (approximately
35,000 analyses) are compared. As a result of the experience gained in building these bases, a new international
*i*gneous data *base* (IGBA) is being organized, which will
supercede eventually the others due to the inclusion of
mineralogical and more textural information.

Recent developments in petrological mixing models
include a better understanding of the principles behind
the various models, in particular the fact that for constant sum major element data, a constrained model should
be used. A completely generalized model capable of deal-
ing with metamorphic reactions of the type A + B + C +..
= D + E + F + C.. also has been developed.

The use of principal-components analysis, factor
analysis, and discriminant analysis in the interpretation
of the chemistry of igneous rocks and mineral groups has
become increasingly popular, but unfortunately, either

through ignorance or the use of statistical packages, some
of the interpretations have been incorrect. In particular, principal-component analysis based on the correlation
matrix seems difficult to justify for major element geochemical data.

The modeling of igneous differentiation trends has
been approached in two different ways. One mainly empirical method predicts the path of crystallization of any
given anhydrous liquid composition at 1 atmosphere pressure. The inclusion of H_2O and pressure into the method
is only a question of   time. The other method is
based on Rayleigh's Law of fractional crystallization.

INTRODUCTION

Possibly one of the most important developments in
computer applications in petrology in the last decade has
been the compilation of major petrological data bases,
for without these it is difficult to obtain unbiased results from the application of statistical methods, such
as principal-components analysis, factor analysis, and
discriminant analysis. The lack of availability of such
data bases also may have been responsible partly for the
slow development in the use of some of these multivariate
statistical methods.

One method which has gained wide acceptance and now
is used almost as routinely as a norm calculation, is the
least-squares fitting of compositional data, usually
known as mixing models. The reason for its popularity is
probably the fact that the results are in a form readily
understandable to petrologists and require no specialized
interpretation. However, perhaps the most exciting, and
potentially the most important, development of recent
years is the application of modeling methods to igneous
differentiation processes. Some aspects of some of these
developments now will be discussed in further detail.

PETROLOGICAL DATA BASES

The last decade has seen the development of three
major petrological data bases. In order of appearance
they are RKNFSYS (Chayes, 1971), CLAIR (Le Maitre, 1973,
1976a), and PETROS (Mutschler and others, 1976, 1978).
These files consist essentially of chemical analyses of
igneous rocks from all over the world, plus additional
information which differs slightly from file to file.

RKNFSYS contains approximately 16,000 analyses of
Cenozoic volcanic rocks only. Stored with each analysis
is the Troger number of the rock type and its location.
The data base is accessed by machine-dependent software
and uses random read/write facilities. Although the data
base has never been distributed, data retrievals always
have been available on request.

CLAIR (approximately 26,000 analyses) and PETROS
(approximately 35,000 analyses) are similar types of sequential files of data of all types of igneous rocks (including some metamorphosed ones) of all ages, together
with latitude and longitude and, where available, age,
and trace-element data. The main difference between the
two files is the manner in which the rock names, as given
in the original publications, are recorded. In CLAIR
they are coded in fixed format, which makes retrieval by
rock name extremely easy. In PETROS, however, they are
in free format, which makes retrieval by rock name difficult, especially as abbreviations also are included. For
example, to locate basalts one not only has to search for
the term "basalt" or "bas" etc., but also to exclude
"trachybasalt", "basaltic andesite", etc. The PETROS
file is available freely at the cost of reproduction and
a simple interactive operating system KEYBAM (Barr, Mutschler, and Lavin, 1977) also is available for data reduc-
tions. The CLAIR file has not been made available freely,
although copies are in use at the C.R.P.G. Nancy, France
and in the Department of Geology at the University of
Leicester, England. To process the data file, a generalized data retrieval, storage, and processing system,
termed the CLAIR DATA SYSTEM, was written (Le Maitre and
Ferguson, 1978). In use, this open-ended system has
proved to be extremely flexible and capable of processing
many types of data, mainly due to the design philosophy
of the system, which is described adequately by Le Maitre
and Ferguson (1978).

One of the interesting things about these three
files is the manner in which they differ. All three
authors of the data files believed that they had collected
a considerable amount of the data available, yet comparisons of the files revealed that only 15 percent of the
total number of analyses in RKNFSYS and CLAIR were common
to both files (Chayes and Le Maitre, 1972). Similarly,
the overlap between CLAIR and PETROS was only 18 percent,
indicating that probably well over 100,000 analyses already are available in the literature. Published maps
of the geographical distribution of data from CLAIR

(Le Maitre, 1973) and PETROS (Mutschler and others, 1978)
reveal that even these differ. Compared to CLAIR, PETROS
contains little data from Europe or Australasia, but far
more from the ocean floors and northwestern U.S.A.

One major deficiency of these three files is that
they contain no mineralogical information apart from what
may be in the rock name. In order to overcome this, and
to avoid duplication of future effort, a new international
data base called IGBA (for *ig*neous *ba*se) came into being.
This was launched as IGCP Project 163 and considerable interest was shown in the concept at the inaugural meeting
at Bochum in 1977 under the chairmanship of Felix Chayes.
Since then some 12 working groups have been set up in
various parts of the world to contribute data to the file.
Eventually, IGBA will supercede the other three files
both in number of analyses and in the type of information
recorded.

The uses to which these files can be put is almost
limitless and many examples of their application can be
cited from the literature. However, their most important
contribution to date probably is in the area of the
classification of igneous rocks (Chayes, 1976, 1979; Le
Maitre, 1976a, 1976b, 1976c; Streckeisen and Le Maitre,
1979) where work is in progress to aid the IUGS Subcom-
mission on Systematics in Igneous Petrology.

PETROLOGICAL MIXING MODELS

The least-squares fitting of compositional data
(usually termed mixing models) was applied first a decade
ago and is one of the few statistical methods to have
achieved wide acceptance and use amongst petrologists.
The method has been described many times elsewhere
(Bryan, 1969; Bryan, Finger, and Chayes, 1969a, 1969b;
Wright and Doherty, 1970; Albarede and Provost, 1977;
Stormer and Nicholls, 1978) so will not be repeated here.
Minor differences in method have arisen, one of which is
the choice of whether to constrain the estimated proportions to sum to unity, or to leave them unconstrained.
Recently, the geometric interpretation of the differences
between the two methods has indicated that, for compositional data with a constant sum, it is more logical to
constrain the proportions to sum to unity (Le Maitre,
1979). This geometric approach also has led to a generalized mixing model that can be applied to metamorphic
reactions of the type:

$$A + B + C \ldots = D + E + F + G \ldots$$

When the proportions on both sides of the equation are constrained to sum to unity, the problem is simply to locate the points of closest approach of two hyperplanes in n-dimensional composition space, one passing through compositions A, B, C, etc., and the other passing through compositions D, E, F, G, etc. The residual sum of squares then is the square of the shortest distance between the two hyperplanes. Prior to this such reactions had to be solved by proposing a model of the type:

$$A = B + C \ldots + D + E + F + G \ldots$$

and hoping that the proportions of B, C, etc. come out negative. However, such a solution, although giving proportions that are of the right order of magnitude, gives residual sums of squares that can be misleading. Used on actual analytical data, this generalized mixing model showed that the metamorphic reaction

Biotite + sillimanite + quartz = garnet + K-feldspar + water

is far from isochemical (Le Maitre, 1979).

PRINCIPAL-COMPONENTS ANALYSIS, FACTOR ANALYSIS, AND DISCRIMINANT ANALYSIS

Although not used as extensively as the mixing modles, these three techniques have become increasingly popular in the last decade. Considerable confusion exists in the literature about the difference between principal-components analysis and factor analysis with many authors considering principal-components analysis to be a part of factor analysis (Joreskog, Klovan, and Reyment, 1976). However, I, like many statisticians, consider principal-components analysis to be a method in its own right and distinct from true factor analysis. Thus, many papers using what is described as factor analysis only are using principal-components analysis.

One of the reasons for using principal-components analysis is to produce an optimal visual representation of complex multivariate data, by projecting the original data into the space of the first few eigenvectors. Fortunately, for most petrological systems, the first three eigenvalues derived from the variance-covariance matrix usually account for over 90 percent of the total variance, so that excellent projections can be produced (Le Maitre, 1968). There remains, however, a choice of whether to extract the eigenvectors and eigenvalues from the variance-covariance or the correlation matrix. In the latter situation, all the variables are scaled to have equal variance and, therefore, are given equal weight so that, for example, a change of 0.2 percent in MnO may be given as much importance as a change of 20 percent in MgO. Although this may be acceptable for variables measured in different units (for which this method of scaling was intended originally, there seems to be little justification for scaling of this type with major element data. There would seem to be some justification in using the correlation matrix if the variables are mixed major and trace elements (i.e. wt% and ppm), but as they are measured basically in the same type of unit (i.e. weight per unit weight), a more logical approach would be to convert all the values to wt% or ppm and to take logarithms. In this manner a major element that doubled in value would be given the same weight as a trace element that doubled in value.

A pitfall that some authors seem to have fallen into (e.g. Till and Colley, 1973; Saxena and Walter, 1974) is to use the correlation matrix to determine the eigenvectors and then to form the cross-product sum of the *raw* data and the eigenvectors in order to produce the plots. Processed in this manner, however, the data are not projected onto the eigenvectors (which is the object of the exercise) but are projected onto a set of axes which are rotated with respect to the original eigenvectors. The correct procedure is to form the cross-product sum of the *standardized* data and the eigenvectors.

Factor analysis has been used successfully by many authors to investigate the chemical variation within mineral and rock groups (e.g. Middleton, 1964; Mottana, Sutterlin, and May, 1971; Shaw, 1974), but the previous comments regarding the disadvantage of using a correlation matrix (the starting point for most factor-analysis procedures) yet apply. More recently, Miesch (1976) used factor analysis in a novel manner as an alternative to conventional mixing models and has achieved similar results.

Because of some of the earlier examples of discriminant analysis (Chayes, 1964, 1968; Le Maitre, 1968), the

method has been accepted generally but has not been used
as widely as it should have been, as many examples can be
cited in the literature of groups being separated on a
variety of simple scatter diagrams, usually constructed
around some preconveived idea. Whether these diagrams
are the only or best way of distinguishing the groups,
seems to be of little interest to the authors. Most
examples of the use of discriminant analysis continue to
be two group examples (e.g. Chayes, 1975) although a few
examples of multiple discriminant analyses also have been
published (Gleadow and others, 1974; Le Maitre, 1978).
The generalization of the classical two group discriminant analysis into multiple discriminant analysis, where
more than two groups are involved, has the advantage that
scatter diagrams can be produced showing the clustering
of the groups in question. Although potentially useful
for delimiting rock types from each other, the general
use of discriminant analysis for classification purposes,
unfortunately, has some disadvantages as pointed out by
Le Maitre (1976c).

MODELING IGNEOUS DIFFERENTIATION TRENDS

The main difficulty with modeling differentiation
trends, given a starting composition, is the problem of
deciding what phases will crystallize from a particular
liquid composition. Theoretically, this problem can be
solved using thermodynamics, but unfortunately the required constants have not been determined yet. Taimre
(1977) successfully modeled crystallization within the
simple system Di-An-Fo using thermodynamic principles
with constants determined empirically from experimental
data. A slightly different method is used by Nathan and
van Kirk (1978) in presenting a generalized model of magmatic crystallization of dry melts at 1 atmosphere pressure. By assuming that the crystallization temperature
of each phase is a smooth function of the composition of
the liquid, they use experimental data and multiple regression to determine the constants of these "mineral
temperature equations". Only two of the "variables" in
these equations, however, are based on "thermodynamics",
the remainder being oxide fractions. With this method
they successfully reproduce the trends of several natural
rock series and the further extension of similar equations
to anhydrous melts under pressure (to simulate plutonic
conditions) is only a matter of awaiting relevant experimental results.

Another rather different approach, based on Rayleigh's Law of fractional crystallization, is used by
Maaløe (1976) to determine the compositional trends within
the simple Ab-An and Ab-An-Di systems. Presenting the solutions of the differential equations graphically, he demonstrates, for example, that with certain starting compositions, marked differences in trends may be expected
depending upon whether perfect or partial fractional
crystallization is involved. Similarly, by applying the
same principles, Allegre and others (1977) and Minster
and others (1977) further develop the theory to explain
the behavior of trace elements during igneous processes
with the object of deducing the main features of the differentiation process, including the initial liquid composition and the phases involved, given a suitable set of
trace-element determinations on the suite of rocks. In
this approach the differentiation trend is defined, and
the possible mechanism of differentiation, which, of
course, is the inverse of the previous applications.

REFERENCES

Albarede, F., and Provost, A., 1977, Petrological and
    geochemical mass-balance equations: an algorithm
    for least-squares fitting and general error analysis:
    Computers & Geosciences, v. 3, no. 2, p. 309-326.

Allegre, C.J., Treuil, M., Minster, J.F., Minster, B.,
    and Albarede, F., 1977, Systematic use of trace ele-
    ments in igneous process. Part 1: Fractional crys-
    tallisation processes in volcanic suites: Contrib.
    Mineral. Petrol., v. 60, no. 1, p. 57-75.

Barr, D.L., Mutschler, F.E., and Lavin, O.P., 1977,
    KEYBAM: a system of interactive computer programs
    for use with the PETROS petrochemical data bank:
    Computers & Geosciences, v. 3, no. 3, p. 489-496.

Bryan, W.B., 1969, Materials balance in igneous rock
    suites: Ann. Rept. Dir. Geophys. Lab. Carnegie Inst.
    Washington, v. 67, p. 241-243.

Bryan, W.B., Finger, L.W., and Chayes, F., 1969a, A least-
    squares approximation for estimating the composition
    of a mixture: Ann. Rept. Dir. Geophys. Lab. Carne-
    gie Inst. Washington, v. 67, p. 243-244.

Bryan, W.B., Finger, L.W., and Chayes, F., 1969b, Estima-
    ting proportions in petrographic mixing equations

by least-squares approximation: Science, v. 163, no. 3870, p. 926-927.

Chayes, F., 1964, A petrographic distinction between Cenozoic volcanics in and around the open oceans: Jour. Geophys. Res., v. 69, no. 8, p. 1573-1588.

Chayes, F., 1968, On locating field boundaries in simple phase diagrams by means of discriminant functions: Am. Mineral., v. 53, nos. 3 and 4, p. 359-371.

Chayes, F., 1971, Electronic storage, retrieval, and re- duction of data about the chemical composition of common rock: Ann. Rept. Dir. Geophys. Lab. Carnegie Inst. Washington, v. 70, p. 197-201.

Chayes, F., 1975, On distinguishing alkaline from other basalts: Ann. Rept. Dir. Geophys. Lab. Carnegie Inst. Washington, v. 74, p. 546-547.

Chayes, F., 1976, Characterizing the consistency of cur- rent usage of rock names by means of discriminant functions: Ann. Rept. Dir. Geophys. Lab. Carnegie Inst. Washington, v. 75, p. 782-784.

Chayes, F., 1979, Partitioning by discriminant analysis: a measure of consistency in the nomenclature and classification of volcanic rocks, *in* The evolution of igneous rocks: Princeton Univ. Press, Princeton, New Jersey, p. 521-532.

Chayes, F., and Le Maitre, R.W., 1972, The number of pub- lished analyses of igneous rocks: Ann. Rept. Dir. Geophys. Lab. Carnegie Inst. Washington, v. 71, p. 493-495.

Gleadow, A.J.W., Le Maitre, R.W., Sewell, D.K.B., and Lovering, J.F., 1974, Chemical discrimination of petrographically defined clast groups in Apollo 14 and 15 lunar breccias: Chem. Geology, v. 14, no. 1, p. 39-61.

Joreskog, K.G., Klovan, J.E., and Reyment, R.A., 1976, Geological factor analysis, *in* Methods in Geomath- ematics 1: Elsevier Sci. Publ. Co., Amsterdam, 178 p.

Le Maitre, R.W., 1968, Chemical variation within and be- tween volcanic rock series - a statistical approach: Jour. Petrology, v. 9, no. 2, p. 220-252.

Le Maitre, R.W., 1973, Experiences with CLAIR: a compu-
    terised library of analysed igneous rocks: Chem.
    Geology, v. 12, no. 4, p. 301-308.

Le Maitre, R.W., 1976a, Chemical variability of some com-
    mon igneous rocks: Jour. Petrology, v. 17, no. 4,
    p. 589-637.

Le Maitre, R.W., 1976b, Some problems of the projection
    of chemical data into mineralogical classifications:
    Contrib. Mineral. Petrol. v. 56, no. 2, p. 181-189.

Le Maitre, R.W., 1976c, A new approach to the classifica-
    tion of igneous rocks using the basalt-andesite-
    dacite-rhyolite suite as an example: Contrib.
    Mineral. Petrol. v. 56, no. 2, p. 191-203.

Le Maitre, R.W., 1978, Numerical petrology: Trans. Lei-
    cester Lit. Phil. Soc., v. 72, in press.

Le Maitre, R.W., 1979, A new generalised petrological
    mixing model: Contrib. Mineral. Petrol. v. 71, no.
    2, p. 133-137.

Le Maitre, R.W., and Ferguson, A.K., 1978, The CLAIR data
    system: Computers & Geosciences, v. 4, no. 1, p.
    65-76.

Maaloe, S., 1976, Quantitative aspects of fractional crys-
    tallisation of major elements: Jour. Geology, v.
    84, no. 1, p. 81-96.

Middleton, G.V., 1964, Statistical studies on scapolites:
    Can. Jour. Earth Sci., v. 1, no. 1, p. 23-34

Miesch, A.T., 1976, Q-mode factor analysis of geochemical
    and petrologic data matrices with constant row-sums:
    U.S. Geol. Survey Prof. Paper 574-G, p. 1-47.

Minster, J.F., Minster, J.B., Treuil, M., and Allegre,
    C.J., 1977, Systematic use of trace elements in ig-
    neous processes: Part II. Inverse problem the frac-
    tional crystallisation process in volcanic suites:
    Contrib. Mineral. Petrol., v. 61, no. 1, p. 49-77.

Mottana, A., Sutterlin, P.G., and May, R.W., 1971, Factor
    analysis of garnets and omphacites: a contribution
    to the geochemical classification of eclogites:
    Contrib. Mineral. Petrol. v. 31, no. 3, p. 238-250.

Mutschler, F.E., Rougon, D.J., and Lavin, O.P., 1976,
    PETROS - a data bank of major-element chemical
    analyses of igneous rocks for research and teaching:
    Computers & Geosciences, v. 2, no. 1, p. 51-57.

Mutschler, F.E., Rougon, D.J., Lavin, O.P., and Hughes,
    R.D., 1978, PETROS a data bank of major element
    chemical analyses of igneous rocks: U.S. Dept. Com-
    merce, Nat. Oceanic Atmos. Admin., Envir. Data Serv.,
    Pamphlet 1978(W), 4 p.

Nathan, H.D., and Van Kirk, C.K., 1978, A model of magma-
    tic crystallisation: Jour. Petrology, v. 19, no. 1,
    p. 66-94.

Saxena, S.K., and Walter, L.S., 1974, A statistical-chem-
    ical and thermodynamic approach to the study of lunar
    mineralogy: Geochim. Cosmochim. Acta, v. 38, no. 1,
    p. 79-95.

Shaw, D.M., 1974, R-mode factor analysis on enstatite
    chondrite analyses: Geochim. Cosmochim. Acta, v.
    38, no. 10, p. 1607-1613.

Stormer, J.C., and Nicholls, J., 1978, XLFRAC: a program
    for the interactive testing of magmatic differentia-
    tion models: Computers & Geosciences, v. 4, no. 2,
    p. 143-159.

Streckeisen, A., and Le Maitre, R.W., 1979, A chemical
    approximation to the modal OAPF classification of the
    the igneous rocks: Neues Jahrb. Mineral. Abh. Band
    136, Heft 2, p. 169-206.

Taimre, T., 1977, Theoretical modelling of liquidus rela-
    tion in silicate systems: unpubl. honours project,
    Univ. Melbourne, 132 p.

Till, R., and Colley, H., 1973, Thoughts on the use of
    principal component analysis in petrogenetic prob-
    lems: Jour. Math. Geology, v. 5, no. 4, p. 341-350.

Wright, T.L., and Doherty, P.C., 1970, A linear program-
    ming and least squares computer method for solving
    petrologic mixing problems: Geol. Soc. America
    Bull., v. 81, no. 7, p. 1995-2008.

STRATIGRAPHIC ANALYSIS: DECADES OF REVOLUTION (1970-1979) AND REFINEMENT (1980-1989)

C. John Mann

University of Illinois

ABSTRACT

Significant progress in stratigraphic analysis has occurred during the 70s in several areas of stratigraphy. Multiband seismic data systems with greater resolution of detail have revolutionized our ability to interpret sub-surface stratigraphic units, distributions, lithologies, physical properties, and contained fluids. For the first time, we are able to predict and map with reasonable accuracy what subsurface stratigraphic sequences will be encountered in poorly explored sedimentary basins.

Progress has occurred in development of quantitative stratigraphic correlation methods ranging from probablistic approaches in biostratigraphy to Fourier analyses in lithostratigraphy. Automated analyses of electrical-geophysical logs from boreholes have improved geological interpretations regarding strata. Multivariate approaches have enhanced our paleoenvironmental and paleoecological interpretations of earth's history. Advances in data representation, mapping methods, geographic analysis, and understanding of trend surfaces have resulted in improved regional stratigraphic analyses and interpretations. Interactive computer technology has permitted the stratigrapher to determine more quickly alternative methods of data display and analysis which leads to better understanding of relations and more rapid solution of problems. All of these advances have been accompanied by, and partially are, a result of improved stratigraphic data bases

and information banks. Finally, the first significant
step toward a more rigorous, theoretical stratigraphy
occurred during the past decade with application of set
theory principles to stratigraphic terminology, definitions, and concepts.

The next ten years predictably will give us improved
and greater usage of existing quantitative methodologies.
Better methods of displaying and depicting stratigraphic
data, relationships, and interpretations will arise
through greater use of three-dimensional displays, color
coding, and improved resolution of output. Better data
bases will provide broader coverage and permit more comprehensive analyses; nonetheless, much progress will remain to be accomplished because the final availability
of all stratigraphic data in computer data banks seemingly is more distant than one decade. Similarly, data
standardization will be greater but, unfortunately, probably will not be universal. Better stratigraphic analyses will result from more sophisticated applications of
existing techniques to multiple data sets. All of this
will become available more readily to geologists by development and marketing of smaller, cheaper, and faster
computers having multiple processors and larger memories.
More field usage of computers by geologists during the
next ten years can be anticipated.

No methodological revolutions can be foreseen for
the next decade; only improved usage of existing methodologies is predictable. This does not indicate that
sudden advances will not occur, for who would have predicted ten years ago that seismic technology would revo-
lutionize subsurface stratigraphy in less than a decade?
One can say only that no revolutionary methodology or
technology has been recognized to be lurking in our world,
ready to surge forth in the 80s to alter some aspect of
stratigraphic analysis as did occur in the 70s.

INTRODUCTION

The 70s were an active and interesting decade in
stratigraphic analysis. With increasing availability
generally of larger computers and increasing appreciation by geologists of benefits to be derived from computers, greater application of computers to the solution
of stratigraphic problems was made. Both were major
factors in seismic stratigraphy and quantitative stratigraphic correlation, two areas which advanced most

significantly during this interval.

This review attempts to identify areas of major progress, trends, and growth in stratigraphy during the 70s.
The bibliography is not exhaustive but hopefully it is
comprehensive in areas of major quantification. Continued use and numerous papers in applications of older
methods generally have not been noted individually.
This does not indicate that these contributions are being ignored nor does it imply that they have been unim-
portant because obviously they are when applications have
been frequent.

SEISMIC STRATIGRAPHY

Undoubtedly the most significant change and advance
in stratigraphy during the past decade has been the rapid
development of seismic stratigraphy. This has been made
possible primarily through more complete integration of
theory with practice in seismic exploration and data enhancement by digital computer (Payton, 1977). Seismic
stratigraphic interpretations are possible now because
resolution of seismic data has been increased and de-
structive signals have been reduced. Although some improvement in seismic data has been a result of improved
seismic equipment, new and improved techniques, and
electronic filtering of seismic signals, the vast major-
ity of improvement has arisen through digital enhancement
of raw data by various computer correction programs
(Dobrin, 1975; Flowers, 1976; Sheriff, 1977).

A basic general improvement in seismic data comes
about merely by repositioning the data to reflect more
accurately subsurface geology in spatially correct relations (Flowers, 1976; Sheriff, 1977). These migrations
are removal of horizontal components of seismic-wave
travel paths which may have significant effects even in
flat-lying strata. Although migration of seismic signals
had been a recognized improvement for seismic data for
sometime, extensive computations necessary to make them
routinely has been prohibitive until recently, about
1969, when larger and more economical computational facilities became available. More recently, three-dimensional migrations have become possible whenever gridded
seismic data are available.

Useless signals in seismic data such as random noise
and reflective multiples have been reduced by a variety

of techniques and computational corrections (Sheriff,
1977). Static correction programs may eliminate differences arising in the vicinity of seismic sources and
geophones at earth's surface. Signature-processing remedies and employment of sources of known signal input
eliminate much noise originating from seismic sources.
Divergence corrections can remove many differences created by subsurface strata. Velocity filtering (common-
depth point stacking) and redundancy recording procedures
permit attenuation of many types of coherent wavetrains
and random noise. Predictive deconvolution and common-
depth point stacking reduce undesirable multiples. Deconvolution helps remove near-surface reverberation noise
and broadens the frequency spectrum to improve or sharpen
seismic wavelets. Wave-equation migration clarifies
stratigraphic evidence arising from dipping strata even
if bedding generally is flat.

Seismic resolution is a function primarily of signal
wavelength that is reflected from subsurface interfaces
(Sheriff, 1977). Generally, the greatest vertical resolution of events or features will be 1/8 to 1/4 the
wavelength and greatest horizontal resolution will be
proportional to the square root of the product of wavelength and depth to interface. Wavelengths normally increase with depth because velocity increases downward
generally and frequency diminishes with depth; therefore
resolution normally decreases with increasing depth.
Because

wavelength = velocity · period = velocity/frequency

and velocity is a function of geologic material and
depth, the only manner that seismic resolution can be
controlled is by altering input frequency and by recording a wide band of frequencies on signal return. Larger
frequencies give greater resolution than do smaller frequencies. Previously most high frequencies were neither
recorded nor retained in processing seismic data. Today,
deliberate procedures are undertaken to generate, record,
and retain during processing a broad band of frequencies.
Nonetheless, earth attenuates higher frequencies
(Sheriff, 1976; Dobrin, 1977) and enhanced resolution
solely by generation of higher input frequencies is
limited. Resolution also is improved by data enhancement, such as zero-phase wavelet extraction, analysis
of amplitudes, and noise reduction (Dobrin, 1977).

   Mathematical modeling (Flowers, 1976; Sheriff, 1976,
1977; Meckel and Nath, 1977; Schramm, Dedman, and Lindsey,
1977; Neidell and Poggiagliolmi, 1977; Farr, 1979; Ruotsala, 1979; Rice, Bakker, and Weinberg, 1979) also is
introduced to improve seismic interpretations of stratigraphy. Many useless signals arise in near-surface geology which generally is well known and can be modeled
effectively in order to reduce these unwanted signals in
seismic data. Synthetic seismograms constructed from
well data are effective in identifying interfaces from
which reflections are arising. Synthetic stratigraphic
columns or pseudologs constructed from seismic data are
helpful in predicting lithologies and bed geometries in
lesser known subsurface areas and detection of possible
stratigraphic traps. All these modeling procedures are
directed toward correcting, refining, and defining more
precisely subsurface geology from raw seismic data.

   Additional improvements in seismic data interpretations have been realized by considering seismic signals
to be a component of a complex signal (Bracewell, 1965;
Farnback, 1975; Taner and Sheriff, 1977; Taner, Koehler,
and Sheriff, 1978). This transformation allows seismic
signals to be examined from a local significance standpoint thereby providing insights that previously were
not available for geologic interpretations. These transformations are comparable to Fourier transformations
which have long been used in time-series and seismic
analyses but which conversely provide an averaged value
for a large portion of the signal trace for various wave
properties. The real portion of a complex signal is
that portion which is recorded by geophones whereas the
imaginary or quadrature portion is not recorded; both
real and imaginary traces are identical except for a 90°
phase shift.

   As a result of complex trace analysis, attributes
may be defined which give point values and which when
incorporated with normal seismic amplitude sections permit enhanced interpretations.

   Reflection strength or amplitude of the complex
   trace is independent of phase and is a function
   of interface reflection quality. Good reflection
   strength is associated with major lithic changes
   and gas accumulations. Constancy indicates a
   single reflecting horizon or persistent composite
   reflectors. It forms a good reference for time-
   interval measurements in seismic stratigraphy

and clearly reveals differential compaction, local
or regional thinning, facies changes, and velocity
variations. Local sharp changes of reflection
strength may be indicative of faulting, hydrocarbon accumulations (bright spots), and rapid
facies changes.

Instantaneous phase of the complex signal emphasizes continuity of subsurface events. It is
good for recognizing pinchouts, angularities in
deposition or structure, discontinuities, faults,
prograding sediments, and offlap.

Instantaneous frequency, the time derivative of
instantaneous phase, is helpful in recognizing
pinchouts and edges of hydrocarbon-water interfaces. Low-frequency shadows may develop in
strata below gas, condensate, and oil accumulations. Shadows also may occur below fracture
zones in brittle rocks. Usually frequency is
smoothed through some finite interval by moving
windows so that an *averaged weighted frequency*
actually is used rather than instantaneous frequency.

Apparent polarity is the sign of the seismic
trace when reflection strength has a maximum
value. It is sensitive to data quality and may
distinguish between different types of bright
spots.

Attributes aid significantly in stratigraphic interpretation of normal seismic amplitude sections.

A final contribution of improved seismic data enhancement during the past decade has been the effective
use of color to convey complex types of multiple data to
geological and geophysical interpreters of attributes for
standard amplitude traces (Balch, 1971). Colors aid more
accurate assimilation and digestion of seismic data by
adding effectively another dimension; color results in
better comprehension and geologic translations. Normally,
attribute values are zoned arbitrarily and coded numerically in computer output so that a user may assign any
color he wishes to various interval values. Colors normally are superimposed over conventional migrated, enhanced seismic amplitude displays.

Seismic stratigraphy originally was concerned only with improved depiction of subsurface geology to identify more accurately and faithfully possible traps of hydrocarbons. However, with increased seismic resolution and complex trace analysis, not only have stratigraphic relations become clearer in the subsurface but lithologies, facies changes, porosities, and fluid content of strata usually can be recognized. Discordances reveal erosional surfaces and depositional cycles. Coupling this knowledge with simple depositional configurations (Vail, Mitchum, and Thompson, 1977) and an assumption that persistently strong regional reflective interfaces are approximate time horizons, extensive inferences may be made concerning depositional histories, marine transgressions and regressions, structural movements, and geologic history of large regions which because of a lack of subsurface drilling exploration previously were unknown geologically. Seismic data from continental shelves have been interpreted in terms of relative sea-level fluctuations (Vail, Mitchum, and Thompson, 1977; Vail and Mitchum, 1979).

Continued improvements in seismic stratigraphy in the future may be expected and correspondingly will increase probabilities of detection of petroleum accumulations in stratigraphic traps by seismic methods. With ever increasing scarcity of hydrocarbons, more and more petroleum effort will be directed toward discovery of stratigraphic accumulations that are independent of geologic structures. Because stratigraphic accumulations remain our last great hope for significant quantities of undiscovered reserves in earth's crust, seismic stratigraphy will play an increasingly important role in the world's economic future.

QUANTITATIVE STRATIGRAPHIC CORRELATION

Considerable progress has been realized during the past decade in efforts to correlate automatically stratigraphic sequences, either biostratigraphically or lithostratigraphically, by computer from data files. Although a fully operational system yet is to be established, numerous methods have been proposed and demonstrated to be capable of quantitative correlations in certain situations. But so far, all have limitations and none has been demonstrated to be general and adequate for handling all situations.

These methods have ranged in biostratigraphy from
two-dimensional graphic approximations (Miller, 1977;
Edwards, 1978) through seriation (Scott, 1974; Davaud
and Geux, 1978) and multivariate analyses of various
types (Hazel, 1970, 1977; Hohn, 1978) to probabilistic
approaches (Hay, 1972; Southam, Hay, and Worsley, 1975;
Rubel, 1976; Worsley and Jorgens, 1977; Edwards and Beaver, 1978). In lithostratigraphy, methods have ranged
from successive pairwise point comparisons (Dienes, 1974a)
through graphic procedures (Leont'ev, 1972; Kemp, 1977;
Shaw, 1978), assumed sedimentation rates (Dienes, 1974a),
slotting (Gordon and Reyment, 1979), cross correlation
(Rudman and Lankston, 1973), zonation (Hawkins and Merriam, 1973, 1974; Webster, 1973; Shaw, 1978; Shaw and
Cubitt, 1979) and pattern recognition (Vincent, Gartner,
and Attali, 1979) to Fourier analysis (Dowell, 1972;
Henderson, 1973; Rudman, Blakely, and Henderson, 1975;
Mann and Dowell, 1978).

Efforts of a great number of workers were coordi-
nated with some modest organization in 1977 when, Quantitative Stratigraphic Correlation, Project 148 of the
International Geological Correlation Program was established. The first meeting and organization of Project
148 was held at Syracuse University during the 6th Geochautauqua when a one-half day session was devoted to
quantitative correlation (Computers & Geosciences, v. 4,
no. 3). The first international meeting and report was
held last year in Jerusalem in connection with the International Sedimentological Association. Numerous national
meetings have been held locally in the past two years.
One technical session is planned for the International
Geological Congress in Paris to report on advances and
accomplishments of Project 148.

                          PROBABILITIES

Applications of probabilities in stratigraphic analyses were more evident during the 70s than previously.
Probabilistic stratigraphy of Hay (1972) and subsequent
workers (Hay and Steinmetz, 1973; Worsley and others,
1973; Southam, Hay, and Worsley, 1975; Rubel, 1976; Edwards and Beaver, 1978) has been a major contribution
to ordering and evaluating dependability of biostratigraphic data. Originally, the probablistic approach was a
simple application of binomial probability density functions to the practical problems of determining the biostratigraphic value of numerous microfaunal forms

encountered in deep-sea drilling data. By assuming that
no two biostratigraphic events occurred simultaneously,
pairwise comparisons of biostratigraphic events can be
made and probabilities of their ordering being a random
occurrence can be calculated. A matrix of probabilities
then may be ordered to establish the most likely sequence
of events. Recent work (Edwards and Beaver, 1978) has
generalized this approach to a trinomial probability density function which recognizes synchroneity of events as
well as earlier than and later than occurrences. Probabilistic stratigraphy also forms an important approach
to biostratigraphic correlation (Hay, 1974; Hay and
Southam, 1978).

     Probabilities were utilized by McCammon (1970; Har-
ris and McCammon, 1971) to estimate lithic components in
stratigraphic sequences with simultaneous evaluation of
sonic, density, and neutron logs. A probabilistic approach is necessary whenever the number of lithologies
in a sequence exceeds the number of response equations
available for their prediction. The method involves determining a relative entropy function because a maximum
entropy estimate is the least biased solution for estimating lithologic components under uncertainty. An example by McCammon (1972), demonstrates that the probabilistic approach is consistent with actual stratigraphic
sequences.

     A probabilistic method of paleobiogeographic analysis
was employed by Henderson and Heron (1977) in a study of
Cretaceous ammonites. Inadequacies of existing binary
coefficients in paleobiogeography analyses are replaced
by a new technique which relates number of shared taxa
to sample size and inferred population size for areas.
The probability frequency function proposed assumes random selection of taxanomic samples in the stratigraphic
record and provides a quantitative assessment of population diversity and error estimates.

     Probabilities also are being employed increasingly
in petroleum exploration (Harbaugh, Doveton, and Davis,
1977; Harbaugh, 1979) in both evaluation of geologic,
stratigraphic, and economic questions and in decision-
making processes. Undoubtedly this trend in stratigraphic analyses will continue.

STOCHASTIC-PROCESS MODELS

Applications of random-process models in stratigraphic studies have increased slowly during the past ten years. Markovian chains, matrices, and transitional probabilities continue to attract many workers (Dacey and Krumbein, 1970; Schwarzacher, 1972; Miall, 1973; Ethier, 1975; Read, 1976; Hattori, 1973, 1976; Smyth and Cook, 1976). These have been used widely in sequential analyses, especially in cyclic sequences. More importantly, however, has been an increasing interest in and application of other forms of stochastic modeling for solution of geologic problems (Krumbein, 1972, 1976; Merriam, 1976). These stochastic studies have ranged in content from general aspects of stratigraphic applications (Krumbein, 1972, 1976; Schwarzacher, 1976, 1978), to specific problems (Mizutani and Hattori, 1972; Switzer, 1976), and exploratory excursions in various geologic processes (Jacod and Joathon, 1971, 1972).

STRATIGRAPHIC DATA SYSTEMS

After considerable inertia during the preceding decade, geologists began the 70s with cautious evaluations of general data systems (Robinson, 1970; Hubaux, 1972b; Burk, 1973), philosophical examinations (Dixon, 1970; Hubaux, 1970, 1972a), and practical concern such as how to formulate geologic data into digits (Morgan and McNellis, 1971; Hubaux, 1971; Conley and Hea, 1972; Greisemer and Costello, 1972). Generalized geologic data systems were developed initially (Jeffery and Gill, 1973; Cubitt, 1976) but were followed quickly by more specialized systems that dominately were oriented stratigraphically (David and Lebuis, 1976; Odell, 1976, 1977a; Shaw and Simms, 1977). A necessary subsequent development was a method to interchange data between two or more systems of dissimilar formating (Sutterlin, Jeffery, and Gill, 1977) and to utilize easily and efficiently available data files in normal geologic fashions (Burns and Remfry, 1976; Odell, 1977b; Baer, 1979; Talley, 1979).

Now at the end of the decade, we see some progress but, except for individual data systems within corporate entities, commercial groups, and governmental agencies, overall progress is disappointing. Stratigraphic data systems are limited. The task of quantification and codification of existing stratigraphic records is monumental; it requires considerable manpower, time, and

money to accomplish.   The Illinois Geological Survey is
perhaps a typical example in this regard of the data-
system situation.   Although starting in 1973 to establish
a state data system consisting of more than one quarter
million boreholes,   only 37 items of perhaps 600 total
stratigraphic and lithic items of geologic interest have
been entered into the system for about 45 percent of the
borings so far.   Additional geological data will be added
after this initial phase is completed for all wells in
about 1982.

Along with establishment of numerous localized data
systems, which are not necessarily compatible, a disappointing lack of standardization of data within data systems (Iglehart, 1979; Baer, 1979) has created additional
problems.

Although continued improvement and greater general
availability of data from data systems will occur during
the next decade, an interval longer than ten years unfortunately will be necessary probably before stratigraphic data systems are fully satisfactory to the users.

QUANTITATIVE LITHIC ANALYSIS

Commercial well-logging groups and petroleum companies have pioneered computerized reduction of electric
and geophysical log data (Konen and Helander, 1970; Poupon and others, 1970; Fertl and Hammack, 1971; Harris and
McCammon, 1971) for obvious economic reasons.   Nearly
all commercial logging companies provide routine computerized analyses for more dependable interpretations of
lithologies, porosities, permeabilities, fluid content,
and other lithic features encountered in strata pene-
trated and logged (Watt, 1977; Schlumberger, n.d.) by
various logging devices.   Computerization of log analyses
has improved lithic interpretations as well as providing
analysis which incorporates all available data.   These
computer analyses and summary logs of lithic properties
now are becoming available at the well site (Anonymous,
1975) and signal an improved and timely formation evaluation capability that is available to the wellsite geologist.

In addition to commercial investigations and systems
of lithic analyses by computer in the petroleum and mineral industries, other geological workers also are exploring methods of quantitative lithic analysis (McCammon, 1970, 1972; Ruoff, 1976; Magara, 1979) for solution

of surface and subsurface problems in stratigraphy.
These range from probabilistic approaches to simple class-
ificational procedures and interactive systems (Doveton
and Cable, 1979).

PALEOENVIRONMENTAL-PALEOECOLOGICAL ANALYSIS

Computer applications continue to contribute heavily
to paleoenvironmental and paleoecological analyses in
stratigraphy as they did during the previous decade.
Analyses during the 70s tended to use more than one form
of quantitative analysis (Feldhausen and Ali, 1976a,
1976b; Warshauser and Smosna, 1979), more sophisticated
forms of analyses (Price and Jorden, 1977; Cisne and
Rabe, 1978), and new methods (Gordon and Birks, 1974).
But largely, no significant changes or radical advances
occurred in environmental reconstructions. Increasingly,
applications were the most noteworthy aspect of computer
applications in paleoenvironmetal and paleoecological
analysis.

INTERACTIVE COMPUTER APPLICATIONS

Interactive computer applications in stratigraphy
have grown during the past decade. So far, use seemingly
resides primarily in two areas: petroleum exploration
(Jones, Johnson, and Phillips, 1976; Abry, 1979; Rice,
Bakker, and Weinberg, 1979; Doveton and Cable, 1979) and
in education (Mann, 1976a, 1976b; Raffin, 1976; Brady,
1978). Although some applications also are being made
by geological surveys in other geological areas (Miesch,
1975, p. 159; 1976, p. 181), stratigraphic applications
seemingly are limited in scope. Advantages of interactive computer programs reside in the ability of a stratigrapher to quickly review available data, to select modes
of presentation and scales, and to identify areas that
have attractive data for further exploration. Actual
programs and methods used by interactive computer applications range greatly.

SET THEORY

Applications of set theory have been made only
slowly in geology. Yet many advantages in this mathematical area seem to exist when computer manipulation of
stratigraphic data is being made. One area is stratigraphic mapping (Bouille, 1976) where graph theory

permits simple and fast digitization of unit boundaries.
Excessive data volume is reduced through gridding. From
an oriented graph composed of arcs associated with stratigraphic boundaries, other graphs may be deduced one of
which is used to structure the data and a second of which
is used to summarize geologic properties of the map.
These in turn are useful for graphic reconstructions,
correlation, and other analyses. Selective reconstructions permit great flexibility of composition by a user.

    Rubel (1976) described biostratigraphic ranges of
taxa in set-theory notation for more efficient evaluation
of biostratigraphic sequences. By using sets, rather
than probabilities, some problems of the latter are
avoided and maximum subdivision of stratigraphic sequences
is accomplished. The method intuitively is suitable for
geologists.

    Formalized statement of traditional geologic concepts
such as stratigraphic units, fossil zonations, temporal
relationships, and stratigraphic order in set-theory notation (Dienes, 1974a, 1974b, 1977; Dienes, and Mann,
1977; Mann, 1977) can facilitate computer manipulation
of stratigraphic data files for geologic correlations and
graphic presentations. More importantly, however, than
obvious advantages to be gained in computer operations is
an opportunity for greater stratigraphic generalization
and abstraction than presently is possible without the
rules and rigor of mathematical set theory. Stratigraphic prediction also will be enhanced under a more theoretical approach to stratigraphic problems and associated
uncertainties. Set theory provides the first practical
basis for a rigorous theoretical approach to stratigraphy.

                    CORRESPONDENCE ANALYSIS

    Correspondence analysis was introduced early during
the 70s (Benzercri, 1970) and was quickly applied to geologic problems (Cazes, 1970; Cazes, Solety, and Vuillaume,
1970; David and Beauchemin, 1974; David, Campigilo, and
Darling, 1974; Dagbert and David, 1974; David and Woussen,
1974; David and Dagbert, 1975; Dagbert and others, 1975;
Teil and Cheminee, 1975; David, Dagbert, and Beauchemin,
1977). Beginning with factor analysis, it is a distri-
bution-free technique which takes advantage of the dual-
ity between R- and Q-mode factor analysis. It detects
associations and oppositions existing between variables
and samples in any data set by measuring the contribution

to total variance jointly for each factor. This reduces
scaling problems between variables and samples in diagrams exhibiting relationships of variables and samples
to factors. Unlike standard R- and Q-mode analyses which
have asymmetrical transformations, scaling and weighting
procedures of correspondence analysis involve a symmetrical transformation that results in both analyses being
equivalent. Thus only one diagram is necessary to exhi-
bit relationships revealed by the analysis. Subsets of
both variables and samples are projected onto the same
set of factoral axes thereby aiding in an interpretation
of the analytical results. The validity of correspondence
analysis as a viable variation of factor analysis has
been questioned (Miesch, 1974, p. 139-140).

GRADIENT ANALYSIS

The term, gradient analysis, unfortunately is used
in at least two specific, but different ways formally in
geology. In addition to these formal meanings, gradient
analysis is used informally when gradients of any type
are being analyzed.

Gradient analysis from applications in structural
geology (Loudon, 1964, 1967; Whitten, 1966, 1968) now has
been extended to stratigraphic problems (Lahiri and Rao,
1974). Gradient analysis, in this sense, is based on
concepts of principal axis and moving averages; it reveals
the direction of dispersion in a data array. Vectorial
decomposition of spatial scalar data in multivariate situations may aid in searching for patterns in many types
of stratigraphic data and analyses. Increased uses of
gradient analysis follows directly from greater accessibility to faster and more economical computing facilities.

Gradient analysis as used more recently in paleoecologic and paleoenvironmental studies is an entirely different mode of analysis. Here percentages of taxa similarities existing at several localities form a basis for
a gradient or complex gradient of environmental variation.
Ordination of community samples provides information on
abundance and distribution of taxa which permits construction of a continuous gradient (Cisne and Rabe, 1978).
This gradient subsequently is useful in establishing co-
encorrelations in stratigraphic sequences.

TREND SURFACES

Now in its third decade of applications in geology, trend surfaces are employed in routine fashion by workers in all areas of geology who would not term themselves mathematical geologists. The geological profession as a whole has embraced enthusiastically this computer method because they appreciate its value in daily geologic operations. Trend surfaces perhaps are most uniquely geological of all computer methodologies that we use today.

Because of the importance that trend-surface analyses have in geology, considerable activity is being directed yet toward improvement and greater understanding of these methods (Whitten, 1970; Rao and Rao, 1970; Watson, 1971, 1972; Jones, 1972; Krumbein and Watson, 1972; Rao, 1975; Lahiri and Rao, 1978). New variations and techniques were initiated during the 70s in the form of extension of orthogonal polynomials to irregularly spaced data (Whitten, 1970), Z-trends (Robinson and Merriam, 1971), and spline-surfaces comparisons (Whitten and Koelling, 1973).

THREE-DIMENSIONAL ANALYSIS AND PRESENTATION

Three-dimensional presentation and analysis of stratigraphic data continues to show slow progress (Tipper, 1976, 1977). However, stratigraphic applications generally have not kept pace with three-dimensional technologies that are available to stratigraphers from other disciplines. Most significant advances perhaps have been in interactive computer technology and seismic exploration. The latter area has demonstrated conclusively beneficial aspects of three-dimensional analysis (Bone, Graebner, and Brown, 1979) but nonetheless, its increased expense may prohibit extensive utilization except for the most complex geologic situations requiring detailed studies and stratigraphic correlations. Certainly more extensive utilization of three-dimensional analyses and presentations in stratigraphy can be expected in the future.

ANTICIPATED ADVANCES DURING NEXT DECADE

Predictions of future advances are easy to make for clearly developed trends in stratigraphic analysis; they are difficult to make in those recently emerged areas which have not yet established a clear direction. Generally, all the present methodologies may be expected to grow and improve with greater usage and better understanding by workers. Better methods of displaying and depicting stratigraphic data, relationships, analytical results, and interpretations are anticipated during the eighties. These advances will ensue from greater use of three-dimensional displays, colors, and greater resolution of analytical methods.

Improved data bases will provide broader stratigraphic coverage, permit more comprehensive analyses, and allow new forms of analyses which previously have not been possible. However, data bases will remain incomplete most likely and much progress will remain to be accomplished in the following decade. Similarly, data standardization, unfortunately, also will be incomplete by the end of next decade, although this shortcoming may be circumvented in many instances. Overall, better stratigraphic analyses will result because of improvement in methodologies, more sophisticated applications of available techniques, and better data bases; in general, a refinement in analyses.

Computer applications in stratigraphy also will grow during the 80s because computers will be smaller, faster, more powerful, and cheaper for geologists to use. Multiple processors and larger memories will facilitate solution of some presently difficult geologic problems due to their complexities or sheer volume of input data required for solution. Greater field usage of computers is anticipated for the next decade. Computer displays in color will accelerate utilization of color in stratigraphic analyses.

No revolution in stratigraphic analysis comparable to seismic stratigraphy is predictable for the 80s. By nature, these type of events are difficult to predict except for moments of sheer genius or soothsayers. This does not indicate that sudden advances will not occur. It indicates merely that a revolutionary methodology or technique has not been recognized to be lying undeveloped, ready to surge forth in the 80s and radically alter some aspect of stratigraphy.

CONCLUSIONS

The 70s have been a period of rapid growth in many areas of computer application in stratigraphic analysis.

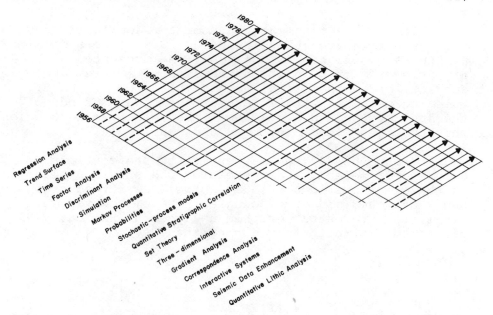

Figure 1.   Quantitative methods used in stratigraphy and
            their approximate date of introduction (after
            Krumbein, 1969).

Seismic stratigraphy has been the most impressive advancement in both total computational effort required and increased stratigraphic capability which has been given to
us.   Quantitative stratigraphic correlation has grown from
small exploratory excursions into considerations and evaluations of possible numerous and sometimes intricate and
complex procedures suitable to either biostratigraphic or
lithostratigraphic data.   Probabilistic approaches to
stratigraphy have radiated from curious examinations of
Markovian matrices and transitional probabilities of
stratigraphic sequences in the 60s into true stochastic
modeling and simple but elegant applications of probability density functions.   Applications of set theory have
been introduced in stratigraphy to handle more efficiently
various difficult stratigraphic concepts and classification problems; it also provides the first viable basis
for a theoretically rigorous stratigraphy.   New modes of
stratigraphic analyses were introduced during the 70s in
the form of correspondence analysis, gradient analysis,
and lithic analysis.   Continued growth and improvement
were seen in three-dimensional analyses and representation of stratigraphic data, interactive computer systems,
stratigraphic data files and all the older methods used
prior to 1970.

Bill Krumbein summarized computer applications in geology through the 60s (Krumbein, 1969) in a symposium at Kansas comparable to this one. He presented a three-dimensional matrix in which the axes were time, geologic subject, and mathematical method (his figs. 1 and 2). Building upon his stratigraphic level, new methods of the 70s have been added (Fig. 1) and older methodologies which he recognized have been updated.

During the 80s, we may expect to see continued growth, refinement, and increasing widespread applications of these methods in use today as well as introduction of new techniques and methodologies. None, however, are likely to alter stratigraphic analyses as radically as did seismic stratigraphy during the 70s.

REFERENCES

Abry, C.G., 1979, Interactive graphics in subsurface stratigraphic methodology (abst.): 10th Ann. APG Symp., West Virginia Geol. Survey Circ. C-15, p. 1.

Anonymous, 1975, New digital logging system improves well data accuracy: World Oil, v. 181, no. 6, p. 79-82.

Baer, C.B., 1979, Computer-compatible handling of geologic data (abst.): Am. Assoc. Petroleum Geologists Bull. v. 63, no. 3, p. 412-413.

Balch, A.H., 1971, Color sonagrams: a new dimension in seismic data interpretation: Geophysics, v. 36, no. 6, p. 1074-1098.

Benzecri, J.P., 1970, Distance distributionnelle et metrique du Chi deux en analyse factorielle des correspondances (3rd ed.): Lab Statis. Math., Fac. Sci. Univ. de Paris, 173 p.

Bone, M.R., Graebner, R.J., and Brown, A.R., 1979, Three-dimensional seismic technology (abst.): 10th Ann. APG Symp., West Virginia Geol. Survey Circ. C-15, p. 2.

Bouille, F., 1976, Graph theory and digitization of geo-
    logical maps: Jour. Math. Geology, v. 8, no. 4,
    p. 375-393.

Bracewell, R.N., 1965, The Fourier transform and its ap-
    plications: McGraw-Hill Book Co., New York, 381 p.

Brady, J.B., 1978, Symmetry: an interactive graphics
    computer program to teach symmetry recognition:
    Computers & Geosciences, v. 4, no. 2, p. 179-187.

Burk, C.F., Jr., 1973, Computer-based storage and retrie-
    val of geoscience information: Bibliography, 1970-
    1972: Geol. Sur. Canada Paper 73-14, 38 p.

Burns, K.L., and Remfry, J.G., 1976, A computer method
    of constructing geological histories from field sur-
    veys and maps: Computers & Geosciences, v. 2, no.
    2, p. 141-162.

Cazes, P., 1970, Application de l'analyse de donnees an
    traitement de problemes geologique: These de 3eme
    cycle, Fac. Sci. Univ. de Paris, 132 p.

Cazes, P., Solety, P., and Vuillaume, Y., 1970, Exemple
    de traitement statistique de donnees hydrochimiques:
    Fr. Bur. Rech. Geol. Minieres Bull. (Ser. 2), Sect.
    3, no. 4, p. 75-90.

Cisne, J.L., and Rabe, B.D., 1978, Coenocorrelation:
    gradient analysis of fossil communities and its
    applications in stratigraphy: Lethaia, v. 11, no.
    4, p. 341-364.

Conley, C.D., and Hea, J.P., 1972, A lithologic data-
    recording form for a computer-based well-data sys-
    tem: Jour. Math. Geology. v. 4, no. 1, p. 61-72.

Cubitt, J.M., 1976, An analysis and management system
    suitable for sedimentological data, *in* Merriam, D.F.,
    ed., Quantitative techniques for the analysis of
    sediments: Pergamon Press, Oxford, p. 1-9.

Dacey, M.F., and Krumbein, W.C., 1970, Markovian models
    in stratigraphic analysis: Jour. Math. Geol., v. 2,
    no. 2, p. 175-191.

230   MANN

Dagbert, M., and David, M., 1974, Pattern recognition and
     geochemical data: an application to Monteregian
     Hills: Can. Jour. Earth Sci., v. 11, no. 11, p.
     1577-1585.

Dagbert, M., Pertsowsky, R., David, M., and Perrault, G.,
     1975, Agpaicity revisited: pattern recognition in
     the chemistry of nepheline syenite rocks: Geochim.
     et Cosmochim. Acta., v. 39, no. 11, p. 1499-1504.

Davaud, E., and Geux, J., 1978, Traitement analgique
     <<manuel>> et algorithmique de problemes complexes
     de correlations biochronologiques: Eclogae Geol.
     Helvetiae, v. 71, no. 3, p. 581-610.

David, M., and Beauchemin, Y., 1974, The correspondence
     analysis method and a FORTRAN IV program: GEOCOM
     Program 10, 14 p.

David, M., Campiglio, C., and Darling, R., 1974, Progress
     in R- and Q-mode analyses: correspondence analysis
     and its application to the study of geological pro-
     cesses: Can. Jour. Earth Sci., v. 11, no. 1, p.
     131-146.

David, M., and Dagbert, M., 1975, Lakeview revisited:
     variograms and correspondence analysis. New tools
     for the understanding of geochemical data: Proc.
     Intern. Geochem. Symposium, Vancouver, p. 163-181.

David, M., Dagbert, M., and Beauchemin, Y., 1977, Statis-
     tical analysis in geology: correspondence analysis
     method: Colorado Sch. Mines Quart., v. 72, no. 1,
     60 p.

David, M., and Woussen, G., 1974, Correspondence analysis,
     a new tool for geologists: Proc. Mining Pribram,
     v. 1, p. 41-65.

David, P.P., and Lebuis, J., 1976, LEDA: a flexible co-
     dification system for computer-based files of geo-
     logical field data: Computers & Geosciences, v. 1,
     no. 4, p. 265-278.

Dienes, I., 1974a, General formulation of the correlation
     problem and its solution in two special situations:
     Jour. Math. Geology, v. 6, no. 1, p. 73-81.

Dienes, I., 1974b, Subdivision of geological bodies into
    ordered parts, *in* Mathemathika es szamitastecknika a
    nyersanyagbutatosban, Proceedings of a conference
    held at Budapest, v. 1: Hungarian Geol. Soc., p.
    138-147.

Dienes, I., 1977, Formalized stratigraphy: basic notions
    and advantages, *in* Merriam, D.F., ed., Recent ad-
    vances in geomathematics: Pergamon Press, Oxford,
    p. 81-87.

Dienes, I., and Mann, C.J., 1977, Mathematical formaliza-
    tion of stratigraphic terminology: Jour. Math.
    Geology, v. 9, no. 6, p. 587-603.

Dixon, C.J., 1970, Semantic symbols: Jour. Math. Geology,
    v. 2, no. 1, p. 81-87.

Dobrin, M.B., ed., 1975, Continuing education course on
    principles of seismic stratigraphy: Am. Assoc. Pet-
    roleum Geologists, Dallas, Texas, 87 p.

Dobrin, M.B., 1977, Seismic exploration for stratigraphic
    traps: Am. Assoc. Petroleum Geologists Mem. 26, p.
    329-351.

Doveton, J.H., and Cable, H.W., 1979, KOALA - minicomputer
    log analysis system for geologists (abst.): Am.
    Assoc. Petroleum Geologists Bull., v. 63, no. 3, p.
    441.

Dowell, T.P.L., Jr., 1972, An automated approach to sub-
    surface correlation: unpubl. master's thesis, Univ.
    Illinois, Urbana, 34 p.

Edwards, L.E., 1978, Range charts and no-space graphs:
    Computers & Geosciences, v. 4, no. 3, p. 247-255.

Edwards, L.E., and Beaver, R.J., 1978, The use of a
    paired comparison model in ordering stratigraphic
    events: Jour. Math. Geology, v. 10, no. 3, p. 261-
    272.

Ethier, V.G., 1975, Application of Markov analysis to the
    Banitt Formation (Mississippian), Alberta: Jour.
    Math. Geology, v. 7, no. 1, p. 47-61.

Farnback, J.S., 1975, The complex envelope in seismic
    signal analysis: Seis. Soc. America Bull., v. 65,
    no. 4, p. 951-962.

Farr, J.B., 1979, High-resolution seismic work as tool to locate stratigraphic traps (abst.): Am. Assoc. Petroleum Geologist Bull., v. 63, no. 3, p. 448.

Feldhausen, P.H., and Ali, S.A., 1976a, Sedimentary environmental analysis of Long Island Sound, USA, with multivariate statistics, *in* Merriam, D.F., ed., Quantitative techniques for the analysis of sediments: Pergamon Press, Oxford, p. 73-98.

Feldhausen, P.H and Ali, S.A., 1976b, A multivariate statistical approach to sedimentary environmental analysis: Trans. Gulf Coast Assoc. Geol. Soc., v. 24, p. 314-320.

Fertl, W.H., and Hammack, G.W., 1971, A comparative look at water saturation computations in shaly pay sands: SPWLA Logging Symp.

Flowers, B.S., 1976, Overview of exploration geophysics - recent breakthrough and challenging new problems: Am. Assoc. Petroleum Geologists Bull., v. 60, no. 1, p. 3-11.

Gordon, A.D., and Birks, H.J.B., 1974, Numerical methods in Quaternary paleoecology, II. Comparison of pollen diagrams: New Phytol., v. 73, p. 221-249.

Gordon, A.D., and Reyment, R.A., 1979, Slotting of borehole sequences: Jour. Math. Geology, v. 11, no. 3, p. 309-327.

Griesemer, A.D., and Costello, D.F., 1972, An attempt at an unambiguous scheme to code the geometry of bedding planes: Jour. Math. Geology, v. 4, no. 4, p. 345-351.

Harbaugh, J.W., 1979, Computer-based oil exploration decision systems (abst.): 10th Ann. APG Symp., West Virginia Geol. Survey Circ. C-15, p. 15-16.

Harbaugh, J.W., Doveton, J.H., and Davis, J.C., 1977, Probability methods in oil exploration: John Wiley & Sons, New York, 261 p.

Harris, M.H., and McCammon, R.B., 1971, A computer-oriented generalized porosity-lithology interpretation of neutron, density and sonic logs: Jour. Petr. Tech., v. 23, no. 2, p. 239-248.

Hattori, I., 1973, Mathematical analysis to discriminate
     two types of sandstone-shale alternations: Sediment-
     ology, v. 20, no. 3, p. 331-345.

Hattori, I., 1976, Entropy in Markov chains and discrim-
     ination of cyclic patterns in lithologic successions:
     Jour. Math. Geology, v. 8, no. 4, p. 477-497.

Hawkins, D.M., and Merriam, D.F., 1973, Optimal zonation
     of digitized sequential data: Jour. Math. Geology,
     v. 5, no. 4, p. 389-395.

Hawkins, D.M., and Merriam, D.F., 1974, Zonation of mul-
     tivariate sequences of digitized geologic data:
     Jour. Math. Geology, v. 6, no. 3, p. 263-269.

Hay, W.W., 1972, Probabilistic stratigraphy: Eclogae
     Geol. Helvetiae, v. 65, no. 2, p. 255-266.

Hay, W.W., 1974, Implications of probabilistic stratigra-
     phy for chronostratigraphy: Verhandl. Naturf. Ges.
     Basel, v. 84, p. 164-171.

Hay, W.W., and Steinmetz, J.C., 1973, Probabilistic analy-
     sis of distribution of Late Paleocene - Early Eoecene
     calcareous nannofossils: Soc. Econ. Paleon. and
     Min., Calc. Nannofossil Symp., Houston, Texas, p.
     58-70.

Hay, W.W., and Southam, J.R., 1978, Quantifying biostrati-
     graphic correlation: Ann. Rev. Earth Planet. Sci.,
     v. 6, p. 353-375.

Hazel, J.E., 1970, Binary coefficients and clustering in
     biostratigraphy: Geol. Soc. America Bull., v. 81,
     no. 11, p. 3237-3252.

Hazel, J.E., 1977, Use of certain multivariate and other
     techniques in assemblage zonal biostratigraphy:
     examples utilizing Cambrian, Cretaceous, and Ter-
     tiary benthic invertebrates, in Kauffman, E.G., and
     Hazel, J.E., eds., Concepts and methods of biostrati-
     graphy: Dowden, Hutchinson & Ross, Inc., Strouds-
     burg, Pennsylvania, p. 187-212.

Henderson, G.J., 1973, Correlation and analysis of geo-
     logic time series: unpubl. doctoral dissertation,
     Univ. Indiana, Bloomington, 289 p.

Henderson, R.A., and Heron, M.L., 1977, A probabilistic
    method of paleobiogeographic analysis: Lethaia, v.
    10, no. 1, p. 1-15.

Hohn, M.E., 1978, Stratigraphic correlation by principal
    components: effects of missing data: Jour. Geology,
    v. 86, no. 4, p. 524-532.

Hubaux, A., 1970, Description of geological objects:
    Jour. Math. Geology, v. 2, no. 1, p. 89-95.

Hubaux, A., 1971, Scheme for a quick description of rocks:
    Jour. Math. Geology, v. 3, no. 3, p. 317-322.

Hubaux, A., 1972a, Dissecting geological concepts: Jour.
    Math. Geology, v. 4, no. 1, p. 77-80.

Hubaux, A., ed., 1972b, Geological data files: CODATA
    Bull., v. 8, 30 p.

Iglehart, C.F., 1979, The API well number: what is it?
    Where is it available? (abst.): 10th Ann. APG
    Symp., West Virginia Geol. Sur., Circ. C-15, p. 18-
    19.

Jacod, J., and Joathon, P., 1971, Use of random-genetic
    models in the study of sedimentary processes: Jour.
    Math. Geology, v. 3, no. 3, p. 265-279.

Jacod, J., and Joathon, P., 1972, Conditional simulation
    of sedimentary cycles in three dimension, *in* Merriam,
    D.F., ed., Mathematical models of sedimentary pro-
    cesses: Plenum Press, New York, p. 139-165.

Jeffery, K.G., and Gill, E.M., 1973, G-EXEC: A general-
    ized FORTRAN system for data handling: Geol. Sur.
    Canada Paper 74-63, p. 59-61.

Jones, T.A., 1972, Multiple regression with correlated
    independent variables: Jour. Math. Geology, v. 4,
    no. 3, p. 203-218.

Jones, T.A., Johnson, C.R., and Phillips, D.C., 1976,
    Interactive computer graphics and petroleum explor-
    ation (abst.): Geol. Soc. America, v. 8, p. 484-
    485.

Kemp, L.F., Jr., 1977, An algorithm for the stratigraphic
    correlation of well logs: Amoco Prod. Co., Research
    Dept. Rept. Cr 77-3, 21 p.

Konen, C.E., and Helander, D.P., 1970, A computer analysis of shaly sands using multiple porosity logging devices: The Log Analyst, v. 11, no. 1, p. 3-12.

Krumbein, W.C., 1969, The computer in geological perspective, *in* Merriam, D.F., ed., Computer applications in the earth sciences: Plenum Press, New York, p. 251-275.

Krumbein, W.C., 1972, Probabilistic models and the quantification process in geology: Geol. Soc. America Sp. Paper 146, p. 1-10.

Krumbein, W.C., 1976, Probabilistic modeling in geology, *in* Merriam, D.F., ed., Random processes in geology: Springer-Verlag, New York, p. 39-54.

Krumbein, W.C., and Watson, G.S., 1972, Effects of trends on correlation in open and closed three-component systems: Jour. Math. Geology, v. 4, no. 4, p. 317-330.

Lahiri, A., and Rao, S.V.L.N., 1974, Gradient analysis: a technique for the study of spatial variation: Modern Geology, v. 5, no. 1, p. 33-45.

Lahiri, A., and Rao, S.V.L.N., 1978, A choice between polynomial and Fourier trend surfaces: Modern Geology, v. 6, no. 3, p. 153-162.

Leont'ev, G.I., 1972, An attempt at a synchronization of old cyclically bedded sediment by the method of graphic connections: Lithology and Mineral Resources, v. 7, p. 103-113.

Loudon, T.V., 1964, Computer analysis of orientation data in structural geology: Ofc. Naval Research, Geography Branch, Tech. Rept. no. 13, ONR Task No. 339-135, 129 p.

Loudon, T.V., 1967, The use of eigenvector methods in describing surfaces: Kansas Geol. Survey Computer Contr. 12, p. 12-15.

Magara, K., 1979, Identification of sandstone body types by computer method: Jour. Math. Geology, v. 11, no. 3, p. 269-283.

Mann, C.J., 1976a, The PLATO system, its language, assets, and disadvantages: Computers & Geosciences, v. 2, no. 1, p. 41-50.

Mann, C.J., 1976b, Geology lessons on PLATO (abst.): Geol. Geol. Soc. America, v. 8, p. 492.

Mann, C.J., 1977, Toward a theoretical stratigraphy: Jour. Math. Geol., v. 9, no. 6, p. 649-652.

Mann, C.J., and Dowell, T.P.L., Jr., 1978, Quantitative lithostratigraphic correlation of subsurface sequences: Computers & Geosciences, v. 4, no. 3, p. 295-306.

McCammon, R.B., 1970, Component estimation under uncertainty, *in* Merriam, D.F., ed., Geostatistics, Plenum Press, New York, p. 45-61.

McCammon, R.B., 1972, Estimating lithologic components in stratigraphic sequences under uncertainty: Geol. Soc. America Sp. Paper 146, p. 11-24.

Meckel, L.D., Jr., and Nath, A.K., 1977, Geologic considerations for stratigraphic modelling and interpretation: Am. Assoc. Petroleum Geologists Mem. 26, p. 417-438.

Merriam, D.F., ed., 1976, Random processes in geology: Springer-Verlag, New York, 161 p.

Miall, A.D., 1973, Markov chain analysis applied to an ancient alluvial plain succession: Sedimentology, v. 20, no. 3, p. 347-364.

Miesch, A.T., 1974, Q-mode factor analysis: U.S. Geol. Survey Prof. Paper 900, p. 139-140.

Miesch, A.T., 1975, Simulation of sampling problems: U.S. Geol. Survey Prof. Paper 975, p. 158-159.

Miesch, A.T., 1976, Statistical geochemistry and petrology: U.S. Geol. Survey Prof. Paper 1000, p. 181-182.

Miller, F.X., 1977, The graphic correlation method in biostratigraphy, *in* Kauffman, E.G., and Hazel, J.E., eds., Concepts and Methods of biostratigraphy: Dowden, Hutchinson & Ross, Inc., Stroudsburg, Pennsylvania, p. 165-186.

Mizutani, S., and Hattori, I., 1972, Stochastic analysis
    of bed-thickness distribution of sediments: Jour.
    Math. Geology, v. 4, no. 2, p. 123-146.

Morgan, C.O., and McNellis, J.M., 1971, Reduction of
    lithologic-log data to numbers for use in the digital
    computer: Jour. Math. Geology. v. 3, no. 1, p. 79-
    86.

Neidell, N., and Poggiagliolmi, E., 1977, Stratigraphic
    modelling and interpretation - geophysical princi-
    ples and techniques: Am. Assoc. Petroleum Geolo-
    gists Mem. 26, p. 389-416.

Odell, J., 1976, An introduction to the LSDO2 system for
    rock description: Computers & Geosciences, v. 2,
    no. 4, p. 501-505.

Odell, J., 1977a, Description in the geological sciences
    and the lithostratigraphic description system,
    LSDO2: Geol. Mag., v. 114, no. 2, p. 81-163.

Odell, J., 1977b, LOGGER, a package which assists in the
    construction and rapid display of stratigraphic
    columns from field data: Computers & Geosciences,
    v. 3, no. 2, p. 347-379.

Payton, C.E., ed., 1977, Seismic stratigraphy - applica-
    tions to hydrocarbon exploration: Am. Assoc. Petro-
    leum Geologists Mem. 26, 516 p.

Poupon, A., Clavier, C., Dumanoir, J., Gaymard, R., and
    Misk, A., 1970, Log analysis of sand-shale se-
    quences - a systematic approach: Jour. Petr. Tech.,
    v. 22, no. 7, p. 867-881.

Price, R.J., and Jorden, P.R., 1979, A FORTRAN IV program
    for foraminiferid stratigraphic correlation and
    paleoenvironmental interpretation: Computers &
    Geosciences, v. 3, no. 4, p. 601-615.

Raffin, T.G., 1976, Oilfield, A PLATO lesson of the
    stratigraphy and economics related to oil drilling
    (abst.): Geol. Soc. America, v. 8, no. 4, p. 505.

Rao, M.S., 1975, Study of trend models: Modern Geology,
    v. 5, no. 2, p. 75-93.

238   MANN

Rao, S.V.L.N., and Rao, M.S., 1970, Geometric properties
    of hypersurfaces (trend surfaces) in three-dimen-
    sional space: Jour. Math. Geology, v. 2, no. 2, p.
    203-205.

Read, W.A., 1976, An assessment of some quantitative
    methods of comparing lithological succession data,
    in Merriam, D.F., ed., Quantitative techniques for
    the analysis of sediments: Pergamon Press, Oxford,
    p. 33-51.

Rice, G.W., Bakker, M.L., and Weinberg, D.M., 1979, Geo-
    seismic modelling - an interactive computer approach
    to stratigraphic and structural interpretation
    (abst.): Am. Assoc. Petroleum Geologists Bull.,
    v. 63, no. 3, p. 515.

Robinson, J.E., and Merriam, D.F., 1971, Z-trend maps
    for quick recognition of geologic patterns: Jour.
    Math. Geology, v. 3, no. 2, p. 171-181.

Robinson, S.C., 1970, A review of data processing in the
    earth sciences in Canada: Jour. Math. Geology, v.
    2, no. 4, p. 377-397.

Rubel, M., 1976, On biological construction of time in
    geology: Eesti NSV Tead. Akad Toim Keem Geol., v.
    25, p. 136-144.

Rudman, A.J., Blakely, R.F., and Henderson, G.J., 1975,
    Frequency domain methods of stratigraphic correla-
    tion: Offshore Tech. Conf., v. 2, p. 265-277.

Rudman, A.J., and Lankston, R.W., 1973, Stratigraphic
    correlation of well logs by computer techniques:
    Am. Assoc. Petroleum Geologists Bull., v. 57, no. 3,
    p. 577-588.

Ruoff, W.A., 1976, A technique for interpreting deposi-
    tional environments of sandstones from the SP log
    utilizing the computer: Log Analyst, v. 17, no. 4,
    p. 3-10.

Ruotsala, J.E., 1979, Seismic modelling (abst.): 10th
    Ann. APG Symp. West Virginia Geol. Survey Circ.
    C-15, p. 23-24.

Schlumberger, no date, Schlumberger engineered open hole
    services: Schlumberger, Houston, Texas, 40 p.

Schramm, M.W., Jr., Dedman, E.V., and Lindsey, J.P., 1977,
    Practical stratigraphic modelling and interpretation:
    Am. Assoc. Petroleum Geologists Mem. 26, p. 477-502.

Schwarzacher, W., 1972, The semi-Markov process as a gen-
    eral sedimentation model, *in* Merriam, D.F., ed.,
    Mathematical models of sedimentary processes: Plenum
    Press, New York, p. 247-267.

Schwarzacher, W., 1976, Stratigraphic implications of ran-
    dom sedimentation, *in* Merriam, D.F., ed., Random
    processes in geology: Springer-Verlag, New York,
    p. 96-111.

Schwarzacher, W., 1978, Mathematical geology and sediment-
    ary stratigraphy, *in* Merriam, D.F., ed., Geomathe-
    matics: past, present, and prospects: Syracuse
    Univ. Geol. Contr. 5, p. 65-71.

Scott, G.H., 1974, Essay review: stratigraphy and ser-
    iation: Newsletters of Stratigraphy, v. 3, p. 93-
    100.

Shaw, B.R., 1978, Quantitative lithostratigraphic corre-
    lation of digitized borehole-log records: Upper
    Glen Rose Formation, Northeast Texas: unpubl. doc-
    toral dissertation, Syracuse Univ., 168 p.

Shaw, B.R., and Cubitt, J.M., 1979, Stratigraphic correla-
    tion of well logs: an automated approach, *in* Gill,
    D., and Merriam, D.F., eds., Geomathematical and
    petrophysical studies in sedimentology: Pergamon
    Press, Oxford, p. 127-148.

Shaw, B.R., and Simms, R., 1977, Stratigraphic analysis
    system, SAS: Computers & Geosciences, v. 3, no. 3,
    p. 395-427.

Sheriff, R.E., 1976, Inferring stratigraphy from seismic
    data: Am. Assoc. Petroleum Geologists Bull., v. 60,
    no. 4, p. 528-542.

Sheriff, R.E., 1977, Limitations on resolution of seismic
    reflections and geologic detail derivable from them:
    Am. Assoc. Petroleum Geologists Mem. 26, p. 3-14.

Smyth, M., and Cook, A.C., 1976, Sequence in Australian
    coal seams: Jour. Math. Geology, v. 8, no. 5, p.
    529-547.

Southam, J.R., Hay, W.W., and Worsley, T.R., 1975, Quantitative formulation of reliability in stratigraphic correlation: Science, v. 188, no. 4186, p. 357-359.

Sutterlin, P.G., Jeffery, K.G., and Gill, E.M., 1977, FILEMATCH: a format for the interchange of computer-based files of structured data: Computers & Geosciences, v. 3, no. 3, p. 429-441.

Switzer, P., 1976, Applications of random process models to the description of spatial distributions of qualitative geological variables, *in* Merriam, D.F., ed., Random processes in geology: Springer-Verlag, New York, p. 124-134.

Talley, B.J., 1979, Lithology data systems - rocks to applications (abst.): Am. Assoc. Petroleum Geologists Bull., v. 63, no. 3, p. 537.

Taner, M.T., Koehler, F., and Sheriff, R.E., 1978, The computation and interpretation of seismic attributes by complex trace analysis: Seiscom Delta, Inc., Calgary, Alberta, Canada, 29 p.

Taner, M.T., and Sheriff, R.E., 1977, Application of amplitude, frequency, and other attributes to stratigraphic and hydrocarbon determinations: Am. Assoc. Petroleum Geologists Mem. 26, p. 301-327.

Teil, H., and Cheminee, J.L., 1975, Application of correspondence factor analysis to the study of major and trace elements in the Erta Ale Chain (Afar, Ethiopia): Jour. Math. Geology, v. 7, no. 1, p. 13-30.

Tipper, J.C., 1976, The study of geological objects in three dimensions by the computerized reconstruction of serial sections: Jour. Geology, v. 84, no. 4, p. 476-484.

Tipper, J.C., 1977, Three-dimensional analysis of geological forms: Jour. Geology, v. 85, no. 5, p. 591-611.

Vail, P.R., Mitchum, R.M., Jr., and Thompson, S., III, 1977, Seismic stratigraphy and global changes of sea level, part 3: relative changes of sea level from coastal onlap: Am. Assoc. Petroleum Geologists Mem. 26, p. 63-97.

Vail, P.R., and Mitchum, R.M., Jr., 1979, Global cycles
of sea-level change and their role in exploration:
Preprint for "Tenth World Petroleum Congress", September 9-14, Bucharest, Romania, 28 p.

Vincent, Ph., Gartner, J.-E., and Attali, G., 1979, An
approach to detailed dip determination using correlation by pattern recognition: Jour. Petr. Tech.,
v. 31, no. 2, p. 232-240.

Warshauser, S.M., and Smosna, R.A., 1979, Multivariate
analysis of carbonate data for paleoenvironmental
interpretation (abst.): 10th Ann. APG Symp., West
Virginia Geol. Survey Circ. C-15, p. 29.

Watson, G.S., 1971, Trend-surface analysis: Jour. Math.
Geology, v. 3, no. 3, p. 215-226.

Watson, G.S., 1972, Trend-surface analysis and spatial
correlation: Geol. Soc. America Sp. Paper 146, p.
39-46.

Watt, H.B., 1977, A complete analysis of complex and sandstone reservoirs: Dresser Atlas Tech. Memo, v. 6,
no. 1, 8 p.

Webster, R., 1973, Automatic soil-boundary location from
transect data: Jour. Math. Geology, v. 5, no. 1, p.
27-37.

Whitten, E.H.T., 1966, Sequential multivariate regression
methods and scalars in the study of fold-geometry
variability: Jour. Geology, v. 74, no. 5, pt. 2, p.
p. 744-763.

Whitten, E.H.T., 1968, FORTRAN IV CDC 6400 computer program to analyze subsurface fold geometry: Kansas
Geol. Survey Computer Contr. 25, 46 p.

Whitten, E.H.T. 1970, Orthogonal polynomial trend surfaces
for irregularly spaced data: Jour. Math. Geology,
v. 2, no. 2, p. 141-152.

Whitten, E.H.T., and Koelling, M.E.V., 1973, Spline-
surface interpolation, spatial filtering, and trend
surfaces for geological mapped variables: Jour.
Math. Geology, v. 5, no. 2, p. 111-126.

Worsley, T.R., Blechschmidt, G., Ralston, S., and Snow,
    B., 1973, Probability-based analysis of the area-time
    distribution of Oligocene calcareous nannofossils:
    Soc. Econ. Paleon. and Min., Calc. Nannofossil Symp.,
    Houston, Texas, p. 71-79.

Worsley, T.F., and Jorgens, M., 1977, Automated biostrat-
    igraphy, *in* Ramsay, A.T.S., ed., Oceanic micropal-
    eontology: Academic Press, London, p. 1201-1229.

COMPUTER METHODS FOR GEOCHEMICAL AND PETROLOGIC MIXING PROBLEMS

A.T. Miesch

U.S. Geological Survey

ABSTRACT

Mixing problems arise frequently in examinations of compositional variations in rock bodies, particularly in studies of magmatic differentiation. At one time the problems were examined graphically, but ten years ago geochemists and petrologists were shown the matrix algebra that could be used to obtain least-squares solutions. Computer programs based on the fundamental matrix operations, and variations of them, have been circulated broadly and used widely by petrologists.

More recently, it has been determined that the methods of Q-mode factor analysis, extended for treating compositional data, are well suited for all types of chemical and mineralogic mixing problems. The methods can be used not only to estimate the mixing proportions, but also to determine the number of end members required in a given problem and to aid in determination of end-member compositions. The first step is to derive a matrix of recomputed data. The recomputed data matrix can approximate closely the original data matrix even though it may be of lower rank. The rank equals the number of end members required in the mixing model. Possible end-member compositions are represented by vectors in the same space as the row vectors in the matrix of recomputed data. Various methods can be used to select end-member vectors that might represent the compositions of materials involved in the mixing process. Also,

selected compositions can be tested individually for
mathematical suitability and modified accordingly.   Interactive computer programs allow one to test geochemical hypotheses by trying various sets of end-member compositions until the derived mixing proportions are compatible with all that is known about the samples and the
geologic environment from which they were collected.

INTRODUCTION

Mixing problems are abundant in geochemistry and
petrology because most rocks have formed by processes of
mixing or unmixing. Mixing occurs, for example, when
sediments from different sources are deposited together
or when magmas incorporate foreign materials. Unmixing
occurs when minerals precipitate from aqueous solutions
or silicate melts or when constitutents are removed from
rocks by chemical or physical processes of alteration.
However, the concept of mixing can be important even
where mixing did not actually occur. Most rocks, for
example, are regarded as mixtures of minerals although
all the minerals may have crystallized in place from a
common solution with no mixing at all. Also, many minerals are regarded as mixtures of theoretical end members even though the end members actually might not
ever have existed in a pure state.

The basic mathematical model assumed in mixing problems is:

$$X_{NM} \simeq P_{Nm}C_{mM} \tag{1}$$

X_{NM} is the matrix of compositional data for M constituents in N samples of rocks, sediments, soils, or
water, and is approximated by the product of matrices
P_{Nm} and C_{mM}. Matrix P_{Nm} contains the mixing proportions
for the m end members in each of the N sam-
ples, and matrix C_{mM} contains the compositions of the m
end members. The elements of matrices X_{NM} and C_{mM}
are generally in units of percent concen-
tration and all the rows of both matrices sum to 100.
Most of the factor-analysis methods discussed here require this constant row-sum. Some of the elements in
P_{Nm} may be negative, but the m values for each of the N
rows must sum to plus one.

Ten years ago Bryan, Finger, and Chayes (1969)
showed that a least-squares solution for the P_{Nm} matrix

may be derived from:

$$P_{Nm} = X_{NM}C'_{Mm}(C_{mM}C'_{Mm})^{-1} \qquad (2)$$

and variations of this method have been proposed and used by Wright and Doherty (1970) and by Stormer and Nicholls (1978). The method allows one to estimate mixing proportions given a particular set of end-member compositions. However, depending on the end-member compositions used, the matrix derived as the product of the derived mixing proportions and the given end-member compositions may or may not approximate the matrix of original data. If it does not, either alternative end-member compositions must be used or others must be added to those used previously. The method provides no information about the number of end-member compositions required for a given problem, although it is generally known that m need be no greater than M in order to account perfectly, in a mathematical sense, for any observed data. There are a great many mixing problems in geochemistry and petrology where the C_{mM} matrix to be used in equation (2) will be obvious, as, for example when determining the proportions of albite and anorthite in a series of plagioclase specimens: or in estimating the proportions of known minerals of known composition in a suite of rock samples. However, there also are a great many problems where determination of a mathematically adequate and geologically plausible C_{mM} matrix is as much as or more of a problem than determination of P_{Nm}. In this type of situation, methods of factor analysis and vector geometry can be useful.

FACTOR ANALYSIS

The methods of Q-mode factor analysis described by Klovan and Imbrie (1971) lead to a matrix of principle components or varimax factor loadings, A_{Nm}, and a matrix of principal components or varimax factor scores, F_{mM}. Each of the N rows of the loadings matrix can be taken as m coordinates of a vector that represents the corresponding sample. Each row of the scores matrix pertains to one of the m reference axes (principal components or varimax) for the vector system. If the extended Q-mode methods (Miesch, 1976a) are used, one can use A_{Nm} and F_{mM} to derive an approximate data matrix, $\hat{X}_{NM}$. A brief description of the procedures is given in the Appendix. The column means of $\hat{X}_{NM}$ are the same as those of the actual data matrix,

X_{NM}; the principal difference between the two matrices
is that $\hat{X}_{NM}$ is of lower rank. The rank of X_{NM} is
always M if ^{NM} it consists of actual chemical ^{NM} or
mineralogic determinations. The rank of $\hat{X}_{NM}$ may be much
less than M without the two matrices ^{NM} differing
by an appreciable amount. Thus, a mixing model with
relatively few end members (m) may be derived to account
for $\hat{X}_{NM}$, whereas M end members are required to account
for ^{NM} X_{NM}. If the two matrices are substantially the
same, as ^{NM} may be the situation, the extra end members
are superfluous and may cause development of the mixing
model to be unncessarily difficult.

VECTOR REPRESENTATION OF COMPOSITIONS

The compositions represented by the vectors defined
by the rows of matrix A_{Nm} (that is, the sample vectors)
are contained in the ^{Nm} corresponding rows of matrix
$\hat{X}_{NM}$. The compositions represented by other vectors may
be determined by the following procedure. Determine
the scores for the vector from:

$$G_M = B_m F_{mM} \tag{3}$$

where B_m contains the coordinates (loadings) of the vector ^{m} with respect to either the principal components
or varimax axes represented by F_{mM}. A scale factor for
the kth set of scores then is ^{mM} derived from:

$$s_k = \frac{K - \sum_j b_j}{\sum_j (g_j(a_j - b_j))} \tag{4}$$

where K is the constant row sum in X_{NM} and $\hat{X}_{NM}$ (generally
100), g_j is an element of the score ^{NM} vector ^{NM} G_M, and
a_j and ^{j} b_j are constants used in the initial ^{M} scaling
of the ^{j} jth variable (see equation 1a of Appendix).
The composition represented by the vector then is given
by:

$$c_j = s_k g_j(a_j - b_j) + b_j \qquad 1 \geq j \geq M \tag{5}$$

On the other hand, to derive the coordinates of a
vector that best represents a given composition, the
composition is first scaled by:

$$w_j = \frac{c_j - b_j}{a_j - b_j} \qquad 1 \geq j \geq M \qquad (6)$$

where c_j is the original compositional value (in the same units as X_{NM}), w_j is the scaled value, and a_j and b_j are the same constants used to scale the original data (see equation 1a of Appendix). The scaled data then are row-normalized by:

$$y_j = w_j / (\sum_j w_j^2)^{1/2} \qquad 1 \geq j \geq M \qquad (7)$$

and the coordinates are obtained from:

$$B_m = Y_M F'_{Mm} \qquad (8)$$

where Y_M is a row-vector containing y_j. If m in equation (8) is equal to M, the sum of squares of the elements in B_m (the vector communality) will equal unity. Otherwise, the sum of squares generally will be less than unity indicating that the composition does not fit perfectly into the m-dimensional vector space. Use of the vector B_m derived with equation (8) in equation (3) followed by use of equations (4) and (5), however, will give the composition represented by the vector after it has been projected into the m-dimensional compositional system. The differences between the c_j values used in equation (6) and those later derived with equation (5) will indicate the degree of departure of the composition tested from the compositional system represented by $\hat{X}_{NM}$.

MIXING MODELS FROM THE RESULTS OF FACTOR ANALYSIS

The basic mixing model is:

$$\hat{X}_{NM} = P_{Nm} C_{mM} \qquad (9)$$

where $\hat{X}_{NM}$ is an approximation of X_{NM} and P_{Nm} and C_{mM} are as defined for equation (1). Each of the m rows of the C_{mM} matrix contains a set of c_j values from equation (5), and the elements of the P_{Nm} matrix are derived from an A_{Nm} matrix by:

$$p_{ik} = a_{ik} / (s_k \sum_k (a_{ik}/s_k)) \qquad 1 \leq i \leq N; \ 1 \leq k \leq m \quad (10)$$

where s_k is the scale factor derived from equation (4) corresponding to the kth row in C_{mM} and the kth column in A_{Nm}.

The principal task in the development of a mixing model by Q-mode factor methods consists of determining reference vectors within the vector space represented by A_{Nm} that lead to matrices of P_{Nm} and C_{mM} that are acceptable on geologic grounds. The compositions contained in C_{mM} must be those of geologic materials that were or, at least, could have been involved in the mixing process, or if the model is conceptual only, the compositions in C_{mM} must be consistent with the model's purpose. Also, the mixing proportions in P_{Nm} must be acceptable for each sample in both sign and magnitude. Once the principal-components or varimax coordinates of m reference vectors have been determined, they are used to form the matrix B_{mm}. Multiplication of the matrix A_{Nm} by the inverse of B_{mm} yields a new A_{Nm} matrix containing the coordinates of the sample vectors with respect to the new reference axes (Imbrie, 1963). Each row of matrix B_{mm} can be used in equation (3) to derive a score vector G_M. Equations (4) and (5) then are used to derive the matrix of end-member compositions, C_{mM}, and equation (10) applied to the new A_{Nm} matrix gives the mixing proportions P_{Nm}. The product of the matrices of mixing proportions and end-member compositions will equal the same matrix of $\hat{X}_{NM}$ as determined, for the corresponding value of m, from the principal components or varimax axes by the procedures outlined in the Appendix.

SEARCHING FOR END-MEMBER COMPOSITIONS

As noted previously, the principal task in the development of a geologic mixing model generally is to determine m end-member compositions that both are satisfactory mathematically and plausible geologically in view of all available geochemical and geologic data. The task is reduced considerably if the matrix $\hat{X}_{NM}$ is accepted as a satisfactory approximation of X_{NM} because, in this situation, the number of end-member compositions necessary is known and all possible end-member compositions that are suitable mathematically are represented by hypothetical vectors contained in the space defined in matrix A_{Nm}. In other words, the m end-member compositions are all linear combinations of the compositions contained in the matrix $\hat{X}_{NM}$.

The compositions represented by the vectors within the space defined by A_{Nm} change systematically across the space in all directions. Moving outward from the approximate center of the space, away from the first principal-components axis, the compositional value for some constitutent will eventually become zero and then negative. If this operation is repeated a large number of times, moving outward in various directions, the points where various constitutents turn negative will define the margin of what can be termed the positive subspace. Because negative compositional values are impossible, vectors representing possible end-member compositions occur not only witnin the space defined by A_{Nm} but within the positive subspace of A_{Nm}.

All vectors within the positive subspace of A_{Nm} represent end-member compositions that are satisfactory mathematically in the sense that any m such vectors represent nonnegative compositions and will yield P_{Nm} and C_{mM} matrices whose product equals $\hat{X}_{NM}$ exactly. Searches for a set of geologically satisfactory end members can be conducted by selecting m vectors from the positive subspace, and then examining the resultant P_{Nm} and C_{mM} matrices. If the end-member compositions contained in the rows of C_{mM} are at least similar to those of geologic materials that might have been involved in the mixing (or unmixing) process, and if the mixing proportions contained in the rows of P_{Nm} are reasonable in both sign and magnitude, the search is ended. Most of these P_{Nm} and C_{mM} matrices, however, will be objectionable on geologic grounds. In this situation, either alternative end-member vectors must be selected, or one or more of the methods discussed next may be tried.

Alternative to trying various sets of vectors, a more direct approach is to begin with compositions that one would expect, from knowledge of the geology, to have taken part in the mixing (unmixing) process. For example, if the mineral magnetite is a prominant constituent in a series of differentiated lavas, it is likely that the separation (unmixing) of magnetite contributed to the differentiation process. Equations (6) to (8) can be used to determine the coordinates of the vector within the space defined by A_{Nm} that most closely represents the composition of magnetite. If the vector

communality is less than one, the composition actually
represented by the vector then must be determined from
equations (3) to (5), and if it happens that the composition is partly negative (that is, not within the positive subspace), or if the composition is different substantially from the composition of magnetite, pure magnetite can be rejected as one of the end members for the
mixing problem. This will not indicate that magnetite
was not involved in the differentiation process, only
that magnetite did not separate independently of other
minerals. It is possible yet that magnetite separated
along with other minerals such as, for example, olivine,
plagioclase, or other iron oxides.

In many geologic environments it is to be expected
that the addition or separation of one mineral will be
accompanied by the addition or separation of one or more
others. Thus, even though the correlations among the
amounts added or separated may not be perfect, the correlated behavior of the various minerals may cause them
to have the effect of a single end member in the determination of m. It is possible to anticipate groups of
minerals that might behave in this manner in various geologic environments. For example, olivine separating from
a magma might be expected to be accompanied by small
amounts of magnetite and, perhaps, a calcic plagioclase,
and clay minerals being deposited in a stream bed generally contain minor particles of other minerals as impuri-
ties. The proportions of the various minerals in the assemblage can be estimated using computer programs that
perform iterative computations. The programs form mathematical mixtures of the various minerals in the assemblage, progressing systematically from zero to 100 percent for each mineral, and test each mixture in the same
manner used to test an individual mineral as described
in the preceeding paragraph. The mixture with the highest vector communality is taken as the most likely mixture in the total assemblage to have been involved in
the mixing process. Examples involving the assemblage
magnetite-limenite and the solid-solution series for
forsterite-fayalite are given in Miesch (1976a, fig. 10,
13, and 15). If a large number of the mixtures in the
assemblage have high vector communalities, a range of
compositions within the assemblage may have been involved
in the mixing process, and the assemblage may contain
more than a single end member for the mixing model. For
an example of this situation, involving the assemblage
hornblende-albite-anorthite-magnetite in granitic rocks,
see Miesch and Reed (1979, fig. 11 and accompanying

discussion). Another example, involving the solid-solution series albite-anorthite-orthoclase, is given in Miesch (1976a, fig. 12).

AN EXAMPLE OF THE PROCEDURES

The procedures discussed in the preceding sections will be illustrated using analyses of five orthopyroxenes from Deer, Howie, and Zussman (1963, table 2, analyses 1, 6, 10, 17, and 19). The analyses used are for SiO_2, Fe_2O_3, FeO, and MgO, and CaO, but Fe_2O_3 was recomputed and combined with FeO as is customary in many types of petrochemical calculations, and all four oxide values then were adjusted to sum to 100 percent. The adjusted analyses form the matrix of original data:

$$
X_{NM} = \begin{array}{cccc}
SiO_2 & FeO & MgO & CaO \\
59.84 & 0.38 & 39.46 & 0.32 \\
57.05 & 9.13 & 33.32 & 0.50 \\
54.25 & 18.74 & 24.29 & 2.72 \\
51.95 & 32.42 & 14.15 & 1.48 \\
48.23 & 43.11 & 7.14 & 1.52
\end{array} \qquad (11)
$$

Orthopyroxenes comprise a mineral group whose members range in composition mainly between enstatite ($MgSiO_3$) and ferrosilite ($FeSiO_3$), but small amounts of the wollastonite molecule ($CaSiO_3$) also may be present. The ideal compositions of these theoretical end members, as percents, are:

$$
C_{mM} = \begin{array}{cccc}
SiO_2 & FeO & MgO & CaO \\
59.85 & 0 & 40.15 & 0 \\
45.54 & 54.46 & 0 & 0 \\
51.72 & 0 & 0 & 48.28
\end{array}
\begin{array}{l}
\text{Enstatite} \\
\text{Ferrosilite} \quad (12) \\
\text{Wollastonite}
\end{array}
$$

Use of matrices (11) and (12) in equation (2) gives the following matrix of mixing proportions:

$$
P_{Nm} = \begin{array}{ccc}
\text{Enstatite} & \text{Ferrosilite} & \text{Wollastonite} \\
0.9854 & 0.0081 & 0.0082 \\
0.8241 & 0.1653 & 0.0069 \\
0.6010 & 0.3425 & 0.0540 \\
0.3682 & 0.6018 & 0.0401 \\
0.1772 & 0.7913 & 0.0311
\end{array} \qquad (13)
$$

And finally, multiplication of matrices (12) and (13) according to equation (9) gives the following approximation of the original data:

$$
\begin{array}{ccccc}
 & SiO_2 & FeO & MgO & CaO \\
 & 59.77 & 0.44 & 39.57 & 0.40 \\
 & 57.21 & 9.00 & 33.09 & 0.33 \\
\hat{X}_{NM} = & 54.36 & 18.65 & 24.13 & 2.61 \\
 & 51.52 & 32.78 & 14.79 & 1.94 \\
 & 48.25 & 43.10 & 7.11 & 1.50
\end{array}
\tag{14}
$$

If each of the rows of matrix P_{Nm} is divided through by the row-sum prior to the computation of $\hat{X}_{NM}$, then the rows of P_{Nm} will sum to unity and those of $\hat{X}_{NM}$ will sum to 100 as is required for a mixing model based on percentages. However, in this example the P_{Nm} and $\hat{X}_{NM}$ matrices are changed only slightly by this procedure. Comparison of the estimated matrix in (14) with the original matrix in (11) is a test of the mathematical adequacy of the mixing model.

RESULTS FROM FACTOR ANALYSIS

Methods of extended Q-mode factor analysis may be used to arrive at a mixing model similar to that contained in matrices (12) and (13), but it is not necessary that the precise end-member compositions be known beforehand. The need for a priori knowledge of the end-member compositions is no problem in treating data of the type used in this example, but is the major obstacle in many other types of geologic mixing problems.

Application of the methods described in the Appendix to the data in matrix (11), but omitting the initial scaling according to equation (1a), leads to the following coefficients of determination between corresponding columns of X_{MN} and $\hat{X}_{NM}$ derived using m = 2 to m = 4 factors:

m	SiO_2	FeO	MgO	CaO	
2	0.9876	0.9997	0.9986	0.2673	
3	0.9879	1.0000	0.9997	0.9425	(15)
4	1.0000	1.0000	1.0000	1.0000	

The coefficients for CaO point clearly to the need for 3 end members in order to account for appreciable portions

of the variances in all four oxide variables. The non-
zero eigenvalues of the cosine-theta matrix derived from
the data in matrix (11) are:

$$4.5690 \qquad 0.4300 \qquad 0.0008 \qquad 0.0002$$

These values give no clear indication that three end members are required. The estimated data matrix derived
with m = 3 is:

$$
\hat{X}_{NM} =
\begin{array}{cccc}
SiO_2 & FeO & MgO & CaO \\
59.52 & 0.48 & 39.53 & 0.46 \\
57.37 & 9.04 & 33.23 & 0.35 \\
54.60 & 18.68 & 24.16 & 2.57 \\
51.23 & 32.44 & 14.51 & 1.82 \\
48.59 & 43.14 & 6.92 & 1.34
\end{array}
\qquad (16)
$$

The matrix of principal-components scores is (first 3
rows only):

$$
F_{mM} =
\begin{array}{cccc}
SiO_2 & FeO & MgO & CaO \\
0.8643 & 0.3368 & 0.3729 & 0.0217 \\
-0.0850 & 0.8287 & -0.5527 & 0.0240 \\
0.2265 & -0.2409 & -0.3582 & 0.8731
\end{array}
\qquad (17)
$$

and the matrix of principal-components loadings is
(first 3 columns only):

$$
A_{Nm} =
\begin{array}{ccc}
PC1 & PC2 & PC3 \\
0.9287 & -0.3707 & -0.0055 \\
0.9718 & -0.2352 & -0.0116 \\
0.9989 & -0.0391 & 0.0232 \\
0.9723 & 0.2333 & 0.0029 \\
0.9048 & 0.4257 & -0.0106
\end{array}
\qquad (18)
$$

Multiplication of matrices (18) and (17) yields a product matrix with rows that can be scaled, using equations (4) and (5), to yield the estimated data matrix
in (16). Alternatively, the rows of matrix (17) can be
scaled according to equations (4) and (5), and matrix
(18) scaled by equation (10), so that the product of the
two will yield matrix (16) directly. Regardless, the
rows of matrix (18) each contain the coordinates of a
vector that represents the composition given in the corresponding row of matrix (16). Because the vector system occupies only three dimensions, it can be represented

on a stereogram as shown in Figure 1. The limits of the
positive subspace also are shown on the stereogram as well
as the positions of the principal components and varimax
reference axes. The five sample vectors cluster about a
plane that occurs near one margin of the positive subspace. The compositions represented by vectors at various locations within the positive subspace can be inferred from the contours in Figure 2. It will be seen
that vectors near the upper-left corner of the subspace
represent compositions close to that of enstatite, those
near the upper-right corner represent compositions close
to that of ferrosilite, and those near the lower corner
represent compositions close to that of wollastonite.
Data for drawing Figures 1 and 2 were derived from programs EQSPIN and EQSTER described in Miesch (1976b).

Four specific methods that can be used to explore
for end-member compositions for the mixing model will be
reviewed. Each of the methods is applicable theoretically
in situations where the vector system occupies any number
of dimensions, but available computer programs are restricted to ten or fewer dimensions (end members) and
most of the successful applications have involved no
more than four.

Method 1 is used in situations where there is a
theoretical basis for assuming what one or more of the
end-member compositions might have been. In the orthopyroxene example being used here the obvious end-member
compositions are those given in matrix (12) - the ideal
compositions of enstatite, ferrosilite, and wollastonite.
Each of these compositions was normalized with equation
(7) and corresponding principal-components vector coordinates were obtained with equation (8) using matrix (17).
[Because the data were not scaled prior to row-normaliza-
tion and derivation of the R_{MM} matrix - see Appendix -
scaling according to   equation (6) prior to the
use of equation (7) can be omitted.] The computed principal-components coordinates and respective vector communalities are:

	(1)	(2)	(3)	Communality	
Enstatite	0.933748	0.357743	0.011441	0.999996	
Ferrosilite	0.194553	0.980077	0.039510	0.999963	(19)
Wollastonite	0.502661	0.409309	-0.761384	0.999908	

Although the communalities are high, all of them
are less than one and the compositions actually

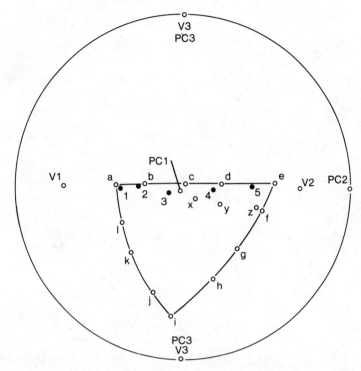

Figure 1. Stereogram showing relative positions of five vectors (solid dots)
that represent compositions of
orthopyroxenes. Open circles
labeled V1, V2, and V3 represent varimax reference axes.
Open circles labeled PC1, PC2,
and PC3 represent principal-
components reference axes. Other
open circles represent vectors
discussed in text. All vectors
have been projected from upper
hemisphere vertically onto plane
of stereogram. Vectors outside
of triangular area represent
compositions that are partly
negative.

represented by the three vectors, determined with equations (3), (4), and (5), are:

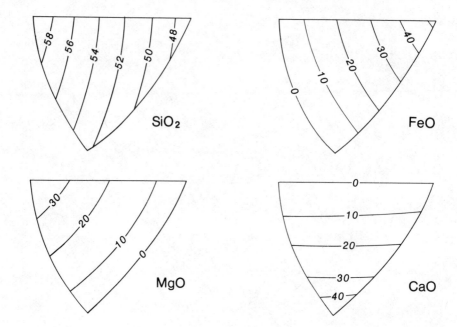

Figure 2.   Contours over triangular area of Figure
            1 showing nature of compositional varia-
            tions.

	SiO$_2$	FeO	MgO	CaO	
Enstatite	59.69	0.05	40.18	0.07	
Ferrosilite	45.94	54.55	-0.28	-0.21	(20)
Wollastonite	52.41	-0.26	-0.45	48.30	

Therefore, although the ideal compositions of these minerals cannot be represented precisely in the 3-dimension-
al space of the sample vectors, vectors that represent
closely similar compositions can be identified. Unfortunately, two of the three vectors lie outside of the
positive subspace; the two recomputed compositions are
partly negative. This difficulty could be overcome by
selecting vectors near those listed in matrix (19), but
within the positive subspace or on its margin. The computations required for method 1 are provided by program
EQEXAM (Miesch, 1976b).

Method 2 is used in situations where one or more of the end-member compositions are thought to be real or conceptual mixtures of two or more other compositions. For example, if an end member is thought to be some type of feldspar, the end-member composition may be a conceptual mixture of albite ($NaAlSi_3O_8$), anorthite ($CaAl_2Si_2O_8$), and orthoclase ($KAlSi_3O_8$). Similarly, if we were unaware that our example data in matrix (11) pertained to orthopyroxenes but suspected that the end members might be iron and magnesium silicate minerals, we could consider the compositional system forsterite (Mg_2SiO_4)-fayalite (Fe_2SiO_4)-silica (SiO_2), as represented in Figure 3. The compositional system then could be examined throughout at small increments by testing each selected composition by the same procedures used in method 1. Using increments of 2 molar percent, 1,326 compositions within the system of Figure 3 were tested and 35 were determined to have communalities equal to or greater than the average of the sample vector communalities (0.9999 - the average row sum-of-squares for matrix 18). These compositions are identified on Figure 3 and range from ideal enstatite to ideal ferrosilite. With the exception of nine compositions close to but slightly outside this range (small row of dots in Fig. 3), no other compositions within the system met the test criterion. Therefore, the extremes in the range of compositions identified in Figure 3 could be taken as two of the end-member compositions for the mixing model. Alternatively, three end-member compositions could be identified by examination of the four-component system forsterite-fayalite-silica-orthosilicate (Ca_2SiO_4). The computational procedures for method 2 are contained in program EQSCAN (Miesch, 1976b).

Method 3 is used to determine an array of compositions that can be added to or subtracted from one composition to produce another. The initial and final compositions may be represented by two vectors in m-dimensional space, and all possible compositions that could produce one from the other are represented by vectors in the plane of these two vectors. For example, in order to change the composition represented by sample vector 2 on Figure 1 to the composition represented by sample vector 3, it is necessary to subtract a composition represented by a vector in the plane of vectors 2 and 3, but to the left of vector 2; or to add a composition represented by a vector in the same plane, but to the right of vector 3. Most vectors in that plane to the left of vector 2 are outside of the positive subspace and

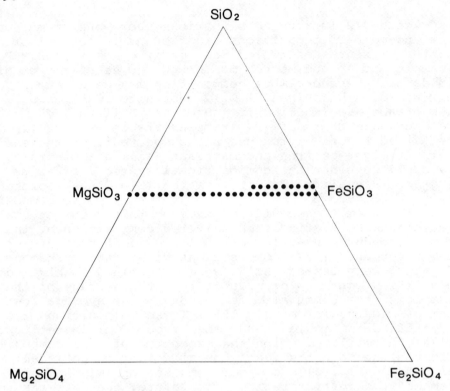

Figure 3.   Triangular diagram representing compositional system enstatite (Mg_2SiO_4)- ferrosilite (Fe_2SiO_4)- silica   (SiO_2)
as   molecular percentages.
Solid dots identify compositions within
system that can be represented in vector
system for orthopyrexene data by vectors
with communalities greater than 0.9999.

therefore, represent compositions that are partly negative. Some of those to the right of vector 3 are located on Figure 3 and represent the following compositions:

Vector	SiO_2	FeO	MgO	CaO	
x	53.58	22.20	20.85	3.37	
y	51.70	28.72	14.70	4.87	(21)
z	47.56	43.10	1.17	8.17	

Examples of the manner in which method 3 can be used to
determine the end members for mixing models are given in
Miesch and Reed (1979) and Miesch (1979). A FORTRAN

computer program that performs the necessary computations
and also derives CIPW norms for the determined compositions (EQFANN) is unpublished but available from the
author (U.S. Geological Survey, Stop 925, Box 25046,
Denver Federal Center, Denver, CO   80225.

Method 4 is based on the premise that many end-member
compositions to be expected in certain petrologic systems
include zero concentrations of one or more of the compositional variables. For example, a precipitate from
basaltic magmas may be the mineral olivine which contains little or no Al_2O_3, CaO, Na_2O, or K_2O, variables
usually represented   in matrices of
petrochemical data. Another precipitate from a broad
range of magmas is plagioclase which contains little or
no FeO or MgO. Because these compositions of interest
contain zero values, the vectors represented by them in
a system of sample vectors will occur on the margins of
the positive subspace. Therefore, it is useful to search
these margins for compositions that might be plausible
geological end-member compositions. Twelve compositions
represented by vectors at approximately regular intervals
along the margins of the positive subspace represented in
Figure 1 are as follows:

Vector	SiO_2	FeO	MgO	CaO	
a	59.72	0.00	40.28	0.00	
b	56.56	12.49	30.96	0.00	
c	53.46	24.71	21.82	0.00	
d	50.81	35.15	13.97	0.00	
e	46.07	53.93	0.00	0.00	
f	47.28	43.66	0.00	9.05	(22)
g	48.83	30.57	0.00	20.59	
h	50.00	20.76	0.00	29.24	
i	52.46	0.00	0.00	47.54	
j	54.39	0.00	10.75	34.86	
k	56.35	0.00	21.59	22.06	
l	57.74	0.00	29.32	12.92	

Compositions on the margins of the positive subspace may
be determined with programs EQSPIN, INSECT, and EQSTER
(Miesch, 1976b) if the sample vector system is 3-dimen-
sional, or with program EQZERO (unpublished but available
from the author) otherwise.

Compositions a, e, and i in matrix (22) are close
to the compositions of ideal enstatite, ferrosilite, and
wollastonite, respectively, as given in matrix (12).
Therefore, in order to illustrate the computational

methods for determining the mixing porportions, these
three compositions will be taken as matrix C_{mM} containing
the end-member compositions for the mixing model.
The coordinates of the end-member vectors with respect
to the principal-components axes may be determined using
equations (7) and (8). These form the matrix B_{mm}:

	PC1	PC2	PC3	
	0.925064	-0.379526	-0.012518	(composition a)
$B_{mm} =$	0.817467	0.574884	-0.036049	(composition e) (23)
	0.655018	-0.046869	0.754127	(composition i)

The product of matrix (18) and the inverse of matrix (23)
gives the coordinates of the five sample vectors with
respect to vectors a, e, and i. These are:

	(a)	(e)	(i)	Sample	
	0.989205	0.009006	0.009557	1	
	0.887927	0.177705	0.007851	2	
A_{Nm}	0.689883	0.392403	0.060973	3	(24)
	0.415913	0.683940	0.043443	4	
	0.189385	0.868018	0.030580	5	

Equations (3) and (4) then are used to derive scale factors for each of the three row-vectors in matrix (23)
and the mixing proportions, matrix P_{Nm}, are derived by
application of equation (10) to matrix (24). The
final mixing model is:

$$X_{NM} \simeq \hat{X}_{NM} = P_{Nm} C_{mM} \qquad (25)$$

where X_{NM} is as given in matrix (11), $\hat{X}_{NM}$ is as given
in matrix (16), and the mixing proprotions and
end-member compositions (from matrix 22) are:

	"Enstatite"	"Ferrosilite"	"Wollastonite"	Sample
	0.9812	0.0091	0.0097	1
	0.8249	0.1677	0.0074	2
$P_{Nm} =$	0.5997	0.3464	0.0540	3
	0.3602	0.6015	0.0383	4
	0.1718	0.7999	0.0282	5

and

	SiO_2	FeO	MgO	CaO	End member
	59.72	0.00	40.28	0.00	"Enstatite"
$C_{mM} =$	46.07	53.93	0.00	0.00	"Ferrosilite"
	52.46	0.00	0.00	47.54	"Wollastonite"

DISCUSSION

Representation of the matrix X_{NM}, which consists of measurements of M compositional variables on N samples, as a vector system requires a vector space of M dimensions. Fortunately, correlation among the compositional variables is a common property of geochemical and petrologic data matrices so that, although the vectors occupy M dimensions, they usually cluster about a space of only m dimensions - as when vectors in three or more dimensions cluster about a plane. When this circumstance occurs the vectors can be projected into the smaller space and only small angles separate the original and projected vectors. Thus, the projected vectors represent compositions close to those represented by the original vectors; the matrix $\hat{X}_{NM}$ represented by the projected vectors is a close approximation of X_{NM}.

Transformation of a matrix of original data, X_{NM}, into a matrix of approximate or recomputed data, $\hat{X}_{NM}$, may be viewed as an attempt to filter the data by removing the effects of random errors in the laboratory measurements and of geologic processes that affected the sample compositions in a minor and random, or at least haphazard, manner. Removal of random effects certainly is possible in computer-simulation experiments and there is no reason to believe that the transformation cannot perform similarly with real data. A comparison of petrographic diagrams constructed from the original and recomputed data by Stuckless and others (1979) suggests that it does.

The recomputed data matrix may be derived directly from the principal-components loadings and scores as shown in the Appendix, or it may be derived from the varimax loadings and scores or from any other reference axes one chooses to use. These initial reference axes are merely devices that serve as a temporary basis for the system of sample vectors. The object of the modeling procedure is to determine a new basis that is interpretable geologically and in accord with whatever is known about the geologic origin of the samples or otherwise in accord with the purpose of the modeling exercise.

The Q-mode approach offers several important advantabes in mixing problems to the basic method introduced to geologists ten years ago. The most important of these are (a) that the number of end members needed for the model can be determined before the end members are known,

and (b) one has the ability to test individual compositions (rather than just groups of compositions) for suitability as end-member compositions for the mixing model
and to modify these when necessary so that they are suitable. It also is possible to prepare lists of suitable
compositions, using various methods, so that the user
may scan these for compositions that are of interest
geologically. Finally, however, the Q-mode method,
similar to other methods, requires that selected sets of
end-member compositions be tested by computing the mixing proportions. The sets must be altered or replaced
if the mixing proportions are determined to be unreason-
able for any substantive reason. The usual reason for
rejection is that the mixing proportions are negative
when geologic evidence calls for addition of the end
member, or positive when the geologic evidence or theory
argues for subtraction.

The Q-mode computations for the orthopyroxene example used here for purpose of illustration were performed
without initial scaling of the data. As a result, the
compositional variables were weighted and affected the
outcome of the analysis in proportion to the variances.
Various methods of initial scaling can be used to avoid
this situation if desired.

Use of the Q-mode method is most effective when
available in an interactive mode on a time-sharing computer system. The methods described here, which are
contained mostly in published FORTRAN programs (Miesch,
1976b), can be used to explore for mathematically suitable and geologically plausible end-member compositions
that yield reasonable mixing proportions so that models
can be developed that are both mathematically sound and
in accord with all available geologic evidence that pertains to the mixing problem.

REFERENCES

Bryan, W.B., Finger, L.W., and Chayes, F., 1969, Esti-
    mating proportions in petrographic mixing equations
    by least-squares approximation: Science, v. 163,
    no. 3870, p. 926-927.

Deer, W.A., Howie, R.A., and Zussman, J., 1963, Rock-
    forming minerals, Vol. 2, Chain silicates: John
    Wiley & Sons, Inc., New York, 379 p.

Imbrie, J., 1963, Factor and vector analysis programs for analyzing geologic data: Office Naval Research, Geography Branch, Tech. Rept. 6 [ONR Task No. 380-135], 135 p.

Klovan, J.E., and Imbrie, J., 1971, An algorithm and FORTRAN-IV program for large-scale Q-mode factor analysis and calculation of factor scores: Jour. Math. Geology, v. 3, no. 1, p. 61-77.

Miesch, A.T., 1976a, Q-mode factor analysis of geochemical and petrologic data matrices with constant row-sums: U.S. Geol. Survey Prof. Paper 574-G, 47 p.

Miesch, A.T., 1976b, Interactive computer programs for petrologic modeling with extended Q-mode factor analysis: Computers & Geosciences, v. 2, no. 4, p. 439-492.

Miesch, A.T., 1979, Vector analysis of chemical variation in the lavas of Paricutin volcano, Mexico: Jour. Math. Geology, v. 11, no. 4, p. 345-371.

Miesch, A.T., and Reed, B.L., 1979, Compositional structures in two batholiths of circum-Pacific North America: U.S. Geol. Survey Prof. Paper 574-H, in press.

Stormer, J.C., and Nicholls, J., 1978, XLFRAC: a program for the interactive testing of magmatic differentiation models: Computers & Geosciences, v. 4, no. 2, p. 143-159.

Stuckless, J.S., Miesch, A.T., Goldich, S.S., and Weiblen, P.W., 1979, A Q-mode factor model for the petrogenesis of the volcanic rocks from Ross Island and vicinity, Antarctica: Am. Geophy. Union Mem., Antarctica Research Series, in press.

Wright, T.L., and Doherty, P.C., 1970, A linear programming and least squares computer method for solving petrologic mixing problems: Geol. Soc. America Bull., v. 81, no. 7, p. 1995-2008.

APPENDIX

Determination of the matrix $\hat{X}_{NM}$

The matrix of original data, X_{NM}, with constant row-sums (generally equal to 100 percent), is scaled initially according to:

$$w_{ij} = \frac{x_{ij} - b_j}{a_j - b_j} \qquad 1 \le i \le N; \; 1 \le j \le M \qquad (1a)$$

where x_{ij} is the value in the ith row and jth column of X_{NM}, w_{ij} is the scaled value, and a_j and b_j are constants for the jth variable. If the data are to be scaled to proportions of the variable ranges, a_j and b_j are set to the maximum and minimum values, respectively, in the jth column of X_{NM}. If the initial scaling is to be omitted, the constants a_j and b_j are effectively set to 1 and 0, respectively, in equation (1a) and in all other equations where they occur.

The scaled data then are row-normalized to produce a Z_{NM} matrix where each element is determined by:

$$z_{ij} = w_{ij}/(\sum_j w_{ij}^2)^{1/2} \qquad 1 \le i \le N: \; 1 \le j \le M \qquad (2a)$$

Following Klovan and Imbrie (1971), then, a cross-products matrix is formed by:

$$R_{MM} = Z'_{MN}Z_{NM} \qquad (3a)$$

The eigenvectors of R_{MM} corresponding to the m largest eigenvalues form the matrix of principal-components scores, F_{mM}, and the matrix of principal-components loadings is obtained from:

$$A_{Nm} = Z_{NM}F'_{Mm} \qquad (4a)$$

The rows of F_{mM} (f_j) are set equal to g_j and scale factors for each of the rows are determined with equation (4); the composition scores for each of the rows then are obtained with equation (5), yielding the matrix C_{mM}. The loading matrix A_{Nm} is converted to a matrix, P_{Nm}, of composition loadings (or

mixing proportions) by use of equation (10). The matrix
$\hat{X}_{NM}$ is obtained with equation (9).

Repetition of all the steps listed after equation
(3a) for values of m from 2 to M will yield M - 1 matrices
of $\hat{X}_{NM}$. The best $\hat{X}_{NM}$ matrix to use in a mixing problem
generally will be the one most similar to
X_{NM} based on the smallest value of m, in accordance
with the principle of parsimony (Imbrie, 1963).
Similarity is measured conveniently by coefficients of
determination (squares of correlation coefficients) between corresponding columns of $\hat{X}_{NM}$ and X_{NM} which can be
summarized effectly on factor-
variance diagrams (Miesch, 1976a). The number of end-
member compositions required to account for all of the
variability in matrix $\hat{X}_{NM}$ is equal to its rank which is
m, the same as the number of columns in A_{Nm} and
P_{Nm} and the number of rows in F_{mM} and C_{mM}.

COMPUTER AS A RESEARCH TOOL IN PALEONTOLOGY

David M. Raup

Field Museum of Natural History

ABSTRACT

In many areas of paleontological research, the computer has taken its place with the microscope and handlens
as a basic research tool. Most of the standard applications are digital and include various types of biometrical analysis, information processing (including collection management), computer graphics, and statistical
testing of hypotheses.

There is some evidence that paleontology, especially
evolutionary paleontology, is undergoing a major transformation: from a primarily idiographic science devoted
to building a chronology of the history of life (who be-
gat whom?) to a more nomothetic science in search of general statistical laws. The computer may not be responsible for this shift of emphasis but it may be the vital
catalyst. In the nomothetic approach species are treated
as particles and the group behavior of large numbers of
species (or evolutionary events) is best treated by computer. This is true for two reasons: (a) testing models
with real data requires massive data-processing capability, and (b) Monte-Carlo and numerical simulations may
be necessary in the formulation and testing of theoretical models.

Along with the search for general statistical laws
in the evolution of life, there is new emphasis on complex Markov processes. Any history and particularly

evolutionary history contains Markovian elements. Whether the computer analysis is done analytically or by simulation, it is important to be able to treat Markov series (especially time series and branching processes) in a massive and rigorous fashion. For this, the computer is indispensable.

THE PAST TEN YEARS

The use of computers in paleontological research has developed on a broad front during the past ten years. For many workers, computers have been absorbed to the point where they are a routine part of the research arsenal - along with the microscope, camera, and calipers. One now rarely sees "by computer" or "computer generated" in the titles of papers - suggesting that the use of computers in paleontology has matured. In fact, it is nearly impossible to survey computer use from the literature alone because it may not state whether computers have been used in a given study.

It cannot be claimed, of course, that all appropriate applications have been explored or that all studies that could benefit from computers actually use computers. By far the most usual applications in paleontology are in aid of fairly standard biometrical analysis of morphologic variation among fossils. Where multivariate methods are used, studies can be done by computer that would be impossible by any other method. Biometrical work thus is no longer restricted to simple univariate and bivariate statistics. Multivariate methods also are being used increasingly in various distributional studies - especially in biofacies analysis and other aspects of community paleoecology.

Certain applications that showed promise ten years ago have developed little. Automatic image analysis in the study of morphology yet has tantalizing possibilities but relatively little actual progress has been made. This is due in part to the lack of suitably efficient and economical hardware and in part to the lack of explicit mathematical models of growth and form in most plant and animal groups. Development of the computerization of biostratigraphy also has been disappointing: much potential but little real progress.

The use of computers in the cataloging and management of large museum collections has not developed to

the extent that many people had hoped. Although not
strictly a research tool, computerization of data on
systematic collections could have important research implications because of the host of interesting and important questions that can be asked of a good electronic
file of museum data. In particular, studies of diversity
and biogeography could be enhanced greatly in this manner.
One problem that yet faces EDP projects in museum collections is the sheer enormity of the data entry problem
(Jones, 1979).

Thus, the past ten years have seen important advances
in computer applications in paleontology but the advances
have been uneven.

THE NEXT TEN YEARS

Any predictions made now probably will be wrong because they will not anticipate technological innovations
nor the influence of ideas generated by a few, key individuals. Nonetheless, some trends are suggestive. My
own hunch is that the next ten years will see increasingly ambitious analyses of large data sets having to do
with distribution of fossil taxa in time and space.
There are several reasons for thinking this:

(1) There is a renewed interest in the search
     for statistical laws or generalizations
     that may be used to predict geographic
     or evolutionary phenomena.
(2) Published compilations of paleontologic
     data are more comprehensive and more avail-
     able than ever before. The *Treatise on In-
     vertebrate Paleontology* and the JOIDES re-
     ports provide a consistent and rigorous
     basis for synthetic studies that has not
     been available before.
(3) The improvement of text-editing systems (such
     as WYLBUR and SUPERWYLBUR) and of basic
     utility programs for sorting and retrieval
     of data has facilitated the building and
     processing of the large data files which
     are the necessary raw material for broad
     synthesis.

Careful analysis of large data sets is applicable
to a wide range of paleoecological, biogeographic, biostratigraphic, and evolutionary problems. Interesting

questions are being asked, especially by the younger research workers, which can be answered only by massive data-processing efforts. We thus may be seeing the convergence of good questions being asked, the availability of appropriate data, and the methods of analysis. The computer may provide the essential catalyst for significant advances in the science. With this in mind, I will devote the remainder of my space to some aspects of the search for statistical laws in evolution and to the contributions that computers are making or are likely to make to this search.

THE SEARCH FOR STATISTICAL LAWS

Paleontology has long been dominated by what has been termed an idiographic approach (Raup and Gould, 1974). That is, the fossil record has been subjected to painstaking and detailed description and chronicling of what happened. Emphasis has been on description of individual species and interpretation of their habitats and on ancestor-descendent relationships (who began whom? and similar questions). This has been necessary and desirable and nearly all fields of natural science have gone through this phase: it has been essential to establish the data base before making large-scale interpretations. This is not to say that paleontologists did not look for generalizations or laws during the idiographic phase. In fact, the literature is strewn with generalizations, particularly in the field of evolution. Examples include the Biogenetic Law, various Cope's Rules, orthogenesis, and many generalizations about evolutionary rates. Therefore it is not fair to say that paleontological research has been idiographic completely in the past and now is nomothetic (roughly the opposite of idiographic). Rather, it seems that the nomothetic aspect is becoming relatively more prominent as a research approach - which is entirely reasonable if we can assume that the data base has improved to the point where synthetic studies are more nearly justified.

At present, there are many paleontologists who feel that the time has come to treat fossil species as particles in a larger dynamic system. To use a rough analogy with the study of gases in physics, it can be argued that we are beyond the point where it is fruitful to describe and track each "molecule"; rather, we should be looking statistically at the group behavior of large numbers of "molecules" so that generalizations having predictive ability can be made (that is, "gas laws" for evolutionary

systems). It is probably safe to assume that an evolutionary system is far more complex than most physical systems; it even may be that simplifying generalizations or
laws are not possible. But the search is on!

MARKOV PROCESSES

Nearly all time sequences in geology and paleontology
can be looked upon as Markov series. Whether the change
is physical (as in a sedimentary sequence) or biological
(as in evolutionary series), the state of the system at
time = t is to some extent dependent upon the state at
time = t-1. A brachiopod species, for example, may change
from one stratigraphic level to the next but the descen-
dent form is constrained to be at least similar to the
ancestral form. This indicates that two succeeding forms
in the series are more similar to each other than each is
to a brachiopod drawn at random from a larger series or
array. In other words, the evolutionary system has memory in the sense that a given step is constrained by the
preceding condition. The state at time = t is not determined fully by the state at t-1, however - at least as
far as we know. A given step is thus a combination of
(a) the influence (legacy) of the preceding step and (b)
an indeterminate array of factors influencing the change
itself. The uncertainty of the change introduces a probabilistic element. The changes from step-to-step even
may be said to contain a random element as long as one
understands that random in this context simply refers to
our inability to predict the changes in advance.

Time series in purely physical systems in geology
can be treated in the same manner, as Krumbein (1969) and
others have shown. In evolution, the two most abundant
Markov processes are the random walk and the branching
process.

RANDOM WALKS

A general exercise in evolutionary paleontology is
to plot the state of a morphological character through
time. Figure 1 shows such a plot for shell diameter in
the classic *Kosmoceras* lineage analyzed by Brinkman
(1929). This example satisfies the requirements of a
Markov chain because the increments in shell diameter
from one sample to the next are small relative to the
differences in diameter between randomly chosen samples:

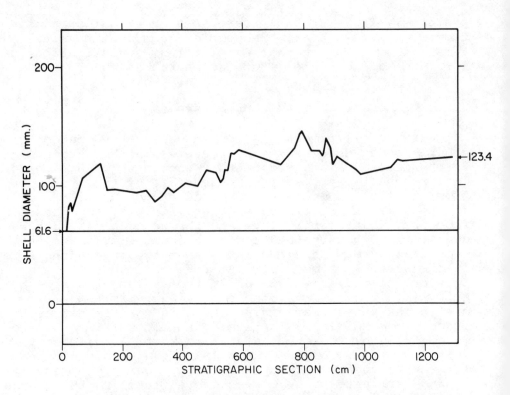

Figure 1.   Change in mean shell diameter for assemblages of Jurassic ammonite *Kosmoceras*
(Zugokosmoceras) through about 12 m of
stratigraphic section.   Data from Brinkmann (1929).

that is, the shell diameter at one horizon is constrained
to be relatively close to that at the preceding horizon.
And there is uncertainty in the direction and magnitude
of any horizon-to-horizon change.   This establishes that
we are concerned with a Markov process and that the simple Markov chain or random walk is a reasonable conceptual and mathematical framework for analysis.

This does not indicate that the evolution of *Kosmo-*
ceras is random in any literal sense - although it may
be.   In the simplest random walk, all changes in the dependent variable (shell diameter, in this situation)
should be equal and the probabilities of upward and downward movement should be the same.   It is clear from Figure 1 that the increments are not constant.   Figure 2
shows a frequency distribution of change in shell

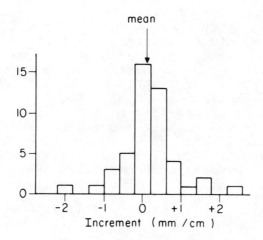

Figure 2.   Histogram of change
             in mean diameter per
             centimeter of section
             for *Kosmoceras* data
             shown in Figure 1.
             Mean change is +0.005
             mm/cm.

diameter per centimeter of stratigraphic section. The
question of whether the upward and downward probabilities
of change are equal need not be answered in the affirma-
tive for a random-walk analysis to be applicable. Although it would be interesting if the probabilities were
equal - suggesting evolution by genetic drift - unequal
probabilities are just as reasonable mathematically and
biologically. If it could be established, for example,
that the probability of an increase in shell diameter in
Kosmoceras was higher than that of a decrease we would
have a measure of the pressure of natural selection fa-
voring a size increase.

     In the *Kosmoceras* example, the mean increment per
centimeter is slightly positive (see Fig. 2). This explains, of course, why there was a net increase in shell
diameter in this particular sequence. But the mean in-
crement per centimeter is not different statistically
from zero and thus, we cannot in this situation reject
the null hypothesis of genetic drift. If directional
selection was operating, it was not significant statistically for the 1200-cm sequence.

The importance of treating Figure 1 as a Markov chain can be illustrated by what happens if conventional independent events statistics are used. Suppose one were to ignore the Markovian aspects of this situation and ask: "Is shell diameter significantly correlated with position in the stratigraphic sequence?" or "Is the increase in shell diameter from bottom to top of the section statistically significant?" To answer the first question one *could* compute a correlation coefficient (r) for all samples, with one variable being shell diameter and the other being centimeters above the base of the section. The r turns out to be 0.74 (N=48) which is different significantly from zero. The second question can be answered by comparing means and variance of the bottom and top samples. A conventional t-test indicates that these two means, in fact, are different. But both exercises are invalid because they ignore the Markovian aspects of the problem.

The bottom line here is that random walks that seem to show significant trends may not. The problem is not limited to evolutionary series of morphologic characters. Any time series in historical geology, such as a sealevel curve or paleotemperature trend is prone to the same difficulty.

COMPUTER ASPECTS OF RANDOM WALKS

The accumulation and processing of data as well as some of the statistical analysis of time series can be carried out most appropriately by computer. But far more important is the use of Monte-Carlo simulations to improve the intuition and generally raise the consciousness of those working with time series. This is particularly important in view of the fact that most people see time series as if they were *non*Markovian, independent-events processes. For these people, the results of random-walk analysis are counter-intuitive.

Figure 3 shows several classic random walks generated by a random-number generator. Each is 50 time units long and the probability of upward and downward change is everywhere constant and equal to 0.5. For each pair of random walks, conventional correlation coefficients (r) have been computed for each series against time and for each series against the other. Using this (invalid) approach, most r values are statistically significant - matching one's intuitive impressions of the graphs. But

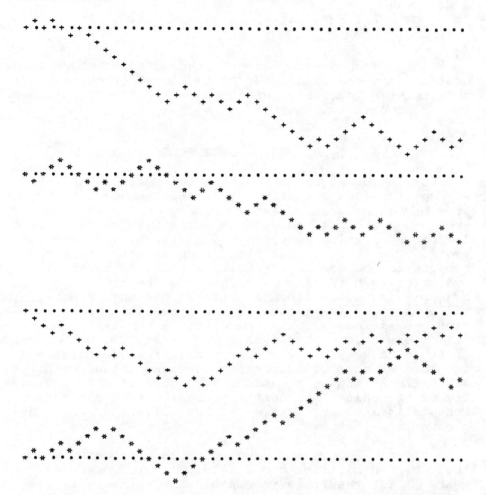

Figure 3.   Four computer-generated random walks.
             Time goes from left to right (50 arbit-
             rary time units). In each time series,
             upward and downward movements had equal
             probabilities. As is typical of all
             time series, path followed by random walk
             gives appearance of being correlated with
             time; also, members of pair of random
             walks may appear correlated with each
             other. This exemplifies Yule's "non-
             sense correlation."

the correlation analysis, of course, is invalid because
none of the several walks show a significant departure
from chance expectations. The end-points of all walks

are within the 95 percent confidence limits of the classic random walk.

Only through study of many random walks known to be unbiased can the student or professional researcher gain an intuitive impression of the normal range of outcomes in a random-walk situation.

BRANCHING PROCESSES

Evolution at or above the species level generally is depicted as a branching tree. Each segment of the tree may be a species, genus, or higher monophyletic group. Segments (lineages) may originate through branching of preexisting lineages and may terminate (extinction). The type of branching process termed time homogeneous is the one most readily applicable to actual evolutionary branching patterns. In the time homogeneous branching process, lineages have a constant probability of termination (expressed as the probability of extinction per lineage million years) and a constant probability of branching. The system may or may not be balanced. If it is balanced, the two probabilities are equal and the total number of coexisting lineages (standing diversity) fluctuates as a random walk. But if the probability of branching exceeds the probability of extinction, the statistical expectation is that diversity will increase through time.

Figure 4 shows a branching pattern produced where the two probabilities are equal (0.1 per lineage million years). The result is reasonable subjectively if compared with real evolutionary trees from the fossil record but the applicability of the time homogeneous branching process to evolution is yet to be established fully. In the real world, there are situations where the frequencies of branching or extinction change through time such that assuming temporal constancy of probabilities would be an oversimplification and lead to error. The most obvious such situations are those where extinction probability suddenly increases or branching probability suddenly decreases to produce what is known as a mass extinction. Also, it is clear that some biologic groups differ consistently from others in the values of the two probabilities. For example, Jablonski (1978) showed that molluscan lineages without a free-swimming larval stage have higher probabilities of extinction and branching than those with a free-swimming larval stage. Even in

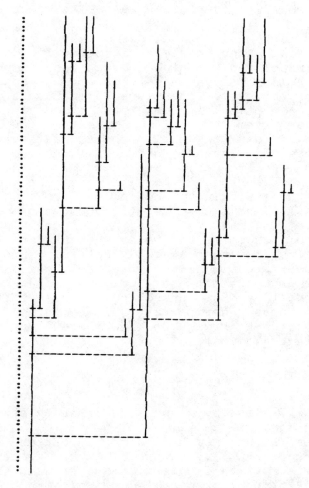

Figure 4. Tree-like branching pat-
            tern. Process starts with
            single lineage at time=0
            (lower left) and proceeds
            through chance branching
            and termination. Thus,
            fact that more branching
            events than termination
            events occurred was mat-
            ter of chance.

these situations, the mathematical framework of the Markovian branching process provides a sensible null hypothesis
against which to test real world data.

COMPUTER ASPECTS OF BRANCHING PROCESSES

The mathematical analysis of the simpler branching processes has been developed in other fields. Equations have been derived by which one can predict the mean expectation (and its variance) for various aspects of the branching pattern. These aspects include standing diversity as a function of time, total progeny produced in a branching system, probability of extinction of the whole system, and many others. In short, if the type of branching process has been defined and if the probabilities of branching and extinction are known or can be postulated, it is possible to describe with rigor the probable anatomy of the resulting branching pattern. Some of the predictions lend themselves to computer processing but as before, the main value of the computer is to raise the consciousness of the researcher by Monte-Carlo simulation of branching patterns. Several examples are shown in Figure 5. All use precisely the same model and the same probabilities as in Figure 4, but the results differ greatly. Some branching systems abort early whereas others undergo what would be termed an adaptive radiation (even through we know there is nothing adaptive about the radiation).

CONCLUSION

I will close by discussing a Markov situation which probably has applicability to the geologic and paleontologic records and which illustrates better than any other the counter-intuitive nature of Markov processes. This is inspired by the excellent and intriguing paper by Cohen (1976) on the so-called Polya's Urn problem. Suppose we have an urn which contains one white ball and one black ball. Chooose a ball at random and note its color; then add a ball of the same color to the urn, thus making a total of three balls (two of one color and one of the other). If this process is repeated many times, the urn gradually fills up. The ratio of colors starts at 1:1; after the first iteration, the ratio is inevitably 2:1 or or 1:2 depending on which color was chosen; after the next iteration, the ratio may revert to 1:1 or move to 3:1, and so on. The problem is to predict statistically the temporal change in the ratio of colors.

The Polya's Urn problem has many obvious biological analogs. Suppose, for example, that the initial balls represent two species of an organism landing as waifs on

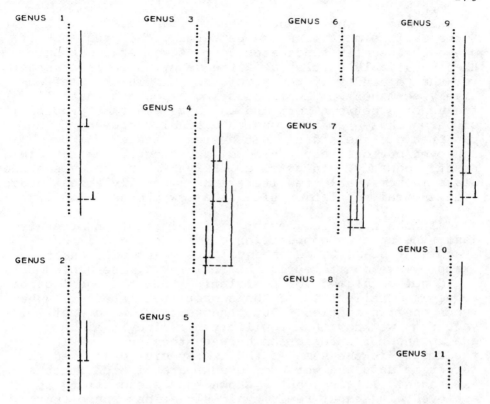

Figure 5.   Eleven branching trees made with same
             program that produced Figure 4. Proba-
             bilities of branching and termination
             were same as in Figure 4 but all eleven
             "genera" went extinct after few time
             iterations and few new branches were
             formed.

an uninhabited island and suppose that the species have
the same probability of population growth through reproduction. How will the ratio of population sizes in the
two species behave over time? As Cohen has indicated,
the answer to the Polya's Urn problem is counter-intuitive
and is missed by most otherwise competent ecologists and
population biologists. Usual scenarios proposed are (a)
that the proportion of one color will fluctuate about
0.5 indefinitely, (b) that one color will dominate the
population quickly (tending toward a frequency of 1.0)
with the dominant color being a matter of chance in the
early iterations, and (c) that frequency will behave as
a random walk through the range from 0.0 to 1.0.

In fact, none of the scenarios are obtained. If
Monte-Carlo simulations are performed, the frequency of
one color usually fluctuates for a few iterations but
then invariably settles at a frequency which is constant
for the remainder of the simulation and which is effectively permanent. The interesting aspect is that all
frequencies between zero and one have the same probability
of being chosen as the constant, final frequency. One
can predict, therefore, that a steady state will be
achieved but one cannot predict anything about that constant frequency. In practice, Polya's Urn achieves steady
state in remarkably few iterations: usually a few hundred
with a total population size of a few thousand individuals.

In the biological example of colonization of an island, the species composition of the island will soon
reach what seems to be an equilibrium and if such an
example were monitored in the real world, the ecologist
could not be blamed for postulating that the equilibrium
value is a reflection of the competitive interaction between the two species. But, thanks to knowledge of Polya's Urn, we know that equilibrium is inevitable even in
the absence of interaction between the species. In fact,
the result is the same if the two species colonized different islands and were not even aware of each other's
existence. It also can be shown that steady state is
achieved with equal rapidity in situations where there
are several species. How many fossil communities which
seem to have fixed species composition were formed by a
Polya's Urn process?

The Polya's Urn case illustrates again the importance
of revising one's intuitive and mathematical approaches
when faced with historical processes which are Markovian
and, as noted earlier, historical geology and paleontology
are primarily Markovian. Computerized simulation techniques are the obvious vehicle for teaching and exploring
the Markov process.

ACKNOWLEDGMENT

This work was supported in part by the Systematic
Biology Program, National Science Foundation, NSF Grant
DEB 78-22568.

REFERENCES

Brinkmann, R., 1929, Statistische-biostratigraphische
    Untersuchungen an mitteljurassischen Ammoniten ueber
    Artbegriff und Stammesentwicklung: Abh. Ges. Wiss.
    Goettingen, Math-Phys Kl., N.F., v. 13, no. 3, p.
    1-249.

Cohen, J.E., 1976, Irreproducible results and the breed-
    ing of pigs: Bioscience, v. 26, p. 391-394.

Jablonski, D., 1978, Transgressions, regressions, and
    endemism in Gulf Coast Cretaceous molluscs (abst.):
    Geol. Soc. America Abstr. v. 10, no. 7, p. 427-
    428.

Jones, B., 1979, Data storage and retrieval for the pal-
    aeontology collections, University of Alberta:
    Palaeont. Assoc., Sp. Papers in Palaeontology, v. 22,
    p. 175-187.

Krumbein, W.C., 1969, The computer in geological perspec-
    tive, *in* International Symposium of Computer Appli-
    cations in the Earth Sciences: Plenum Press, New
    York, p. 251-275.

Raup, D.M., and Gould, S.J., 1974, Stochastic simulation
    and evolution of morphology -- towards a nomothetic
    paleontology: Syst. Zoology, v. 23, no. 3, p. 305-
    322.

THE COMPUTER IN PALEOECOLOGY

R.A. Reyment

Uppsala Universitet

ABSTRACT

Access to electronic computers is necessary for modern quantitative paleoecology, as almost all problems are
highly multivariate. Diversity studies are becoming increasingly abundant in computer-based paleoecology. Multivariate statistical applications are the most important
area of computerized paleoecology, involving both standard multivariate methods as well as special adaptations.
A useful concept in paleoecological reconstructions based
on borehole data is the ecolog, a union of physical and
biological values.

INTRODUCTION

Paleoecology is clearly a complicated subject. It
involves not only the whole range of complications proper
to ecology but also geologic problems of a specific nature. When quantified, the subject easily becomes highly
multivariate. It therefore is obvious that the computer
has a self-appointed role and it is no exaggeration to
say that there would not be much advanced quantitative
paleoecology in research if there were no computers.
This can be seen in another way, notably, by reference
to the literature. There is little significant work in
multivariate ecology of any type before 1960 and most has
been done since 1970. The theoretical background was
available, to a large extent, but not the means for prac-
tically testing it.

For most purposes, it is convenient to think of a quantitative paleoecologic analysis at two levels:

(i)   The most adequate and relevant of the available models or methods of statistical ecology applicable to the problem.

(ii) Special methods of geostatistics designed to give the approximate results obtained under (i) more substance and geologic meaning.

There can be no simple approach of the "problem-solution" type.

DIVERSITY STUDIES

Diversity is currently a popular subject among statistical ecologists and therefore it is appropriate to note some applications from the sphere of paleoecology.

Paleoecologists seem to use techniques developed mostly by numerical taxonomists which all rely heavily on computers. Some examples are cited here.

Birks and Deacon (1973) used lists of species of Recent and fossil vascular plants in 12 geographic regions in Britain for paleoecologic purposes. Using 4 similarity indices (the coefficients of Jaccard, Dice, Simpson, and Braun-Blanquet), converted to dissimilarity coefficients, and nonmetric scaling, two-dimensional dispositions of points representing the regions were determined for each time interval. A marked north-south gradient was demonstrated.

Cheetham and Hazel (1969) studied the performances of various similarity coefficients, 23 in all, for analyzing associations of microfossils. Henderson and Herron (1977), in their paper on a probabilistic method of paleobiogeographic analysis, concluded that diversity studies in paleontology tend to suffer from a number of troublesome defects, most of which are obvious to the quantitative worker. Further references to diversity work are Hazel (1970), Kaesler (1969), and Kaesler and Mulvany (1976). Another paper that can be mentioned here is by Forester (1977), who considered the problem of measuring the relative abundance of microorganisms - in this connection he uses the Poisson parameter for producing an abundance coefficient.

G.P. Patel and his co-workers as a matter of fact
have shown that there is really only one similarity index. Most if not all the variants proposed in the past
by numerous workers reduce algebraically to the same
formula.

ORIENTATION ANALYSIS

An important area of statistical paleoecology is
that of the quantitative study of the orientations of
fossils. Two main problems belong here, (1) the orientions of fossils in situ and (2) the orientions of
transported fossils. The analysis of the former may
yield significant information on the mode of life of the
organism or organisms involved. The latter can provide
details concerning the water currents prevailing during
the time at which the biological flotsam and jetsam was
stranded.

In regard to the statistical theory for these analyses, we are in a strong position today thanks to the developments of the mathematical analysis of geomagnetism.
Thus, the entire field of directional statistics can be
taken over without modification (cf. Mardia, 1972).

Neoecology does not have the same interest in analysis of directions, although I can conceive of several situations in which this type of approach could be put to
better use than hitherto has been done. The most reward-
ing area of research in paleoecology has been that of the
dispersal of cephalopod shells, after the death of the
organism. The essentially trivariate nature of the ma-
jority of orientational problems in paleoecology remains
to be exploited fully and almost all studies made are
based on the circular distribution.

POPULATION DYNAMICS

Population dynamics is one of the main fields of
activity in the neoecologist. A large part of the books
on statistical ecology by Pielou (1974, 1977) are concerned with this aspect of the subject. For understandable reasons, population dynamics cannot be given the
same prominence in statistical paleocology.

Nonetheless, in favorable situations, it is possible
to develop an approximate analysis using a classical

population dynamic approach. Micropaleontology offers
opportunities, as complete growth sequences of ostracods
may occur in sediment that has not been reworked. In
fact, the preparation of a life table (Reyment, 1971, p.
112) for a sample of ostracods may be used with great effect to judge whether a deposit has been reworked, a secondary outcome of the study. For example, life tables
have been prepared for fossil pelecypods, Pleistocene
bears, and other vertebrates, although, perhaps, not always correctly.

For more than one species, the number of analyzable
paleoecological situations is rare, being limited, for
all practical purposes, to the predator-prey relationship
and semiquantitative inferences on competition between
species (c.f. Reyment, 1971, fig. 24). The predation
relationship can be given only adequate statistical study
in paleontology for situations where the predator has
left an observable trace on the shell of the prey. The
best example of this is provided by drilling gastropods,
(c.f. Reyment, 1971, p. 130-150). For marine inverte-
brate paleontologists, at least, predation by drills is
of considerable significance and therefore it is a re-
warding subject for paleoecological research. Fossil
ostracods, pelecypods, and gastropods may be drilled by
naticids, less frequently by muricids, and inasmuch as
the first-mentioned group is an abundant component of
borehole samples, sufficient material can usually be obtained to permit a satisfactory statistical study.

It should be noted here that the analysis of a predator-prey relationship in paleoecology is much of a gam-
ble in that the observed prey and predator frequencies
cannot be claimed with certainty to represent the actual
maxima attained by them. Not only are the sampling fluctuations dependant on factors outside the normal limits
of statistics, but there is the added vexation of the unknown extent of migration as well as post-mortem trans-
port of the drilled shells. A statistical analysis
therefore must be preceded by a detailed qualitative
study of the material.

SPATIAL PALEOECOLOGY

Within certain limits, it is possible to carry out
useful studies on spatial paleoecology (Reyment, 1971,
chapter 6). The confines for such studies of necessity
are narrow, and may verge on paleobiogeography. I have

had occasion to discuss morphometric variations in Paleocene ostracods occurring throughout the Early Paleocene
epicontinental transgression across West and North Africa
(Reyment and Reyment, 1980). The morphometric difference
identified could be related to the possible existence of a
a climatic gradient. This example certainly is not re-
ferable to the main concept of spatial ecology (cf.
Pielou, 1974). Only sessile organisms, such as corals
and bryozoans, are liable to leave sufficiently good
traces of their erstwhile spatial relationships to permit
a usual type of spatial analysis such as developed by
Matern (1960), although the study of Pleistocene plant
associations would seem to offer certain possibilities.

ECOLOGICAL DIVERSITY

Ecological diversity for fossil species may be analyzed with a fair degree of accuracy and perhaps there
are more examples of this category of statistical paleoecologic analysis in the literature than of any other.
These may be in the form of semiquantitative comparisons
of faunal lists, usually involving percentages. Considerable use also has been made of "indices" of which
many variants have been proposed (Reyment, 1971, p. 160,
ff).

One of the preferred tools for analyzing ecological
diversity is the "Shannon-Wiener Index" (or "Shannon-
Weaver Index"), which uses relative abundances (Pielou,
1974, p. 290) and which is gaining some vogue of late in
statistical paleoecology thanks to its desirable mathematical properties (see also the discussion on Diversity
Studies).

ANALYSIS OF SPECIES FREQUENCIES

Seventeen species of ostracods of Early Paleocene
age were analyzed by Joreskog's maximum likelihood model
of factor analysis (Joreskog, Klovan, and Reyment, 1976).
These data were treated originally in Reyment (1963).
Here, it was determined that the relative frequencies
of different species in samples may be interpreted in
terms of the major environmental factors to which the
organisms reacted, that is five unspecified major environmental components. It also was concluded here that
although the factor analysis of fossil species associations seldom can be expected to disclose whether a

species is stenohaline or euryhaline, and stenothermal,
or eurythermal, it can indicate whether it is stenooic
or euryoic. In connection with the more detailed analysis of the material given in Reyment (1966) it was
thought possible to identify one factor as bathyal, ex-
trapolating from our knowledge of the depth distribution
of living ostracods.

The Shannon-Weaver index, previously mentioned, was
introduced into geology by Pelto (1954) and modified by
Miller and Kahn (1962) as a method of studying multispe-
cies systems [in part, analogous to the examples of Pielou (1977)]. Pelto's (1954) suggestion was to use the
function

$$H = -\sum_i p_i \log_e p_i$$

for studying multicomponent systems. Here, p_i is the
percentage of the i-th component, and
$\sum_i p_i = 100\%$. Pelto made use of the concept of relative
entropy, Hr, which is defined as the ratio of the
actual entropy to the maximum entropy, Hm, for the number
of components under consideration:

$$100 \ Hr = \frac{-100 \sum_{i=1}^{N} p_i \log_e p_i}{Hm}.$$

Here, p_i is the proportion of the i-th component in an
N-component system and Hm is

$$Hm = -\sum \frac{1}{N} \log_e \frac{1}{N} = \log_e N.$$

In the application devised by Miller and Kahn (1962), it
is required that the species be divided into "biofacies".
For my study of the Lower Paleocene ostracods, I accepted
the seven factors as representing paleobiofacies based on
the 17 most abundant species. It was found that the entropy approach yields valuable additional information,
particularly for the identification of environmental components that may have been overlooked in the earlier
analysis. Thus, in addition to the bathyal component
outlined in the factor analysis, calcareous and pelitic
components were isolated (Reyment, 1966, p. 48).

SECULAR FLUCTUATIONS IN THE ABUNDANCE OF SPECIES

The study of secular fluctuations in the relative frequencies of species is one that has a specific paleo-ecologic flavor. A classical, early study is that of Chaney (1924), reanalyzed in Reyment (1971, p. 174 ff). Chaney was concerned with attempting to identify shifts in relative abundances of plants in the Bridge Creek flora of Late Oligocene age in Oregon, U.S.A.

THE SPECIES x LEVELS MATRIX

The simplest sequential representation of chronological variations in a set of species can be produced in terms of the categories + (= an increase in average size), − (= a decrease in average size), 0 (= no change). The species by stratigraphic levels matrix of these observations is a useful indicator for picking out a sustained ecologic trend in a multicomponent set of observation, that is a common mode of reaction to the totality of environmental fluctuations. An example is given in Table 1. This representation shows that in the earlier levels of the sequence, most species follow the same pattern of variation, presumably ecologically controlled. Further aspects of the interpretation of this material are given in Reyment (1966, p. 90-93).

THE ECOLOG

I shall now consider an example in which the correlations between frequencies of organisms, on the one hand and geochemical components of the host sediment, on the other, are used to produce what can be referred to as an *ecolog*, that is a log in which diagnostic chemical elements are related to fluctuations in the frequencies of species through time. The example is taken from Reyment (1976).

Samples from 26 levels in a Nigerian borehole in sediments of Late Campanian (Cretaceous) age were analyzed with respect to the 14 elements Si, Fe, Mg, Ca, Na, K, Ti, P, Mn, V, Mo, Sr, Pd, and Zn. The frequencies of the foraminifers *Afrobolivina afra* Reyment, *Gabonella elongata* de Klasz & Meijer, and *Valvulineria* sp. were recorded for those levels. The ostracods, being relatively rare, were pooled for the purposes of the analysis.

Table 1. Size-directional changes
          in a series of seven spe-
          cies of Nigerian Paleo-
          cene ostracods (based on
          fluctuations in the length
          of the carapace).

Species	Direction of change upwards in borehole
Cytherella sylvesterbradleyi	- 0 - 0 0 - + 0 +
Ovocytheridea pulchra	- + + 0 - 0 0 - -
Leguminocythereis lagaghiroboensis	- + + 0 - - - - -
Trachyleberis teiskotensis	0 + + 0 + - + + +
Buntonia beninensis	- 0 + + 0 - + + 0
Buntonia bopaensis	0 + + 0 - - - 0 0
Buntonia livida	0 + + 0 - - - 0 0

The aim of the study was to facilitate the graphical expression of a difficult paleoecologic and biostratigraphic problem. In one direction, it was thought to be of interest to show how all variables considered in the one connection change through time. In another direction, interest was concentrated on tracing temporal covariation in frequencies and geochemical variables.

The method of canonical correlations (Blackith and Reyment, 1971) was used for studying the relationships between sets. Canonical correlations have been little used in ecology owing to certain problems of interpretation, not the least of which is that a high canonical correlation is not associated necessarily with the greatest part of the information in the material. A biological example of the application of canonical correlation to an ecological problem is given by Reyment (1975) for ostracods in the Niger Delta. In this study, pH, Eh, bathymetry, phosphorus, and sulfur formed the predictor set; the response set was composed of total organic substance, Σ $CaCO_3$, and the total frequencies of ostracods. The most significant results of the analysis are (1) a significant canonical correlation with Ss weighed against ostracods (a thanatocoenetic relationship), and (2) the distribution of the ostracod species is controlled by depth in a negative association with phosphorus. Canonical-correlation analysis has an added useful side, that is the graphical presentation of the

transformed partitioned observational vectors. In this
situation, it was ascertained that the samples rich in
ostracods form a well-defined cluster. The example reviewed here however is more complex, as direct observations on known ecologic components could not be obtained.
Si is correlated significantly and positively with Fe,
Mn, and V, and negatively and significantly with Mg, Ca,
Na, P, and Sr. The variable Fe is correlated significantly and positively with Mn, V and Mo, and significantly
negatively with Na, P, and Sr, whereas Na is correlated
significantly and positively with K, P, and Sr. Further
significant correlations are as follows: Ti is correlated
positively with V, Mo, Pb, and Zn, and P is correlated
positively with Sr. Mn is correlated positively with V
and Mo. Mo is correlated positively with Pb and Zn and
negatively with Sr.

For the microfossils, the following significant relationships between sets occur. There is a negative
correlation between ostracod frequencies and Zn, whereas
Afrobolivina afra is not correlated significantly with
any of the geochemical variables. The frequencies for
the *Valvulineria* are correlated positively with Mn and
Fe and negatively with Ca, whereas *Gabonella elongata* is
correlated positively with Fe and Mo, and negatively with
Ca and Sr.

In the following, the vector variable z_1 contains
the chemovariables and the vector variable z_2, the
frequencies of the microfossils. The roots of the
determinantal equation for the two sets (the R_{ij} are
submatrices of the correlation matrix R)

$$|R_{22}^{-1}R_{21}R_{11}^{-1}R_{12} - \lambda_j I| = 0 \qquad\qquad (1)$$

are $\lambda_1 = 0.849$, $\lambda_2 = 0.752$, $\lambda_3 = 0.414$, and $\lambda_4 = 0.182$.
The first two of these roots are statistically signifi-
cant. These roots are the squares of the canonical correlations, that is $R_{c1} = 0.922$ and $R_{c2} = 0.867$ which are
the maximum correlations between two linear
functions of the two sets of variables.

The structure coefficients for two canonical factors
for all 18 variables are given in Table 2. The main
steps involved are as follows (extracted from Cooley and
Lohnes, 1971). Having determined the roots of equation
(1), the vector d is obtained from

Table 2. Structure coefficients (Cooley
          and Lohnes, 1971) for two ca-
          nonical factors of the geochem-
          ical and species-frequencies
          data (after Reyment, 1976).

Variable	Geochemical set		Set of species frequencies		
	Factor 1	Factor 2	Variable	Factor 1	Factor 2
Si	0.31	-0.22	ostracods	-0.39	-0.66
Fe	0.36	-0.23	Afrobolivina	0.12	0.14
Mg	-0.26	-0.08	Valvulineria	0.67	-0.74
Ca	-0.38	0.24	Gabonella	0.62	-0.20
Na	-0.08	0.31			
K	0.21	0.23			
Ti	0.12	0.39	Factor redundancy	0.217	0.197
P	0.05	0.37	Total redundancy	0.565	
Mn	0.49	-0.21			
V	0.26	0.33			
Mo	0.67	0.23			
Sr	-0.27	0.24			
Pb	0.31	0.67			
Zn	0.51	0.36			
Factor redundancy	0.102	0.078			
Total redundancy	0.218				

$$(R_{22}^{-1}R_{21}R_{11}^{-1}R_{12} - \lambda_j I)d_j = 0, \qquad (2)$$

with the constraint that $d_j R_{22} d_j = 1$. The d_j are the
weights for the j-th canonical factor of
z_2. The corresponding weights for the j-th canonical
factor of z_i are obtained from the relationship

$$c_j = \frac{(R_{11}^{-1}R_{12}d_j)}{\sqrt{\lambda_j}} .$$

Up to now, these steps are the usual ones of canonical
correlation. The expansion of the method into a "redundancy analysis" Cooley and Lohnes, 1971) is done by extracting the variance by the canonical variables,
$s_1 s_1 / p_1$, where p_1 denotes the number of variables in z_1

(here, this comprises the 14 chemical elements) and
$s_2's_2/p_2$, where p_2 denotes the number of variables in
vector z_2 (in this example, this is
4). We also have $s_1 = R_{11}c$ and $s_2 = R_{22}d$.
The redundancy of set 1 in the
presence of set 2 (set 1 contains the chemovariables,
set 2 contains the frequencies of the organisms) is defined as

$$R_{d_x} = s_1's_1R_{c1}^2/p_1,$$

where R_{c1} denotes the canonical correlation for the
first pair of canonical variates and the subscript
x labels the canonical factor x. The reverse relationship is expressed by the formula

$$R_{d_y} = s_2's_2R_{c1}^2/p_2.$$

The first canonical factors are $x_1 = c_1'z_1$ and $y_1 = d_1'z_2$.
Likewise, the second canonical
factors are $x_2 = c_2'z_1$ and $y_2 = d_2'z_2$.

The first canonical factor (Table 2) for the left
set of variables comprises significant loadings for most
of them. Only Na, Ti, and P are so low as to indicate
nonsignificant correlation. The first canonical factor
for the right set contains significant loadings for all
frequencies except that of *Afrobolivina afra*. The left-
hand canonical variate is correlated positively with Si,
Fe, K, Mn, V, Mo, Pb, and Zn, and negatively correlated
with Mg, Ca, and Sr. This canonical variate seems to be
explainable as a dipolar relationship between sediment
richer in carbonates and clastic sedimentary components.
The right-hand canonical variate is correlated positively
with the frequencies of *Valvulineria* sp. and *Gabonella
elongata*, and negatively with ostracods.

Ecolog from the Canonical Correlations

The plot of the scores obtained by substituting the
partitioned mean vectors into the first pair of linear
relationships can be used to produce a paleoecologic log
in which the fluctuations in the frequencies of the organisms are weighted against variations in the chemical
components of the host sediment. As to be expected from

the rather high corresponding canonical correlation, the
oscillations follow the same general trends, although
there are numerous deviations in the middle and upper
thirds of the plots. These deviations are small but
might mark periods during which the chemical influences
were overprinted by other environmental factors. The
lower third of the figure might be an indication of a
phase in development during which the chemical components
of the environment dominated, such as arises during periods of pronouncedly chemical sedimentation, as in the
formation of a marl.

Ecolog by Principal Coordinates

Using Pythagorean distances between individuals,
all 18 variables of the foregoing analysis were grouped
into a single principal-coordinates analysis (Gower,
1966). The plot of the first set of coordinates against
location in the borehole, illustrated in Figure 1, shows
the existence of trend in the points. This could indicate that there was a largely unidirectional ecological
trend in the paleoenvironment through the time-interval
covered by the samples. An interesting property of this
ecolog is that the youngest samples seem to be in a state
of ecological equilibrium (levels 17-26 inclusive),
whereas the older samples may reflect an ecologically
perturbed system. The system could have been in the process of becoming stabilized in some manner or other, not
necessarily optimal, for the proliferation of benthic
microorganisms.   In fact, the youngest samples are
characterized by the predominance of *Afrobolivina afra*.

STABILIZED CANONICAL VARIATES IN
PALEOECOLOGICAL ANALYSIS

Canonical-variate analysis of living and fossil
organisms, based on morphological characters, can be
distorted, from the aspect of the biological interpretation of the coefficients of the eigenvectors forming the
canonical variates, through the inclusion of redundant
within-group directions. Instability is associated with
the smallest eigenvalues, particularly if these do not
differ greatly from zero. In a study of borehole samples of *Afrobolivina afra* Reyment from Nigeria, stability
of the canonical-variate coefficients was attained by
removal of a near-redundant direction of within-group
variation. This leads to improved interpretability of

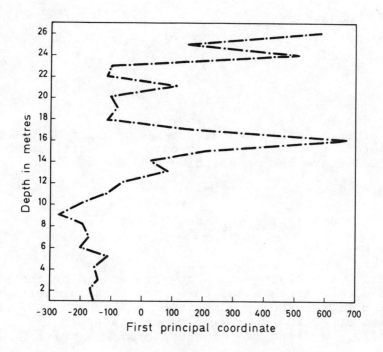

Figure 1. Ecolog of fluctuations in fre-
            quencies of microorganisms con-
            structed from first set of
            principal coordinates.

the morphometric relationships in this species (Campbell
and Reyment, 1978). The characters measured on *Afrobolivina afra* are: (1) = length of the test, (2) = width,
(3) = width of final chamber, (4) = height of final chamber, (5) = height of second last chamber, (6) = diameter
of proloculus, (7) = breadth (measured at right angles to
variable 2), (8) = width of aperture, (9) = location of
aperture on second last chamber. The main computational
steps are set out here.

    The within-groups sums of squares and cross-products
matrix W on n_W degrees of freedom, and the between-groups
sums of   squares and cross-products matrix B are
computed in the usual manner of canonical-variate analysis, together with the matrix of sample means. It then
is recommended that the matrix W then be standardized
to correlation form, with similar scaling for B. The
standardization is obtained by pre- and post-multiplying
by the inverse of diagonal matrix S, the diagonal elements
of which are the square roots of the diagonal elements

of W. Consequently,

$$W* = S^{-1}WS^{-1},$$

and

$$B* = S^{-1}BS^{-1}.$$

The eigenvalues e_i and eigenvectors u_i of W* then are computed; the corresponding orthogonalized variables are the principal components.

With

$$E = \text{diag}(e_i,\ldots,e_v) \text{ and } U = (u_1,\ldots,u_v),$$

$$W* = UEU^T.$$

Usually, the eigenvectors now are scaled by the square root of the eigenvalue; this is a transformation for producing within-groups sphericity. Shrunken estimators are formed by adding shrinking constants k_i^* to the eigenvalue e_i before scaling the eigenvectors.   Write

$$K = \text{diag}(k_1,\ldots,k_v) \text{ and define}$$

$$U* = U(E + K)^{-\frac{1}{2}} = U*(k_1,\ldots,k_v).$$

Next form the between-groups matrix in the within-groups principal-component space, that is,

$$G_{(k_1,\ldots,k_v)} = U*^T_{(k_1,\ldots,k_v)}\ B*U*_{(k_1,\ldots,k_v)}$$

and set d_i equal to the i-th diagonal element of G. The i-th diagonal element d_i is the between-groups sums of squares for the i-th principal component.

An eigen-analysis of the matrix $G_{(0,\ldots,0)}$ yields the usual canonical roots f and canonical vectors for the principal components, a^u. The usual canonical vectors c^u are given by

$$c^u = U*_{(0,\ldots,0)}a^u.$$

Generalized shrunken (or generalized ridge-) estimators are determined directly from the eigenvectors a^s of

$G_{(k_1,\ldots,k_v)}$, with $c^S = U^*_{(k_1,\ldots,k_v)} a^S$. A generalized-

inverse solution results when $k_i = 0$ for $i \leq r$ and $k_i =$

∞ for $i > r$. This gives $a_i^{GI} = a_i^u$ for $i \leq r$ and $a_i^{GI} = 0$

for $i > r$. The generalized inverse solution results from
forming $G_{(0,\ldots,0,\infty,\ldots,\infty)} = U_r^{*T} B^* U_r^*$, where U_r^* corres-

ponds to the first r columns of $U^*_{(0,\ldots,0)}$. The general-

ized canonical vectors $c^{GI} = c^S_{(0,\ldots,0,\infty,\ldots,\infty)}$ are

given by $c^{GI} = U_r^* a^{GI}$, where a^{GI}, of length r, corres-

ponds to the first r elements of a^u. In practice, marked
instability is associated with a small value of e_v and
a correspondingly small diagonal element d_v of G. A
generalized inverse solution with r=v-1 frequently
provides stable estimates and usually is simpler conceptually than using shrinking constants.

An easy rule to use is to examine the contribution
of d_v to the total group separation, trace ($W^{-1}B$); the
latter is merely trace ($G_{(0,\ldots,0)}$) or
$\sum_{i=1}^{v} d_i$. In situations where one or two canonical variates
describe much of the between-groups variation,
it may be better to examine the relative magnitudes of
the first one or two canonical roots derived from
$G_{(0,\ldots,0)}$ and $G_{(0,\ldots,0,\infty)}$ rather than a composite measure. Either way, if $d_v/\sum d_i$, or the corresponding ratio
of canonical roots, is small (say, less than
0.05), then little loss of discrimination will result
from excluding the smallest eigenvalue-eigenvector combination ($k_v = \infty$) or, equivalently, from eliminating the
last principal component.

The eigenvalues and eigenvectors for all nine variables are listed in Table 3. The smallest eigenvalue accounts for only 1.8 percent of the variation within
groups. The eigenvector corresponding to the smallest
eigenvalue (hereinafter referred to as the smallest
eigenvector) reflects a contrast between variables 2 and

Table 3. Eigenvalues and eigenvectors of within-
          groups correlation matrix W* for all
          nine variables; between-groups sums of
          squares for each principal component
          (after Campbell and Reyment, 1978).

Eigenvalues (e_i)	1	2	3	4	5	6	7	8	9
	4.31	1.25	1.00	0.69	0.48	0.43	0.38	0.29	0.16
Eigenvectors	v1	v2	v3	v4	v5	v6	v7	v8	v9
u_1	0.35	0.43	0.42	0.37	0.37	0.15	0.35	0.21	0.23
u_2	0.33	0.09	0.20	0.19	0.21	-0.30	-0.31	-0.55	-0.53
u_3	0.28	-0.15	-0.03	-0.10	-0.07	-0.85	0.23	0.31	0.09
u_4	-0.08	-0.06	0.03	0.09	0.05	0.13	0.01	0.64	-0.74
u_5	-0.44	-0.05	-0.18	0.44	0.51	-0.25	-0.42	0.17	0.24
u_6	-0.01	-0.10	0.03	0.74	-0.66	-0.02	0.01	-0.03	0.03
u_7	0.27	0.26	0.24	-0.20	-0.28	0.03	-0.73	0.33	0.20
u_8	0.64	-0.48	-0.44	0.14	0.19	0.29	-0.11	0.08	0.10
u_9	-0.10	-0.69	0.70	-0.05	0.08	0.06	-0.04	0.00	0.10
	1	2	3	4	5	6	7	8	9
diag$\{G_{(0,\ldots,0)}\}$	1.01	0.25	0.23	0.27	0.26	0.07	1.57	0.18	0.21

trace $\{G_{(0,\ldots,0)}\}$ = 4.05.

3, to wit the width of the test, and the width of the
last chamber.

These loadings are large and , it may be suspected
that if the corresponding between-groups sum of squares
is small, as is the situation in our example, instability
in the corresponding canonical variate coefficients may
result.

The between-groups sums of squares for all principal
components shows that 39 percent of the between-groups
variation is associated with the seventh principal component and 17 percent with the first principal component.
The variation for the seventh principal component results
from a contrast between variable 7 and most of the other
variables; the first principal component is a "size component" (cf. Blackith and Reyment, 1971).

The canonical variate analysis can be carried out in
terms of the principal components (the coefficients for
the original variables are estimated by projecting back
to the space of the original variables). The coefficients for the first canonical variate (a_i^u in Table 4)
highlight the contribution from the   seventh

PALEOECOLOGY   299

Table 4.   Standardized canonical vectors for nine varia-
           bles, including shrunken estimates (from Camp-
           bell and Reyment, 1978).

	v1	v2	v3	v4	v5	v6	v7	v8	v9	Canonical roots
a_1^u	0.54	-0.11	-0.01	0.11	0.06	-0.07	0.79	-0.18	-0.13	
a_2^u	-0.64	-0.32	0.14	-0.13	-0.44	-0.11	0.39	0.05	-0.32	
c_1^u	0.00	-0.59	-0.09	0.43	0.44	0.07	0.99	-0.51	-0.10	2.28
c_2^u	0.65	0.81	-0.27	-0.44	-0.40	0.15	0.04	0.28	0.25	0.76
$c_{1(0,\ldots,\infty)}^{GI}$	0.04	-0.37	-0.31	0.43	0.41	0.06	1.01	-0.51	-0.12	2.25
$c_{2(0,\ldots,\infty)}^{GI}$	0.58	0.29	0.31	-0.53	-0.36	0.25	-0.03	0.37	0.32	0.70
$c_{1(0,.,\infty,\infty)}^{GI}$	-0.17	-0.21	-0.17	0.32	0.42	-0.04	1.06	-0.53	-0.16	2.17
$c_{2(0,.,\infty,\infty)}^{GI}$	0.53	0.32	0.35	-0.40	-0.50	0.22	-0.03	0.36	0.33	0.68

principal component. The coefficients for the original
variables are determined explicitly from the principal-
component canonical vector; any inflation in these latter coefficients results in inflated coefficients for
those among the original variables contributing to the
eigenvector from which the principal component is derived.
Note that the first principal component contributes most
to the second canonical variate (see a_2^u in Table 4).

     The first canonical variate amounts to 56 percent
of the between-group variation. The first two canonical
variates account for 75 percent of the variation between
groups. The coefficients for the standardized original
variables for the first two canonical variates are shown
in Table 4, namely c_1^u and c_2^u.

                    SHRUNKEN ESTIMATES

     The effect of shrinking the contribution of the
smallest eigenvector (and associated eigenvalue), namely,
the ninth principal component, is shown in Table 4 (here,
$k_9 = \infty$ implies the elimination of the ninth principal
component from the analysis).

     The two sets of coefficients for the original var-
bles (c_i^u) and $k_9 = \infty$ ($c_{i(0,\ldots,\infty)}^{GI}$) are similar, except

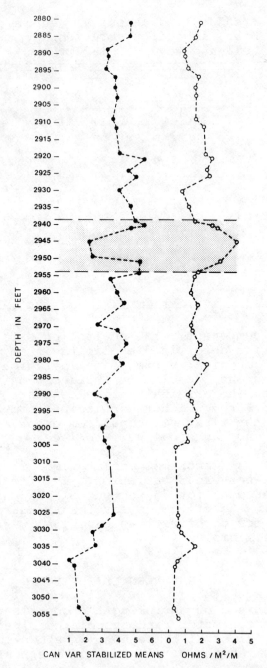

Figure 2.   Biolog formed from growth-
            reduced principal coordinates
            of 10 samples of *Afrobolivina
            afra*.   Right-hand curve is
            short-normal electrical re-
            sistivity log.

for variables 2 and 3. The decrease in the magnitude of
the coefficient for the second variable and the change in
sign of the coefficient for variable 3 are apparent. The
sum of the coefficients for these two variables is relatively stable and the canonical roots are little affected
by the elimination of the smallest eigenvector.

A plot of the shrunken estimates for all nine variables of the canonical variate means for the first canonical variate against location indicates that there is a
general drift over time in the morphology of the species,
manifested here as a trend to the right. This shift
seems to be due to a long-term environmental effect (Fig.
2).

The improved interpretability of paleoecological
data brought about by the foregoing approach to canonical variate analysis offers attractive prospects for the
future. From the aspect of computing, the procedure, of
necessity, is an interactive one.

REFERENCES

Blackith, R.E., and Reyment, R.A., 1971, Multivariate
    morphometrics: Academic Press, London and New York,
    412 p.

Burnaby, T.P., 1966, Growth-invariant discriminant func-
    tions: Biometrics, v. 22, no. 1, p. 96-110.

Campbell, N.C., and Reyment, R.A., 1978, Discriminant
    analysis of a Cretaceous foraminifer using shrunken
    estimators: Jour. Math. Geology. v. 10, no. 4, p.
    347-359.

Chaney, R.W., 1924, Quantitative studies of the Bridge
    Creek flora: Am. Jour. Sci., v. 8, no. 44, p. 127-
    144.

Cooley, W.W. and Lohnes, P., 1971, Multivariate data
    analysis: John Wiley & Sons, New York, 364 p.

Gower, J.C., 1966, A Q-technique for the calculation of
    canonical variates: Biometrika, v. 53, pts. 3/4,
    p. 588-590.

Gower, J.C., 1976, Growth-free canonical variates and
    generalized inverses: Geol. Inst. Univ. Uppsala
    Bull. (new ser.), v. 7, p. 1-10.

Joreskog, K.G., Klovan, J.E., and Reyment, R.A., 1976,
    Geological factor analysis: Elsevier, Amsterdam,
    178 p.

Mardia, K., 1972, Statistics of directional data: Aca-
    demic Press, London and New York, 357 p.

Miller, R.L., and Kahn, J.S., 1962, Statistical analysis
    in the geological sciences: John Wiley & Sons, New
    York, 357 p.

Pelto, C.R., 1954, Mapping of multicomponent systems:
    Jour. Geology, v. 62, no. 5, p. 501-511.

Pielou, E.C., 1974, Population and community ecology:
    Gordon & Breach, New York, 424 p.

Pielou, E.C., 1977, Mathematical ecology: John Wiley
    & Sons, New York, 385 p.

Reyment, R.A., 1963, Multivariate analytical treatment of
    of quantitative species associations: an example
    from palaeoecology: Jour. Anim. Ecology, v. 32,
    p. 535-547.

Reyment, R.A., 1966, Studies on Nigerian Upper Creta-
    ceous and Lower Tertiary Ostracoda. III, Strati-
    graphical, palaeoecological and biometrical conclu-
    sion: Stockh. Contr. Geol., v. 14, 151 p.

Reyment, R.A., 1971, Introduction to quantitative paleo-
    ecology: Elsevier, Amsterdam, 226 p.

Reyment, R.A., 1975, Canonical correlation analysis of
    hemicytherinid and trachyleberinid ostracodes in
    the Niger Delta: Bull. Am. Paleontologist, v. 65,
    no. 282, p. 141-145.

Reyment, R.A., 1976, Chemical components of the environ-
    ment and Late Campanian microfossil frequencies:
    Geol. Foren. Stockh. Forh., v. 98, p. 322-328.

Reyment, R.A., and Banfield, C., 1976, Growth-free canon-
    ical variates applied to fossil foraminifers: Geol.
    Inst. Univ. Uppsala Bull. (new ser.), v. 7, p. 11-
    21.

Reyment, R.A., and Reyment, E.R., 1980, The Paleocene
    trans-Saharan transgression and its ostracod fauna:
    Proc. 2nd Conf. on Geology of Libya, Tripoli,
    in press.

THE FUTURE OF INFORMATION SYSTEMS IN THE EARTH SCIENCES

P.G. Sutterlin

Canada Centre for Mineral

and Energy Technology

ABSTRACT

Much of the effort in modern information systems
has been concentrated in two aspects. The first is in
the design and generation of various types of data
bases. The second is in the design and development of
methods to retrieve selectively relevant information
from these data bases. These activities have had the
effect of forcing the geoscientist to reexamine the
methods in which earth-science data has been collected,
recorded, and stored. As a result some fundamental progress has been made in geoscience information systems
apart from the fields of computer and information sciences. The next phase already seems to be in progress.
The use of distributed processing techniques, the availability of relatively inexpensive microcomputers and an
emerging communications technology will significantly
affect the manner in which geoscientists will gather,
store, and access information.

INTRODUCTION

The rate of change in technology of computer-aided
data processing and electronic data communications is
mind-boggling. It is difficult to anticipate future
developments in geoscience information systems which
undoubtedly will be affected by these new techniques.
Perhaps the best that can be done is to review the

progress of the past couple of decades and, in the light of technology already in place, attempt to gauge the impact this may have on the geoscience community in the coming decade.

The word SYSTEM is being used more and more frequently as a tool to market a whole host of products. There are stereophonic sound systems, home rug-cleaning systems and, most recently, word-processing systems. These systems probably would be described as respectively: one or more electronic components designed to reproduce music from a plastic disk or magnetic tape; a machine with a set of fancy attachments designed to apply a cleaning agent to wall-to-wall carpeting; and a stand-alone mini- or microcomputer which allows direct entry, dynamic revision, and composition of textual material. The emphasis would be focussed most likely on the physical "things" which serve to process music, clean rugs, and manipulate alphanumeric characters. In the same vein, an information system has come to indicate in most instances nothing more than a set of computer programs or a "software package" which permits the processing of various types of information. This, however, is a much too restricted point of view.

In a recent report to the Provincial Ministers of Mines in Canada, C.F. Burk (1979) of the Canada Centre for Geoscience Data defined an information system as follows:

"Things, people, procedures and information
   organized and managed to achieve an objective."

In this context, perhaps the two most common information systems are a library and a room full of filing cabinets, each with their respective staffs who acquire information and data in order to:

(A)   Develop and maintain an information resource, and
(B)   Apply procedures and management techniques to insure efficient and effective utilization of the information resource.

To determine the impact of the application of computer-aided techniques on development of information systems for the earth sciences, it is useful to analyze in a bit more detail the functions involved in information-resource development and information-resource

utilization, using the library and the file room as
models.

INFORMATION-RESOURCE DEVELOPMENT

The development of an information resource involves,
in general terms:

   (A)   Information Resource Acquisition
          1.   Information selection
          2.   Information collection
   (B)   Information Processing
          1.   Information classification
          2.   Information indexing and abstracting
          3.   Information cataloging
   (C)   Information Storage
          1.   Information storage medium design
          2.   Information organization.

INFORMATION-RESOURCE ACQUISITION

The manner in which the basic information resource
of any information system is acquired has been affected
only marginally by computer technology. Only where information and data are recorded directly in analog or
digital form onto a permanent storage medium has the
methodology of selection and collection of information
changed, and then only in response to a change in the
information-generation methods. In all other situations,
collection and selection of information to comprise the
resource remains a manual operation. This, however, is
one area in which the emerging communications technology
may have a marked impact in the near future.

INFORMATION PROCESSING

The processing of information as part of the re-
source-development function becomes necessary when the
number of individual items in an information resource
reaches the point where time constraints preclude item-
by-item examination of all information sources pertinent to a particular problem. Information is classified, indexed and, in some situations, cataloged to
produce subject and author indexes in the form of card
catalogs in libraries, or various indexes to the contents of a series of filing cabinets. These indexes

constitute "secondary" or "derived" information resources
designed to facilitate identification and selective retrieval of those items of information (the books, documents, and file folders) which are most likely to contain pertinent information. In fact, they are organized
or "structured" compilations of information or data. In
this sense, these indexes can be regarded as data bases.
It thus would seem that one of the major objectives in
the processing of an information resource in its development phase is the generation of data bases. The manner in which those data bases are to be accessed has a
definite influence on their design. Therefore, the design of the data bases has been, and is yet, the objective of much research and study.

DATA BASES

There is an almost continuous gradation from a data
base whose records contain only numerical measurement
information (presumably unsullied by any subjective interpretation or regurgitation) to one whose records contain only references to the sources of information (with
or without keywords or abstracts). It has been popular
to contend that the former "numeric" data base comprises
"real" data whereas the latter "bibliographic" data base
is composed of information. It has been contended further that failure to recognize the difference between
data and information, particularly as it pertains to
information-systems design, will lead only to disaster.
However, the point at which objectivity ceases and sub-
jectivity begins, particularly in the earth sciences,
is not easy to determine. Hence, many of the more frequently used geoscience data bases contain within their
records some elements of both these "information end
members (Fig. 1). It would seem, then, that the design
of a geoscience information data base - and consequently
the design of the information system to process the
data base - is more sensitive to the "mix" of information types which form the information resource than to
some arbitrary distinction between data and information.
Therefore it is convenient to regard "data" as a part
of the total spectrum of information, and a data base
as structured information. In that manner it is possible to use the terms data and information interchange-
ably.

DATA BASE ASPECT	END MEMBER 1		END MEMBER 2
Type of Information	Secondary (Information)	Mixed (Infordata)	Primary (Data)
Relative volume of Information	Large	Small	Large
Information Structure	Simple	Complex	Simple
Information Contents	Bibliographic citations	Measurements Observations	Digitized log data

Figure 1. Range of data bases in geoscience.

INFORMATION STORAGE

There is not much point in processing information
and creating data bases to identify the resources unless
they are arranged and stored in such a manner as to relate to the data bases and can be retrieved readily.
Generally, in manual information systems, this involves
some sort of sequential ordering within specified
classes, and the whole arranged physically to optimize
access time. Again, we are reminded of the file room
and the library shelves. As more and more information
became available, most storage facilities became inadequate physically, and many methods have been devised
which will enable the storage of more and more information in less per unit space. Computer technology first
made significant inroads on the information resource
development function with respect to the storage of information.

INFORMATION-RESOURCE UTILIZATION

The utilization of an information resource involves,
in general terms:

```
    (A)   Information Resource Utilization
          1.   Information Processing
               I.    Information problem definition
               II.   Information resource identification
               III.  Information search strategy defini-
                     tion
               IV.   Information selective retrieval
    (B)   2.   Information Acquisiton
               I.    Information transmission
               II.   Information (document) delivery.
```

The conventional methodology of information retrieval
presupposes a relative physical location for each item
of information within the information resource. Given
a well designed set of data bases and an orderly storage algorithm, items of information can be identified,
selected and retrieved directly. The search strategy
will depend on the number of data bases or indexes
available to be used to narrow down the search. The
definition of the information required and the search
strategy employed yet remains a problem. On the one
hand, not many librarians or file clerks are sufficiently
subject-oriented. On the other hand, not many users are
sufficiently familiar with information systems. This
point will be elaborated next.

THE ROLE OF THE COMPUTER INFORMATION SYSTEM

    During the past four decades, the rate of increase
in the amount of information has been staggering. All
predictions point to the fact that this rate of increase
will be at least maintained (if not accelerated) in the
next twenty years. There have been essentially two
stimuli in the application of computer technology to
information systems.

    1. The indexes to most of the major information-
        resource depositories have themselves become
        sufficiently large, in terms of the number of
        records they contain, that item-by-item manual
        searching of these data bases has become im-
        practical.
    2. The volume of material encompassing the infor-
        mation on any one subject - or even one sub-
        discipline - has become sufficiently great that
        storage of this information at a single loca-
        tion is becoming impractical. This has resulted
        in the development of indexes which cover more
        than one information resource. Depository ac-
        cess to these composite indexes, some of which
        by now have assumed gargantuan proportions, is
        impractical using solely manual techniques.

    No single geoscience library is capable of select-
ing, acquiring, and storing all of the earth-science
information now available and which will be generated
in the future. Similarly, although a single exploration
company may be able to organize and store its own field
data and information, but is unlikely to have the

manpower, facilities, or inclination to store centrally
all exploration data available.

The electronic computer therefore has been used
extensively for the last fifteen years as a tool in those
parts of information systems which have to do with information storage - and consequently data-base design - and
with the retrieval of information from these data bases.
The application of computer technology to geoscience information then should have been relatively straightforward. After all, card catalogs and file folders have
been in existence for a long time. What more could have
been required than a simple transposition of information
and data from one storage medium to another? Is there
something unique about geoscience information which
seemingly has required the development of specialized
data bases and information systems? Or perhaps is it
the nature of the science itself, or the methodology of
its practitioners which has produced the host of data
bases and information systems which now are being used
by geoscientists? The answer is - probably a little
bit of both (Hubaux, 1973).

BIBLIOGRAPHIC DATA-BASE DESIGN

It is relatively easy on a library catalog card to
determine which combination of alphanumeric characters
refer to the author (or authors), the title, the citation, the abstract (if present), and the keywords. The
information in each of these "records" does not have to be
ordered or "structured" precisely. The record contents
are decipherable regardless of their internal consistency. However, a computer, not being able to make the
same type of value judgments, requires internal record
consistency. This immediately raises the question not
only of what information should be included in each record of such a data base but how this information should
be structured. Although this question has not been resolved entirely among the indexers, abstractors, and
catalogers of bibliographic data, progress is being
made. In any situation, each document or book can be
described in terms of a record containing one or more
author names, a title, a series of keywords which summarize the essence of the document's contents, a citation or reference, and an abstract. In one way or another, each of these items of information can be assigned
a field which must be "flagged" in such a manner as to
identify the contents of the fields. Although there may

be many authors, a host of appropriate keywords, a lengthy
citation, and a comprehensive abstract making up each record, the information in each field applies equally to the
entire record (Fig. 2). This permits the structure of the
record to remain essentially linear because each field is
linked to a common root, giving rise to a simple tree.
Moreover, as long as each individual item of information
within the record which might be used as a search key is
assigned a separate field, the fields can be readily rearranged - that is to say that their sequence can be revised easily and altered. This indicates that many, if
indeed not most, bibliographic data bases can be adapted
for processing by a number of generalized "data-base systems" or computer programs designed to accommodate simple
data structures. This is not to say that, from a systems
analyst's point of view, these "systems" are simple or
unsophisticated - to the contrary. It does indicate,
however, that the data-base design need not be governed
directly by the nature of the computer programs which may
be used eventually to process the information.

     Because much of the information collected by geo-
scientists is not yet "quantifiable", the definition of
the language used to communicate data and concepts perhaps has not been as precise in the geosciences as it has
in the other physical and natural sciences. Much reli-
ance has been placed on the context in which certain
words and phrases are used. However, when bibliographic
data bases were being converted to those to be processed
by computer, it became apparent that many so-called "descriptors" were meaningless, especially (as is usually
the situation) when they were used as keywords out of
context. This has provided the need for the development
of a number of thesauri to control the vocabulary of com-
puter-processable geoscience bibliographic data bases.
Ultimately, the use of these thesauri in conjunction with
the general availability of the data bases should serve
to help "tighten up" geological terminology to the point
where communication of information will be less ambiguous
and more complete and effective. This is a benefit which
has been the direct result of the application of computer
concepts to bibliographic data-base design, and which may
not have taken place otherwise. Certainly, without the
stimulus of computer-processible data bases, it is unlikely that the development of a multilingual geoscience
thesaurus would have been initiated. This joint undertaking of COGEODATA, IUGS, and the ICSU Abstracting

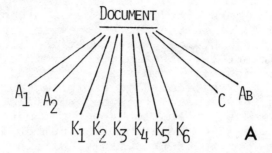

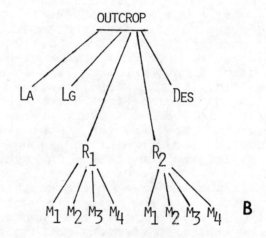

Figure 2. Distinction between structure of
secondary (A) and
primary (B) infor-
mation.

Board, under the Chairmanship of Dr. Harm Glasshof of
West Germany will have a major international impact on
geoscience information systems apart from the aspects of
computer processing which prompted this project.

NONBIBLIOGRAPHIC DATA-BASE DESIGN

Now, let's turn to the other information-system
model. When looking at the geological information and
data on the sheets of paper within a single file folder -
which is a record analagous to a bibliographic citation -
the items of information contained by implication are related to a geological concept or object and therefore

also to one another. However, because geological objects
and concepts are in themselves the product of the interaction of many physical, chemical, and biological phenomena, the interrelations among the items of information
required to describe them adequately tend to be more complex than when the record is a bibliographic reference.
Let's take the example of an outcrop file in which each
record contains information about the outcrop itself as
well as information relating to a number of rock types
within that outcrop. Presumably, within the file folder,
there would be one sheet of paper containing general information relating to the location and description of the
outcrop itself, and a series of sheets of paper each containing information relating to a separate rock type
within the outcrop. We see immediately that there are
within this outcrop record a number of subrecords, the
fields of which do not necessarily relate to the outcrop
as a whole (Fig. 2). In manual systems, the nature of
the recording and storage techniques used usually makes
it unnecessary to spell out every single link between information items. However, the computer again is unable
to make such implied correlations among a set of complexly
interrelated information items. The example I have given
is a relatively simple one. It should be easy to imagine,
however, that complex tree, hierarchy, and network information structures can result easily when working with
geological objects, concepts, and phenomena. Much care
then must be exercised when designing data bases which
contain purely numerical or a combination of numerical
and observational information in order that the item-to-
item relationships are preserved. This problem has led
to the development of a wide array of data bases. The
data-base design to a large degree has come to be dic-
tated by the perceived availability of a set of computer
programs to process a specific data set. This, however,
has not always been the situation.

     When geoscientists first began employing computers
to store and retrieve structured information, the generalized software packages designed to process data were
able only to accommodate the most simple information
structures (Sutterlin and May, 1978). These had been
developed to respond to the need for computer-aided
financial and bookkeeping functions which had to accommodate relatively uncomplicated data structures. Therefore,
there evolved a conviction among geoscientists that it
was necessary to develop a specific software package to
accommodate each of the data structures which were being
encountered. Unfortunately, this belief yet exists to a
large degree. However, the fact that the content of a

set of items of information may be unique scientifically
is no longer justification for this specific systems design approach. It is possible now to accommodate the
structure of almost any set of geological information
using one of the generalized "data-base management systems" available today. However, unlike the example with
bibliographic data bases, the nature of the computer programs selected to process a particular data set can have
a direct influence on the design of the data base. This
is because it is not always a simple matter to rearrange,
without loss of information, the data as they become
structured more complexly.

It is precisely these constraints and considerations
which can serve to benefit geoscientists. One of the
more significant outcomes of designing geoscience data
bases for computer processing has been the discovery (or
affirmation, if you like) that geoscientists with few exceptions have a rather cavalier attitude towards "primary"
information (what could be termed data). The prevailing
point of view seems to have been, perhaps unconsciously,
that as long as no one other than the generator or collec-
tor of information was likely to use a field book or a
"personal" file, it was of little consequence how information was recorded or stored as long as the records were
decipherable by the original observer. In other situations, the volumes of information have been too great and
this has precluded attempts to communicate "primary" information. Therefore, geoscientists have become accustomed to communicating in terms of concepts and conclusions, which are synthesized or "secondary" information
(Hubaux, 1973). These two factors have served to foster
the notion that the communication of "primary" geoscience
information is at best unnecessary and at worst potentially incriminating.

Computer technology, however, has made it possible
to communicate economically and rapidly hitherto unpre-
cedented volumes of "primary" information. So, it is
slowly becoming unacceptable to describe and record the
location of an outcrop as being "about a quarter of a
mile northeast of the upper end of Lake Skaneateles".
This description might lead the original observer back
to the spot, but anyone else would be unlikely to find
it. In this respect, the application of the computer
has forced some reevaluation of information collection
and recording methods.

BIBLIOGRAPHIC INFORMATION RETRIEVAL SOFTWARE

There are many geoscience bibliographic data bases in existence, and almost as much corresponding computer software designed to retrieve information from these data bases. However, it seems that in the last two years or so, there is beginning to be some recognition that perhaps a few large bibliographic data bases which are accessable widely are in the best interests of the geoscience community. As a result, the AGI Geo.Ref data base and Geosystem's GeoArchives data base have been implemented using respectively Lockheed's DIALOG software and SDC's ORBIT software. These data-base vendors have made their data bases widely available through the TYMSHARE, TYMNET, and DATAPAC communications networks. A software package named DIANE is available through the European Economic Commission and uses the EURONET communications network. Retrieval of bibliographic information from these data bases is fast, efficient, and relatively inexpensive. Records are stored randomly on magnetic disk so that access is direct. Comprehensive indexes to the data bases allow a great amount of flexibility in the search strategy used and the form of output desired. Experience has shown that the average retrieval cost is one dollar per minute of connect time.

As long as care is taken in the design of a bibliographic data base, computer conversion of such a data base for processing by a generalized software package is relatively straightforward on a one-to-one basis. Indexes can be generated automatically for each separate field in the record, so that only the indexes are searched in order to identify the storage location of these records which satisfy the search criteria. This not only greatly reduces retrieval time, but also permits a certain amount of Boolean logic to be applied if the search criteria involve more than a single descriptor. Most of the commerically used software packages permit searching of text where the record contains an abstract. However, it should be noted that this latter capability should not be taken as indication that the control of vocabulary, and thus thesaurus development, is no longer important, even though from a strictly computing point of view, it may no longer be a requirement to effect comprehensive search searches of bibliographic records. The benefits of thesaurus construction as an aid to indexers and as an important adjunct to "sharpen up" communication effectiveness.

Other refinements of software design continually are emerging. One example is the QUIKLAW System developed and operated as a data-base vending service by QL Systems in Kingston, Canada. This software computes a ranking for each of the records retrieved which fulfill the search criteria on the basis of the frequency of occurrence of all the search terms (including those in the abstract) used in the retrieval request. The user then may pre-select the number of records which he may wish to see displayed or printed on his terminal based on this statistical ranking. Search strategy commands in DIALOGUE and ORBIT may be preserved and subsequently modified, obviating the need to "start from scratch" every time a similar search or modification of an analogous search is desired. The command language required to use these systems is being simplified constantly so that even the uninitiated user with one day's instruction can master the basics of search techniques. In fact, it is becoming almost easier now to formulate the search commands than it is to master the commands required to insure that one is identified correctly by the system as a legitimate user.

NONBIBLIOGRAPHIC INFORMATION RETRIEVAL SOFTWARE

As has been mentioned before, in the late 1960's and the 1970's many data-specific as well as generalized software packages were developed to process what essentially were nonbibliographic or "primary information" data bases (Fig. 3). This has not been an attempt on the part of geoscientists to seek greener fields in the areas of information and computer science, although many geoscience grant committees seem convinced that this continues to be the sole motification. The fact remains that, until the middle 70's, when System 2000 and Honeywell's IDS II were developed, computer scientists who were developing data-processing software packages were not being faced with information which is structured as complexly as it is in the geosciences. Information which arranges itself in trees, hierarchies, and networks is not as abundant in other fields and where it has occurred, the practical solution was to divide the information into less complexly structured subsets.

As a result of this dilemma, geoscientists developed, in conjunction with (and sometimes over the protests of) the computer professional, a whole host of *data specific* as well as a few *generalized* software packages, some of which are displayed in Figure 3. These represent an

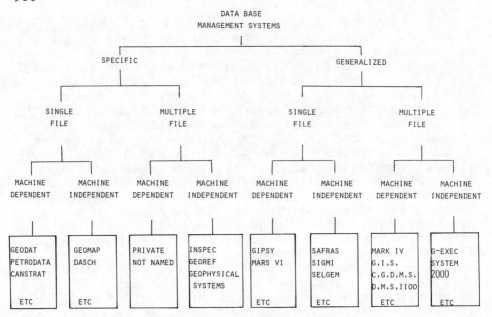

Figure 3.   "Primary information" data bases.

almost total spectrum with respect to the degree of programming sophistication incorporated in them.   The primary aim, of course, has been to design and develop "The
Software Package" which would accommodate readily any
conceivable geoscience information structure, and then
to convince the geoscientific community to use this system.   The analogy to the DIALOGUE, ORBIT, and DIANE systems is clear.   Communication, using automated techniques,
then would become a reality because a common system would
force adherence to standards of both information content
as well as basic information structures.

Unfortunately, the conversion of primary information
data bases from one form to another is not at all
straightforward.   When information structures become more
and more complex, it becomes desirable from a practical
point of view to use the structure embodied in the programming language being used to program the software
package in order to define some of the interrelationships
among the items of information in each record.   Then, unlike the situation with the bibliographic data base, conversion from one form to another involves more than a
mere rearrangement of fields within the records - in the
worst situation it may involve considerable redesign and
manual regeneration of the data base itself.

Even conversion of a data base to another "format" by developing a computer program to do so is not always easy, and becomes more difficult as the information structures become more complex. It can be done, but in many situations is not justifiable if the costs are taken into account. The FILEMATCH concept, which was enunciated three years ago, was an attempt at solving this problem (Sutterlin, Jeffery, and Gill, 1977). This concept suggested that each item of information in a data base have appended to it, in one way or another, enough structural information to define explicitly its relationship to all of the other items of information in the record, apart from the structural information embodied in high-level programming languages. Even though the implementation of FILEMATCH may have been somewhat unsophisticated, it may be time to revive the idea in the light of modern distributed processing concepts. Until something like this is done, communication of large amounts of primary information in machine-processable form will lag behind the significant progress in this direction which are evidenced with the bibliographic information systems.

FUTURE TRENDS

Future trends in information systems, including those which will be used in the earth sciences, will be a product of the interrelated developments in the areas of microcomputer design, distributed processing techniques, and communications technology.

Information processing may come to revolve around the types of functions which mini- and microcomputers are able to perform (Wigington, 1979). Present costs of the these machines is about \$15,000 per megabyte of storage which includes an input-output console, a printer, and operating system as well as applications software. For double this amount, such equipment can be configured with a hard disk capable of storing up to 12 megabytes of information and a number of input-output terminals. The software is sophisticated sufficiently to permit on-line entry and editing of information as well as some data-base search capabilities independent of a large mainframe computer. The potential of these machines to generate small data bases at the point where the data originate and are used is becoming obvious. The cost benefits of file generation using mini- and microcomputers in terms of the efficient use of personnel and physical resources is becoming more and more attractive

as the power of these machines increases in relation to
their cost.

It is possible, using primarily hardware features
included with most of these mini- and microcomputers to
transfer files of information from their storage media,
usually floppy disks, to the storage media of mainframe
computers. The generation of data bases using one mainframe computer and several microcomputers can form a powerful and effective distributed processing network when
the primary information resource (as may be the situation) is deposited in several physically separated locations.

Most microcomputers have available some sort of data-
base management file software which permits generation of
nonbibliographic data bases and selective retrieval, in
random access mode, of information from these data bases.
Presumably, the time is not far off when some of these
software packages will be able to accommodate fairly complex information structures. It would be ideal then to
incorporate these data bases into larger data bases using
distributed processing methods. However, much of the
structural information will continue to be part of the
high-level programming languages which are used in developing the software packages, making communication of the
generated files to another computer for incorporation in
a large data base difficult without first converting the
data bases to the format compatible with that of the
software package implemented on the other machine.

Now, given the potential benefits of distributed
data processing in the generation of primary information
data bases, it might be appropriate to reexamine the
FILEMATCH concept. It may be advantageous to study the
feasibility of establishing some sort of protocol whereby
structural information, hopefully automatically generated
by the software as the data base is being generated, can
be appended to every item of information in the records
of a data base. At present, data-base management systems
which produce random access files do generate as the file
is built (in the form of indexes) information as to the
precise location of records in the storage medium. Could
this technique not be applied in the manner suggested?

The one area where there has been technologically
the least progress, has been in the delivery of the
information to the user. It is not justifiable economically to store the entire contents of a document

or notebook in a data base for reproduction and transmission to a cathode-ray terminal or a high-speed printer. However, there are times when a user requires the
information more quickly than is possible using inter-
library loan and other similar transmission and delivery facilities. The answer, already tried in Great
Britain, seems to be to utilize radio transmission rather
than telephone lines for packet switching of information.
If cable television companies were to make available one
frequency or channel for radio packet switching, about
55,000 users at one time could be accommodated. The cost
of data transmission, as opposed to the present telecommunications networks, could be reduced dramatically.
This technology, coupled with a videodisk capable of
storing 54,000 frames of information, could make the
problem of document delivery and data transmission a
thing of the past. It would be prudent for geoscientists
to closely monitor these developments.

There is one aspect of information systems which
purposely has been left to the last, but not because it
it is the least important. This discussion began by defining an information system as:

"Things, people, procedures and information
organized and managed to achieve an objective".

Much has been said about things, procedures, and information, but little about people. Of course, many people including the information generators, indexers, abstractors,
data-base designers, software developers, and users all
have an impact on information systems. But, in research
centers, industry, and government, the task of making
efficient and effective use of the new information technology has been treated rather lightly. The trained
librarian generally is given these responsibilities.
However, the library staff may be ill-equipped to handle
these responsibilities. The person charged with this
task must be a subject-matter specialist. Then, knowing
where the information is available, where to obtain it,
and how to prepare it for use assumes more than a super-
ficial understanding of the technological changes which
are affecting the information-systems functions. This
person is one of a new breed - the information specialist.

The modern geoscience information professional must
be truly interdisciplinary - so much so that he has in
the past and continues to suffer from a lack of identity.

There is an almost urgent need for people trained to merge the geoscience, information science and computer science disciplines to help in the solution of complex information problems. It is not too drastic to predict that, if such people are not produced, the discipline of geology ultimately will be assimilated by those other scientific disciplines which better understand the vital part that information is playing, and will continue to play, in the evolution of research and development in their fields.

However, it must be remembered that geoscience data bases at present in reality are generated by those interested in geoscience information primarily for their own use. One of the goals which must be kept in mind is that, through research and further development, information technology should be simplified to the point where the tools can be put into the hands of the end user.

REFERENCES

Burk, C.F., 1979, National system for geological informa-
    tion: Rept. Provincial Ministers of Mines, Canada
    Centre for Geoscience Data, Energy, Mines and Re-
    sources Canada, Ottawa.

Hubaux, A., 1973, A new geological tool - the data:
    Earth Science Reviews, v. 9, no. 2, p. 159-196.

Sutterlin, P.G., Jeffery, K.G., and Gill, E.M., 1977,
    FILMATCH: A format for the interchange of computer-
    based files of structured data: Computers & Geo-
    sciences, v. 3, no. 3, p. 429-442.

Sutterlin, P.G., and May, R.W., 1978, Geology, *in* Ency-
    clopedia of computer science and technolgoy: v. 9,
    Marcel Dekker Inc., New York, p. 27-56.

Wigington, R.L., 1979, Minis and micros in perspective,
    unpublished paper presented at Spring Meeting,
    Assoc., Information and Dissemination Centres
    (ASIDIC), Ottawa, Ontario.

TRENDS IN COMPUTER APPLICATIONS IN STRUCTURAL GEOLOGY: 1969-1979

E.H. Timothy Whitten

Northwestern University

ABSTRACT

A brief review of the journal literature since 1969 (supplementing an earlier review covering 1959-1969) indicates the manner in which computer-based techniques have permeated most fields of structural geology. The biggest new thrust has been in the application of finite-element methods, which seem destined to play an increasingly important role in structural-geology research.

INTRODUCTION

Ten years ago, at the beginning of a paper with the same principal title, it was asserted that "Relatively few attempts have been made to exploit the potential usefulness of computers to structural geology" (Whitten, 1969, p. 223). At that time, computers generally had been available only to academic geologists for a little more than a decade, and producing a complete review of the use of computers in structural geology was a relatively simple task. Several goals and objectives could be identified clearly. Now, after a further decade of research publication, the situation is radically different. The computer and quantitative thinking have permeated most domains of the geological sciences. The availability of computers and the widespread ability of students to program and use computers on a routine basis allows these tools to be used without particular comment

in a large proportion of modern structural-geology research. "Computer applications" is ceasing to be a dis-
tinctive subdiscipline of structural geology; rather the
use of computers is tending to be just one of the useful
techniques that qualified structural geologists currently
use.

        As ten years ago, "structural geology" is limited
deliberately here so as to exclude structural work primarily based on geophysical data, rock mechanics, and
theoretical research on strain and stress, although, in
such fields, computers continue to play significant roles.
In this context, in 1969, I used "experimental work" instead of "rock mechanics," but recently an important class
of computer experiments has emerged that is based on
finite-element methods.

        Before proceeding further, it is appropriate to sum-
marize the situation that was reported in 1969. Whitten
(1969, p. 223-224) was able to categorize published work
on the use of computers in structural geology under four
headings:

    (1)   storage and collation of structural observa-
          tions,
    (2)   calculation of generalized structural properties
          from arrays of observations
    (3)   description of the morphology of structural fea-
          tures, and
    (4)   mapping and analyses of the spatial variability
          of structural elements.

Obvious future potentialities were seen to include the
development of computer programs to permit:

    (i)   identification of the multiplicity of geological
          factors that control the nature and spatial va-
          riability of the geometry of actual folds,
   (ii)   objective evaluation of the relative importance
          of the identified controlling geological fac-
          tors, and
  (iii)   erection of process-response models to permit
          simulation of fold systems and objective (quan-
          titative and qualitative) comparison of such
          simulations with the nature of actual fold
          systems.

        These categories remain useful in classifying papers
published in the past decade, although papers in categories (1), (2) and (3) have declined in relative numbers

as the methods became well known and the topics did not
warrant new journal articles. As new techniques for spatial analysis were developed within the past decade, many
of them have been applied to structural geology; hence,
there is a considerable volume of new work under category
(4). So far as future developments anticipated in 1969
are concerned, items (i) and (ii) have received considerable attention, but most of the new research does not fall
within the subject matter of this review. For example,
there has been significant quantitative and qualitative
work on the genesis of foliation and whole folds, but it
has not relied primarily on computer technology. By contrast, the finite-element method, made possible by the
use of large computers, permitted the development of process-response models (item iii) for a wide variety of
structural problems; this is a fast-growing and powerful
new field of research.

The principal purpose of this article is to review
the actual published work in these several fields. However, a major problem is that the total volume of literature has expanded so greatly within the past 10 years
that this review (a) cannot claim to be complete - many
important papers from the world literature may well have
been missed inadvertantly, and (b) can make only cursory
allusion to most of the publications cited. The bibliography at the end of this paper is long, and the references cited are worldwide and frequently from little-
known sources. However, a principal contribution of this
paper is the bibliography, which serves to (a) place individual contributions in a global perspective, and (b)
provide a brief annotated reference to all computer applications in structural geology within the past decade.
This paper is concerned with only work published since
Whitten (1969), although reference is made to a few
articles that had not been seen when that review was
written.

STORAGE AND COLLATION OF STRUCTURAL OBSERVATIONS

In the previous review (Whitten, 1969), the largest
number of articles was attributed to Prof. R.E. Adler,
who has continued to champion the use of computer methods
for the collation, storage, and interpretation of structural data. Abundant papers by Adler and his coworkers
early in the decade reviewed speak for themselves (Adler,
1968a, 1968b, 1968c, 1968d; 1969a, 1969b, 1969c, 1969d,
1969e; 1970a, 1970b; 1971a, 1971b, 1971c; 1972a, 1972b;

Adler and Bodechtel, 1970; Adler, Fenchel, and Pilger, 1965; Adler and others, 1969, 1970; Adler and Paffrath, 1972; Kruckeberg, 1968). The initial steps, begun before 1969, were development of punch cards (Adler, 1968d), field-data sheets (Haugh, Brisbin, and Turek, 1967; Berner and others, 1972; Pferd, 1975a, 1975b), coding devices (Adler, 1972b), and storage of the quantitative data (Adler, 1969d; Burns, 1973). Numerous computer-based systems for the processing, reporting, and storage of such geological data have been developed (e.g., in Australia, Burns and Dunnet, 1973; in the USSR, Vaytekunas and Yankunayte, 1975), although most systems have been set up for general geological information, rather than specifically for structural geology. Allen and Herriott's (1976) system was for tiltmeter, strainmeter, and magnetometer data from southern California.

Electronic-data processing was applied specifically to tectonic analysis of the Weyebusch-Siegerland area of Germany (Eckert, 1970), and to the Grenville Province of Canada (Wynne-Edwards and others, 1970; Laurin and others, 1972).

CALCULATION OF GENERALIZED STRUCTURAL PROPERTIES FROM ARRAYS OF OBSERVED DATA

Whitten (1969, p. 225-227) cited numerous papers in which computer methods were used to plot and analyze β- and π- diagrams. More recently, Kruhl (1974) and Nuttall and Cooper (1978) reviewed the use of computers for the statistical processing of structural measurements (cf. Shatagin and Dergachev, 1978). Numerous computer programs have been published since 1969 for the preparation and contouring of Schmidt stereographic projections. Adler, Fenchel, and Pilger (1965) and Krausse (1970) dealt with Schmidt nets, and La Fountain (1970), Franssen and Kummert (1971), and Behrens and Siehl (1975) provided computer programs; Lam (1969) and Arpat (1970) also published FORTRAN programs for β- diagrams. Tocher (1979) showed how continuous flowing curved-line contours on such diagrams can be computer generated. General purpose computer programs for stereographic structural analyses are included in Braun (1969), Bonyun and Stevens (1971), Brandle and Aparicio (1973), Bouchez and Mercier (1974), Shatagin and Sandomirskiy (1974), and Cubitt and Celenk (1976). Ramsden and Cruden (1979a, 1979b) recently analyzed in detail the problem of estimating densities on contoured orientation diagrams.

Dumitrescu (1974) briefly described a useful method for computer preparation of block diagrams, and Srivastava and Merriam (1975, 1976) described a technique for computer construction of optical-rose diagrams.

There has been considerable recent interest in statistical analyses of linear and vectoral data in structural geology. For example, Venkitasubramanyan (1971) discussed ambiguities in evaluating conical folds on the basis of unit-vectoral data, Mark (1973) showed that, in use of computer time, eigenvalue methods are more efficient for analyzing axial-orientation data than is the rotational-vector approach, and Allredge, Mahtab, and Panek (1974) provided a method for estimating the confidence region for the mean of certain axial data. Venter and Spang (1974) considered numerical analyses of multimodal directed (e.g., cross beds) and nondirected (e.g., joint poles) orientation data, Bailey (1975) used cluster analysis for polymodal structural-orientation data, and Dudley, Perkins, and Gine M (1975) in a detailed critical review, showed the inadequacy of existing tests of preferred orientation in fabric diagrams, and because valid tests involve such lengthy computations, they advocated use of a convenient manual test. Ramsden (1975) wrote his thesis on numerical methods in fabric analysis, whereas Ramsden and Cruden (1979b) used computer simulations for estimating densities on orientation diagrams. Published computer programs for the analysis of directional data are less abundant, but they include those of Lutzner and Maaz (1969) and Schuenemeyer, Koch, and Link (1972); Winchell (1967) alluded in an abstract to another.

In petrofabric studies, computer-based methods have been used occasionally. For example, Siemes (1967) used a FORTRAN program to evaluate fabric data measured by X-ray diffractometer. Burger (1972) described a computer technique that involved the solution of a series of spherical triangles for universal-stage data in order to calculate calcite compression and tension axes. Starkey (1974) described three computer programs for quantitative analyses of orientation data obtained by X-ray fabric analyses; he used quartz-orientation information for Bergsdalen quartzites, Norway, for illustrations. Groshong (1974) compared observed calcite petrofabric data with those predicted by a computer-based model, whereas Spang (1974) and Spang and van der Lee (1975) showed that detailed numerical dynamic analyses of quartz, calcite, and dolomite deformation lamellae gave excellent agreement with the results of conventional dynamic petrofabric

techniques. Lister, Paterson, and Hobbs (1978) used the
Taylor-Bishop-Hill model for polycrystalline deformation
as the basis for a computer program to simulate preferred
crystallographic orientations in deforming quartzites.

DESCRIPTION OF THE MORPHOLOGY OF STRUCTURAL
FEATURES - FOLDS

There has been relatively little computer-based work
on the shape of folds, although reference should be made
to Stabler's (1968) Fourier analysis of a wide range of
fold shapes. In the USSR, Goncharov (1971) extended his
earlier research with a new mathematical model of fold
structure, and Vikhert (1967, 1973) and Vikhert and Goncharov (1969) continued their development of deterministic
and probabilistic models for the description and classification of folds. Shcherbakov (1973) used automatic-
data processing to enhance interpretation of the structure of the sedimentary rocks of western Latvia. Edel'-
shteyn (1972) used quantitative methods to study folds
of platform areas and Kulyndyshev (1972) also used "logical analysis" to describe elementary structural surfaces.
Hudleston (1973) showed the value of harmonic analysis
for describing fold shapes. In an abstract, George and
Sowers (1975) alluded to comparison of folds computed for
elastic, viscous, viscoelastic, and plastic models, and
concluded that the latter may be the dominant rheological
response in relatively shallow geological folding.

Wray (1973) provided a FORTRAN computer program to
construct cross sections of curved and faulted structural
surfaces; his illustrative example from Butte, Montana,
showed the geometry prior to three stages of faulting.
Nidd and Ambrose (1971) discussed computerized solutions
for some geometric problems of conical folds, whereas
more recently, Cheshire, Spang, and Stockmal (1978)
briefly outlined an empirical nonlinear computer technique for evaluating conical-fold structural elements.
Cruden and Charlesworth (1972) used an APL program to
generate cylindrical and conical folds and then tested
for optimum methods of calculating their fold axes;
Charlesworth, Langenberg, and Ramsden (1975, 1976) subsequently described computer methods for determining the
axes, axial planes, and sections of four folds from the
Canadian Rocky Mountains. In an extension of this technique, Langenburg, Rondeel, and Charlesworth (1977) used
computer methods to produce structural sections through
five homogeneous domains within a 50 km^2 area of the
Belgian Ardennes.

For the Kriging method of spatial analysis (see the
section on Mapping and Analysis of Spatial Variability..),
semivariograms with respect to a selection of azimuths
are computed first to determine the weighting factors to
be used for the moving-average calculations; the preparation of a semivariogram involves calculating the spectrum
of variance (along a particular azimuth across the map
area) of the dependent variable at all spacing intervals
between samples. Whitten (1977a) determined that such
semivariograms provide a novel method of describing quantitative attitudes of fold shape, and, because the variance of the elevation on a bed is a minimum parallel to
the axis and a maximum normal thereto, semivariograms have
proved to be useful tools in identifying the fold axes in
subsurface terrain. Whitten (1977a, 1979) used this technique to locate fold-axial trends in the Michigan Basin.

In petroleum exploration, computer applications to
structural problems have become widespread, although for
proprietary reasons they rarely are alluded to in the
literature. A few unusual examples are cited here.
Kontorovich and others (1971) used computer methods to
predict productivity of structures in the western Siberian
Platform on the basis of recognition-pattern algorithms.
Petrov, Ellanskiy, and Zverev (1972) discussed general
problems of utilizing mathematical methods in petroleum
geology, whereas Davis, Doveton, and Hambleton (1975)
briefly alluded to a case history of using probabilistic
analysis for oil exploration. Interactive graphics (*Interactive Exploration*) as a tool in petroleum search per-
mitting direct control of large central, but remote, computers by field-based explorationists was referred to in
abstracts by Branisa and Johnson (1975) and Jones, Johnson, and Herron (1976). Juneman (1971) earlier had used
interactive computer graphics for analyzing three-dimensional geological data sets.

Burns, Marshall, and Gee (1969) and Borrmann (1972a)
were responsible for some of the early exercises in computer-assisted geological structural mapping. Of course,
cartography now is an extensively computerized discipline,
but no attempt is made here to assay the tremendous advances in this field and in computer graphics generally,
despite their immediate and direct usefulness to structural geology.

The analysis of strain in folded rocks has received
considerable attention in the past decade, although most
studies did not use computer computations. However, the

detailed analyses of strain in folded layered rocks by
Ramberg (1970) and Hobbs (1971) involved considerable computation. Matthews, Bond, and van den Berg (1974) used a
FORTRAN IV program in their algebraic analysis of strain
using elliptical markers. Flinn's (1978) computation of
three-dimensional progressive deformations also is relevant here. Finally, Kruhl (1978) published a useful computer program for unravelling the structural complexity
of highly strained current-bedding in Scottish Precambrian
quartzites.

     During the past decade there has been a steady growth
of interest in using computer technology and satellite
imagery for geological structural interpretation. This
is a computer application that is going to expand considerably in the next few years. Representative studies
include the papers by Short (1973a, 1974a, 1974b) and
Kronberg (1975) on geological structures seen from the
Earth Resources Technology Satellite (ERTS-1) imagery.
In analyzing structural geology, ERTS imagery also was
used by Bodechtel and Lammerer (1973) for the Alps and
Appenines, by Bodechtel and Nithack (1974) for northern
and central Italy (also using SKYLAB data), by Lambert
(1975) for the northwestern part of the Massif Central
of France, by Burkhardt and Endlicher (1977) for the
eastern Bavarian basement, and by Offield and others
(1975) for the southern copper region of Brazil. More
recently, Cassinis (1977) illustrated the value of satellite imagery in interpreting the structural geology of
Italy. In the USSR, satellite imagery also has been used
extensively to elucidate tectonic and major structural
features; for example, one may cite the work of Bush and
Kats (1978) on the Sredizemnomorsk Alpine Region, of Kapustin, Przhiyalgovskiy, and Trofimov (1978) on the tectonic
framework of the Caspian Depression, of Grishkyan, Parfenov, and Ufimtsev (1977) on the Baikal Rift Region, of
Solov'yeva (1978) on central Asia, and of Volchegurskiy
and Pronin (1978) on the major structural forms within
the Russian and Turanian plates.

          DESCRIPTION OF THE MORPHOLOGY OF STRUCTURAL
             FEATURES - FAULTS, LINEAMENTS, ETC.

     The rate of publication on faults and faulting has
increased enormously within the past 10 years, and in
attempting to obtain objective quantitative answers to
problems, computer syntheses and analyses have been used.
The distribution of faulting in space and time (e.g.,

Cogbill, 1979) has important implications in earthquake-
prediction studies.

Numerous descriptive studies of fissures, fractures,
and faults have been made. For example, Jeran and Mashey
(1970) used a FORTRAN program for stereographic analysis
of coal fractures and cleats, Altinli and Eroskay (1971)
used automatic data-processing techniques to analyze the
fractures of the Ikizdere Granitic Complex, and Ghez and
Janot (1974) described a method for statistically computing the matrix-block volume of a fissured reservoir. The
relationship between joint spacing (frequencies and orientation) and bed thickness was analyzed by Bock (1971).
Borrmann (1972b) described a computer program for the
statistical analysis of fracture and joint orientation
data, and Vychev (1976) a program for fracture-density
determination in rocks from field observations. Podwysocki (1973) developed computer methods for analyzing
fracture patterns identified from remote-sensing imagery.

Whitten (1969) referred to James' (1968) earlier
work on faulted surfaces using least-squares methods with
discontinuous functions. James (1970) applied his method
to subsurface data for the Ramsey Oil Pool, Payne County,
Oklahoma, where there was independent evidence of high-
angle faulting. More recently, Attoh and Whitten (1979)
published a FORTRAN program that extends this method and
permits estimates of the throw of one or more faults to
be computed on the basis of subsurface data. Peikert
(1970) also described an interactive computer-graphics
system for elucidating subsurface faulted structures. As
mentioned, most geophysical studies are excluded from this
review, but Sharma and Geldart's (1968) use of Fourier
transforms in the analysis of gravity anomalies associated
with two-dimensional faults such as the Canadian Logan
Fault, and Szumilas' (1977) brief report on a computer
time-to-depth conversion and structure mapping system designed for evaluating complexly faulted areas are relevant
here.

Serra (1973) described a computer program for calculating and plotting the stress distribution and possible
fault trajectories under specified crustal boundary conditions. Dabovski (1975) provided a mathematical model
for stress and displacements around faults (and magma
chambers), whereas Alarcon Guzman, Fernandez, and Gonza-
lez-Rubio (1975) published a computer program for stress
analysis of structures.

A major new development in the computer-based study
of faults and faulting involves simulation with finite-
element methods. This topic is discussed in the section
on Finite-Element Methods..., where reference is made to
Dieterich's (1969) work on the mechanical properties of
seismically active fault zones, Kosloff's (1976) model of
creep zones of finite width (associated with faults) resembling the Palmdale Uplift, California, Miyatake's
(1977) simulation of dynamic faulting processes, Rodgers
and others (1977) thrust-fault mechanisms, Stein and
Wickham's (1978) study of drape-fold development associated with faulting, and the analyses of Stein and
Wickham (1979) on fault-zone propagation, and of Wickham,
Stein, and Reddy (1979) on various faulting models.

Stearns (1978) developed an analog model to produce
simulations of fault patterns during the deformation of
thick, homogeneous, isotropic continuous rock masses;
analogies were drawn with structures in the Rocky Mountain Foreland Province.

Terrestrial lineaments recently have received considerable attention because of the general availability
of air photos and satellite imagery. Crain (1972, 1973)
reviewed in detail lineaments at different levels of geotectonic analysis, and he analyzed Monte-Carlo simulations of such structures. Short (1973b) briefly alluded
to mapping joints, faults, and contacts from ERTS imagery.
Various aspects of computer-assisted analysis of lineaments from air photographs have been discussed by many
authors; for example, Maffi and Marchesini (1964), Hanley
(1975) for the fracture pattern of Catawba Mountain, Virginia, Huntington (1975) for fracture systems of the
Arabian Shield, the Karroo Basin, and some Paleozoic
folded rocks of northern Wales, Podwysocki, Moik and
Shoup (1975), Burns, Huntington, and Green (1977),
Arakelyan and Karakhanyan (1978), and Yeromenko and
Katterfel'd (1978). Rice, Davis, and Johnson (1976)
specifically alluded to inferences about subsurface geological structure based on computer analyses of lineaments.

The acquisition of satellite imagery involves extensive use of computers. Kowalik (1975) compared lineaments
read from SKYLAB and LANDSAT images with actual joint
orientations in north-central Pennsylvania, whereas
Correa and Lyon (1976) analyzed Californian linear features on the basis of optical Fourier analyses of ERTS-1
imagery. Tricart (1976) presented evidence for lineaments

in the French Vosges Mountains read from LANDSAT-1 imagery. Burns, Shepherd, and Berman (1976) investigated the
reproducibility of lineaments read from satellite imagery.
Cardamone and others (1977) used LANDSAT-2 images to study
lineaments in the Friuli earthquake area, and Masson (1978)
also used LANDSAT data to analyze structures of the Levan-
tine Rift. Artamonov, Vostokov, and Sheremet (1978) combined satellite and geologic-geophysical data in a study
of the fracture tectonics of the Peri-Baltic Syneclise.

MAPPING AND ANALYSIS OF SPATIAL VARIABILITY OF
STRUCTURAL ELEMENTS - FILTERING SYSTEMS

Whitten (1969, p. 229-233) gave a detailed review of
the use of trend-surface and other filtering analyses for
subsurface structural mapping. Although work in this area
has expanded considerably, several problems identified in
1969 remain today (e.g., most mathematical models require
data on a regular grid, whereas actual data are almost
always irregularly spaced).

The basic purpose of trend-surface analysis is to
separate three components of the total variability: (a)
regional effect or trend, (b) localized features of geological significance, and (c) error and other random
components (including significant geological variability
produced by features smaller than the data-point spacing).
A detailed guide to the practical use of trend-surface
analysis methods was published by Whitten (1975); perhaps
the most important advance since 1969 was the introduction of orthogonal-polynomial trend-surface analysis for
irregularly spaced data (Whitten, 1970), which eliminates
the troublesome task of inverting large matrices and permits the Z^2-array and the contribution of each coefficient to be identified; a FORTRAN computer program is available (Whitten, 1974). Trend-surface analyses of folded
subsurface strata now have become relatively routine and
tend not to be noted specially in English-language publications; we may note the use of mathematical trend analysis by Lokhmatov and Alayev (1967) and Lokhmatov, Alayev,
and Yevdokimova (1968) for Lower Cambrian strata of the
upper Angara River Region, Sibera, by Belonin and Zhukov
(1970) for the surface of the Aleksevvku Uplift in the
Kuibyshev District, and by Kumar (1977) for structural
analysis of the Miocene rocks in part of southern Louisiana. In the Peoples' Republic of China, Xu and Sun
(1966) described trend-surface analyses of stratigraphic
data, and Zhang (1977) used polynomial and Fourier

trend-surface analyses for evaluating subsurface structure on the basis of 71 irregularly spaced data points in
682 km^2. Myasnikova and Shpil'man (1973) used trend analyses to investigate the interrelationships between sediment accumulation and structural evolution.

Recently, numerous additional techniques for the
analysis of subsurface structure have been developed that
approximate surfaces to the actual observed data. Such
artifices, which, unlike trend-surface analyses, make no
attempt to separate component (c) from (a) and (b), necessarily make the implicit assumption that all observed data
are accurate (error free) and deserve equal weight being
placed on them. Although these factors can be a disadvantage in some spatial analyses, stratum-elevation data used
in structural work usually are determined with virtually
no error. However, the fact that irregularly spaced data
can be used directly in orthogonal-polynomial trend-surface analyses gives a powerful advantage over most techniques which construct surfaces that pass precisely
through the data-point values, because computation of almost all of the latter requires gridded data. Approxima-
ting gridded from irregularly spaced data can introduce
significant unacceptable errors and biases (Whitten and
Koelling, 1973).

Experiments with numerous slightly different techniques have been made, but perhaps the most important in
the past decade have been:

(1)   a method of spatial filtering in which two-
      dimensional Fourier transforms are used with
      gridded raw data,
(2)   bicubic-spline surfaces, and
(3)   surfaces developed by a variety of Kriging
      techniques.

(1)   The early work on spatial filtering with two-
dimensional Fourier transforms developed by Robinson,
Charlesworth, and coworkers in Alberta was reviewed by
Whitten (1969, p. 232-233). This useful technique for
identifying and enhancing subsurface structural patterns
was elaborated and further described in a series of papers
(Robinson, 1969, 1970; Robinson and Charlesworth, 1969a,
1969b, 1975; Robinson and Merriam, 1972). Recently,
Eschner, Robinson, and Merriam (1979) discussed the comparison of spatially filtered geological maps. Unfortunately, gridded data (or data interpolated on a grid) are
a prerequisite of this method.

(2) Spline surfaces are used widely by engineers for
continuous smooth surfaces passing precisely through specified points. In principle, spline surfaces should be useful in modeling subsurface structure (cf., Davis, 1975).
Koelling and Whitten (1973) published a FORTRAN program
for computing bicubic-spline surfaces for gridded data,
but as they (Whitten and Koelling, 1973) pointed out, the
necessity of interpolating values on a grid introduces unacceptable errors in subsurface structural analyses where
only irregularly spaced raw data are available. It seems
that it should be possible to develop a system of equations to permit construction of bicubic-spline surfaces
for irregularly distributed data points. Whitten and
Koelling (1975, 1978) described a set of equations and
directly computed a spline surface on the basis of irregularly spaced data for the top of the Devonian Dundee
Limestone in Michigan; although, in this example, problems did not arise, their set of 15 equations to solve
for 16 coefficients should not always yield a complete
solution.

(3) Prof. G. Matheron expanded the weighted moving-
average methods developed by Dr. D.G. Krige (for gold and
uranium assay data) to a sophisticated series of techniques generally referred to as Kriging. Although initially developed in France by Matheron and coworkers for
mine assay and development, Kriging is valuable in many
other domains in which spatial variability is important.
In a general article on stochastic models in geology,
Whitten (1977b) drew attention to the extensive background
literature on Kriging. Several authors have used Kriging
to construct structural stratum-contour maps. Agterberg
(1970) exposed the problems of estimating autocorrelation
functions from irregularly spaced data; he approximated
autocorrelation functions for top of the Arbuckle Group
(Kansas) and used Kriging and polynomial trend surfaces
to portray its subsurface structure. Sampson (1975a,
1975b) illustrated contoured maps (and maps of the expected errors) for the top of the subsurface Pennsylvanian Lansing Group in Stafford and Graham Counties, Kansas,
based on universal Kriging of orthogonal data interpolated
from the original irregularly spaced observations. Olea
(1975) illustrated similar maps for the top of the Tobi-
fera Series, Magellan Basin, Chile, which also were based
on universal Kriging of orthogonalized data. Whitten
(1977a, 1979) also used Kriging for a structure map of
the Dundee Limestone of part of the Michigan Basin. Two
computer programs for computing such maps by Kriging are
available (David, 1977; Sampson, 1975b); unfortunately,

both of these programs require gridded-data input, so
that the questionable interpolation of values at the nodes
of a rectangular grid is necessary with virtually all real
subsurface data. In addition, these programs use simple
Kriging, rather than universal Kriging. The latter provides superior results when a significant regional gradient (trend) is present, but computer programs for universal Kriging are only available in proprietary sources.

       Trend surfaces and these three additional types of
surface approximation all make the assumption of continuous variation across the study area, whereas, in practice, faults may be a complicating factor. As mentioned
previously, in 1968 James introduced a simple nonlinear
model that permitted faulted surfaces to be mapped, by
using what in fact are faulted polynomial trend surfaces.
James (1970) applied the method to faulted subsurface
structures in Oklahoma. Attoh and Whitten (1979) extended
James' technique and their FORTRAN program permits estimation of subsurface-fault throws. Bolondi, Rocca, and
Zanoletti (1975) and Dahlberg, Deland, and Creed (1975)
provided brief abstracts concerned with mapping faulted
surfaces; to augment customary methods of inferring subsurface faults, the latter used computer statistical
methods to correlate stratigraphic features with possible
faults.

       In conclusion, a few additional studies must be
cited. Arabadzhi, Vasil'yev, and Mil'nichuk (1967) described the use of correlation analysis in the compilation of structural maps of the Caspian Basin area, and
Berlyand (1971) investigated the use of autocorrelation
analysis in studying the structure of a gravity field.
Demirmen (1972, 1973) published details of a numerical-
description technique for folded surfaces. Srivastava
and Merriam (1974) and Srivastava (1975) described quantitative optical- and digital-processing methods which
they applied to numerous subsurface horizons in Kansas.
Jones and Jordan (1975) briefly alluded to an automated
procedure for structural mapping with data containing
points that do not intersect the horizon of particular
interest. Whitten (1977a, 1979) published surfaces (prepared by Kriging) depicting areal differential-subsidence
rates of certain Cretaceous units in the southeastern
USA; this technique should have value in analyzing the
rate of warping and folding during sedimentation (Whitten, 1976).

FINITE-ELEMENT METHODS, SIMULATION, AND
RELATED TECHNIQUES

Without doubt, the most dramatic advances in computer applications in structural geology in the past decade have occurred in this domain. Finite-element methods were explained simply in Zienkiewicz's (1971) text, which gives a computer program that can be adapted readily to many structural problems. Zienkiewicz (1974, 1976), a civil engineer, recently contributed some geological papers on flow and geophysical topics.

An impressive array of papers has been based on finite-element methods to analyze various aspects of folds. In the compass of this review, one can do little apart from catalog the types of problems that have been assayed. The following list of about 40 papers and abstracts indicates the chronological development of analyses of folding and folds that used finite-element and related types of computer methods:

Date	Author/s	Subject
1964 1968	Chapple	Solution of finite-difference equations by computer in study of finite-amplitude folding.
1968	Fumagalli	Simulation of rock-mechanics problems.
1969	Chapple	Fold shape through time that results from folding of a viscous-plastic layer.
1969	Dieterich and Carter; Dieterich and Onat	Finite-element determination of the stress field in two-dimensional, large-amplitude folding of a viscous layer and other solids.
1970	Voight and Dahl	Analysis of nonlinear rock deformation by numerical continuum approaches.
1970	Dieterich	Computer simulation of time-dependent deformation: mechanics of finite-amplitude folding.
1970a 1970b	Chapple	Growth of folds from shape perturbations in layered rocks and instability during growth of folds.

1971	Stephansson and Berner	Finite-element methods for analyzing folds, boudinage, and isostatic adjustments.
1972	Fujii	Finite-element methods in structural analysis.
1973	Bridwell	Finite-element applications for mechanical problems in structural geology.
1973	Parrish	Nonlinear finite-element fold model involving steady-state flow of quartzite and marble.
1973	Stephansson	Finite-element solution of various structural-geology problems.
1973	Heinze and Goetze	Computer simulation of stresses and strains in heterogeneous polycrystalline solids.
1973	Hudleston and Stephansson	Experiment, analog modeling, and finite-element study of single-layer buckling.
1974	Ikeda and Shimamoto	Numerical experiment on viscous bending folds.
1974	Chapple and Spang	19 samples of Greenport Center syncline, NY, used for comparison with layer-parallel slip folding simulated by finite-element methods.
1974	Bridwell	Stress-strain finite-element model of nonlinear bending.
1974	Bridwell and Swolfs	Stability analysis (using finite-elements) of experimentally deformed Indiana limestone.
1974	Hardy and others	Computer simulation of inelastic-beam behavior.
1974	Heinze and Goetze	Numerical simulation of stress concentrations.
1974	Owens	Mathematical modeling of magnetic anisotropy of deformed rocks.
1975	Bird, Toksoz, and Sleep	Finite difference models of continent-continent convergences.
1975 1976	Parrish, Krivz, and Carter	Finite-element folds of similar geometry.

1976	Cosgrove	Finite-element study of growth of buckling instabilities into finite fold structures.
1976	Stephansson	Finite-element analysis of folds.
1976	Robinson	Computer simulation of folds.
1976	Wickham and Anthony	Compares actual Appalachian structures in carbonates to finite-element models.
1976	DeBremaecker and Becker	Numerical simulation of folding taking incompressibility into account.
1977	Cobbold	Finite-element analysis of fold propagation.
1978	DeBremaecker and Becker	Finite-element models of folding.
1978	Anthony and Wickham	Fold shape and strain studied in finite-element simulation of asymmetric folding.
1978	Lewis and Williams	Finite-element study of fold propagation in a viscous layer.
1978	Williams, Lewis, and Zienkiewicz	Finite-element analysis of the significant role of initial perturbations in folding.
1978	Stein and Wickham	Drape folds and related faulting.
1978	Neugebauer and Spohn	Finite-element modeling of flexure of US Atlantic continental margin.
1979	Cobbold	Removal (by finite-elements) of finite deformation, using strain trajectories.
1979	Reddy and Wickham	Finite-element studies of incompressible flow due to gravity in rocks, etc.
1979	Reches and Johnson	Finite-element analysis of monocline development.

In addition, numerous other structural problems have been assayed with the versatile finite-element method. Again, the list of applications is long. Voight and Samuelson (1969) discussed the application of finite-element methods to stress analysis in the earth sciences.

Douglas (1970) calculated the crustal displacement under sediment loading by finite-element methods, and Sturgul and Grinshpan (1975) modeled possible isostatic rebound of the Grand Canyon by finite elements. By using a three-dimensional finite-element relaxation model, Kosloff (1976) modeled a structure resembling the Californian Palmdale Uplift. Feenstra and Wickham (1976) used fin-ite-element methods to model simple-shear deformation superimposed on symmetrical folds that is relevant to understanding the development of structures similar to those of the Ouachita Mountains. Salt domes and other diapiric structures have been studied by several authors; for salt domes, Howard (1971) used computer-simulation models and Woidt (1978a, 1978b) used finite-element meth-ods, whereas Fletcher (1972) studied mantled gneiss domes with finite elements. Finite-element modeling of surface deformation associated with intrusion of magma in reser-voirs within the Kilauea Volcano, Hawaii (Dieterich, 1972; Dieterich and Decker, 1975), Himalayan Orogeny (Bird and Toksoz, 1976), and strain paths and folding in carbonate rocks near the Blue Ridge (central Appalachians) (Wickham and Anthony, 1977) further illustrated the versatility of the method. Forster and Leonhardt (1972) used mathemati-cal simulation to study kinematic stream lines within the Eastern Alps. At a smaller scale, Stromgard (1973) exam-ined the stress distribution during boudinage and pres-sure-shadow formation with photoelastic and finite-ele-ment techniques, and Selkman (1978) used finite elements for displacement analysis of boudinages.

Hattori and Mizutani (1971) described computer simu-lations of fracturing in layered rocks, whereas finite-element studies of the responses of jointed rock under quasistatic loading (Baligh, 1972), and of preexisting fractures on the scale of laboratory experiments (Minear, 1972) were followed by Tapp and Wickham's (1978) finite-element study of predicted fracture occurrence during folding, and Tapp, Wickham, and Reddy's (1979) numerical modeling of fracture density in single-layer folds. Cun-dall (1971) developed a computer model for simulating progressive large-scale movements in blocky rock systems, and, in the field of petroleum geology, du Prey and Boisse-Codreanu (1975) generated numerical simulations of fissured-reservoir production.

Dieterich (1969) modeled by finite-element methods the mechanical properties of a seismically active fault zone. Miyatake (1977) and Wickham, Stein, and Reddy (1979) prepared numerical simulations of the dynamical-faulting process, Stein and Wickham (1979) of fault-zone propagation, and Rogers and others (1977) of thrust-fault mechanisms.

Three additional abstracts are relevant here. Jackson (1972) dealt with numerical simulation of the main and aftershock earthquake sequence of a fault system, whereas finite-element techniques were used by Alewine and Jungels (1972) in a study of the 1964 Alaskan earthquake, and by Clancy, Turcotte, and Kulhawy (1977) in analysis of strain accumulation and release on the San Andreas Fault.

MISCELLANEOUS APPLICATIONS

As mentioned earlier, computer applications have permeated thoroughly virtually all domains of structural geology. Because they have become so commonplace, it is an elusive task to track down all of the interesting and useful developments that are important in modern work. Also, several applications do not fit neatly into the major headings dealt with here. A few examples may be briefly cited.

Nonlinear-regression models were used by Mundry (1972) to determine rheological constants in time-dependent stress-strain measurements. Deist, Salamon, and Georgiadis (1973) described a new digital method for three-dimensional stress analysis in elastic media, whereas Pollard and Holzhausen (1978) provided a FORTRAN program for calculating stress intensity factors, stresses, and displacements associated with a fluid-pressurized fracture.

Kinematics and strain can be tackled at widely dissimilar domain sizes. In geodynamics, innumerable papers are based on computer computation; for example, papers range from those of Coode (1966, 1967) on spherical harmonic analyses of major tectonic features to the least-squares Bullard-type plate-tectonic continent-fit reconstructions of Smith and Hallam (1970) for the southern continents and of Smith (1971) for the Mediterranean area, and to Neugebauer and Spohn's (1978) work on buckling along the trailing edge of a passive plate margin and its effect on sediment accumulation rates. Attempts to model the creep deformation of solids using modified finite-difference equations (Andrews, 1971) and to model the tectonic flow behind island arcs (Andrews and Sleep,

1974) are examples of a further class of computer-based
geodynamical structural study. Smith and Kind (1972) developed a least-squares strain-variation picture for
southern Nevada on the basis of a regional strain-meter
array; at a different size level, Watson and Smith (1975)
developed a computer simulation of grain shape during
isotropic growth of grains in an aggregate, a study of
potential value in numerous strain studies. Using homo-
geneous-strain transformation in plane-polar coordinates,
Hirsinger (1976) estimated total strain by matching the
deformed shape of fossils with their initial geometries.

CONCLUDING REMARKS

It seems clear that in the next decade the use of
computer techniques will have permeated and revolutionized so thoroughly all facets of structural geology that
it probably will be simpler to identify those fields of
structural geology in which computers are not used, rather
than those in which they have been utilized. Perhaps the
most significant new insights will be derived from ex-
ploiting (a) the potential of the finite-element techniques for structural simulation and prediction and (b)
the interface between geophysics and structural geology.

REFERENCES

Adler, R.E., 1968a, Gelandevermessung mit einfachen Hilfs-
    mitteln: Breithaupt Mitteilungen, Kassel II, p.
    1-61.

Adler, R.E., 1968b, Der Einfluss der Tektonik auf maschi-
    nell mit der Streckenvortriebsmaschine Wohlmeyer
    aufgefahrene Flozstrecken: Gluckauf-Forschungshefte,
    29 Jahr., no. 3, p. 149-156.

Adler, R.E., 1968c, Zur Tektonik des Polsumer und Huls-
    dauer Sprunges im nordlichen Ruhr-Karbon: Neues
    Jahrb. Geol., Palaont., Monat., no. 5, p. 257-276.

Adler, R.E., 1968d, Lochkartc.., ein Hilfsmittel der
    modernen Tektonik: Clausthaler Tekt. Hefte., v. 8,
    p. 93-149.

Adler, R.E., 1969a, Electronische Datenverarbeitung in
    der Tektonik: Z. deutsch. Geol. Ges., Jahr. 1967,
    v. 119, p. 219-244.

Adler, R.E., 1969b, Kleintektonische Beobachtungen aus
    dem Ruhrkarbon: Forschunsber. Land. Nordrh.-Westf.,
    no. 2008, p. 5-53.

Adler, R.E., 1969c, Moderne Daten- und Informationsgewin-
    nung und -verarbeitung in der Tektonik: Zbl. Geol.
    Palaontol., Teil ID, no. 6, p. 1053-1079.

Adler, R.E., 1969d, Instrumentelle Aufnahme und elektron-
    ische Auswertung von tektonischen Flachen und
    Linearen: Geol. Rundsch., v. 59, no. 1, p. 152-162.

Adler, R.E., 1969e, Neue Arbeitsmethoden in der tekonishen
    Forschung: Geol. Mitt. (Aachen), v. 9, no. 2, p.
    97-108.

Adler, R.E., 1970a, Tektonische Geologie, photogrammet-
    rische Datenerhebung und elektronische Datenbearbei-
    tung: Gluckauf-Forschungshefte, 31 Jahr., no. 6,
    p. 318-332.

Adler, R.E., 1970b, Elektronische Datenverarbeitung in
    der modernen Tektonik: Clausthaler Tekt. Hefte,
    v. 10, p. 25-47.

Adler, R.E., 1971a, Mathematische Geologie: Zbl. Geol.
    Palaontol. Teil I, p. 3-14.

Adler, R.E., 1971b, Praktische Tektonik 2 - Geschicht-
    liche Entwicklung: Zbl. Geol. Palaontol., Teil I
    for 1970, no. 7-8, p. 915-938.

Adler, R.E., 1971c, Tektonik und Datenverarbeitung: Zbl.
    Geol. Palaontol., Teil I, no. 1-2, p. 15-28.

Adler, R.E., 1972a, Praktische Tektonik Stellung, Bedeu-
    tung, Moglichkeiten: Zbl. Geol. Palaontol. Teil I
    for 1971, no. 5-6, p. 333-357.

Adler, R.E., 1972b, Ableitung einer Kennzahl zur Charak-
    terisierung tektonischer Deformationen: Neues Jahrb.
    Geol. Palaont., Monat., no. 5, p. 257-259.

Adler, R.E., Berling, D., Bodechtel, J., and Vieten, W.,
    1970, Anwendung der Photogrammetrie zur Erfassung
    tektonischer Daten: Clausthaler Tekt. Hefte, 10,
    p. 337-358.

Adler, R.E., and Bodechtel, J., 1970, Tektonische Daten-
    erfassung aus terrestrischphotogrammetrischen Aufnah-
    men sowie deren Weiterverarbeitung in der EDV:
    Bildmessung und Luftbildwesen, v. 38, no. 5, p. 267-
    272.

Adler, R.E., Fenchel, W., and Pilger, A., 1965, Statis-
    tische Methoden in der Tektonik II. Das Schmidtsche
    Netz und seine Anwendung im Bereich des makroskopi-
    schen Gefuges: Clausthaler Tekt. Hefte, 4, p. 1-111.

Adler, R.E., Kruckeberg, F., Pfisterer, W., Pilger, A.,
    and Schmidt, M.W., 1969, Elektronische Datenverar-
    beitung in der Tektonik: Clausthaler Tekt. Hefte,
    8 for 1968, p. 1-157.

Adler, R.E., and Paffrath, A.A., 1972, Ein neues Schema
    zur Fixierung geologischtektonischer Informationen:
    Neues Jahrb. Geol. Palaont., Abh., v. 140, p. 1-32.

Agterberg, F.P., 1970, Autocorrelation functions in geo-
    logy, *in* Merriam, D.F., ed., Geostatistics, a collo-
    quium: Plenum Press, New York, p. 113-142.

Alarcon Guzman, J.A., Fernandez T, D.A., and Gonzalez-
    Rubio, H.E., and others, 1975, Stress analysis of
    structure by computer with dynamic option: Intern.
    Inst. Seismol. Earthquake Engineer., Individ. Stud.,
    v. 11, p. 106-146.

Alewine, R.W., and Jungels, P., 1972, A study of the 1964
    Alaskan earthquake using finite element and general-
    ized inversion techniques (abst.): Am. Geophys.
    Union Trans., v. 53, no. 11, p. 1119.

Alldredge, J.R., Mahtab, M.A., and Panek, L.A., 1974,
    Statistical analysis of axial data: Jour. Geology,
    v. 82, no. 4, p. 519-524.

Allen, S.S., and Herriot, J.W., 1976, A computer graphics
    data system for low-frequency geophysical data
    (abst.): Am. Geophys. Union Trans., v. 57, no. 3,
    p. 154.

Altinli, I.E., and Eroskay, S.O., 1971, Toplam vektor
    metodu ile Ikizdere Granit Karmasiginin Yonelim
    Tahlili: Istanbul Univ. Fen Fak Macm., Ser. B.,
    v. 36, no. 3-4, p. 115-136.

Andrews, D.J., 1971, A numerical method for creep defor-
    mation of solids (abst.): Am. Geophys. Union
    Trans., v. 52, no. 4, p. 347.

Andrews, D.J., and Sleep, N.H., 1974, Numerical modelling
    of tectonic flow behind island arcs: Roy. Astron.
    Soc., Geophys. Jour., v. 38, no. 2, p. 237-251.

Anthony, M., and Wickham, J., 1978, Finite-element simu-
    lation of asymmetric folding: Tectonophysics, v.
    47, no. 1-2, p. 1-14.

Arabadzhi, M.S., Vasil'yev, Y.M., and Mil'nichuk, V.S.,
    1967, Postroyeniye strukturnykh kart metodom kor-
    relyatsionnogo analiza na primere Prikaspiyskoy
    vpadiny: Prikl. Geofiz., v. 50, p. 133-139; (English
    translation) Exploration Geophysics, 1969, v. 50,
    p. 107-113.

Arakelyan, R.A., and Karakhanyan, A.S., 1978, Opoznavaniye
    i deshifrirovaniye razlomov na kosmicheskikh snimkakh
    razlichnykh urovney yestestvennoy generalizatsii:
    Vysshoe Uchebnoye Zavedeniye, Izv., Geol. Razved.,
    no. 10, p. 35-39.

Arpat, E., 1970, A computer method for preparing beta
    diagrams (program in FORTRAN IV-H, using an IBM 360/
    67 computer): Mineral Res. Explor. Inst. Turkey
    Bull. (foreign edit.), no. 74, p. 34-42.

Artamonov, M.A., Vostokov, Y.N., and Sheremet, O.G., 1978,
    Razlomnaya tektonika Baltiyskoy sineklizy i prile-
    gayushchikh territoriy po kosmicheskim i geologo-
    geofizicheskim dannym: Vysshoye Uchebnoye Zavedeniye,
    Izv. Geol. Razved., no. 10, p. 141-146.

Attoh, K., and Whitten, E.H.T., 1979, Computer program
    for regression model for discontinuous structural
    surfaces: Computers & Geosciences, v. 5, no. 1,
    p. 47-71.

Bailey, A.I., 1975, A method of analyzing polymodal dis-
    tributions in orientation data: Jour. Math. Geology,
    v. 7, no. 4, p. 285-293.

Baligh, M.M., 1972, Finite element study of the response
    of jointed rock (abst.): Am. Geophys. Union Trans.,
    v. 53, no. 11, p. 1118.

Behrens, M., and Siehl, A., 1975, GELI 2 - ein Rechenpro-
    gramm zur Gefuge- und Formanalyse: Geol. Rundsch.,
    v. 64, no. 2, p. 301-324.

Belonin, M.D., and Zhukov, I.M., 1970, Geometrical pro-
    perties of the surface of the Alekseevka uplift in
    the Kuibyshev district, *in* Topics in mathematical
    geology, Romanova, M.A., and Sarmanov, O.V., eds.:
    Consultants Bureau, New York, p. 186-199.

Berlyand, N.G., 1971, O vozmozhnostyakh avtokorrelyat-
    sionnogo analiza pri izuchenii struktury gravitat-
    sionnogo polya: Fizika Zemli, no. 1, p. 68-78.

Berner, H., Estrom, T., Lilljequist, R., Stephansson, O.,
    and Wikstrom, A., 1972, Geomap - a data system for
    geological mapping: Proc. 24th Intern. Geol. Con-
    gress (Montreal), Sect. 16, p. 3-11.

Bird, P., and Toksoz, M.N., 1976, Himalayan orogeny mo-
    delled with finite elements (abst.): Am. Geophys.
    Union Trans., v. 57, no. 4, p. 334-335.

Bird, P., Toksoz, M.N., and Sleep, N.H., 1975, Thermal
    and mechanical models of continent-continent con-
    vergence zones: Jour. Geophys. Res., v. 80,
    no. 32, p. 4405-4416.

Bock, H., 1971, Uber die Abhangigkeit von Kluftabstanden
    und Schichtmachtigkeiten: Neues Jahrb. Geol.
    Palaont., Monat., no. 9, p. 517-531.

Bodechtel, J., and Lammerer, B., 1973, New aspects on the
    tectonic of the Alps and the Apennines revealed by
    ERTS-1 data: NASA Sp. Publ. 327, p. 493-499.

Bodechtel, J., and Nithack, J., 1974, Geologisch-tekton-
    ische Auswertung von ERTS-1 und SKYLAB-Aufnahmen von
    Nordund und Mittelitalien: Geoforum, no. 20, p. 11-
    24.

Bolondi, G., Rocca, F., and Zanoletti, S., 1975, Contour-
    ing faulted surfaces (abst.): Soc. Explor. Geophys.
    Annual Intern. Meet., no. 45, p. 58.

Bonyun, D., and Stevens, G., 1971, A general purpose com-
    puter program to produce geological stereo net dia-
    grams, *in* Data processing in biology and geology,
    Cutbill, J.L., ed.: Academic Press, London, p. 165-
    188.

Borrmann, H.-G., 1972a, Automatische Kurven- und Karten-
    konstruktionen (abst.): Dtsch. Gesell. Geol. Wissen.
    Ber., Reihe A., Geol. Palaont., v. 17, no. 1, p. 13.

Borrmann, H.-G., 1972b, Programm zur statistischen Aus-
    wertung von Richtungsmessungen (Kluft und Gefuge-
    statistik) mit Hilfe der EDV (abst.): Dtsch. Gesell.
    Geol. Wissen. Ber., Reihe A, Geol. Palaont., v. 17,
    no. 1, p. 14.

Bouchez, J.-L., and Mercier, J.-C., 1974, Construction
    automatique des diagrammes de densite d'orientation:
    Sci. Terre, v. 19, no. 1, p. 55-64.

Brandle, J.L., and Aparicio, A., 1973, Un programa basico
    para diagramas de petrofabricas: Estud. Geol.
    (Instit. Investig. Geol. 'Lucas Mallada'), v. 29,
    no. 4, p. 315-317.

Branisa, F., and Johnson, C.R., 1975, Interactive explo-
    ration: an application of interactive computer
    graphics (abst.): Geophysics, v. 40, no. 1, p. 130.

Braun, G., 1969, Computer calculated counting nets for
    petrofabric and structural analysis: Neues Jahrb.
    Mineral., Monat., no. 10, p. 469-476.

Bridwell, R.J., 1973, Finite element applications to
    mechanical problems in structural geology: unpubl.
    doctoral dissertation, Univ. Utah.

Bridwell, R.J., 1974, Nonlinear in-plane bending of a
    plane stress-strain finite element model: Jour.
    Geophys. Res., v. 79, no. 11, p. 1674-1678.

Bridwell, R.J., and Swolfs, H.S., 1974, Stability analysis
    of an experimentally deformed single layer of Indiana
    limestone using finite elements: Jour. Geophys.
    Res., v. 79, no. 11, p. 1679-1686.

Burger, H.R., 1972, Computerized solution for calculating
    calcite compression and tension axes: Geol. Soc.
    America Bull., v. 83, no. 8, p. 2439-2442.

Burkhardt, R., and Endlicher, G., 1977, Geologische In-
    terpretation des ERTS-2-Satellitenbildes des Ost-
    bayerischen Grundgebirges und angrenzender Gebiete:
    Acta Albertina Ratisbonensia, v. 37, p. 91-102.

Burns, K.L., 1973, Structural data files: Tectonics Struct. Newsl., Geol. Soc. Australia, no. 2, p. 21-22.

Burns, K.L., and Dunnet, D., 1973, Structural data processing: Tectonic Struck. Newsl., Geol. Soc. Australia, no. 2, p. 20-21.

Burns, K.L., Huntington, J.F., and Green, A.A., 1977, Computer-assisted photointerpretation of geological lineaments: perception method: Intern. Symp. Applic. Comput. Oper. Res. Mineral Indust., Papers, no. 15, p. 275-285.

Burns, K.L., Marshall, B., and Gee, R.D., 1969, Computer-assisted geological map: Australas. Inst. Mining Metall., Proc., no. 232, p. 41-47.

Burns, K.L., Shepherd, J., and Berman, M., 1976, Reproducibility of geological lineaments and other discrete features interpreted from imagery: measurement by a coefficient of association: Remote Sensing Environ., v. 5, p. 267-301.

Bush, V.A., and Kats, Y.G., 1978, Tektonicheskoye rayonirovaniye Sredizemnomorskogo al'piyskogo poyasa po rezul'tatam deshifrirovaniya kosmicheskikh snimkov: Vysshoye Uchebnoye Zavedeniye, Izv., Geol. Razved., no. 10, p. 74-79.

Cardamone, P., Leche, G.M., Cavallin, A., and others, 1977, Application of conventional and advanced techniques for the interpretation of LANDSAT 2 images for the study of linears in the Friuli earthquake area: Intern. Symp. Remote Sens. Environ., Proc., no. 11, p. 1337-1353.

Cassinis, R., 1977, Applications of satellite studies for structural geology in Italy *in* Remote sensing of the terrestrial environment, Peel, R.F., and others, eds., Butterworths, London, p. 169-181.

Chapple, W.M., 1964, A mathematical study of finite-amplitude rock folding (abst.): Am. Geophys. Union Trans., v. 45, no. 1, p. 104.

Chapple, W.M., 1968, A mathematical theory of finite-amplitude rock-folding: Geol. Soc. America Bull., v. 79, no. 1, p. 47-68.

Chapple, W.M., 1969, Fold shape and rheology: the fold-
    ing of an isolated viscous-plastic layer: Tectono-
    physics, v. 7, no. 2, p. 97-116.

Chapple, W.M., 1970a, The initiation and spacing of folds
    in viscous multilayered media (abst.): Geol. Soc.
    America,Abs. Prog., v. 2, no. 4, p. 276.

Chapple, W.M., 1970b, The finite-amplitude instability
    in the folding of layered rocks: Can. Jour. Earth
    Sci., v. 7, no. 2, pt. 1, p. 457-466.

Chapple, W.M., and Spang, J.H., 1974, Significance of
    layer-parallel slip during folding of layered sedi-
    mentary rocks: Geol. Soc. America Bull., v. 85,
    no. 10, p. 1523-1534.

Charlesworth, H.A.K., Langenberg, C.W., and Ramsden, J.,
    1975, Determining axes, axial planes and profiles
    of macroscopic folds using computer-based methods
    (abst.): Geol. Soc. America, Abs. Prog., v. 7, no.
    6, p. 734.

Charlesworth, H.A.K., Langenberg, C.W., and Ramsden, J.,
    1976, Determining axes, axial planes, and section
    of macroscopic folds using computer-based methods:
    Can. Jour. Earth Sci., v. 13, no. 1, p. 54-65.

Chesire, S.G., Spang, J.H., and Stockmal, G.S., 1978,
    Am empirical non-linear technique for the analysis
    of conical folds (abst.): Geol. Soc. America, Abs.
    Prog., v. 10, no. 5, p. 212-213.

Clancy, R.T., Turcotte, D.L., and Kulhawy, F.H., 1977,
    Finite element studies of strain accumulation and
    release of the San Andreas fault (abst.): Am. Geo-
    phys. Union Trans., v. 58, no. 12, p. 1227.

Cobbold, P.R., 1977, Finite-element analysis of fold
    propagation - a problematic application?: Tectono-
    physics, v. 38, no. 3-4, p. 339-353.

Cobbold, P.R., 1977, Removal of finite deformation using
    strain trajectories: Jour. Struc. Geol., v. 1, no.
    1, p. 67-72.

Cogbill, A.H., 1979, The relationship between crustal
    structure and seismicity in the western Great Basin:
    unpubl. doctoral dissertation, Northwestern Univ.

Coode, A.M., 1966, An analysis of major tectonic fea-
    tures: Roy. Astron. Soc., Geophys. Jour., v. 12,
    no. 1, p. 55-66.

Coode, A.M., 1967, The spherical harmonic analysis of
    major tectonic features, in Mantles of the Earth
    and terrestrial planets, Runcorn, S.K., ed.: Inter-
    science Publ. London, p. 489-498.

Correa, A.C., and Lyon, R.J.P., 1976, Application of
    optical Fourier analysis to the study of geological
    linear features in ERTS-1 imagery of California:
    Utah Geol. Assoc., Publ. no. 5, p. 462-479.

Cosgrove, J.W., 1976, The formation of crenulation clea-
    vage: Jour. Geol. Soc., London, v. 132, no. 2, p.
    155-178.

Crain, I.K., 1972, Statistical methods for geotectonic
    analysis (abst.): 24th Intern. Geol. Congress
    (Montreal), Abst., p. 70-71.

Crain, I.K., 1973, A statistical approach to the analysis
    of geotectonic elements: unpubl. doctoral disserta-
    tion, Australian National Univ.

Cruden, D.M., and Charlesworth, H.A.K., 1972, Some obser-
    vations on the numerical determination of the axes
    of cylindrical and conical folds (abst.): Geol.
    Soc. America, Abs. Prog., v. 4, no. 6, p. 372-373.

Cubitt, J.M., and Celenk, O., 1976, FORTRAN program for
    producing stereograms in geology: Computers & Geo-
    sciences, v. 1, no. 3, p. 207-211.

Cundall, P.A., 1971, A computer model for simulating pro-
    gressive, large-scale movements in blocky rock sys-
    tems, in Rock fracture: Intern. Soc. Rock. Mech.,
    unpaginated.

Dabovski, K., 1975, Matematicheskaya model' napryazheniy
    i peremeshcheniy okolo magmaticheskikh kamer i
    razlomov: Geotektonika, Tektonofiz., Geodinamika,
    v. 3, p. 17-30.

Dahlberg, E.C., Deland, C.R., and Creed, R.M., 1975,
    Probability mapping of subsurface faults from strati-
    graphic data (abst.): Geol. Soc. America, Abs.
    Prog., v. 7, no. 1, p. 45.

David, M., 1977, Geostatistical ore reserve estimation:
    Elsevier Scientific Publ. Co., New York, 364 p.

Davis, H.T., 1975, Multivariate prediction and spline
    functions, *in* The search for oil: some statistical
    methods and techniques, Owen, D.B., ed.: v. 13,
    Marcel Dekker, Inc., New York, p. 33-40.

Davis, J.C., Doveton, J.H., and Hambleton, W.W., 1975,
    Oil exploration by probabilistic analysis: a case
    history (abst.): Am. Assoc. Petroleum Geologists
    Soc. Econ. Pal. Miner., Ann. Mtg., v. 2, p. 18.

De Bremaecker, J.-C., and Becker, E.B., 1976, Numerical
    simulation of folding (abst.): Am. Geophys. Union
    Trans., v. 57, no. 4, p. 321.

De Bremaecker, J.-C., and Becker, E.B., 1978, Finite
    element models of folding: Tectonophysics, v. 50,
    no. 2-3, p. 349-367.

Deist, F.H., Salamon, M.D.G., and Georgiadis, E., 1973,
    A new digital method for three-dimensional stress
    analysis in elastic media: Rock Mechan. (Vienna),
    v. 5, no. 4, p. 189-202.

Demirmen, F., 1972, Mathematical procedures and FORTRAN
    IV program for description of three-dimensional sur-
    face configurations: Kansas Geol. Survey, KOX Tech.
    Rept., 131 p.

Demirmen, F., 1973, Numerical description of folded sur-
    faces depicted by contour maps: Jour. Geology,
    v. 81, no. 5, p. 599-620.

Dieterich, J.H., 1969, Mathematical modeling of fault
    tectonic and seismicity (abst.): Geol. Soc. America,
    Abs. Prog., pt. 7, p. 47-48.

Dieterich, J.H., 1970, Computer experiments on mechanics
    of finite amplitude folds: Can. Jour. Earth Sci.,
    v. 7, no. 2, p. 467-476.

Dieterich, J.H., 1972, Numerical modeling of deformations
    associated with volcanism (abst.): Geol. Soc.
    America, Abs. Prog., v. 4, no. 3, p. 146.

Dieterich, J.H., and Carter, N.L., 1969, Stress-history
    of folding: Am. Jour. Sci., v. 267, no. 2, p. 129-
    154.

Dieterich, J.H., and Decker, R.W., 1975, Finite element
    modeling of surface deformation associated with
    volcanism: Jour. Geophys. Res., v. 80, no. 29, p.
    4094-4102.

Dieterich, J.H., and Onat, E.T., 1969, Slow finite defor-
    mations of viscous solids: Jour. Geophys. Res.,
    v. 74, no. 8, p. 2081-2088.

Douglas, A., 1970, Finite elements for geologic modelling:
    Nature, v. 226, no. 5246, p. 630-631.

Du Prey, E.J.L., and Bossie-Codreanu, D.N., 1974, Simulat-
    ion numerique de l'exploitation des reservoirs fiss-
    ures: World Petrol. Congr., Proc. IX, v. 4, p. 233-246

Dudley, R.M., Perkins, P.C., and Gine M, E., 1975, Stat-
    istical tests for preferred orientation: Jour.
    Geology, v. 83, no. 6, p. 685-705.

Dumitrescu, V., 1974, Blocdiagrame realizabile la com-
    puter: Stud. Cercet. Geol., Geofiz., Geogr., Ser.
    Geogr., v. 21, no. 1, p. 117-119.

Eckert, H.U., 1970, Einsatz der elektronischen datenver-
    arbeitung bei kleintektonischen Untersuchungen auf
    Blatt Weyerbusch/Siegerland; 1:25000: Clausthaler
    Tekt. Hefte, 10, p. 191-228.

Edel'shteyn, A.Y., 1972, O kolichestvennyhk metodakh
    izucheniya platformennoy skladchatosti: Geol. Geo-
    fiz (Akad. Nauk. SSSR, Sib. Otd.), v. 11, p. 120-
    124.

Eschner, T.R., Robinson, J.E., and Merriam, D.F., 1979,
    Comparison of spatially filtered geologic maps:
    summary: Geol. Soc. America Bull., pt. I, v. 90,
    no. 1, p. 6-7; pt. II, p. 104-134.

Feenstra, R., and Wickham, J.S., 1976, Computer models
    of simple shear deformation superposed on symmetric
    folds applied to deformation in the Ouachita Moun-
    tains (abst.): Geol. Soc. America, Abs. Prog.,
    v. 8, no. 1, p. 20.

Fletcher, R.C., 1972, Application of a mathematical model
    to the emplacement of mantled gneiss domes: Am.
    Jour. Sci., v. 272, no. 3, p. 197-216.

Flinn, D., 1978, Construction and computation of three-
    dimensional progressive deformations: Geol. Soc.
    London Jour., v. 135, pt. 3, p. 291-305.

Forster, H., and Leonhardt, J., 1972, Mathematische
    Simulation ptygmatischer Strukturen: Geol. Rundsch.,
    v. 61, no. 3, p. 883-896.

Franssen, L., and Kummert, P., 1971, Presentation d'un
    programme de traitement des donnees en geologie
    structurale: Soc. Geol. Belgique, Annal., v. 94,
    no. 1, p. 39-43.

Fujii, K., 1972, Structural analysis by the finite ele-
    ment method, *in* Prof. Jun-ichi Iwai Memorial Volume,
    Hatai, K., Asano, K., and others, eds.: Tohoku
    Univ., Inst. Geol. Paleont., Japan, p. 471-480.

Fumagalli, E., 1968, Model simulation of rock mechanics
    problems, *in* Rock mechanics in engineering practice,
    Stagg, K.G., and Zienkiewicz, O.C., eds.: John
    Wiley & Sons, London, p. 353-384.

George, L., and Sowers, G.M., 1975, Comparison of com-
    puted folds in multilayered media: elastic, vis-
    cous, viscoelastic, and plastic cases (abst.):
    Geol. Soc. America, Abs. Prog., v. 7, no. 2, p.
    167-168.

Ghez, F., and Janot, P., 1974, Calcul statistique du
    volume des blocs matriciels d'un gisement fissure:
    Inst. Francais Petrole Rev., v. 29, no. 3, p. 375-
    386.

Goncharov, M.A., 1971, Matematicheskaya model'skladchatoy
    struktury: Geol. Geofiz. (Akad. Nauk SSSR, Sib.
    Otd.), no. 4, p. 117-123.

Grishkyan, R.I., Parfenov, L.M., and Ufimtsev, G.V.,
    1977, Kosmicheskiye izobrazheniya Baykal'skoy rift-
    ovoy oblasti i yeye vozmozhnaya kinematicheskaya
    model', *in* Rol' riftogeneza v geologicheskoy istorii
    Zemli, Florensov, N.A., ed.: Izd. Nauka, Novosibirsk,
    p. 104-108.

Groshong, R.H., Jr., 1974, Experimental test of least-squares strain gage calculation using twinned calcite: Geol. Soc. America Bull., v. 85, no. 12, p. 1855-1863.

Hanley, J.T., 1975, Numerical techniques for areal fracture analysis (abst.): Geol. Soc. America, Abst. Prog., v. 7, no. 1, p. 70.

Hardy, M.P., Crouch, S.L., Fairhurst, C., and others, 1974, A hybrid computer system simulating inelastic seam behavior: Intern. Soc. Rock. Mech., Congr. Proc., III, v. 2B, p. 1015-1021.

Hattori, I., and Mizutani, S., 1971, Computer simulation of fracturing of layered rock: Engineer. Geology, v. 5, no. 4, p. 253-269.

Haugh, I., Brisbin, W.C., and Turek, A., 1967, A computer-oriented field sheet for structural data: Can. Jour. Earth Sci., v. 4, no. 4, p. 657-662.

Heinze, W.D., and Goetze, C., 1973, Computer simulation of fracturing of layered rock (abst.): Am. Geophys. Union Trans., v. 54, no. 4, p. 450.

Heinze, W.D., and Goetze, C., 1974, Numerical simulation of stress concentrations in rocks: Intern. Jour. Rock Mech. Min. Sci., v. 11, no. 4, p. 151-155.

Hirsinger, V., 1976, Numerical strain analysis using polar coordinate transformations: Jour. Math. Geology, v. 8, no. 2, p. 183-202.

Hobbs, B.E., 1971, The analysis of strain in folded layers: Tectonophysics, v. 11, no. 4, p. 329-375.

Howard, J.C., 1971, Computer simulation models of salt domes: Am. Assoc. Petroleum Geologists Bull., v. 55, no. 3, p. 495-513.

Hudleston, P.J., 1973, Fold morphology and some geometrical implications of theories of fold development: Tectonophysics, v. 16, no. 1-2, p. 1-46.

Hudleston, P.J., and Stephansson, O., 1973, Layer shortening and fold-shape development in the buckling of single layers: Tectonophysics, v. 17, no. 4, p. 299-321.

Huntington, F., 1975, A photogeological study of fracture
    trace patterns using data-processing techniques
    (abst.): Inst. Min. Metall. Trans., v. 84B, no.
    828, p. 156.

Ikeda, Y., and Shimamoto, T., 1974, Numerical experiments
    on the viscous bending folds (in Japanese): Geol.
    Soc. Japan Jour., v. 80, no. 2, p. 65-74.

Jackson, D.D., 1972, Numerical simulation of main shock
    and aftershock sequence (abst.): Am. Geophys.
    Union Trans., v. 53, no. 11, p. 1047.

James, W.R., 1968, Least-squares surface fitting with
    discontinuous functions: Tech. Rept. 8, ONR Task
    389-150, Contract Nonr-1228(36), 51 p.

James, W.R., 1970, Regression models for faulted struc-
    tural surfaces: Am. Assoc. Petroleum Geologists
    Bull., v. 54, no. 4, p. 638-646.

Jeran, P.W., and Mashey, J.R., 1970, A computer program
    for the stereographic analysis of coal fractures
    and cleats: U.S. Bur. Mines Info. Circ. 8454, 34 p.

Jones, T.A., Johnson, C.R., and Herron, S.R., 1976, An
    application of interactive computer graphics to
    petroleum exploration (abst.): Geol. Soc. America,
    Abs. Prog., v. 8, no. 1, p. 26-27.

Jones, T.A., and Jordan, N.F., 1975, Structural mapping
    with data containing points that do not intersect
    the horizon of interest: an automated procedure
    (abst.): Am. Assoc. Petroleum Geologists Mtg.
    Abst., v. 2, p. 40-41.

Juneman, P.M., 1971, Geological applications of interac-
    tive computer graphics and "graphic analysis of
    three dimensional data" (G.A.T.D.): Sci. Terre,
    v. 16, no. 3-4, p. 303-316.

Kapustin, I.N., Przhiyalgovskiy, Y.S., and Trofimov, D.
    M., 1978, Primeneniye kosmicheskoy informatsii pri
    sostavlenii tektonicheskoy karty Prikaspiyskoy
    vpadiny i yeye obramleniya (stat'ya I): Vysshoye
    Uchebnoye Zavedeniye, Izv., Geol. Razved., no. 10,
    p. 40-46.

Koelling, M.E.V., and Whitten, E.H.T., 1973, FORTRAN IV
    program for spline-surface interpolation and contour-
    map production: Geocom Programs, v. 9, p. 1-12.

Kontorovich, A.E., Fotiadi, E.E., Berilko, V.I., and
    others, 1971, Prognoz produktivnosti lokal'nykh
    struktur tsentral'noy i yugo-vostochnoy chastey
    zapadno-Sibirskoy plity s primeneniyem algoritmov
    raspoznavaniya obrazov: Geol. Geofiz. (Akad. Nauk
    SSSR Sib. Otd.), Novosibirsk, no. 7, p. 84-91.

Kosloff, D., 1976, Numerical investigation of a mechanism
    of formation of the Palmdale Uplift (abst.): Am.
    Geophys. Union Trans., v. 57, no. 12, p. 898.

Kowalik, W.S., 1975, Application of satellite photographic
    and MSS data to selected geologic and natural re-
    source problems in Pennsylvania: III, Comparison
    of Skylab and Landsat lineaments with joint orien-
    tations in north central Pennsylvania: NASA Tech.
    Memo, no. X-58168, p. 958-969.

Krausse, H.F., 1970, Uber eine erste statistische Aus-
    wertung von Gefugedaten mit elektronischen Rechen-
    anlagen: Clausthaler Tekt. Hefte, v. 10, p. 49-62.

Kronberg, P., 1975, ERTS-1 shows buried structures *in*
    Geoscientific studies and the potential of the
    natural environment, Deutsche UNESCO-Komm., Koln,
    Verlag Dok. Munchen, p. 122.

Kruckeberg, F., 1968, Eine Programmiersprache fur gefuge-
    kundliche Arbeiten: Clausthaler Tekt. Hefte, v. 8,
    p. 7-53.

Kruhl, J., 1974, Mitteilung uber die Benutzung von Sicht-
    geraeten bei der statischen Auswertung von Gefuge-
    messungen: Geol. Mitt. (Aachen), v. 12, no. 4, p.
    319-326.

Kruhl, J., 1978, Current bedding in the Moinian quart-
    zites at eastern Loch Leven, Scottish Highlands:
    Neues Jahrb. Mineral., Abh.,v. 132, no. 1, p. 52-
    66.

Kulyndyshev, V.A., 1972, Logicheskiy analiz metodov
    opisaniya elementarnykh strukturnykh poverkhnostey:
    Geol. Geofiz. (Akad. Nauk SSSR, Sib. Otd.), Novosi-
    birsk, no. 1, p. 142-144.

Kumar, M.B., 1977, Computer-aided subsurface structural
    analysis of the Miocene formations of the Bayou
    Carlin-Lake Sand area, South Louisiana: Louisiana
    Geol. Surv., Geol. Bull., no. 43, pt. I, 177 p.

LaFountain, L.J., 1970, Plotted and point-counted stereo-
    grams by computer X-Y plotter or microfilm devices:
    Geol. Soc. America Bull., v. 81, no. 4, p. 1267-
    1271.

Lam, P.W.H., 1969, Discussion: computer program for
    plotting beta-diagrams: Am. Jour. Sci., v. 267,
    no. 9, p. 1114-1117.

Lambert, P., 1975, La structure impactitique de Roche-
    chouart (Haute-Vienne) et la structure de la partie
    nord-ouest du Massif central francais, interpreta-
    tion de "photographies obtenues par satellite";
    image ERTS (abst.): France, Bur. Rech. Geol.
    Minieres Bull. (Ser. 2), Sect. 2, no. 1, 21 p.

Langenberg, C.W., Rondeel, H.E., and Charlesworth, H.A.
    K., 1977, A structural study in the Belgian Ardennes
    with sections constructed using computer-based meth-
    ods: Geol. Mijnb., v. 56, no. 2, p. 145-154.

Laurin, A.-F., Sharma, K.N.M., Wynne-Edwards, H.R., and
    Franconi, A., 1972, Application of data processing
    techniques in the Grenville Province, Quebec, Canada:
    Proc. 24th Intern. Geol. Congress (Montreal), Sect.
    16, p. 22-35.

Lewis, R.W., and Williams, J.R., 1978, A finite-element
    study of fold propagation in a viscous layer:
    Tectonophysics, v. 44, no. 1-4, p. 263-283.

Lister, G.S., Paterson, M.S., and Hobbs, B.E., 1978, The
    simulation of fabric development in plastic deforma-
    tion and its application to quartzite: the model:
    Tectonophysics, v. 45, no. 2-3, p. 107-158.

Lokhmatov, G.I., and Alayev, G.T., 1967, Metod razdeleniya
    strukturnykh i izopakhicheskikh kart na sos-
    tavlyayushchiye: Geol. Nefti Gaza, v. 11, no. 4,
    p. 32-38.

Lakhmatov, G.I., Alayev, G.T., and Yevdokimova, V.N.,
    1968, Matematicheskiy metod paleotektonicheskogo
    analiza platformennykh struktur v usloviyakh monok-
    linal'nogo sklona: Geol. Nefti Gaza, v. 12, no. 5,
    p. 46-50.

Lutzner, H., and Maaz, H., 1969, Ein Rechenprogramm zur
    statistischen Beschreibung von Richtungsmessungen
    mit geringer Streuung und dessen Anwendung: Deutsche
    Gesell. Geol. Wissen., Ber., Reihe A, Geol. Palaont.,
    v. 14, no. 5, p. 561.

Maffi, G., and Marchesini, E., 1964, Semi-automatic
    equipment for statistical analysis of airphoto
    linears: Photogram. Engineer., v. 30, no. 1, p.
    139-141.

Mark, D.M., 1973, Analysis of axial orientation data,
    including till fabrics: Geol. Soc. America Bull.,
    v. 84, no. 4, p. 1369-1374.

Masson, P., 1978, Essai d'analyse structurale du Rift
    Levantine d'apres les donnees Landsat: Photo inter-
    pret., v. 17, no. 1, p. 17-33.

Matthews, P.E., Bond, R.A.B., and Van den Berg, J.J.,
    1974, An algebraic method of strain analysis using
    elliptical markers: Tectonophysics, v. 24, no. 1-
    2, p. 31-67.

Minear, J.W., 1972, Finite-element models of preexisting
    fractures (abst.): Am. Geophys. Union Trans., v.
    53, no. 11, p. 1118.

Miyatake, T., 1977, Numerical simulation of dynamical
    faulting process (in Japanese): Zisin Seismol.
    Soc. Japan Jour., v. 30, no. 4, p. 449-461.

Mundry, E., 1972, Nonlinear regression models in geology
    (abst.): Proc. 24th Intern. Geol. Congress (Mon-
    treal) Abst., p. 522-523.

Myasnikova, G.P., and Shpil'man, V.I., 1973, Izucheniye
    svyazi kharaktera osadkonakopleniya i rosta struktur
    s primeniniyem trend-analiza: Geol. Nefti Gaza,
    v. 4, p. 12-16.

Neugebauer, H.J., and Spohn, T., 1978, Late stage devel-
    opment of mature Atlantic-type continental margins:
    Tectonophysics, v. 50, no. 2-3, p. 275-305.

Nidd, E., and Ambrose, J.W., 1971, Computerized solutions
    for some problems of fold geometry: Can. Jour.
    Earth Sci., v. 8, no. 6, p. 688-693.

Nuttall, D.J.H., and Cooper, M.A., 1978, Computer pro-
    grammes for the analysis and presentation of orien-
    tation data: Geol. Soc. London Jour., v. 135, pt.
    2, p. 243-244.

Offield, T.W., Abbott, E.A., Gillespie, A.R., and others,
    1975, Enhanced ERTS images for mapping of structural
    control in the southern Brazil copper region (abst.):
    Soc. Explor. Geophys., Ann. Intern. Mtg., Abst.,
    no. 45, p. 76.

Olea, R.A., 1975, Optimum mapping techniques using re-
    gionalized variable theory: Kansas Geol. Survey,
    Ser. on Spatial Analysis, 137 p.

Owens, W.H., 1974, Mathematical model studies on factors
    affecting the magnetic anisotrophy of deformed rocks:
    Tectonophysics, v. 24, no. 1-2, p. 115-131.

Parrish, D.K., 1973, A nonlinear finite element fold
    model: Am. Jour. Sci., v. 273, no. 4, p. 318-334.

Parrish, D.K., Krivz, A., and Carter, N.L., 1975, Finite
    element folds of similar geometry (abst.): Geol.
    Soc. America,Abs. Prog., v. 7, no. 2, p. 223-224.

Parrish, D.K., Krivz, A., and Carter, N.L., 1976, Finite-
    element folds of similar geometry: Tectonophysics,
    v. 32, no. 3-4, p. 183-207.

Peikert, E.W., 1970, Interactive computer graphics and
    the fault problem (abst.) Am. Assoc. Petroleum Geo-
    logists Bull., v. 54, no. 3, p. 556-557.

Petrov, A.P., Ellanskiy, M.M., and Zverev, G.N., 1972,
    Ispol'zovaniye matematicheskikh metodov pri reshenii
    zadach klassifikatsii geologicheskikh ob'yektov *in*
    Matematicheskiye metody v gazoneftyanoy geologii i
    geofizike, Izd. Nedra, Moscow, p. 10-32.

Pferd, J.W., 1975a, A computer-based system for the col-
    lection of detailed structural data from metamorphic
    terrains (abst.): Geol. Soc. America, Abs. Prog.,
    v. 7, no. 1, p. 106.

Pferd, J.W., 1975b, Computer-compatible collection of de-
    tailed structural data in metamorphic terrains:
    published privately, Amherst, Massachusetts, 39 p.

Podwysocki, M.H., 1973, Computer applications in the
    analysis of fracture patterns (abst.): Geol. Soc.
    America,Abs. Prog., v. 5, no. 2, p. 207-208.

Podwysocki, M.H., Moik, J.G, and Shoup, W.C., 1975, Quan-
    tification of geologic lineaments by manual and ma-
    chine processing techniques: NASA Tech. Memo., no.
    X-58168, p. 885-903.

Pollard, D.D., and Holzhausen, G., 1978, FORTRAN computer
    program for calculation of stress-intensity factors,
    stresses, and displacements associated with a fluid-
    pressurized fracture near the Earth's surface: U.S.
    Geol. Survey open-file rept. 78-160, 26 p.

Ramberg, H., 1970, Folding of laterally compressed multi-
    layers in the field of gravity, II Numerical exam-
    ples: Phys. Earth Planet. Interiors, v. 4, no. 2,
    p. 83-120.

Ramsden, J., 1975, Numerical methods in fabric analysis:
    unpubl. doctoral dissertation, Univ. Alberta.

Ramsden, J., and Cruden, D.M., 1979a, Estimating densi-
    ties in contoured orientation diagrams: summary:
    Geol. Soc. America Bull., v. 90, no. 3, pt. I, p.
    229-231.

Ramsden, J., and Cruden, D.M., 1979b, Estimating densities
    in contoured orientation diagrams: Geol. Soc. Amer-
    ica Bull., v. 90, pt. II, p. 580-607.

Reches, Z., and Johnson, A.M., 1979, Development of mono-
    clines: Part II Theoretical analysis of monoclines:
    Geol. Soc. America Mem. 151, p. 273-311.

Reddy, J.N., and Wickham, J.S., 1979, Numerical modeling
    of geologic structures I. Finite element formula-
    tions of viscous, incompressible flows: in press.

Rice, L.F., Davis, J.H., and Johnson, A.C., 1976, Computer
    analysis of lineaments to infer existence of sub-
    surface geologic structures (abst.): Am. Assoc.
    Petroleum Geologists Bull., v. 60, no. 4, p. 714.

Robinson, J.E., 1969, Spatial filters for geological data: Oil and Gas Jour., v. 67, no. 37, p. 132-134, 138, and 140.

Robinson, J.E., 1970, Spatial filtering of geological data: Rev. Inst. Intern. Statist., v. 38, no. 1, p. 21-34.

Robinson, J.E., 1976, Computer simulation of real folds (abst.): Geol. Assoc. Canada, Mineral. Assoc. Canada jt. mtg., prog. abs., v. 1, p. 51.

Robinson, J.E., and Charlesworth, H.A.K., 1969a, Spatial filtering illustrates a relationship between tectonic structure and oil occurrences in southern and central Alberta: Can. Inst. Min. Metall., 20th Ann. Mtg., Edmonton, paper 6935, p. 1-8.

Robinson, J.E., and Charlesworth, H.A.K., 1969b, Spatial filtering illustrates relationship between tectonic structure and oil occurrence in southern and central Alberta: Kansas Geol. Survey Computer Contr. 40, p. 13-18.

Robinson, J.E., and Charlesworth, H.A.K., 1975, Relation of topography and structure in south-central Alberta: Jour. Math. Geology, v. 7, no. 1, p. 81-87.

Robinson, J.E., and Merriam, D.F., 1972, Enhancement of patterns in geologic data by spatial filtering: Jour. Geology, v. 80, no. 3, p. 333-345.

Rodgers, D.A., Gallagher, J.J., Jr., Rizer, W.D., and Spang, J.H., 1977, Analysis of thrust fault mechanisms: II. Mathematical models (abst.): Am. Geophys. Union Trans., v. 58, no. 6, p. 507.

Sampsom, R.J., 1975a, The SURFACE II graphics system, in Display and analysis of spatial data, Davis, J.C., and McCullagh, M.J., eds.: John Wiley & Sons, New York, p. 244-266.

Sampson, R.J., 1975b, SURFACE II graphics system: Kansas Geol. Survey, Ser. on Spatial Analysis, 240 p.

Schuenemeyer, J.G., Koch, G.S., Jr., and Link, R.F., 1972, Computer program to analyze directional data, based on the methods of Fisher and Watson: Jour. Math. Geology, v. 4, no. 3, p. 177-202.

Selkman, S., 1978, Stress and displacement analysis of
    boudinages by the finite-element method: Tectono-
    physics, v. 44, no. 1-4, p. 115-139.

Serra, S., 1973, A computer program for calculation and
    plotting of stress distribution and faulting: Jour.
    Math. Geology, v. 5, no. 4, p. 397-407.

Sharma, B., and Geldart, L.P., 1968, Analysis of gravity
    anomalies of two dimensional faults using Fourier
    transforms: Geophys. Prospect., v. 16, p. 77-93.

Shatagin, N.N., and Dergachev, A.L., 1978, A modified
    procedure for the computer preparation of diagrams
    of the orientations of structural elements: Moscow
    Univ. Geol. Bull., v. 33, p. 90-91.

Shatagin, N.N., and Sandomirskiy, S.A., 1974, Postroyeniye
    krugovykh diagramm oriyentirovok na EVM: Akad.
    Nauk SSSR, Izv. Ser. Geol., no. 9, p. 97-104.

Shcherbakov, V.S., 1973, Rezul'taty prımeneniya nekotorykh
    matematicheskikh metodov i ETSVM pri izuchenii stro-
    yeniya osadochnogo chekhla zapadnoy chasti Latviyskoy
    SSR, in Problemy regional'noy geologii Pribaltiki i
    Belorussi: Minist. Geol. SSSR, Vses. Nauchno-Issled.
    Inst. Morsk. Geol. Geofiz., Riga, p. 189-200.

Short, N.M., 1973a, Mineral resources, geological struc-
    ture, and landforms surveys: Symp. Signif. Result.
    Obtain. ERTS-1, v. III (Goddard Space Flight Cent.),
    p. 30-46.

Short, N.M., 1973b, ERTS: Applications to tectonics,
    volcanology, mineral resources, and landforms analy-
    sis (abst.): Am. Geophys. Union Trans., v. 54, no.
    7, p. 700.

Short, N.M., 1974a, Mineral resources, geological struc-
    tures, and landform surveys: Third ERTS Symp., v.
    II, NASA spec. publ. no. 356, p. 147-167.

Short, N.M., 1974b, Mineral resources, geological struc-
    ture, and landform surveys: Third ERTS Symp., v.
    III, NASA spec. publ. no. SP-357, p. 33-51.

Siemes, H., 1967, Ein Rechenprogramm zur Auswertung von
    Rontgen-Texturgoniometer-Aufnahmen: Neues Jahr.
    Mineral., Monat., no. 2-3, p. 49-60.

Smith, A.G., 1971, Alpine deformation and the oceanic
    areas of the Tethys, Mediterranean, and Atlantic:
    Geol. Soc. America Bull., v. 82, no. 8, p. 2039-
    2070.

Smith, A.G., and Hallam, A., 1970, The fit of the south-
    ern continents: Nature, v. 225, no. 5228, p. 139-
    144.

Smith, S.W., and Kind, R., 1972, Observations of regional
    strain variations: Jour. Geophys. Res., v. 77, no.
    26, p. 4976-4980.

Solov'yeva, L.I., 1977, Neotektonika i informativnost'
    kosmicheskikh snimkov (na primere Sredney Azii):
    Vysshoye Uchebnoye Zavedeniye, Izv., Geol. Razved.,
    no. 12, p. 47-54 (English translation) Intern.
    Geol. Rev., 1978, v. 20, no. 11, p. 1281-1286.

Spang, J.H., 1974, Numerical dynamic analysis of calcite
    twin lamellae in the Greenport Center syncline:
    Am. Jour. Sci., v. 274, no. 9, p. 1044-1058.

Spang, J.H., and van der Lee, J., 1975, Numerical dynamic
    analysis of quartz deformation lamellae and calcite
    and dolomite twin lamellae: Geol. Soc. America
    Bull., v. 86, no. 9, p. 1266-1272.

Srivastava, G.S., 1975, Optical and digital processing of
    geological surfaces in Kansas: unpubl. doctoral
    dissertation, Syracuse Univ., 326 p.

Srivastava, G.S., and Merriam, D.F., 1974, Quantitative
    comparison of maps using optically derived parameters
    (abst.): Geol. Soc. America, Abs. Prog., v. 6, no.
    7, p. 964-965.

Srivastava, G.S., and Merriam, D.F., 1975, Computer con-
    structed optical-rose diagrams (abst.): Geol. Soc.
    America, Abs. Prog., v. 7, no. 1, p. 121.

Srivastava, G.S., and Merriam, D.F., 1976, Computer con-
    structed optical-rose diagrams: Computers & Geo-
    science, v. 1, no. 3, p. 179-186.

Stabler, C.L., 1968, Simplified Fourier analysis of fold
    shapes: Tectonophysics, v. 6, no. 4, p. 343-350.

Starkey, J., 1974, The quantitative analysis of orientation data obtained by the Starkey method of X-ray fabric analysis: Can. Jour. Earth Sci., v. 11, no. 11, p. 1507-1516.

Stearns, M.T., 1978, The deformation of thick, homogeneous, isotropic continuous rock masses. Part III Analog model studies (abst.): Geol. Soc. America, Abs. Prog., v. 10, no. 1, p. 26.

Stein, R.J., and Wickham, J.S., 1978, Computer models of drape folding and related faulting (abst.): Geol. Soc. America,Abs. Prog., v. 10, no. 7, p. 497.

Stein, R.J., and Wickham, J.S., 1979, Numerical models of fault zone propagation, in press.

Stephansson, O., 1973, The solution of some problems in structural geology by means of the finite-element technique: Geol. Forenin. Forhandl., v. 95, pt. 1, no. 552, p. 51-59.

Stephansson, O., 1976, Finite element analysis of folds: Roy. Soc. London, Philos. Trans., Ser. A, v. 283, no. 1312, p. 153-161.

Stephansson, O., and Berner, H., 1971, The finite element method in tectonic processes: Phys. Earth Planet. Interiors, v. 4, no. 4, p. 301-321.

Stromgard, K., 1973, Stress distribution during formation of boudinage and pressure shadows: Tectonophysics, v. 16, no. 3-4, p. 215-248.

Sturgul, J.R., and Grinshpan, Z., 1975, Finite-element model for possible isostatic rebound in the Grand Canyon: Geology, v. 3, no. 4, p. 169-171.

Szumilas, D., 1977, Using computer for time-to-depth conversion and structure mapping in complexly faulted areas (abst.): Am. Assoc. Petroleum Geologists Bull., v. 61, no. 5, p. 834-835.

Tapp, G., and Wickham, J.S., 1978, Fracture predictions using finite element computer models (abst.): Geol. Soc. America,Abs. Prog., v. 10, no. 1, p. 26.

STRUCTURAL GEOLOGY   365

Tapp, G., Wickham, J.S., and Reddy, J.N., 1979, Numerical
    modeling of geologic structures III. Fracture den-
    sity in single layer folds, in press.

Tocher, F.E., 1979, The computer contouring of fabric
    diagrams: Computers & Geosciences, v. 5, no. 1, p.
    73-126.

Tricart, J.L.F., 1976, Evidence offered by LANDSAT-1
    imagery of tectonic lineaments in the Vosges Moun-
    tains (eastern France), in Rilevanmento spaziale
    delle risorse terrestri; Tecnologie dei sistemi e
    componenti spaziali; Rilevamento spaziale dei feno-
    meni atmosferici; Energia solare e fonti di energia
    terrestre non convenzionali: Intern. Tech. Sci.
    Mtg. Space Proc., no. 16, p. 53-59.

Vaytekunas, I.P., and Yankunayte, I.I., 1975, Informat-
    sionno-poiskovaya sisteme po glubokim skvazhinam
    Yuzhnoy Pribaltiki (abst.): Izd. Litov. Nauch.-
    Issled. Geologorazved Inst. Vilna, p. 70.

Venkitasubramanyan, C.S., 1971, Least-squares analysis
    of fabric data: a note on conical, cylindroidal
    and near-cylindroidal folds: Can. Jour. Earth
    Sci., v. 8, no. 6, p. 694-697.

Venter, R.H., and Spang, J.H., 1974, Numerical analysis
    of multimodal orientation data (abst.): Am. Geo-
    phys. Union Trans., v. 55, no. 2, p. 73-74.

Vikhert, A.V., 1967, Tipovyye matematicheskiye modeli
    raspredeleniya vysot (glubin) strukturnykh poverkh-
    nostey, izobrazhennykh na kartakh v izoliniyakh
    (abst.): Mosk. Obshchest. Ispyt. Prir., Byull.,
    Otd. Geol., v. 42, no. 3, p. 160.

Vikhert, A.V., 1973, O metodike i vozmozhnostyakh postro-
    yeniya morfologicheskoy klassifikatsii skladchatosti
    v chislennykh statisticheskikh merakh: Mosk. Obsh-
    chest. Ispyt. Prir., Byull., Otd. Geol., v. 48, no.
    1, p. 148-149.

Vikhert, A.V., and Goncharov, M.A., 1969, O determinist-
    skikh i verayatnostnykh modelyakh strukturnykh
    poverkhnostey: Geol. Geofiz. (Akad. Nauk SSSR,
    Sib. Otd.), Novosibirsk, no. 5, p. 66-71: (English
    translation) Intern. Geol. Rev., 1970, v. 12, no.
    11, p. 1310-1313.

Voight, B., and Dahl, H.D., 1970, Numerical continuum approaches to analysis of nonlinear rock deformation: Can. Jour. Earth Sci., v. 7, no. 3, p. 814-830.

Voight, B., and Samuelson, A.C., 1969, On the application of finite-element techniques to problems concerning potential distribution and stress analysis in the earth sciences: Pur. Appl. Geophys., v. 76, p. 40-55.

Volchegurskiy, L.F., and Pronin, V.G., 1977, Vozmozhnosti vyyavleniya krupnykh strukturnykh form v predelakh Russkoy i Turanskoy plit (po materialam deshifriro-vaniya televizionnykh kosmicheskikh snimkov): Vysshoye Uchebnoye Zavedeniye, Izv., Geol. Razved, no. 9, p. 14-19 (English translation) Intern. Geol. Rev., 1978, v. 20, no. 11, p. 1276-1280.

Vychev, V., 1976, Programma dlya opredeleniya rustoty treshchin v porodakh po polevym nablyudeniyam: Geotektonika, Tektonofiz., Geodinamika, v. 4, p. 59-64.

Watson, D.F., and Smith, F.G., 1975, A computer program and study of grain shape: Computers & Geosciences, v. 1, no. 1-2, p. 109-111.

Whitten, E.H.T., 1969, Trends in computer applications in structural geology, in Computer applications in the earth sciences: an international symposium, Merriam, D.F., ed.: Plenum Press, New York, p. 233-249.

Whitten, E.H.T., 1970, Orthogonal polynomial trend sur-faces for irregularly spaced data: Jour. Math. Geology, v. 2, no. 2, p. 141-152.

Whitten, E.H.T., 1974, Orthogonal-polynomial contoured trend-surface maps for irregularly spaced data: Computer Applications, v. 1, no. 3-4, p. 171-192.

Whitten, E.H.T., 1975, The practical use of trend-surface analyses in the geological sciences, in Display and analysis of spatial data, Davis, J.C. and McCullagh, M.J., eds.: John Wiley & Sons, England, p. 282-297.

Whitten, E.H.T., 1976, Geodynamic significance of spas-modic, Cretaceous, rapid subsidence rates, contin-ental shelf, USA: Tectonophysics, v. 36, no. 1-3, p. 133-142.

Whitten, E.H.T., 1977a, Kriging in subsurface structural
    analyses: Pribram Mining Conf. (Czechoslovakia),
    Proc., v. 3, p. 801-819.

Whitten, E.H.T., 1977b, Stochastic models in geology:
    Jour. Geology, v. 85, no. 3, p. 321-330.

Whitten, E.H.T., 1979, Semi-variograms and Kriging: pos-
    sible useful tools in fold description, *in* Future
    trends in geomathematics, Craig, R., and Labovitz,
    M., eds.: Pion Press, London, in press.

Whitten, E.H.T., and Koelling, M.E.V., 1973, Spline-
    surface interpolation, spatial filtering, and trend
    surfaces for geological mapped variables: Jour.
    Math. Geology, v. 5, no. 2, p. 111-126.

Whitten, E.H.T., and Koelling, M.E.V., 1975, Computation
    of bicubic-spline surfaces for irregularly spaced
    data: Northwestern Univ., ARO-D Grant Rept. 3,
    57 p.

Whitten, E.H.T., and Koelling, M.E.V., 1978, O bikubiche-
    skikh splain-poverkhnostiakh dlia neravnomerno
    raznesennikh dannikh nabliodenii, *in* Issledovania
    po matematicheskoi geologii, Romanova, M.A., and
    Sapagov, N.A., eds.: Leningrad, p. 150-162.

Wickham, J.S., and Anthony, J.M., 1976, Incremental
    strain paths and folding of carbonate rocks near
    the Blue Ridge, central Appalachians (abst.): Am.
    Geophys. Union Trans., v. 57, no. 4, p. 321.

Wickham, J.S., and Anthony, J.M., 1977, Strain paths and
    folding of carbonate rocks near Blue Ridge, central
    Appalachians: Geol. Soc. America Bull., v. 88,
    no. 7, p. 920-924.

Wickham, J.S., Stein, R.J., and Reddy, J.N., 1979, Numer-
    ical modeling of geologic structures II. Computer
    models of faulting: in press.

Williams, J.R., Lewis, R.W., and Zienkiewicz, O.C., 1978,
    A finite-element analysis of the role of intial
    perturbations in the folding of a single viscous
    layer: Tectonophysics, v. 45, no. 2-3, p. 187-200.

Winchell, H., 1967, A computer program concerned with
    statistics of rock fabrics (abst.):   Geol. Assoc.
    Canada, Mineral. Assoc. Can., Intern. Mtg. Abst.
    Pap., p. 103-104.

Woidt, W.-D., 1978a, Numerical calculations applied to
    salt dome dynamics (abst.):   Am. Geophys. Union
    Trans., v. 59, no. 4, p. 386.

Woidt., W.-D., 1978b, Finite element calculations applied
    to salt dome analysis: Tectonophysics, v. 50, no.
    2-3, p. 369-386.

Wray, W.B., Jr., 1973, A computer program to construct
    cross sections of curved surfaces: Jour. Math.
    Geology, v. 5, no. 2, p. 149-161.

Wynne-Edwards, H.R., Laurin, A.F., Sharma, K.N.M., Nandi,
    A., Kehlenbeck, M.M., and Franconi, A., 1970, Com-
    puterized geological mapping in the Grenville pro-
    vince, Quebec: Can. Jour. Earth Sci., v. 7,
    no. 6, p. 1357-1373.

Xu, D., and Sun, H., 1966, Trend-surface analysis of
    stratigraphic data (in Chinese):   Stratigraphy Maga-
    zine, v. 1, p. 1.

Yeromenko, V.Y., and Katterfel'd, G.N., 1978, Ispol'
    zovaniye kosmicheskikh snimkov pri izuchenii re-
    gional'nykh i global'nykh sistem lineamentov Zemli:
    Vysshoye Uchebnoye Zavedeniye, Izv., Geol. Razved.,
    no. 10, p. 23-29.

Zhang, Q.R., 1977, An example of trend-surface analysis
    of gentle folds (in Chinese):   Scientia Geologica
    Sinica, v. 4, p. 377-389.

Zienkiewicz, O.C., 1971, The finite element method in
    engineering science: McGraw-Hill Publ. Co. Ltd.,
    London, 521 p.

Zienkiewicz, O.C., 1974, Finite element methods in flow
    problems: an introduction, *in* Finite element meth-
    ods in flow problems, Oden, J.T., and others, eds.:
    Univ. Alabama, Huntsville Press, Huntsville, p. 3-4.

Zienkiewicz, O.C., 1976, The finite element method and
    the solution of some geophysical problems: Roy.
    Soc. London, Philos. Trans., Ser. A, v. 283, no.
    1312, p. 139-151.

A FORECAST FOR USE OF COMPUTERS BY GEOLOGISTS IN THE
COMING DECADE OF THE 80s

D.F. Merriam

Syracuse University

ABSTRACT

The first two decades of computer applications in
geology have resulted in many advances. The decade of
the 80's promises continued rapid development of hardware
and software, both areas generally outside the influence
of earth scientists. We can expect continued trends in
smaller, faster, cheaper, and more accessable computers,
especially in the form of micros and minis. Software
will be more user oriented and telecommunications will
become commonplace. New and improved algorithms for
solving geological problems will be developed. Simulation of geological processes and realistic three-dimensional models also will be important in the coming decade. It is possible that a language to express geological concepts and terminology in mathematical terms will
be formulated.

INTRODUCTION

Geologists have been involved with computers now
for about 20 years. Early computer use was restricted
because of limited background of geologists in quantification. Geophysicists, engineering geologists, and hy-
drologists, however, readily applied computer-oriented
techniques in their work as soon as available. Much has
been written on the development and application of computers in geology so rather than look back, it is appropriate to see where we are today and then look ahead.

The discovery (conceptual phase) of computers by geologists took place in the 1950's (Fig. 1). The date of computerization can be given as 1958, when W.C. Krumbein and L.L. Sloss published a simple computer program written in SOAP in the Bulletin of the American Association of Petroleum Geologists. This program was designed to calculate three percentages and two ratios. During the 50's most of the papers (there were very few) were of a general nature and contained only suggestions of possible uses (Table 1).

The 1960's brought development and rapid growth in uses. Papers demonstrated uses for different techniques (mostly borrowed from other disciplines such as biology, engineering, statistics, etc.) with test geological data sets. Research and teaching centers of the subject of geomathematics, geostatistics, and computer applications appeared as well as special publication outlets to handle this new aspect of geology.

Many applications were reported during the 1970's and some specific developments to solve geological problems took place. As the use of computers spread through the subdisciplines of geology (and none have been immune) many problems and shortcomings were found not only in the applications but in the content and generation of the data base itself. Now, as we enter the 1980's, computer use will be integrated completely in geologic studies as this aspect of the science matures.

In some respects this introduction of computers into geology can be likened to the introduction of the petrographic microscope and the seismograph. The computer is an extension of the mind as the microscope extended seeing and the seismograph extended hearing. Also parallel to development and integration of the microscope and seismograph into geology, two groups have developed - those interested in the applications as a science unto itself and those who simply want to use the techniques as a tool. Thus, the subdiscipline of geomathematics (which encompasses geostatistics and computer applications) is at a similar cross roads as geophysics and geochemistry were a decade or two ago.

PRESENT STATUS OF COMPUTER USE IN GEOLOGY

Many of the borrowed techniques used to solve geological problems have been successful. Time-trend,

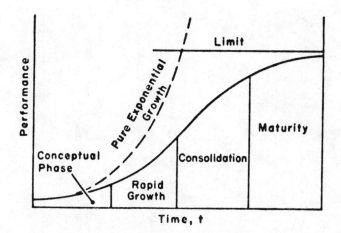

Figure 1.   Graphic representation of
            performance and limit to
            growth of ideas and appli-
            cations (from Starr and
            Rudman, 1973).

cross-correlation and cross-association (which include
autocorrelation and autoassociation), and time-series
analyses have been used to study sequences. Trend and
Fourier analyses and spatial filtering along with numerous enhancement techniques have been used to treat spatial data both two and three dimensions. Multivariate
analysis, including cluster, disciminant, principal components, and factor analyses, has been used extensively
in a variety of conditions (Merriam, 1980).

     Data bases have been assembled and storage and re-
trieval systems built to use them. Systems such as G-
EXEC, GIPSY, SASFRAS, GRASP, and CLAIR are available
readily to interrogate these large data bases. Included
in this category are the information systems such as
Geo.Ref and GeoArchives. Unfortunately, many of the
bases are proprietary information.

     Graphics have been important especially recently.
Geologists are oriented visually and for the most part
prefer their data in summary form, for example as maps,
cross sections, graphs, etc. Therefore much effort has
gone into presenting raw data in some palatable form.

     In all of these developments, each step has been more
complex (Fig. 2). As geologists became more astute and

Table 1. Historical record of stage of integration of computer concepts or techniques in geology (from Merriam, 1975).

	Publications	Data	Computer Programs	References
Discovery	Papers general with suggestions of possibilities.	None	None	Practically none.
Development	Papers demonstrate use of different techniques.	Madeup	"Borrowed" from other fields intact	Mostly from other disciplines.
Application	Papers acknowledge use of computers and source of programs. Different problems tried.	Sample data sets	Modified and adapted from other fields with some geological bent.	Everything written on the subject in geology.
Assimilation	Completely integrated.	Real data in quantities necessary to solve problems.	Programs written with only parts of "canned" programs used but specific for purpose.	Citation of only those papers of pertinence to work.

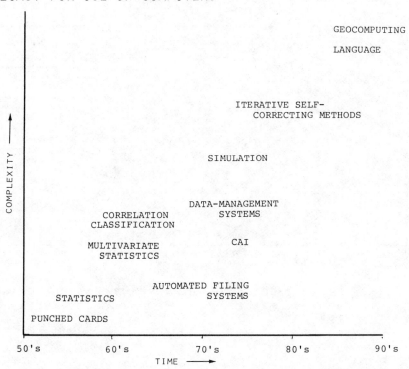

Figure 2. Increasing sophistication of applying computer-oriented techniques to
solve geological problems (Merriam,
1980).

competent, more complex analyses were made of more complex problems. Starting with punched cards and sorting
machines, we now have advanced to solving highly involved, complex multivariate situations with sophisticated techniques.

As previously stated no subdiscipline of geology
has escaped the effect of computers. In the past ten
years however, the distribution of interest has shifted.
In general it can be seen (Fig. 3) that the use of computers has decreased in relation to other subjects for
structure-tectonics, mineralogy-petrology, geochemistry,
and stratigraphy-paleontology. Part of the relative decrease has been brought about by an increase in geomathematics (per se), oceanography, geomorphology, and environmental and engineering geology.

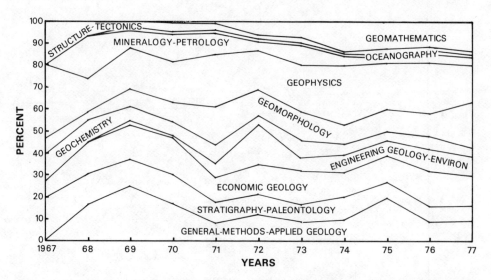

Figure 3.   Percentage of papers concerned with geologic
            subject material for past decade (Merriam,
            1980).

PROBLEMS

        Along with this computer "revolution" in geology
have come many problems with the benefits. These problems, however, have helped emphasize the need for additional studies which in the long run will improve geolo-
ical predictions.

        Many of the techniques adapted from other disciplines
have been incorrectly used - in other words applied to
problems for which they were not intended. In some instances the data did not fit the requirements needed for
the analysis, in some applications the technique was simply misused, in others the example was not appropriate
or realistic (Sutterlin and May, 1978).

        In the construction of data bases it was found that
there was a sampling problem, or the data were incomplete
or of poor quality. In some situations the desired data,
especially proprietary and historical data, were not
available. The transcription of visual data bases presented problems in quality control and required decisions
on what and how much was to be transcribed (often these
decisions were not realistic).

One of the main problems at this point in time is the inability (or unwillingness) of geologists to use what is available. Part of the problem is updating the education of practicing geologists and part is just the knowledge of what is available and where. For example, Geo.Ref, the online bibliographic reference system for geologists, is being utilized only now and its potential is essentially untested. This system alone contains about 500,000 entries and grows at about 4,500 citations per month (incidentally, Australia accounts for only 3 percent of the file in contrast to 42 percent for the US). Coverage unfortunately extends back only to 1961 for North America and to 1967 for areas outside North America. Also 60 percent of the material (from 1967- 1978) is in English! And less than 2 percent is concerned with mathematical geology in contrast with 19 percent for structure-geophysics (as determined in 1976-1978 interval of coverage). How many geologists effectively use the system? Probably very few.

CAI (computer-aided instruction) offers tremendous possibilities as a supplemental teaching aid. However, to date little use has been made of it in geology (Merriam, 1976).

WAYS OF THE FUTURE

Now that geology is changing from an observational and historical science to a more quantitative and rigorous one we can look ahead and make some predictions of things to come. Several things should be noted here - first of all we are passing from a stage of "where" to one of "how." In understanding the processes, we seek an understanding of "why" (Merriam, 1975). Second, we have come to appreciate our inherent problems in data distribution and acquisition and now can cope with it. Thirdly, we are dependent on and closely linked with hardware and software developments outside geology. And lastly, it will take an education effort and perhaps a new generation of geologists to develop geologically oriented techniques to solve geological problems.

Hardware

We can expect the continuing development of smaller but bigger capacity, faster machines (Branscomb, 1979b). Recent developments of large-scale integration (LSI and

VSLI), optical fibers, and storage technology in the form
of magnetic bubble storage devices have contributed to
these trends (Frazer, 1979). They also have contributed
to the continued decrease in cost per bit of about 28
percent per year for random access memory (RAM) and 15
percent per year for cost performances for large systems
(Branscomb, 1979a). The increase in speed is enormous
(Table 2), in fact the difference is much greater than
the difference in a person walking 4 miles per hour and
the Concord flying at 1200 miles per hour. Size for
physical space required for a megabyte of storage has
decreased greatly (Table 3) in just 16 years (IBM, 1979).
Remember the old first generation machines with their
tubes and water-cooling systems? What a spectacular
change in such a short time.

     There will be improved and easier accessibility of
hardware. Minis and micros now are commonplace and
the personal computer has arrived. A personal computer
consists of a microprocessor (miracle chip), keyboard,
memory unit, and TV screen and may be programmed in
BASIC for example. They sell for as little as $99 for
National Semi-Conductors SC/MP model, $350 for INTEL's
SD-80, and $499 for Radio Shack's TRS-80 or $600 for
their popular PET. Personal computers accounted for $5
million in sales in 1975 and $55 million three years
later in 1978! In a few years every geologist will have
one of these personal computers for his work.

                           Software

     Computers will become easier to use; the software
will be more user oriented. Eventually synthesizers will
be used - that is, machines will be available which
hear, speak, and understand (Robinson, 1979). Optical
scanners are available already to convert the written
word into sound (readers for the blind for example).

     Table 2. Computation speeds (Knuth, 1976).

man (pencil and paper)	0.2/sec
man (abacus)	1/sec
mechanical calculator	4/sec
medium-speed computer	200,000/sec
fast computer	200,000,000/sec

Table 3.   Cubic feet/1 million
           characters of storage
           (IBM, 1979).

1953	400 ft^3
1959	100 ft^3
1970	8 ft^3
1976	0.3 ft^3
1979	0.03 ft^3

Some progress has been made to date in speech recognition
for the purpose of automating writing. Imagine being
able to dictate your field notes or a manuscript and get
a written draft! Many other manual operations will be
automated as well so data-acquisition methods will be improved.

Fast algorithms will be developed which in turn will
speed up analyses (Kolata, 1978). Already the FFT (fast
Fourier transform) has revolutionized some aspects of
computing. Now comes the manipulation of polynomials
and power series and a system to solve simultaneous
linear equations (Davis, David, and Belisley, 1978) which
will allow faster computations. Many computations now
will become available in practice rather than just in
theory.

Also witness the solution of the four-color problem
which involved some 1,200 hours of high-speed computing.
Does this type of problem solving signal a revolution in
the theory of knowledge?

Telecommunications (the marriage of communications
equipment and computer technology) will appear commonplace on the geological scene in the not too distant future. Already computer conferencing has been tested in
the geoscience community. Many benefits were demonstrated
including sharing data bases, joint writing, improving
group conferences, maintaining communications on a continuing basis, and ease in dissemination of scientific
information (Vallee, Askevold, and Wilson, 1977). Increased useage can be expected with decreasing costs and
increased accessibility of hardware and software. The
nearest communications network (e.g. TYMSHARE or TYMNET)
is only a telephone call away from wherever you are to
put you in voice contact with analytical methods, data
bases, information systems, other workers in the field.

Geological

In addition to improving the methods already being
used in geology new ones will be developed. They will
be geologically oriented algorithms designed specifically
to solve geological problems. Some of these will be improved simulation methods, some self-correcting iterative
methods, and development of a language to express geological concepts and terminology in mathematical terms.

Simulation is important in geology because it allows
the condensation of time (an element so important in geological studies). It does not tell you what to do but
what happened - an important aspect in unraveling earth
history. Models have been simple and straightforward.
In the future these models will become more complex (and
thus more realistic) as they are tested in three dimensions for real situations. In this respect, CAI also
will become more important than now in transferring and
demonstrating complex concepts to students.

Iterative self-correcting methods and fast algorithms will be used with increasing efficiency and enhancing results of geological applications. As a result predictions should be improved.

A geocomputing language will be developed specifically to solve geological problems. An example is formalized stratigraphy where stratigraphic concepts and
terminology are expressed in terms of mathematical set
notation to facilitate computer manipulations (Dienes
and Mann, 1977). This will allow stratigraphic problems
to be formulated with mathematical definitions and nota-
tions and therefore can be solved by more exact methods.
To paraphrase Charles Babbage, any branch of mathematics
can advance only as far as its notation permits - the
same can be said for geology.

SUMMARY

Many exciting changes in geology can be anticipated
during the coming decade. The 1980's will show a continued and rapid expansion in the use of computers in
the geological profession as this aspect of the science
matures. Computers will continue to decrease in size
and price as they increase in capacity and efficiency.
They will be easier and cheaper to communicate with on
a worldwide basis as networks develop and each geologist

acquires his own personal equipment. A simple connection
will allow him to browse (or if you like, have it read
to him) through current abstracts of leading journals,
teleconference with other workers on recent developments,
access anyone of many data bases for a quick study and
call on any one of numerous techniques available for
analyses in order to test an idea, check the most recent
grants made by any one of several federal, state, or private organizations, or just plain relax and watch a ball-
game or play games.

REFERENCES

Branscomb, L.M., 1979a, Computing and communications - a
    perspective of the evolving environments: IBM Sys-
    tems Jour., v. 18, no. 2, p. 189-201.

Branscomb, L.M., 1979b, Information: the ultimate fron-
    tier: Science, v. 203, no. 4376, p. 143-147.

Davis, M.W.D., David, M., and Belisle, J.-M., 1978, A
    fast method for the solution of a system of simul-
    taneous linear equations - a method adapted to a
    particular problem: Jour. Math. Geology, v. 10,
    no. 4, p. 369-374.

Dienes, I., and Mann, C.J., 1977, Mathematical formaliza-
    tion of stratigraphic terminology: Jour. Math.
    Geology, v. 9, no. 6, p. 587-603.

Frazer, W.D., 1979, Potential technology implications
    for computers and telecommunications in the 1980's:
    IBM Systems Jour., v. 18, no. 2, p. 333-347.

IBM, 1979, Price performance: Data Processor, v. 22,
    no. 2, p. 1-6.

Knuth, D.E., 1976, Mathematics and computer science:
    coping with finiteness: Science, v. 194, no. 4271,
    p. 1235-1242.

Kolata, G.B., 1978, Computer science: surprisingly fast
    algorithms: Science, v. 204, no. 4370, p. 857-858.

Krumbein, W.C., and Sloss, L.L., 1958, High-speed digital
    computers in stratigraphic and facies analysis:
    Am. Assoc. Petroleum Geologists Bull., v. 42, no.
    11, p. 2650-2669.

Merriam, D.F., 1975, Computer perspectives in geology, *in* Concepts in geostatistics: Springer-Verlag, New York, p. 138-149.

Merriam, D.F., 1976, CAI in geology: Computers & Geosciences, v. 2, no. 1, p. 3-7.

Merriam, D.F., 1980, Computer applications in geology - two decades of progress: Proc. Geologists' Assoc., v. 91, no. 182, p. 53-58.

Robinson, A.L., 1979, Communicating with computers by voice: Science, v. 203, no. 4382, p. 734-736.

Starr, C., and Rudmann, R., 1973, Parameters of technological growth: Science, v. 182, no. 4110, p. 258-364.

Sutterlin, P.G., and May, R.W., 1978, Data and information management, *in* Encyclopedia of computing science and technology, v. 9: Marcel Dekker, Inc., New York, p. 27-56.

Vallee, J., Askevold, G., and Wilson, T., 1977, Computer conferencing in the geosciences: Inst. for the future, Melo Park, California, 85 p.

INDEX